IN SEARCH OF WISDOM

IN SEARCH OF WISDOM

Essays in Memory of John G. Gammie

Edited by
LEO G. PERDUE
BERNARD BRANDON SCOTT
WILLIAM JOHNSTON WISEMAN

WESTMINSTER/JOHN KNOX PRESS
Louisville, Kentucky

Unless noted otherwise, scripture quotations are the authors' own translations.

Book design by Publishers' WorkGroup
Cover design by Frank Perrone

First edition

Published by Westminster/John Knox Press
Louisville, Kentucky

This book is printed on acid-free paper that meets the American National Standards Institute Z39.48 standard. ♾

PRINTED IN THE UNITED STATES OF AMERICA
2 4 6 8 9 7 5 3 1

Library of Congress Cataloging-in-Publication Data

In search of wisdom : essays in memory of John G. Gammie / Leo G. Perdue, Bernard Brandon Scott, and William Johnston Wiseman, editors. — 1st ed.

p. cm.

Includes bibliographical references and indexes.

ISBN 0-664-25295-8 (alk. paper)

1. Wisdom (Biblical personification) 2. Bible—Criticism, interpretation, etc. I. Gammie, John G. II. Perdue, Leo G. III. Scott, Bernard Brandon, 1941– . IV. Wiseman, William Johnston.

BS680.W6I5 1993
220.6—dc20 93-31957

CONTENTS

Contributors vii

Foreword
JAMES BARR ix

Abbreviations of Periodicals, Reference Works, and Serials xv

1. The Concept of God in Old Testament Wisdom
JAMES L. CRENSHAW 1

2. Wisdom in the Chronicler's Work
JOSEPH BLENKINSOPP 19

3. Scribal Wisdom and Theodicy in the Book of the Twelve
RAYMOND C. VAN LEEUWEN 31

4. Wisdom in the Psalter
SAMUEL TERRIEN 51

5. Wisdom in the Book of Job
LEO G. PERDUE 73

6. Wisdom in Proverbs
CAROLE R. FONTAINE 99

7. Wisdom in Qoheleth
MICHAEL V. FOX 115

8. The Meaning of Wisdom in Ben Sira
ALEXANDER A. DI LELLA, O.F.M. 133

9. Wisdom in the Wisdom of Solomon
DAVID WINSTON 149

10. Wisdom, Apocalypticism, and Generic Compatibility
JOHN J. COLLINS 165

11. Wisdom in Q and *Thomas*
STEPHEN J. PATTERSON 187

12. Wisdom and Apocalypticism in Mark
RICHARD HORSLEY 223

13. The Gospel of Matthew:
A Sapiential Performance of an Apocalyptic Discourse
BERNARD BRANDON SCOTT 245

14. Wisdom and Apocalyptic in Paul
E. ELIZABETH JOHNSON 263

15. Wisdom and Apocalyptic in the Apocalypse of John:
Desiring Sophia
TINA PIPPIN 285

Index of Scriptural and Deuterocanonical References 297

Index of Modern Authors 313

CONTRIBUTORS

JAMES BARR is Professor of Hebrew Bible at the Divinity School, Vanderbilt University.

JOSEPH BLENKINSOPP is John A. O'Brien Professor of Biblical Studies at the University of Notre Dame.

JOHN J. COLLINS is Professor of Old Testament at the University of Chicago.

JAMES L. CRENSHAW is Professor of Old Testament at the Divinity School, Duke University.

ALEXANDER A. DI LELLA is Andrews-Kelly-Ryan Professor of Old Testament at the Catholic University.

CAROLE R. FONTAINE is Professor of Old Testament at Andover Newton Theological School.

MICHAEL V. FOX is Max and Frieda Weinstein-Bascom Professor in Jewish Studies in the Department of Hebrew and Semitic Studies at the University of Wisconsin.

RICHARD HORSLEY is Professor and Director of the Religious Studies Program at the University of Massachusetts, Boston.

E. ELIZABETH JOHNSON is Associate Professor of New Testament at New Brunswick Theological Seminary.

CONTRIBUTORS

STEPHEN J. PATTERSON is Assistant Professor of New Testament at Eden Theological Seminary.

LEO G. PERDUE is Professor of Hebrew Bible and Dean at Brite Divinity School, Texas Christian University.

TINA PIPPIN is Assistant Professor of Bible and Religion at Agnes Scott College.

BERNARD BRANDON SCOTT is Darbeth Distinguished Professor of New Testament at Phillips Graduate Seminary, Tulsa Center, the University of Tulsa.

SAMUEL TERRIEN is Emeritus Professor of Hebrew and Cognate Languages at Union Theological Seminary, New York.

RAYMOND VAN LEEUWEN is Professor of Religion and Theology at Calvin College.

DAVID WINSTON is Professor of Hellenistic and Judaic Studies at the Graduate Theological Union.

WILLIAM WISEMAN is Pastor Emeritus at First Presbyterian Church and Former Dean of the Chapel and Professor of Religious Studies at the University of Tulsa.

FOREWORD

James Barr

John Gammie was the first doctoral student I ever had; we met in 1955, within the first few weeks of my Edinburgh professorship. He had just arrived and was starting research for his Ph.D.: he worked on the figure of Melchizedek. From the beginning we became close friends. He came to our home and was soon familiar with our family. We talked of every sort of subject: having been in Korea, he already had wide experience outside the United States. I remember him expressing admiration of the "economic democracy" of Britain as it then was, a country much more socialistic than it now is. He had a true American love of democracy, but not everyone saw it in these social-economic terms. He was also, of course, deeply concerned with the struggle over racial discrimination back in the United States, which spilled over into our student community in Scotland, where American students were numerous, and many were appalled by the injustices back in their own country, of which they had hardly known when they had lived there themselves. John did much to foster a spirit of reconciliation.

In Tübingen, where he was studying for a time, I managed to meet him — this was my first visit to Germany — and I still remember the alfresco lunch we had together. A year later a series of events brought us even closer together. When giving a course of summer lectures on the Isle of Iona, where St. Columba founded his mission to the Scots, I was taken seriously ill and was in hospital for some weeks in the small town of Oban. Jane, my wife, was back in Edinburgh with three small children, and in those days she did not drive a car. Other means of transport were slow and difficult; but it was desperately necessary for us to see each other. John at once volunteered to drive her, complete with all three children, up in our car. Our car in those days was a Volkswagen, what was later called a Beetle — that name was not then used, because there was no other kind. John had never driven such a vehicle. Characteristically, before starting out, he went to the local VW dealer and demanded full information on the mysteries of driving it — its oversteer (or was it understeer?), its gearshift, its zany reserve tank system (for there was no fuel gauge, and one had to change to the reserve at a moment's notice). Needless to say, the family was safely transported up to Oban and back. It was only one example of his care for others.

This was not all. During such journeys Jane talked with him a lot. In the conversations John communicated the information that he had realized he was in love with Catherine. But Catherine was then far away, in Korea. What should he do? Jane said: "Send her a telegram and ask her to marry you." And that is what he did. So we had plenty of connection with the Gammie family.

And so it continued. In 1961, when we came to the United States, considering an invitation to Princeton, John met us at Idlewild, as the airport was then called, and we enjoyed the hospitality of John's father in his beautiful house in Great Neck, Long Island. And after that we had many other contacts. John, once settled in academic work, had a great gift of friendship with other workers in similar areas. Several times we came to Tulsa to lecture, my wife as well as myself, and always he had arranged for additional visits to places all over the Southwest, and through these we met all sorts of colleagues whom but for John we might never have met, or not until much later.

This was one of the keynotes of John Gammie's scholarship throughout: he could work with almost everybody, and saw good in the ideas and efforts of almost all. He overcame barriers between denominations and traditional, fossilized oppositions. When we came to Tulsa, we found we were talking not only in the university department, but in Roman Catholic convents, in the Southern Baptist student center, in forums that brought together the most heterogeneous groups of people. John was always irenic. He might differ from some points of view, but he would always argue a courteous and reasoned case: he never got into cliques or partisan groups; he never engaged in polemics. And this is one reason why so many remember him with honor.

I believe he should have got sooner to higher position in academic life. His mind was first-rate, but he also had humility. From the beginning I knew there were appointments for which he had been recommended, but which never turned out as they should have. He had not always done the "right" things to get ahead, and others, who had followed the customary and accepted tracks, were preferred, even though their minds were narrower and more conventional. He never complained about this to me, and I never talked about it to him. As a man, he stood head and shoulders above most of us who are in scholarship.

He owed much to the Union Theological Seminary (New York) of his own generation, and he spoke much of James Muilenburg and especially of Samuel Terrien. His life and mind were a tribute to the enormous contribution that Union made to American religion. The volume in honor of Terrien, which he edited along with others, was a landmark in his work: it pointed back to Union Seminary and forward to the special interests in Hebrew wisdom and in general Hebrew concepts, such as that of holiness, that were to mark his mature work.

The swift escalation of interest in Hebrew wisdom, which began — shall we say? — in the early 1970s, fitted his needs and his ethos admirably. Though he was not so much younger than myself — about six years — we had come through very different layers of theological experience. He had been less touched by the times of Barthianism and neo-orthodoxy, when theological study was more like a kind of warfare than a kind of intellectual discussion, and when a certain sharpness in controversy seemed almost necessary in order to keep alive at all. His atmosphere was a gentler one; but that at the same time made it less easy to know at once in what direction one should go. There was no one overwhelming problem — such as, for many of us, "revelation in history" had been — that had to be surmounted before any progress was made. And John by training and background was not obviously a specialist, the kind of person of whom one would say: he or she is the known expert on one book, or one problem, or one writer. He was much more a generalist. And thus at Tulsa, teaching in a department of religion and philosophy, as distinct from a theological school, his scholarship grew and expanded in a variety of directions. The biblical world had to converse with the surrounding worlds of knowledge — just as, his scholarship was to make clear, it had done in its own time, and especially as the Hebrew Bible merged into the Greco-Roman world.

Here again there was a shift of emphasis. Long before there was any talk of a "canonical approach" there was, for many people, a difference between two worlds. The Bible was one canon; the Greek and Latin classics were another. The less they made contact, the easier it felt. Even when the mistaken contrasts between the Hebrew mentality and the Greek came to grief, it was not easy for biblical scholars to move back confidently and happily across the dividing fences — even for those of us who had a very excellent classical knowledge. Further, by the mid–twentieth century that sort of classical knowledge could no longer be assumed: by then many Hebrew Bible scholars had only slight experience in Greek and Latin. And it should not be supposed that the separation made between the two worlds came entirely from the biblical side. Classics, as it was taught in the older times, was also a sort of canon, and, as a subject, it was commonly understood to come to a stop before contact with the biblical world took place: in Greek, before the Septuagint — indeed, for the most part, before Alexander; in Latin, before Christian writing began. All these considerations were a hindrance that lamed many of us in our thinking and held back its development.

By the latter decades of the century this unhappy situation was dissolving. Work on the apocryphal books, on apocalyptic and late wisdom, was flourishing; the Dead Sea Scrolls were a major stimulant; and important works of research were appearing: one thinks of Hengel, of Momigliano, and many others. John Gammie committed himself readily to this current. The Septuagint and the other Greek versions of the Bible were part of traditional biblical scholarship; but the hellenization of Jewish wisdom in Aristeas represented a move more distinctly into the Greek context, and by 1985 he had published an article on Stoicism and anti-Stoicism in Qoheleth, and by 1986 one on Herodotus himself. Though the Stoicism article was a comparative piece related to a biblical book, the striking thing about it was the depth at which Gammie had gone into the original Stoic material itself, as distinct from the many studies that worked from a few simple textbook formulae. The interesting thing about the article on Herodotus is that it was a direct study of the historian for himself and was not written with any explicit bearing on the Bible at all (though admittedly a final footnote carried a message for biblical scholarship too).

The wisdom literature, equally, was a powerful attraction to him; not surprisingly, for Terrien was honored as a supreme commentator on Job. I do not know how widely John's explanation of the section on Behemoth and Leviathan is accepted, but it certainly shows originality and power in deploying information and argument. The field of wisdom and apocalyptic, including Daniel, along with their dualism, and their later integration in the Hellenistic world, continued to be a major interest throughout his life.

His *Holiness in Israel* was a major work, which appeared at a time when he was already severely ill with the sickness that led to his death. It was supremely appropriate that the Society of Biblical Literature provided a symposium on this volume, at which he was present in person, at its annual meeting, not long before he died. Walter Brueggemann in his introduction specified three areas of distinction in the book: first, the recognition of *theological diversity* within the text; second, the *broad base of learning* within which the interpretive comments are set; third, the fact that the work is a *theological statement* and not a study of religious phenomenology only. All these aspects are certainly characteristic of John Gammie's work.

This being so, one has to add that John thought deeply and continually about the total role of biblical study, within the academic world on the one hand and within the world of synagogue and church on the other. Had he lived longer, he might have written an approach to the "theology" of the Hebrew Bible (or Old Testament — for he had thought carefully about the problems that these different designations of the subject imply). He spoke in favor of an "ecumenical, critical theology of the Old Testament/Hebrew Bible." In a paper on this subject he noted factors that will affect the shape and complexion of any work articulated by any single biblical scholar. These included: (1) the academic context within which the scholar works (and here he included "pragmatic theological" interests, which would include work for a particular segment of humanity: women, particular racial groups, particular areas like Latin America); (2) the intellectual/ecclesial context; (3) the kind of audience that the scholar addresses; (4) the degree of interest the scholar may have in systematic theology; and (5) the mode of perception of the internal relations, structures, or proportions of the Hebrew Bible. All these are certainly considerations that are structurally inherent in the subject and will have to be weighed in future approaches to it. The conception of the way in which they hang together typifies Gammie's personal consciousness of, and involvement with, these numerous contexts within which biblical theology has to be tried and constructed.

John was very aware of the competing tendencies and pressures that have run through modern discussion. One that he found it impossible to accept was the idealization of a "pre-Enlightenment mentality" that he felt was implied in some recent theological directions. He thought that biblical theology, as he conceived it, because it was "critical," must also accept the reality and the liberating aspects that reason and the Enlightenment had afforded to theology. It followed that the Christian scholar engaging in the theology of the Old Testament/ Hebrew Bible could not press christological interpretations without casting doubt upon the ecumenical nature of the enterprise. In the long run, the endeavor called for restraint: and he himself sincerely followed these rules.

John was, I think, a liberal in the best sense of the word. I think I still have, somewhere, a typescript of a talk I gave in Tulsa at his invitation on "The Idea of Liberalism as a Factor in Christian Theological Discourse" (or something of the sort); and, whether that was the exact title or not, he liked the talk and we discussed it quite a lot. For I said then, and still think, that the idea of liberalism split, early this century, into two (or more) contrary currents, and that much of the disagreement between religious "liberals" and religious "conservatives" is really between different factions of the older liberal tradition. And this fracturing of the liberal tradition has taken place in several ways. Some of what now counts as "liberal" is a very narrow, heavily politicized, legalistic, and often intolerant sort of pressure group, often unwilling to recognize that the majority of people want to go another way. John belonged to a liberalism that was broad, sympathetic, understanding, tolerant, and democratic. I think he also thought that much of the Reformed church tradition to which he belonged had led toward this and stood behind him in it, and there too he was right.

His scholarship was integrated with what he believed, and by what he believed he lived. The thoughts of Hebrew wisdom, in which his mind moved so freely, go with him:

> The souls of the righteous are in the hand of God. . . .
> They are at peace. . . .
> Their hope is full of immortality. . . .
> Those who trust in the Lord will understand truth.

ABBREVIATIONS OF PERIODICALS, REFERENCE WORKS, AND SERIALS

AB	Anchor Bible
ABD	D. N. Freedman (ed.), *Anchor Bible Dictionary*
AnBib	Analecta biblica
ANET	J. B. Pritchard (ed.), *Ancient Near Eastern Texts*
ATD	Das Alte Testament Deutsch
BA	*Biblical Archaeologist*
BBB	Bonner biblische Beiträge
BETL	Bibliotheca ephemeridum theologicarum lovaniensium
BHT	Beiträge zur historischen Theologie
Bib	*Biblica*
BR	*Biblical Research*
BTB	*Biblical Theology Bulletin*
BZ	*Biblische Zeitschrift*
BZAW	Beihefte zur *ZAW*
BZNW	Beihefte zur *ZNW*
CBQ	*Catholic Biblical Quarterly*

CBQMS	Catholic Biblical Quarterly — Monograph Series
CJT	*Canadian Journal of Theology*
CRINT	Compendia rerum iudaicarum ad novum testamentum
EKKNT	Evangelisch-katholischer Kommentar zum Neuen Testament
EstBib	*Estudios bíblicos*
EvT	*Evangelische Theologie*
ExpTim	*Expository Times*
FBBS	Facet Books, Biblical Series
FRLANT	Forschungen zur Religion und Literatur des Alten und Neuen Testaments
HBC	*Harper's Bible Commentary*
HBD	*Harper's Bible Dictionary*
HR	*History of Religions*
HTR	*Harvard Theological Review*
HUCA	*Hebrew Union College Annual*
ICC	International Critical Commentary
IDBSup	Supplementary volume to *IDB*
Int	*Interpretation*
JAAR	*Journal of the American Academy of Religion*
JBL	*Journal of Biblical Literature*
JJS	*Journal of Jewish Studies*
JQR	*Jewish Quarterly Review*
JSJ	*Journal for the Study of Judaism in the Persian, Hellenistic and Roman Period*
JSNTSup	Journal for the Study of the New Testament — Supplement Series
JSOT	*Journal for the Study of the Old Testament*

JSOTSup	Journal for the Study of the Old Testament — Supplement Series
JSPSup	Journal for the Study of the Pseudepigrapha — Supplement
JTS	*Journal of Theological Studies*
KAT	Kommentar zum Alten Testament
NHS	Nag Hammadi Studies
NICOT	New International Commentary on the Old Testament
NovT	*Novum Testamentum*
NovTSup	Novum Testamentum, Supplements
NTS	*New Testament Studies*
OBO	Orbis biblicus et orientalis
OBT	Overtures to Biblical Theology
OTA	*Old Testament Abstracts*
OTL	Old Testament Library
OTP	J. H. Charlesworth (ed.), *The Old Testament Pseudepigrapha*
OTS	*Oudtestamentische Studiën*
RB	*Revue biblique*
RevExp	*Review and Expositor*
RevQ	*Revue de Qumran*
RHPR	*Revue d'histoire et de philosophie religieuses*
RSR	*Recherches de science religieuse*
RTL	*Revue théologique de Louvain*
SBLDS	SBL Dissertation Series
SBLMS	SBL Monograph Series
SBLSP	SBL Seminar Papers
SBT	Studies in Biblical Theology

SJT	*Scottish Journal of Theology*
SNTSMS	Society for New Testament Studies Monograph Series
SVTP	Studia in Veteris Testamenti pseudepigrapha
TDNT	G. Kittel and G. Friedrich (eds.), *Theological Dictionary of the New Testament*
TLG	Thesaurus Linguae Graecae
TLZ	*Theologische Literaturzeitung*
TS	*Theological Studies*
TSK	*Theologische Studien und Kritiken*
VT	*Vetus Testamentum*
VTSup	Vetus Testamentum, Supplements
WBC	Word Biblical Commentary
WMANT	Wissenschaftliche Monographien zum Alten und Neuen Testament
WO	*Die Welt des Orients*
WUNT	Wissenschaftliche Untersuchungen zum Neuen Testament
ZAH	*Zeitschrift für Althebraistik*
ZAW	*Zeitschrift für die alttestamentliche Wissenschaft*
ZDMG	*Zeitschrift der deutschen morgenländischen Gesellschaft*
ZNW	*Zeitschrift für die neutestamentliche Wissenschaft*
ZTK	*Zeitschrift für Theologie und Kirche*

1

THE CONCEPT OF GOD IN OLD TESTAMENT WISDOM

James L. Crenshaw

As a corrective to abstract treatments in biblical theology, Claus Westermann has proposed that ancient Israelites understood God by means of two fundamental categories: saving and blessing.[1] In his view, canonical literature describes a saving God, except for the wisdom corpus and Psalms, which characterize the deity as one who blesses all living creatures. I find this distinction both provocative and problematic. As savior, God acts on behalf of a favored people, who gratefully conduct their lives according to the divine will and in each generation actualize the memory of former deliverances. The blessing God makes life possible by creating an orderly universe in which all creatures benefit from divine generosity. Although the saving God actively participates in the ongoing drama of salvation, the blessing God acts primordially to establish conditions essential to life.

In general, the saving God disregards worth when entering into a covenant relationship with a special group, although inconsistently applying this standard in subsequent dealings with the elect. The blessing God lavishly dispenses bounty without regard to merit and does not play favorites with any group. Yet individual worth determines access to life and riches, so that for many the world of blessing presents itself as a curse, a universe foundering on broken promises. Hence the saving

1. C. Westermann, *What Does the Old Testament Say about God?* (London: SPCK, 1979).

God benefits the few and relates to them and to their enemies with violent jealousy, whereas the blessing God smiles only on those persons who act wisely and virtuously, but that smile, too, lacks consistency.

Of course, the saving God resembles ancient Near Eastern patron deities, and the blessing God is remarkably like high gods of Egypt and Mesopotamia. The rarity of saving deeds,[2] which made their recitation all the more poignant, and the perceived indifference or hostility of the blessing God suggest that ancient Israel's perception of the holy does not lend itself to easy categorization.[3]

The essential problem isolated by these remarks surfaces grandly in those rare attempts within the Bible to reflect on God's essential nature, specifically Exod 34:6–7; Gen 18:22–33; Job 1–2; and Jonah 4.[4] The interplay of justice and mercy permeates these texts, each of which addresses the issue in a distinct manner. Does the quality of mercy extend itself so far that human conduct, even willful idolatry, cannot provoke divine wrath? Can the virtuous character of a few people redound to the benefit of unrepentant sinners? Does God ever act with total disregard for human worth? Does not justice require strict retribution, repentance notwithstanding? These probing explorations into God's character do not mute the unresolved tensions throbbing beneath the surface. At the same time, the several texts take definite moral positions. The Lord's extraordinary capacity for compassion offers no basis for presuming that this gracious, long-suffering deity will be indifferent to sin. In truth, the judge of the whole earth cares more for the well-being of the group than for exacting strict justice; hence God endorses a principle of vicarious merit. Confronted with a prophet who has personally enjoyed divine forgiveness, God defends the higher principle of spontaneous graciousness that cancels punishment for a repentant city's inhabitants, both human and animal. On the other hand, circumstances occasionally arise that prompt the deity to afflict a supremely virtuous man and to destroy his children and numerous slaves for no discernible reason.

It appears that the categories of justice and mercy cancel one an-

2. J. D. Levenson observes that "most of the time, God in the Hebrew Bible is doing nothing; the *magnalia Dei* are celebrated in part because of their rarity" (*Creation and the Persistence of Evil* [San Francisco: Harper & Row, 1988] 163 n. 7; punctuation altered).

3. J. G. Gammie explores anew the appropriateness of the category of holiness in understanding Israel's God (*Holiness in Israel* [Minneapolis: Fortress Press, 1989]).

4. L. Schmidt, *De Deo* (BZAW 143; Berlin and New York: Walter de Gruyter, 1976). Schmidt's analysis suffers from rigid application of source criticism.

other, necessitating that God opt for one or the other. Even the effort to combine the two qualities by virtue of an elect people encounters difficulty here. The texts concur in the insistence that justice be constituted by compassion. Furthermore, only one of the four texts has a restricted understanding of divine solicitude, the other three addressing God's relationship with non-Israelites.

Although the tension between justice and mercy extends beyond Israel's sapiential literature, it has occasioned wide discussion among modern interpreters of ancient wisdom, for whom the operative term in characterizing the deity, "retributor," poses the problem with stark directness. In short, the sages viewed God primarily as the guarantor of a strict system of reward and retribution. According to Johannes Fichtner, whose comprehensive analysis of the wise's view of God remains essential reading,[5] early Israelite wisdom literature maintained complete silence about divine mercy, just as this corpus does not mention such dominant ideas and persons outside the wisdom texts as Abraham, Moses, David, the exodus, Sinai, the covenant, the holy city. Fichtner attributes the introduction of a concept of mercy to Sirach's nationalization of wisdom, an unfortunate term for a very real process of integrating older Yahwistic traditions into sapiential teachings.

This understanding of religious development convinced J. Coert Rylaarsdam, who tried to refine and strengthen the argument.[6] On the basis of a fresh study of Israel's wisdom literature in its ancient Near Eastern setting, Horst Dietrich Preuss reached the radical conclusion that biblical wisdom is pagan in all essentials.[7] Unlike Fichtner, who thought Israelite wisdom in its early form excluded divine forgiveness from consideration, although that concept was widely attested in Mesopotamian wisdom, Preuss subsumed biblical wisdom under the encompassing umbrella of Egypt and Mesopotamia. I find myself reacting strongly against Preuss's conclusions and wondering about the accuracy of Fichtner's interpretation of the data. I wish therefore on this occasion to reexamine the sages' understanding of justice and mercy.

5. J. Fichtner, *Die altorientalische Weisheit in ihrer israelitisch-jüdischen Ausprägung* (BZAW 62; Giessen: A. Töpelmann, 1933).

6. J. C. Rylaarsdam, *Revelation in Jewish Wisdom Literature* (Chicago: University of Chicago Press, 1946).

7. See, above all, H. D. Preuss, "Das Gottesbild der alteren Weisheit Israel," VTSup 23 (1972) 117–45, and idem, *Einfuhrung in die alttestamentliche Weisheitsliteratur* (Stuttgart: W. Kohlhammer, 1987).

On the surface, the data seem absolutely compelling. Within the book of Proverbs only 28:13 even remotely accommodates itself to the idea of a compassionate deity, and the sense may well be restricted to human forgiveness.

> Whoever hides an offense will not thrive,
> but whoever admits (fault) and abandons
> (perfidy) will obtain favor.

The rigid insistence on divine justice within the speeches of Job's three friends is nevertheless tempered by an occasional concession that God inclines toward lenience rather than exact quid pro quo (11:6), but the exasperated sufferer, who asks for his right, not for mercy, adamantly denies any compassion toward him, human or divine. On the basis of content alone, the divine speeches apparently confirm Job's suspicion, for God's solicitude is restricted to the natural world and the animal kingdom. In Qoheleth's view, no distinction between animals and humankind relieves the absurdity of all things. Thus it seems that Fichtner rightly identifies retribution as the dominant notion, albeit a concept that brought considerable consternation because of the indifferent way it manifested itself.

The prominence of divine mercy in Sirach contrasts sharply with this virtual silence in earlier wisdom. Ben Sira seems never to tire of exploring the way God holds justice and mercy in delicate balance. Human weakness and life's brevity evoke divine compassion on all living creatures; this universality of God's mercy differs from human sympathy, which is limited to immediate neighbors (18:8–14). Two powerful forces exist within God, wrath and mercy, neither squelching the other but together issuing in exact reward and retribution (16:11–14). Charitable deeds purchase favorable response from God (29:9, 12), and prayer for forgiveness avails nothing apart from a readiness on the part of the supplicant to forgive human offenses (28:2–4). Delayed punishment offers no reason to presume that wrath is inoperative (5:6), even if God resembles a shepherd and teacher (18:13). Sinners who repent of their deeds obtain forgiveness, although God shows no partiality (35:12).

In the midst of such assertions about God's nature, Ben Sira alludes to ancient Yahwistic texts, most notably the divine proclamation of the so-called thirteen attributes in Exod 34:6–7 and the story of David's offense against God in taking a census, for which he is offered various types of punishment and chooses to fall into divine hands rather than human ones (2 Sam 24:14). Believing that present distress is somehow God's loving means of testing an individual, Ben Sira often resorts to prayer and even expresses himself in the form of a national lament in which he pleads for renewed wonders and deliverance for Israel from its enemies (36:1–17). This prayer, which breathes hatred for foreigners, is worlds removed from earlier wisdom, Israelite or otherwise. The concluding hymn recalls God's mercy, and the praise of the High Priest Simon II mentions his prayer to the merciful Most High. In the final resort, when Ben Sira invites young people to come to his house of study, he explicitly encourages them to rejoice over divine mercy. Nevertheless, in all this reflection on God's mercy Ben Sira tenaciously holds on to a belief in retribution (51:30).

The special relationship between God and the elect surfaces again in Wis 3:9, but the reverse side of that bond comes to expression as well. The author remarks that if strict justice befalls the nations hostile to Israel, even after a time of divine indulgence to allow for repentance, those who enjoy God's favor will be punished all the more exactingly when they sin (12:20–21). This notion of lenience in the interest of generating repentance occurs elsewhere: "But thou art merciful to all, for thou canst do all things, and thou dost overlook people's sins, that they may repent" (11:23). This author argues that divine justice is beyond question, and because the deity has supreme authority, God manifests mildness and patience (12:12–18). In this book we find the usual allusion to God as creator, along with a number of interesting epithets: Lord of your elect, savior, and father.

When we ask how Israel's sages sum up their experience of God, at least two texts come to mind. In response to the divine speeches, Job renounces his previous understanding of God, calling it derivative, and contrasts that earlier rumor about deity with immediate sight. Still, the author exercises extraordinary restraint, and readers do not become privy to the nature of such knowledge. At best, we intuit the silencing effect of new insight on a chastened sufferer. More typical is the response of Elihu to a frightening display of divine power. This awesome manifestation of thunder, lightning, and hail was sufficiently ambiguous to evoke different possibilities in explanation: "Whether for correction, or for land, or for love, [God] causes it to happen" (37:13). To this we compare Qoheleth's bewilderment, presumably about God's actions: "Whether it is love or hate one cannot know" (9:1).

Neither Elihu nor Qoheleth ruled out the possibility that God might smile on humankind. In the former instance, the formulation may suggest all three possibilities as real, the only uncertainty being the actual determination about specific natural manifestations. Indeed, Elihu may even imply that he can identify each of these divine disclosures, for he boasts of having perfect knowledge. Such bold claims are the exception; Israel's sages, like their counterparts in Mesopotamia and Egypt, usually possessed a healthy agnosticism.

The reason was divine freedom, of course, and the sages seem always to have recognized that reality. Human beings may propose, but God disposes; they make plans, but God's will works itself out; the lot may fall into the human lap, but the deity determines its outcome. Gerhard von Rad has brought this idea into the center of discussion,[8] particularly as it relates to the concept of order that has received considerable attention as a result of Klaus Koch's hypothesis about fate producing deeds,[9] a kind of exact reward and retribution that enslaved the deity also, who at best functioned as midwife assisting an action to reach its specific goal for good or ill. Roland E. Murphy's rejection of order as the controlling concept in biblical wisdom[10] reacts against such excess, which Patrick D. Miller assessed negatively in a study of biblical prophecy.[11] In this connection, Hans Heinrich Schmid has demonstrated the widespread emphasis on order in ancient Near Eastern wisdom, particularly the imagery associated with the goddess Maat in Egypt.[12]

The sages held another idea as unflinchingly as they did divine freedom. They insisted on the intellect's capacity to assure the good life by word and deed. By using their intellectual gifts the sages hoped to steer their lives safely into harbor, avoiding hazards that brought catastrophe to fools. Unfortunately, the two ideas impinged on one another. God was free to ignore human merit, and responsible conduct guar-

8. G. von Rad, *Wisdom in Israel* (Nashville: Abingdon Press, 1972).

9. K. Koch, "Gibt es ein Vergeltungsdogma im Alten Testament?" *ZTK* 52 (1955) 1–42; Eng. trans. in *Theodicy in the Old Testament* (ed. J. L. Crenshaw; Philadelphia: Fortress Press; London: SPCK, 1983) 57–87.

10. Assessed in J. L. Crenshaw, "Murphy's Axiom: Every Gnomic Saying Needs a Balancing Corrective," *The Listening Heart* (ed. K. G. Hoglund et al.; JSOTSup 58; Sheffield: JSOT Press, 1987) 1–17.

11. P. D. Miller, *Sin and Retribution in the Prophets* (SBLMS 27; Chico, Calif.: Scholars Press, 1981).

12. H. H. Schmid, *Wesen und Geschichte der Weisheit* (BZAW 101; Berlin: A. Töpelmann, 1966).

anteed life's bounty, specifically prosperity, honor, health, and progeny. The interplay of these conflicting ideas lends considerable complexity to the concept of God in biblical wisdom. One can venture the hypothesis that ancient wisdom rested on a fundamental delusion that its concept of God exposed, but in doing so the sages introduced ideas about deity that evoked sharply opposing reactions. In other words, the conviction that one escapes vulnerability through proper use of the intellect collapsed before the exercise of divine freedom. At the same time, divine arbitrariness generated skepticism in some people and surrender before a merciful deity in others. These two reactions merely develop implications of earlier wisdom. This statement is obvious with respect to divine freedom and its debilitating consequences, but what about the basis for believing in God's compassion? This one is less obvious, but I think ancient biblical wisdom does offer a rationale for such an understanding of God.

Where shall we begin? With a study of divine names as Fichtner did? The information here certainly seems to substantiate his claim. The absence in early biblical wisdom of allusions to divine compassion contrasts with the many references to God's mercy in Sirach and Wisdom of Solomon. Sometimes texts can be deceiving. Take, for instance, the sayings of Agur in Prov 30:1–14, which, on the surface at least, appears to be the most God-intoxicated textual unit in wisdom literature. Those who study the divine names could have a field day here, for one finds the following names: El (twice), Qedoshim, Elohim, YHWH, Elohai. So much God-talk fails to conceal the substantial distance between Agur and traditional belief in God.[13]

The same point applies to the expressions "fear of YHWH" and "abomination of YHWH," for the first can mean as little as the modern word "religion" and the second may suggest no more than "displeasing," having lost its cultic nuance. In any event, the effort to exclude such references from the oldest wisdom does not seem altogether successful, although that literature does exemplify no great proclivity toward use of the divine name. Furthermore, this early wisdom did not understand YHWH as a patron deity who had entered into an intimate

13. See my essay, "Clanging Symbols," *Justice and the Holy: Essays in Honor of Walter Harrelson* (ed. D. A. Knight and P. J. Paris; Atlanta: Scholars Press, 1989) 51–64. Contrast, however, D. Burkett, *The Son of Man in the Gospel of John* (JSNTSup 56; Sheffield: JSOT Press, 1991) 51–75.

relationship with the nation Israel or any of its official representatives. Instead, YHWH functioned as a precise equivalent of El or Elohim, the more general names for God.

The unique feature of Yahwism, the deity's violent jealousy,[14] makes no appearance in wisdom literature. Job does refer to a *gō'el,* a personal vindicator, but the meaning of this allusion is far from clear. If *gō'el* refers to the institution of redeemer, Job is terribly confused, for he is still very much alive, and if his monotheism rules out another deity who could overpower Job's divine oppressor, we are left with an implausible theory about a split within the deity that throws little light on the text.

On the other hand, Job occupies a special place in God's esteem, and this favoritism brings calamity in its wake. The designation of Job as "my servant" implies a close relationship between deity and human worshiper like that underlying Yahwistic literature. According to Prov 23:10–11, widows occupy a special place in the mind of a redeemer, who pleads their cause forcefully. It is not clear whether the author thought of royalty here or of the ultimate sovereign.

This brief reference to a social institution indicates the complexity of all attempts to clarify the social location of wisdom literature itself.[15] The family must surely have been the primary locus for early wisdom, and this setting offers at least one possibility of thinking about God as merciful. The aphorism about the deity chastening loved ones, an instance of argument by analogy with parental discipline, hardly describes a neutral or indifferent sovereign. Another social locus, the royal court, also provides a strong possibility for compassion to enter the picture. Royal ideology throughout the ancient Near Eastern world emphasized care of widows and orphans, persons on the margins of society who were not thought to have deserved their misfortune. A third social locus, the school, seems ill disposed toward cultivating an emphasis on divine mercy, for scribal discipline was particularly harsh. Yet Sirach, a

14. "YHWH's violent 'jealousy,' which tolerates no rival, is without parallel in the religious literature of the ancient Near East" (T. Mettinger, *In Search of God* [Philadelphia: Fortress Press, 1988] 74).

15. R. N. Whybray, "The Social World of the Wisdom Writers," *The World of Ancient Israel* (ed. R. E. Clements; Cambridge: Cambridge University Press, 1989) 227–50; idem, *Wealth and Poverty in the Book of Proverbs* (JSOTSup 99; Sheffield: JSOT Press, 1990); R. Albertz, "Der sozialgeschichtliche Hintergrund des Hiobbuches und der 'Babylonischen Theodizee,'" *Die Botschaft und die Boten* (ed. J. Jeremias and L. Perlitt; Neukirchen: Neukirchener Verlag, 1981) 349–72; F. Crüsemann, "The Unchangeable World: The 'Crisis of Wisdom' in Koheleth," *God of the Lowly* (ed. W. Schottroff and W. Stegemann; Maryknoll, N.Y.: Orbis Books, 1984) 57–77.

member of this institution, nourished such thoughts in the early second century BCE and permitted them to flourish.

These social locations of wisdom did not give rise to metaphors that convey special understandings of deity. This astonishing fact has occasioned little comment, all the more noteworthy in light of Thorkild Jacobsen's illuminating analysis of Mesopotamian symbolism in terms of three root metaphors: natural, royal, and familial.[16] We search in vain for comparable metaphors in Israel's wisdom literature, where an occasional allusion to a creator almost exhausts the possibilities, unless shepherd in Qoh 12:11 points beyond King Solomon to the divine source of Qoheleth's teaching. The absence of metaphors from the family and school is puzzling, for parental metaphors were certainly familiar in the ancient world, and nothing could be more natural for the wise than to call God the heavenly teacher (cf. Sir 18:13).

The pervasive influence on biblical wisdom of ideology derived from speculation about Maat introduced solicitous concern as an important aspect of the relationship between this intermediary figure and human beings. In her biblical expression, she woos young men with exquisite rhetoric, offering them life and riches. Her invitation assumes the character of demand, punctuated with prophetic-sounding threats. This aggressive figure boasts of special relationship with God in primordial times, even of participation in the act of creation, at least as appreciative observer. Nevertheless, she restricts her love to those who love her, thus failing to break out of the mold cast by retributive thinking. In fact, even Mesopotamian wisdom maintains the concept of merit in those places where divine compassion abounds. For example, those individuals who, like Job, suffer afflictions for no apparent reason experience the deity's favor in response to appropriate ritual acts. The correct ritual thus earns restoration and assures divine favor. In this view, mercy is actually the underside of justice, making it possible for deserving persons to climb out of a morass.

Is such forgiveness possible in biblical wisdom? As we have seen, only one text in Proverbs mentions forgiveness, and the silence with respect to the agent conceals its meaning from readers. Does the individual acknowledge a mistake, motivated by a desire to acquire human compassion from an offended person? That reading is certainly possible, but so is the alternative understanding, that the confession of

16. T. Jacobsen, *The Treasures of Darkness* (New Haven: Yale University Press, 1976).

guilt addressed a higher court successfully. On this reading, the text corresponds to Mesopotamian confessions, except for the ritual accompaniments, about which the biblical text is silent. The customary context for creation language in Proverbs indicates that it bears a tiny ingredient of compassion, for the association of creator with the poor stands out. The rich are reminded that their maker also fashioned the poor, and anyone who heaps insults on the unfortunate would do well to recall his or her creator. The royal obligation to rescue the perishing and give them strong drink to dull their awareness of misery also suggests that strict justice was not always the best thing (Prov 31:1–9).

Analogy with Ben Sira's discussion of physicians implies that comparable questions about favoring the poor might logically have arisen. If the physician risks divine anger by interfering with sickness understood as punishment for sin, an assumption Ben Sira endeavors to undermine, do not those who offer assistance to the lowly undertake a comparable risk?[17] That conclusion would follow upon the strict application of a retributive principle, according to which all people received their proper deserts. We hear no argument against helping the poor; in fact, such kindness is encouraged (cf. Zech 7:9–10). In a society governed by an exact retribution there would be no undeserved misery, but the sages were not that divorced from reality.

Although the conservative ideology of the wise brought distinct rewards, their motive was not entirely selfish. Their understanding of the cosmic order placed a premium on ethical behavior, which constituted society and prevented the incursion of chaos into daily life. Those individuals who behaved like fools allowed their passions to control them, leading to violence and wholesale destruction of law and order. Such conduct threatened the very fabric of society and the universe, creating a topsy-turvy world in which former slaves rode on horses and individuals who once enjoyed high social status were reduced to traveling on foot. Naturally, the losers in this exchange of status directed thoughts to the heavens, accusing the sovereign of lapsing into a state of unconsciousness.

Such a threat of returning to chaos was real in ancient Israel, as Jeremiah's exquisite poem describing this event attests (4:23–26). The sages as a group never quite abandoned a conviction that God had

17. See my essay "Poverty and Punishment in the Book of Proverbs," *Quarterly Review* 9 (1989) 30–43.

everything firmly under control, but the divine speeches in Job come very close to acknowledging an area beyond the deity's power. When YHWH challenges Job to overcome human pride in others, does the question conceal an admission that God has found that task formidable? Job stands before God as the supreme example of pride that refuses to bend before the majestic creator. To be sure, this deity was more successful in negating the threat from Behemoth and Leviathan, creatures who represent the chaotic forces within the universe itself.[18] The divine victory over these elements is virtually complete, for they are depicted as little more than playthings with seriously restricted movement. To humans they pose terror on every hand, but God has the primordial beasts under complete control.

If societal turmoil could not be explained as the result of a resurgence of power on the part of Behemoth and Leviathan, and if human perfidy failed to explain the destruction of order, the logical explanation pointed to a change in the face of God. Job saw no other reason for the calamity that befell him, and the possibility of inconstancy in God threatened his worldview with collapse. The prospect of serving a useless corvée was distressing, for such an admission struck at the foundation of the sages' understanding of reality. An orderly universe depended on a creator who guaranteed the dispensing of reward and punishment, and when the deity became derelict in this important duty the entire system shattered.

The understanding of God in the book of Job is complex, necessitating separate analyses of the prose, the individual speeches, and the poem about wisdom's hiddenness. The portrayal of deity in the story combines folkloristic simplicity with an astonishing assumption that human beings do actually worship without thought of the carrot or the stick. On the one hand, the author presents Job as a man who will serve God in all circumstances, gladly accepting divine bounty and refusing to complain about inflicted harm. Job's reasoning, foreign to his wife's comprehension, assumes that we ought to be grateful for anything that God sends our way. In Job's view, humans have no claim on God, and the correct response in all circumstances is gratitude. On the

18. On these two beasts, see J. Gammie, "Behemoth and Leviathan: On the Didactic and Theological Significance of Job 40:15–41:26," *Israelite Wisdom: Theological and Literary Essays in Honor of Samuel Terrien* (ed. J. G. Gammie et al.; Missoula, Mont.: Scholars Press, 1978) 217–31, and O. Keel, *Jahwes Entgegnung an Ijob* (FRLANT 121; Göttingen: Vandenhoeck & Ruprecht, 1978).

other hand, this story describes God as one who stops at almost nothing, even murder, to prove a point. Furthermore, God admits that the adversary moved the deity to afflict Job without justification. Surprisingly, the deity makes no concession about the deaths of Job's children and servants, who are eradicated and then replaced without a word of apology. Such disregard for human worth stands alongside an amazing acknowledgment of exceptional goodness in one person, whom God twice praises for exemplary conduct in all areas of life and whose words, in the end, God endorses as well. This deity expects proper ritual, particularly sacrifice, and responds favorably to Job's intercession for friends after having ignored a similar act on behalf of his children. The God of the story also ties up all loose ends where Job is concerned, guaranteeing that he receives an appropriate reward for his trouble. Having suspended the operation of the retributive worldview for a season, God reinstates the system for the benefit of his servant. The disturbing feature of this depiction of God is that a heavenly courtier wields sufficient power to manipulate God and thus to inflict grievous suffering on earth — with God's explicit consent.

Job's God, as presented in his speeches within the dialogue, is paradoxically both present and absent, an oppressive presence and a hiding friend. Job thinks of God as an enemy determined to destroy him, the imagery fluctuating from wild animal to warrior. Like a lion, God tears apart his prey, and like a strong warrior, God hurls arrows at an exposed target. This tyrant has cast off all capacity for justice, treating Job like a sinner. Eventually, Job charges God with injustice on a much wider scale, mentioning the miserable wretches of society who are victims of oppressive rule. Their cries for help fail to move the deity to pity, leading Job to the conclusion that God turns away from them and thus encourages violence. This picture of the Lord of a chaotic world does not altogether conceal Job's secret hope that God will come to his assistance if only Job can make contact. This search does not reveal a compassionate deity anywhere, and Job despairs over finding the former friend. Of one thing Job is convinced: God is making a mistake and will eventually regret Job's departure. In all this bold accusation and appeal for a trial, Job never abandons his conviction that God has sufficient power to do anything.

The three friends emphasize divine justice and power. They cannot accept Job's insistence on innocence, for that concession would condemn the deity as unjust. Therefore they press relentlessly the point of

Job's guilt, urging humble repentance and assuring him of God's forgiveness. They, too, celebrate the majesty of the creator of the universe; in doing so, they lessen the status of moral deed on the part of humans. In their view human actions do not affect the deity in any way, so majestic and pure is God. Elihu also emphasizes God's sovereignty and justice, although bringing the disciplinary and educative activity of the deity into focus. Ironically, by depicting God as a "merciless engineer of the mechanization of divine retribution"[19] they imprison the deity in a rigid system that human beings actually control by their conduct.

The hymn on wisdom's inaccessibility stresses divine remoteness, like that of wisdom. Human beings perform incredible feats in search of rare gems; before their efforts, the deepest recesses of the earth yield their precious secrets. Nevertheless, the quest for wisdom ends in frustration, for no human being has access to it, and even Sheol and Abaddon can only boast about having heard a rumor of wisdom's whereabouts. God alone has access to wisdom. In context this celebration of divine intelligence and human ignorance pronounces a powerful negative verdict on Job's bold claim to know the failings of divine conduct. The final declaration that religion is the equivalent of wisdom and hence accessible to everyone seriously negates the force of this poem.

The understanding of God in the whirlwind is the subject of considerable discussion in recent literature. The most comforting reading of the divine speeches emphasizes their aptness as response to Job's two accusations: that God is guilty of criminal activity and that the world lacks any discernible plan. God's twofold response points to human insignificance and ignorance that renders meaningless any charge leveled at the ruler of the universe, and the majesty of the created order contains so much splendor that all creatures are assured a chance to attain their true nature. On this reading, human beings also live in a setting that permits them to achieve their potential. A less positive understanding of this divine lecture on natural wisdom recognizes the creator's virtual silence about humankind. To be sure, this line of argument on God's part exposes anthropocentricity, substituting the mystery of creation and indirectly its creator as the center of all legitimate reflection. In doing so, however, it silences the fundamental questions about human suffering, for God completely ignores the issue and offers no explanation for Job's misfortune.

19. Mettinger, *In Search of God*, 178.

Still, Job ultimately bends the knee before this deity and places a hand over his mouth, leaving unanswered all kinds of questions. Has he been vindicated because God appeared to Job without crushing him? Has Job seen the error of his argument and repented? Has he given up on his hope of obtaining a fair trial before the heavenly tribunal? Does he acquiesce outwardly but harbor inner rebellion that he determines to stifle for his own protection? How ought one to understand the dismissal of his previous relationship with God as derivative, amounting to hearsay? How can we reconcile the presence of theophany in wisdom literature?

The last question raises the issue of genre, which evokes a variety of suggestions: a lament, a dispute, a drama, a paradigm of an answered lament, a lawsuit. Similarities with lament psalms are obvious, although the dominant genre is not lament. Moshe Weinfeld's typological comparisons with laments in Mesopotamian parallels reinforce Claus Westermann's arguments, but not at the expense of dispute.[20] Here, too, close parallels exist with the acrostic poem known as the Babylonian Theodicy. Does Job's literary form influence the treatment of divine justice?

Qoheleth echoes traditional understandings of God as creator, albeit in quite different language. All things were created beautiful in their time, perhaps in the sense of appropriate for the moment, and God placed something quite valuable within the human mind but rendered it inaccessible (3:11). Before the created world humans stand powerless, either to change the nature of God's finished work or to grasp the mystery of life and death. Qoheleth does not deny God's generosity, but he insists that a probing intellect cannot discern any rationale for the distribution of divine favor. Insofar as Qoheleth can determine, chance reigns and makes a mockery of all sapiential efforts to secure life (the same theme occurs in Papyrus Insinger). This state of affairs is possible because God dwells in remote realms and remains indifferent to the human condition. In God's absence, death has stolen the scene, and its arbitrariness strikes despair in human hearts. Some interpreters view Qoheleth's teachings quite differently, claiming that his summons to enjoyment grows out of complete confidence in divine goodness rather

20. M. Weinfeld, "Job and Its Mesopotamian Parallels — A Typological Analysis," *Text and Context* (JSOTSup 48; Sheffield: Almond Press, 1988) 217–26; C. Westermann, *The Structure of the Book of Job* (Philadelphia: Fortress Press, 1981).

than representing the counsel of despair.[21] Although not wholly rejecting a cultic practice such as making vows to God, Qoheleth advises caution rather than outright negligence, and he calls attention to the vast distance separating God from human beings. For him, all things are futile or absurd. This negative assessment of everything on earth offers no support to those critics who understand the *Deus absconditus* in a comforting manner. Qoheleth's positive evaluation of life, wine, wisdom, and so forth makes all the more poignant his protest against a system that fails to promote virtue. In a society where accident or chance has the final word, one can do absolutely nothing to master the circumstances of existence. In this situation, wisdom has lost its power.

Several wisdom psalms explore the problem of the prosperity of the wicked, but these reflect the communal setting and consequently offer consoling words, either divorced from reality or in spite of all appearances. The author of Psalm 37 serves notice that nothing under the heavens suffices to call into question divine justice. Here is another example of hardening dogma like that espoused by Job's three friends and Elihu. For this psalmist, no one in immediate purview has ever experienced undeserved want. In short, always and in every circumstance God dispenses good things to deserving persons and misfortune to offenders. Perhaps, like Job's friends, the psalmist rejects the possibility of achieving the status of righteousness, so that divine injustice is excluded on principle. For the author of Psalm 49 the enigmas of human existence fade before God's mystery. Momentary prosperity counts for nought, and death speaks the final word, canceling all supposed gain. Psalm 73 traces the movement from doubt to trust in great detail. At first the psalmist begins to doubt traditional belief in God's goodness toward the upright, for experience presents far too many examples of prosperous villains. Conscious of teetering on the brink of folly, the psalmist makes a concerted effort to purify such thoughts, receiving support in the assembled congregation of the faithful. Here the psalmist recognizes the insubstantiality and ephemerality of the success enjoyed by the wicked, but, more importantly, acquires a fresh awareness of di-

21. Contrast R. N. Whybray, *Ecclesiastes* (Grand Rapids, Mich.: Wm. B. Eerdmans Publishing Co., 1989) and G. S. Ogden, *Qoheleth* (Sheffield: JSOT Press, 1987) with J. L. Crenshaw, *Ecclesiastes* (Philadelphia: Westminster Press, 1987) and M. V. Fox, *Qohelet and His Contradictions* (Sheffield: JSOT Press, 1989). On this matter I cannot agree with Gammie (*Holiness in Israel*, 151–55).

vine nearness. Bolstered by a sense of God's touch and leadership, the psalmist realizes that nothing else in all of the universe quite compares with God's presence. That nearness alone confirms the accuracy of the original credo, and it now becomes permissible to entertain the bold thought that even death's power may yield to a greater force, the God of glory.

What has this survey indicated? That Fichtner overlooked a few sure signs that Israel's sages believed in divine compassion. Still, his essential point stands, requiring explanation. Why did the situation change dramatically with Ben Sira? Does the key reside in the shift from individual concerns to those of a people who thought of themselves as chosen? In Westermann's terms, the saving God has become dominant over the blessing God. That is, the scandal of particularity has triumphed over universalism. If this is indeed the answer, why does Ben Sira make so little of national concerns outside the encomium in 44–51?[22] Except for occasional allusions to canonical traditions, the lament in chap. 36 alone sounds this particularistic theme.

Perhaps we have not really discerned the nature of the problem. Ben Sira offers a clue when observing that nothing we give our parents can repay them for the gift of life. Perhaps that argument is carried to a higher level in Job 41:11, where God seems to ask, "Who has given to me, that I should repay him?" and then declares that everything under heaven belongs to God, a theme also found in Ps 50:10–12. If human existence is a gift entirely outside the domain of calculating morality, we are already recipients of grace exceeding any merit we may possibly acquire through virtuous conduct.[23] Israel's sages may well have understood reward and retribution in light of an encompassing love of God, a compassionate act of self-manifestation that created the conditions essential to life. To accuse God of failing to maintain an exact correlation between human merit and divine reward amounts to colossal ingratitude for prior generosity.[24] If this point has validity, it follows

22. B. L. Mack, *Wisdom and the Hebrew Epic* (Chicago: University of Chicago Press, 1985), and T. R. Lee, *Studies in the Form of Sirach 44–50* (SBLDS 75; Atlanta: Scholars Press, 1986).

23. S. Ben Joseph Al-Fayyumi emphasizes this point (*The Book of Theodicy* [New Haven, Conn.: Yale University Press]). Goodman's introduction to Saadia's argument is a model of clarity.

24. Resulting in bitterness, according to J. T. Wilcox, *The Bitterness of Job* (Ann Arbor: University of Michigan Press, 1989).

that justice has always been tempered with mercy, whether or not the sages recognized the interrelationship of the divine attributes.

Why did Ben Sira suddenly articulate this unstated presupposition of wisdom? Did the theological impact of Job's hellish nightmare and Qoheleth's indifference to religious commitment weigh so heavily on Ben Sira's mind that they led to an emphasis on God's mercy and a recovery of the national heritage for a group of sages who had tried to make it on their own abilities? One thing is certain: for Ben Sira, justice alone does not adequately describe God, who turns toward all creatures in abundant mercy. In short, the blessing God is also the saving Lord.

Perhaps this decisive transition from universality to particularism coincides with historical developments in ancient Israel. Although wisdom literature obscures its genesis extremely well, Joseph Blenkinsopp has recently described a plausible social setting for polemic against the strange women in Proverbs 1–9, which he relates to the struggle against marriage between Jews and foreign women in the time of Ezra and Nehemiah.[25] A confident community of sages may well have existed during the expansionism of the eighth century, particularly Hezekiah's rule. Believing themselves capable of controlling their future, these optimists relied on their own knowledge and goodness to face all eventualities. Their confidence was shared by the society at large, one that found expression eventually in the Josianic reforms that turned their ideology into national policy. The catastrophic events of 609–587 BCE and the loss of self-government amid a humiliating exile, followed by intense rivalry[26] upon returning to Jerusalem and economic hardship for more than a century, gave ample inspiration to someone who fictionalized the problem of suffering and a religious response to injustice. The collapse of family relationships and the emergence of commercialization at the cost of societal obligations and kinship ties seem to lie behind Qoheleth's egocentrism and fascination with wealth. The unreliability of riches, their tendency to vanish overnight as a result of risky ventures, left a society enamored of wealth highly vulnerable.

Furthermore, the political situation under the Persians and Ptolemies offered little basis for confidence, for the ever-watchful officials

25. J. Blenkinsopp, "The Social Context of the 'Outsider Woman' in Proverbs 1–9," *Bib* 72 (1991) 457–73.

26. C. A. Newsom gives a brilliant analysis of rival discourse among the sages ("Woman and the Discourse of Patriarchal Wisdom: A Study of Proverbs 1–9," *Gender and Difference in Ancient Israel* [ed. P. L. Day; Minneapolis: Fortress Press, 1989] 142–60).

of government exacted their taxes and kept the population in check. The Seleucid authorities and rising Hellenistic influence created an anxious populace who desperately needed assurance that God would have mercy on those faithfully turning from sin. In this unprecedented historical setting, belief in the moral order became highly problematic and dependence on God's mercy offered hope to those who had lost confidence in the correspondence between worth and well-being.

For many years I have pondered the puzzling endings of Job and Goethe's *Faust,* both of which seem to "cop out" after having pressed intellectual honesty to the breaking point. Is René Girard right that human societies value order so highly they will go to any extreme, even violence, to maintain it?[27] One can think of ample testimony to belief in reward for effort expended, but rare indeed is the voice of the ancient prophetess who walked through a city with a torch in one hand and a bucket of water in another, her cry echoing through the streets: "Would that I could burn heaven with this flame and extinguish hell's fires with this water, that people would love God for God's sake alone." Can we bear the thought of forsaking all without getting much in return? That dilemma has changed little if any in the centuries since ancient sages struggled with it. On the one hand, we desire a sovereign who rules the universe justly; on the other hand, we earnestly wish for a solicitous champion of our interests who overlooks human frailty. The sages, too, vacillated in this respect, and this fact demonstrates the validity of Schmid's claim that wisdom literature is in a very real sense historical.[28] The changing views reflect historical events, although obliquely and grudgingly. I do not pretend to have resolved the matter of a shift within wisdom thinking to give greater prominence to divine mercy, but I hope I have shown the complexity of the problem and the rewards of pursuing the question Fichtner posed in his ground-breaking monograph on ancient Oriental wisdom in its Israelite-Jewish expression.

27. R. Girard, *Job: The Victim of His People* (Stanford, Calif.: Stanford University Press, 1987).

28. Schmid, *Wesen und Geschichte der Weisheit.*

2

WISDOM IN THE CHRONICLER'S WORK

Joseph Blenkinsopp

I

The historiographical work comprising 1–2 Chronicles and Ezra-Nehemiah (hereafter C)[1] forms part of the third section of the Hebrew Bible canon often imprecisely subsumed under the rubric of "wisdom writings." But it will be at once obvious that this work has little in common with those writings — at a minimum, Job, Proverbs, and Qoheleth — which exhibit linguistic and thematic features that more properly and precisely may be designated sapiential. On the contrary, C's single-minded concentration on explicitly religious and cultic concerns would seem to justify placing it at the opposite extreme of those writings whose orientation is generally taken to be much more secular, discursive, and international in character.

What has been said of C could, of course, also be said of much of the extant corpus of Jewish writings from the early centuries of the Second Commonwealth. As we survey these writings, we have the impression of a very limited degree of intellectual activity outside of cultic circles. In this respect, the contrast with the Greek-speaking world from the sixth to the fourth century BCE is quite remarkable. For this was the

1. I allow for the possibility of additions to a basic draft, e.g., the genealogies in 1 Chronicles 1–9, the latter part of the Davidic line in 1 Chronicles 3, and the Nehemiah material. For the view that Chronicles and Ezra-Nehemiah form one continuous history see my *Ezra-Nehemiah: A Commentary* (Philadelphia: Westminster Press, 1988) 47–54.

age of decisive advances in metaphysics, cosmology, astronomy, mathematics, and geometry; the age of Xenophanes, Heraclitus, the Eleatics, and Sophists; the age of Socrates, a contemporary of Ezra. One might attempt an explanation of the difference by appealing to the social and economic conditions obtaining in the respective regions. As a later Jewish writer would point out at some length, intellectual activity requires leisure and therefore a degree of wealth (Sir 38:24–39:11), both of which may have been hard to come by in the province of Judah during these two centuries. Economic conditions on the Greek mainland, in Ionia and Magna Graecia, seem to have favored the emergence of a leisured class of lay thinkers, whereas in Judah we hear frequent complaints of economic distress exacerbated by the fiscal policies of the Persian monarchy.[2] Another factor was the loss of royal patronage on which much of the intellectual activity in Israel and Judah depended; hence the frequent attribution of "wisdom writings" to kings (e.g., Prov 1:1; 25:1; 31:1; Qoh 1:1). After the debacle in the sixth century the priesthood was in the ascendancy, in some respects taking the place of the monarchy; hence the preponderant emphasis on the cult in exilic and postexilic writings. In the Greek-speaking city-states the social situation was quite different, and did not permit cult personnel to attain such a position of power and prestige. There therefore developed in Judah a situation uncongenial to the emergence of a lay intelligentsia and a tradition of independent critical inquiry.

We might also take note of a constraint of a more general nature that had been in evidence long before the period in question. Max Weber drew attention to it in commenting on what he called "culture hostility" in Israelite prophecy, by which he meant an attitude unsympathetic to cultural expressions outside of the specifically religious sphere.[3] That this attitude was not confined to prophecy may be seen in the generally negative attitude to professional purveyors of wisdom throughout the biblical period. Professional sages (*ḥăkāmîm*) no doubt existed under the monarchy, but the almost total absence of allusion to them in preexilic writings is remarkable, and may be explained by the preemptive association of the term with foreign sages.[4] This deterrent attitude to

2. Hag 1:6, 8–11; Zech 8:10; Mal 2:13–16; 3:10–11; Isa 58:3–4; 59:6, 9–15; Jonah 1–2; Neh 5:15.

3. M. Weber, *Ancient Judaism* (New York: Free Press, 1952) 285.

4. The incidence of the term is surveyed, with negative results, by R. N. Whybray, *The Intellectual Tradition in the Old Testament* (Berlin: Walter de Gruyter, 1974); see

the more speculative and discursive kind of intellectual activity comes through clearly in the comments appended to Qoheleth (Qoh 12:12–14) and perhaps also in the verse added at the end of the poem on wisdom in Job 28. And the lack of esteem for the intellectual traditions of other nations surfaces at several points, for example in the dismissive attitude of the exilic Isaiah to Babylonian astronomy, divination, and omen lore, all prominent elements of Mesopotamian intellectual life (Isa 44:25; 47:8–13).

We should, perhaps, qualify what has been said by allowing that the limitations alluded to might be explained by the very definite religious criteria according to which only certain writings were allowed to survive. In other words, the literary output of early Second Temple Judaism may have been more extensive and varied than the extant canonical corpus would suggest. C itself refers to sources which, assuming that they actually existed, have not survived.[5] To judge by frequent allusions to "discourses of the sages" (*dibrê ḥăkāmîm*) in Proverbs and Qoheleth,[6] it was the custom to put together collections of the sayings of notable teachers, and it is unlikely that Prov 31:1–9 is all that existed of the sayings of Agur and Lemuel. It is also possible to exaggerate the contrast between Greek and Israelite literature, as Josephus did in his tract against Apion (*Ag. Ap.* 1 §37–41). Like Xenophanes, Agur expresses a religious skepticism at odds with current beliefs. Job also seems to presuppose a lay readership and intellectual milieu. Like his contemporary Pindar, the author is wary of attempts to plumb the deep complexities of human existence; witness the list of unanswered and presumably unanswerable questions posed in the theophany (Job 38). At the same time, he stands in the tradition of learned reflection on the cosmos, including the movements of the heavenly bodies (9:6–10; 26:7–14) and the phenomena of nature in general (8:11–12; 12:7–9; 36–37). The poem on inaccessible wisdom in chap. 28, generally thought to be a later addition

---

also G. Fohrer, "Sophia" in *TDNT* (1971) 7.476–96. Foreign sages are referred to, and disparaged, in Gen 41:8; Exod 7:1; Isa 19:11–12; Jer 10:7; 50:35; 51:57; Obad 8.

5. 1 Chr 29:29; 2 Chr 9:29; 12:15; 13:22; 20:34; 26:22; 32:32; 33:19.

6. Prov 1:6; 22:17; Qoh 12:11. Whybray (*The Intellectual Tradition,* 50–54) argues against a professional connotation at Prov 22:17 on the grounds that *dibrê ḥăkāmîm* is a title, therefore in prose and hence indeterminate. The sense may have been originally indeterminate, i.e., "discourses of wise people," but once it begins to be used as a title this need no longer be the case. The category persisted into the Roman period and is represented in early Christianity; see J. M. Robinson, "'Logoi Sophon': On the Gattung of Q," *Trajectories through Early Christianity* (ed. J. M. Robinson and H. Koester; Philadelphia: Fortress Press, 1971) 71–113.

to the book,[7] is not so far removed from some aspects of the thinking of Heraclitus: "the unexpected is not to be tracked down, and no path leads to it" (frg. 18; cf. Job 28:7–8, 13).[8] This kind of reflection and writing did not take place in a social vacuum, but unfortunately we do not have the means to reconstruct the milieu in which it flourished.

II

The author of C, therefore, moves in a world far removed from that of the Greek philosophers or, for that matter, the sages of Israel; a world centered on the temple and its cult, the prerogatives and duties of the cultic personnel, and the moral and ritual obligations of the ethnic community whose history he rewrites and reinterprets. An outside observer will inevitably view that world as narrow and confining. One can therefore understand, even if one does not share, the reaction of a liberal humanist like Wellhausen, who found in our author's work what he took to be the most stultifying traits of the emergent Judaism that C helped to shape. In speaking of the section of the work dealing with David as founder of the temple cult he wrote:

> The whole section I Chron. xxii–xxix is a startling instance of that statistical phantasy of the Jews which revels in vast sums of money on paper (xxii. 14), in artificial marshallings of names and numbers (xxiii–xxvii), in the enumeration of mere subjects without predicates, which simply stand on parade and neither signify nor do anything. The monotony is occasionally broken only by unctuous phrases, but without refreshing the reader. Let the experiment of reading the chapters through be tried.[9]

Wellhausen's aversion to Judaism, and indeed to any developed form of religious institution, is well known and need not detain us here. Later commentators have expressed themselves with more moderation, but without abandoning this negative view of the author of C as one of the epigoni. The point that can easily be missed is that the worldview of C, which Wellhausen so deplored, resulted from a deliberate opting

7. It follows a passage (27:13–23) attributed to Job that could hardly have been spoken by him. It is therefore out of context, but much of the imagery in the poem occurs elsewhere in the book, and Zophar had already made much the same point about the inaccessibility of wisdom (11:5–8).

8. Quoted from E. Hussey, *The Pre-Socratics* (New York: Charles Scribner's Sons, 1972) 38–39.

9. J. Wellhausen, *Prolegomena to the History of Ancient Israel* (New York: Meridian Library, 1957) 181 (original German ed. of 1883, 179–88).

for an alternative form of wisdom, the practical wisdom of fidelity to a law conceived to have been available from the beginning of the nation's history. Observance, therefore, is for Israel the equivalent of the wisdom of other peoples. This position, which first emerged clearly as a cardinal point of Deuteronomic orthodoxy, was fully internalized by the author of C. Others would develop it along theoretical lines by hypostatizing *tôrâ* as the embodiment and comprehensive expression of *ḥokmâ,*[10] but this was not a concern of the author of our work. The peculiar form assumed by wisdom in C is, therefore, the fruit of a specifically Israelite reaction to encounter with other intellectual traditions, and one that was developed only within one segment, albeit a dominant one, of late Israelite–early Jewish society.

As noted a moment ago, the point of departure for this development is the Deuteronomic corpus. Just as the Deuteronomic History, in its final exilic form, served as the principal source for 1–2 Chronicles, so the Deuteronomic law and program provided the author of C with his basic orientation. A fundamental point is the assertion that law observance is to be for Israel the equivalent of the wisdom of other peoples. If, therefore, the law is studied and observed, Israel will be regarded by these other peoples as a wise and discerning nation (*ʿam-ḥākām wĕnābôn,* Deut 4:6–8). This peculiarly Israelite form of wisdom has been revealed once and for all, and is therefore attainable without the kind of speculation about "hidden things" (*nistārôt*) characteristic of foreign wisdom (Deut 29:28). It is to be sought neither in heaven, namely, through the quest for arcane knowledge, nor overseas, namely, from the wisdom traditions of other peoples (Deut 30:11–14). It is available in an authoritative written law[11] that Moses as teacher gave to his people[12] and that they in their turn must study and teach their children.[13] True to this perspective, the author of C regards the law, which certainly included the laws in Deuteronomy as its principal component,[14] as having been available from the outset in writing.[15] Movements of renewal through-

10. Prov 8:22–31; Sir 24:1–29.

11. The Deuteronomists appear to have been the first to apply the term *tôrâ* to the corpus of laws as a whole rather than, as previously, to an individual stipulation of law. See B. Lindars, "Torah in Deuteronomy," *Words and Meanings* (ed. P. R. Ackroyd and B. Lindars; Cambridge: Cambridge University Press, 1968) 128–29.

12. Deut 4:1, 5, 14; 5:31; 6:1; 31:19, 22.

13. Deut 4:10; 5:1; 11:19; 17:18–19; 31:13.

14. On the identity of the law in Chronicles-Ezra-Nehemiah see my *Ezra-Nehemiah,* 152–57.

15. 1 Chr 10:13; 16:40; 22:12–13; 28:7, 19; 2 Chronicles 5–10.

out the history always begin with a return to this law and its demands. In a departure from his principal source, the author describes how Jehoshaphat sent a panel of lay and clerical officials round the cities of Judah to teach the people out of a written law that they took with them (2 Chr 17:7–9), an incident that may reflect practice in the author's own day. Jehoshaphat also set up a regional and central judicial system based on Deuteronomy (2 Chr 19:4–11; Deut 1:16–18; 17:8–13). Deuteronomy expressly places judges among the wise (*ḥăkāmîm,* Deut 16:18–19; cf. Exod 23:8), and we may be sure that for the author of C the custodians, teachers, and interpreters of the law were the true depositories of the wisdom peculiar to Israel.

In view of what has been said, it is not surprising if language associated with wisdom is used sparingly in C, and where it occurs the reference is never to a class of professional sages. A brief glance at terms occurring frequently in sapiential compositions will suffice to make the point. With the exception of those places where it refers to the skill of the artisan, the substantive *ḥokmâ* and the adjective *ḥākām* are restricted to Solomon as paradigm of judicial wisdom.[16] The associated quality of *śēkel* (discretion, good sense) and the related verbal form *haśkîl* also occur in connection with Solomon, and even more frequently with reference to the functions of Levites and the qualities needed to carry them out.[17] The teaching activity of Levites is highlighted during the reign of Jehoshaphat in the incident already noted (2 Chr 17:7–9; verbal stem *lmd,* Piel), and elsewhere *habîn* (lit.: to impart understanding) and the participle *mēbîn* (instructor) occur in connection with their task of teaching the law and performing (perhaps also composing) liturgical music.[18]

The author of C explicitly associates wisdom with law observance in the charge addressed by David to Solomon in which discretion and understanding (*śēkel ûbînâ*) are expressed in observance of the law that in its turn brings success (1 Chr 22:12–13). In his night vision at Gibeon, Solomon himself requested wisdom and knowledge (*ḥokmâ ûmaddā*) with a view to successful government that, in the author's view, and following the Deuteronomic line, meant the conscientious and judicious

16. 2 Chr 1:10–12; 2:11; chap. 9 passim.

17. Solomon: 1 Chr 22:12; 2 Chr 2:11; Levites: 1 Chr 28:19; 2 Chr 30:22; Ezra 8:18; Neh 8:8, 13.

18. 1 Chr 15:22; 25:6–7; 2 Chr 26:5; 34:12; 35:3; Neh 8:2–3, 7–9, 12. Note the phrase *mēbîn ʿim-talmîd* (instructor with pupil) at 1 Chr 25:8.

implementation of the laws (2 Chr 1:7–12; Deut 17:14–20). Following Solomon's example (the author prudently omits his involvement with foreign women), the wise kings of Israel — Asa, Jehoshaphat, Hezekiah, and Josiah — were those who "sought YHWH" by obeying his will revealed in a written law.[19] These rulers embody the model of kingship set out in Deuteronomy (17:14–20), according to which constant reference to a written law in the ruler's possession guarantees a long and successful reign. The Deuteronomic equation of nomism with wisdom also appears in the Ezra material, and specifically in the imperial firman authorizing Ezra to enforce the law among Jews in the Trans-Euphrates satrapy and set up appropriate judicial procedures (Ezra 7:11–26). This decree of Artaxerxes (probably Artaxerxes I Long Hand, 465–424 BCE) may be based on an authentic document, but if so it has quite clearly been extensively edited by the author of the history as a whole.[20] One of the clearest indications is the parallelism between "the law of your God which is in your hand" (*dāt ʾĕlāhāk dî bîdāk*, 7:14) and "the wisdom of your God which is in your hand" (*ḥokmat ʾĕlāhāk dî bîdāk*, 7:25). This phrase, totally out of place in a Persian imperial decree, recalls the identification of law observance with wisdom in Deut 4:6 and here and there in psalms of Deuteronomic inspiration (Pss 37:30–31; 119:98). The establishment of judicial procedures and the command to give instruction in the law (7:25) are also in keeping with the Deuteronomic program (Deut 1:16–17; 16:18; 17:8–13; cf. the *šāpĕtîn* and *dayyānîn* of Ezra 7:25 with the *šopĕṭîm* and *šoṭĕrîm* of Deut 16:18), and the distinction between "the law of your God" and "the law of the king" in Ezra 7:26 corresponds to that between "the matter of YHWH" and "the matter of the King" in C's account of Jehoshaphat's judicial reforms (2 Chr 19:11). There is, in fact, a close parallelism between the legal and judicial measures attributed to Jehoshaphat in C's history and those with which Ezra was charged in the decree.

It would be widely agreed that critical judgment on our author as historian must be tempered by an appreciation of the fact that his primary intent was to edify and convey moral teaching, and specifically by demonstrating the consequences of observance or nonobservance of the laws. Beginning with the divided monarchy, the history may in fact be read as a series of moral exempla that, though arranged chronologi-

19. 2 Chr 14:3, 7; 17:4; 19:3; 20:4; 22:9; 31:21; 34:3. "Seeking YHWH" (stem *drš*) is characteristic of the Deuteronomic circle.

20. See my *Ezra-Nehemiah*, 144–52.

cally, could be taken independently. In this respect at least the author's work overlaps with that of the sages, and we cannot help noticing how themes familiar from the work of the sages keep on recurring; for example, the consequences of fidelity and infidelity, humility before God and pride. Particularly in evidence is the principle of individual retribution, a familiar theme in the so-called wisdom writings. To illustrate this principle the author does not hesitate to alter the record, as in his account of Manasseh's repentance following on captivity in Babylon, an account that neatly disposes of the problem of how a bad king could have had such a long reign (2 Chr 33:10–13). While the point is never made explicitly, it is clear that for the author piety and wisdom are interchangeable terms.

Whatever, therefore, is subsumed under the rubric of wisdom is here concentrated exclusively on conduct evaluated according to the prescriptions of a revealed and written law. Though the analogy is partial and imperfect, we might think of the way in which certain sectors in Islam have at different times neglected a rich tradition of intellectual inquiry in favor of a single-minded concentration on the *shāriʿa,* the law based on divine revelation, tradition, and consensus. It is therefore hardly surprising if we find little reference in C to intellectual activity outside the legal and cultic spheres. Perhaps the only exception, if it is that, is the obscure allusion to those of the tribe Issachar "who had understanding of the times, to know what Israel ought to do" (1 Chr 12:33). The Targum is no doubt correct in understanding this to refer to astronomical matters, but even here the intent is practical and ethical.[21] The author does not polemicize against intellectual speculation and inquiry, but his lack of interest in these matters anticipates the ambiguity toward foreign learning ("Greek wisdom") in certain rabbinic writings of the Tannaitic and Amoraic periods.[22]

21. See R. Le Déaut and J. Robert, *Targum des Chroniques I: Introduction et Traduction* (Rome: Biblical Institute Press, 1971) 70–71. H. G. M. Williamson (*1 and 2 Chronicles* [Grand Rapids, Mich.: Wm. B. Eerdmans Publishing Co., 1982] 112) suggests that "to know what Israel ought to do" has been interpolated, but without adequate warranty.

22. S. Lieberman, *Greek in Jewish Palestine* (New York: Jewish Theological Seminary of America, 1942) 15–28; and again in *Hellenism in Jewish Palestine* (2d ed.; New York: Jewish Theological Seminary of America, 1962) 100–114, Lieberman warned against interpreting certain baraitot dealing with "Greek wisdom" (*ḥokmat yavanîm, ḥokmâ yavanît*) in the sense of an absolute prohibition of learning the Greek language or studying Greek philosophy. The principal relevant passages are: *b. B. Qam.* 82b; *b. Soṭa* 49b; *b. Menaḥ.* 64b, 99b.

III

One would not need to be deeply versed in the sociology of knowledge to suspect that the distinctive tradition in which the author of C stood, a tradition concentrating single-mindedly on legal and cultic matters including ritual law (*tāhorat haqqodeš*, 2 Chr 30:19), is of clerical origin. The world of C is the temple community in the province of Judah, probably in the last years of Persian rule, and more specifically the social elite referred to often in Ezra-Nehemiah as the *gôlâ* or *běnē-haggôlâ* originating in the Mesopotamian diaspora during the Neo-Babylonian period.[23] Exclusive control of the temple and its considerable revenues by this group, secured during the first century of Iranian rule, assured social and economic as well as religious dominance for this social entity in general and the temple personnel in particular. And it goes without saying that an important instrument of social control was the interpretation and administration of the laws that, as was the case elsewhere in the Persian empire, formed the civil constitution of the Jewish *ethnos*.[24]

The point has been made that the most important formative influences on the author of C derive from the Deuteronomic corpus and especially the Deuteronomic law. At the literary level, a fairly clear line of continuity can be traced between the homiletic material in Deuteronomy (e.g., 4:1–40) and the Levitical sermons in 1–2 Chronicles. In an important article published in 1934, Gerhard von Rad argued that these generally fairly brief addresses, even when not actually delivered by Levites, derive from Levitical instruction delivered either orally, as they went in circuit about the province (2 Chr 17:7–9; 30:6–10), or in epistolary form (2 Chr 21:12–15; 30:1). Typically, these addresses or sermons, presumably much abbreviated in the form in which they appear in Chronicles, would contain doctrine, application by means of historical examples, and concluding exhortation. They also incorporated allusions to earlier authoritative writings, especially from the prophetic books.[25] Von Rad maintained that the basic model for the genre is to be found in the Deuteronomic homily, especially the war homily (e.g.,

23. Ezra 1:11; 2:1 = Neh 7:6; Ezra 3:8; 4:1; 6:16, 19–21; 8:35; 10:7, 8, 16.

24. On the social situation in Judah during the Persian period see my "Temple and Society in Achaemenid Judah," *Second Temple Studies*, vol. 1: *Persian Period* (ed. P. R. Davies; Sheffield: JSOT Press, 1991) 22–53.

25. G. von Rad, "The Levitical Sermon in I and II Chronicles," *The Problem of the Hexateuch and Other Essays* (Edinburgh and London: Oliver & Boyd, 1966) 267–80.

Deut 7:16–26; 9:1–6; 31:3–8), which he attributed to Levites, the forerunners of those who, according to the author of C, "instructed all Israel" (2 Chr 35:3). One could therefore make out a good case that the bearers of the tradition in which the author of C stood, and out of which he wrote, were Levites who specialized in legal matters, including legal exposition and instruction.

Who, then, were these Levites? With the exception of one reference in a late redactional strand (Deut 27:14, in which the Levites pronounce the covenant curses), the distinction between first- and second-order clergy, priests, and Levites is not attested in Deuteronomy, and allusions to Levites in the history are among the clearest instances of Deuteronomistic or post-Deuteronomistic editing (Josh 3:3; 1 Sam 6:15; 2 Sam 15:24; 1 Kgs 8:4). In Deuteronomy cultic personnel are routinely referred to as "Levitical priests" (*kohănîm lĕviyyîm*), and all have *in principle* the same status and enjoy the same privileges, even though many are unemployed and in need of public support.[26] While the Deuteronomic law speaks of several functions performed by these "Levitical priests" (e.g., the diagnosis of skin disease, Deut 24:8), the emphasis falls heavily on the study, teaching, and administering of the laws.[27] At the same time, the silence of Deuteronomy on Aaron and his descendants, with the exception of one reference that is not at all complimentary,[28] suggests that this presentation of the priestly office in Deuteronomy is deliberate and polemical. The Priestly source (P), on the contrary, regards Aaron as the prototypical priest and has nothing to say about instruction as a priestly task. The obscurity surrounding the history of the priestly families during the preexilic and exilic periods rules out any clear and certain interpretation of these data, but it seems as if the authors of the Deuteronomic law and history were active at a time when the Aaronite priestly class was struggling for but had not yet attained

26. On Levites living outside Jerusalem and in need of public support see Deut 12:12, 18–19; 14:27, 29; 16:11, 14; 26:11–13. Their right to serve at the central sanctuary is clearly stated in Deut 18:6–7.

27. The law tablets, deposited in the ark, are confided to them (Deut 31:9–13, 25–26), and their involvement in judicial proceedings is alluded to several times (17:9, 12; 19:17; 21:5). The oracle on Levi also refers to a teaching function (33:8–11).

28. See Deut 9:20, where Aaron is saved from death during the Golden Calf incident by the intercession of Moses. The incidental allusions to Aaron's death (10:6; 32:50) are acknowledged to be later additions in the P manner. The negative image of P in Deuteronomic circles would emerge even more clearly if, as L. Perlitt argued (*Bundestheologie im Alten Testament* [Neukirchen-Vluyn: Neukirchener Verlag, 1969] 203–32), Exodus 32–34 is essentially a D composition.

complete ascendancy, and had in mind a rather different understanding of the priestly office.

By the time of the composition of C, however, the distinction between the Aaronite priesthood, now claiming descent also from Zadok (1 Chr 27:17), and the Levites as a distinct and inferior class of cult personnel, was a fait accompli. The circumstances under which the Aaronite branch of the priesthood achieved ascendancy are unknown, though some hints of the internecine strife within priestly families that led to it can be gleaned from the P narrative and genealogical material in the Pentateuch and from Ezekiel 40–48.[29] In this respect it is also worth noting that Levites were not represented in the original caravan of Babylonian *olim* assembled by Ezra (Ezra 8:15). Throughout the two centuries of Persian rule several classes of cult personnel, including musicians and gatekeepers, were co-opted into the Levitical ranks, and the minimum age was progressively lowered to accommodate these additions.[30] But in spite of his obvious enthusiasm for liturgical music, the Chronicler clearly regarded exposition of and instruction in the law as the most important Levitical function. The Levites are closely associated with the ark that contained the tablets of the law (e.g., 2 Chr 5:4–12; 7:6). They play an important role in the reforming activity of the "good" kings, Jehoshaphat (2 Chr 17:7–9; 19:4–11), Hezekiah (2 Chr 31:4), and Josiah (2 Chr 35:3), and are especially prominent as educators in Ezra's public reading of the law (Nehemiah 8), which perhaps reflects a kind of proto-synagogal practice at the time of writing. The author misses no opportunity to highlight the contribution of Levites, even at the expense of the Aaronite priests (e.g., 2 Chr 29:34), and it may be significant that on more than one occasion he lists them before priests (2 Chr 19:8; 30:21; Neh 10:1).

As von Rad observed, one of the principal vehicles of Levitical instruction in C was the sermon, and an important component of the Levitical sermon was the illustration by historical example of the con-

29. See especially Num 16:1–17:15, the rebellion of the Kohathite Levite Korah supported by lay leaders, and Ezek 44:10–14; 48:11. A. H. J. Gunneweg (*Leviten und Priester* [Göttingen: J. C. B. Mohr, 1965] 138, 185–87) discussed the contribution of the P genealogies in this respect.

30. Liturgical musicians and gatekeepers are listed separately in Ezra-Nehemiah (Ezra 2:40–41, 70 = Neh 7:43–44, 73; also Ezra 7:7; Neh 13:10), but by the time of C they are assumed to be Levites (1 Chr 9:33–34; 15:16–22; 23:2–32; 25:1–31; 26:1–19). The minimum age for Levites is thirty in Num 4:3 and 1 Chr 23:3, twenty-five in Num 8:24, and twenty in 1 Chr 23:24, 27.

sequences of fidelity and infidelity. Azariah ben Oded, for example, attributes the anomie of the period of the Judges to the absence of a *kohēn môreh* (teaching priest, 2 Chr 15:1–7). Accounts of military actions, many of them clearly fictitious, seem to have served largely as narrative context for these sermons. Indeed, as suggested earlier, the history of the monarchy as a whole could be read as a series of lessons or exempla illustrating the importance of the law as *the* source of Israel's wisdom and well-being.[31] If the author was himself a Levite, which seems overwhelmingly probable, adoption of the literary medium of edifying history would make sense in view of his conviction that the Levites had inherited a share of the prophetic office. We note that where his source speaks of priests and prophets participating in the reforms of Josiah (2 Kgs 23:2), he refers to priests and Levites (2 Chr 34:30). The composition and rendition of liturgical music by the Levitical guilds are forms of prophecy (1 Chr 25:1–31), and the brief sermon preached by the Levite Jahaziel during the reign of Jehoshaphat is attributed to prophetic inspiration (2 Chr 20:13–19). Furthermore, the author cites as sources so many prophets and seers as to leave little doubt that he regarded the writing of history, or at least his kind of history, as a prophetic activity, a view later stated explicitly by Josephus (*Ag. Ap.* 1 §37–41). In this sense, therefore, clearly a very limited and idiosyncratic sense dictated by the tradition within which it was written, Chronicles-Ezra-Nehemiah may be regarded as sapiential.

31. A similar point is made by P. R. Ackroyd in "The Age of the Chronicler," *The Chronicler in His Age* (Sheffield: JSOT Press, 1991) 63–65.

3

SCRIBAL WISDOM AND THEODICY IN THE BOOK OF THE TWELVE

Raymond C. Van Leeuwen

Israelite wisdom appears in varied guises in the Hebrew Bible. At the last stage of canon formation, wisdom became a "hermeneutical construct,"[1] guiding scribal sages in their task of theological pattern-making, stitchery, and embroidery by which the quilt-work of centuries became one great tapestry as single and complex as life itself. Ben Sira's grandson construed the tripartite *Tanakh* in wisdom terms, as writings "on account of which we should praise Israel for *instruction and wisdom.*"[2] The grandson's Prologue and Ben Sira's work itself show that wisdom had become literary and learned in character, with primary sources in the law, prophets, and "other books" (see Sir 24:23, 33; 38:24; 39:1–3; 44–50). The sapiential prelude to Ben Sira's synthetic wisdom was the scribal activity of the final redactors of the *Tanakh*.

Scholars have begun to trace the handiwork of this end-redaction in various parts of scripture. Gerald Wilson, for example, shows that the wisdom redaction of the Psalter is crucial for its interpretation.[3] The

I would like to thank Simon J. De Vries, Leo Perdue, and members of the Religion Department of Calvin College for comments on an earlier draft of this essay.

1. G. T. Sheppard, *Wisdom as a Hermeneutical Construct: A Study in the Sapientializing of the Old Testament* (BZAW 151; Berlin: Walter de Gruyter, 1980) 13.

2. *Paideia kai sophia*, Prologue, line 3; cf. line 12. Cf. the Greek wisdom vocabulary of 2 Tim 3:15–16.

3. G. H. Wilson, "The Shape of the Book of Psalms," *Int* 46 (1992) 138. In addition to using ordinary redactional techniques such as insertions, the sages who edited the Psalter created larger theological matrices of meaning through arranging

study of the scribal, literary aspect of wisdom in the prophetic corpus is relatively new.[4]

The present essay will focus on a specific corpus, the Book of the Twelve, to detail certain techniques by which the scribes added hermeneutical patches at key junctures, arranged and stitched together previously existing works, all to shape this prophetic scroll into a theological whole.[5] In this essay the question of earlier stages of wisdom in the Twelve must be left aside.[6] My particular focus is on the quasi-midrashic and redactional use of a pentateuchal text that appears repeatedly in the first six books of the Twelve.[7] The base text, Exod 34:6–7, is an elaboration of the name YHWH expressing the bipolar attributes of mercy and retributive justice. As R. C. Dentan has shown, Exod 34:6–7 has certain affinities with the wisdom books of the Hebrew Bible.[8] (The broader golden calf tradition and text of Exodus 32–34 also plays a role in Hosea-Micah.)[9]

---

macrostructures, sequences, juxtapositions, and clusters of psalms. A major aspect of this scribal editing was theodicy in connection with the Babylonian exile (see ibid., 139–41, on the pivotal role of Psalm 89).

4. For the methodological issues that inform this essay, see R. C. Van Leeuwen, "The Sage in the Prophetic Literature," *The Sage in Israel and the Ancient Near East* (ed. J. G. Gammie and L. G. Perdue; Winona Lake, Ind.: Eisenbrauns, 1990) 295–306; M. Fishbane, *Biblical Interpretation in Ancient Israel* (Oxford: Clarendon Press, 1985); and R. E. Clements, "Patterns in the Prophetic Canon," *Canon and Authority: Essays in Old Testament Religion and Theology* (ed. G. W. Coats and B. O. Long; Philadelphia: Fortress Press, 1987) 42–55; idem, "Prophecy as Literature: A Re-appraisal," *The Hermeneutical Quest: Essays in Honor of James Luther Mays on his Sixty-fifth Birthday* (ed. D. G. Miller; Allison Park, Pa.: Pickwick Publications, 1986) 59–75. See also the essay (with bibliography) by C. R. Seitz and R. J. Clifford, "Isaiah, Book of" *ABD* (1992) 3.472–507. The present essay will not pursue the much-discussed question of wisdom as an aspect of original prophecy or of earlier stages of prophetic redaction.

5. See D. A. Schneider, "The Unity of the Book of the Twelve" (Ph.D. Diss.; Yale University, 1979), and P. R. House, *The Unity of the Twelve* (JSOTSup 97; Sheffield: Almond Press, 1990). Despite his title, Schneider's work is mainly concerned with the historical evolution of the Twelve into their present form. House employs categories from literary criticism (genre, character, structure, plot, point of view) that in practice appear not always apt nor able to illuminate crucial data.

6. Much work remains to be done in this area. For an initial orientation to the literature and problems, see Van Leeuwen, "The Sage."

7. See also Nah 1:3a as treated below.

8. R. C. Dentan, "The Literary Affinities of Exodus XXXIV6f.," *VT* 13 (1963) 34–51. Dentan's conclusion, that the formula has its origin in wisdom, may be too strong and has been criticized. But the general affinity of the concepts in Exod 34:6–7 to wisdom are undeniable. Cf., for example, Psalms 111 and 112 in their use of the attribute formula (111:4b; 112:4b). Because these psalms, as Zimmerli saw, are "twins," they should *both* be considered wisdom psalms. As far as theological concept formulation is concerned, the *imitatio Dei* is necessarily a two-way street. See also J. Scharbert, "Formgeschichte und Exegese von Ex 346f. und seiner Parallelen," *Bib* 34 (1957) 130–50.

9. Fishbane, *Biblical Interpretation*, 335–50; T. B. Dozeman, "Inner-Biblical In-

The scribal redactors of the MT (as opposed to the LXX) have used this base text as it existed in preexisting prophetic works, and have found pattern and thread to elaborate a theodicy in the first six books of the Twelve.[10] The wisdom character of the theodicy is signaled by its first explicit redactional appearance in Hos 14:10. The arrangement and editing of the first six books as wisdom theodicy prepare the *general* movement in the Twelve from judgment to salvation,[11] via Nahum and Habakkuk, which more explicitly vindicate God's justice relative to the respective destroyers of Israel and Judah.[12] Here the whole is more than the sum of the parts. Exodus 34:6–7, in the final form of the Twelve, is used as the redactors' crucial commentary on the bitter eighth-century prophets, Hosea, Amos, and Micah, thus combining judgment with theodicy and hope for the future.[13]

Fundamental to my essay is the insight of R. E. Clements "that the literary form of prophecy in the Old Testament establishes not simply a medium of preservation, but also a medium of interpretation." Drawing on studies concerning orality and literacy, Clements argues that the creation of a written prophetic corpus enabled the creation of a genuine prophetic theology where the diverse divine attributes, notably of justice and mercy, were seen "to cohere in a single divine Being." The literary character of prophecy enables "the more profound dimensions of genuine theologizing [, which appears] only when a given range of human experiences are interpreted in the light of this justice and mercy." For Clements, "the corpus of prophetic writings as a whole is profoundly and firmly hopeful in its message. The message of doom serves . . . to explain the past . . . in the manner of a theodicy . . . and to provide a groundwork of hope." . . .[14]

---

terpretation of Yahweh's Gracious and Compassionate Character," *JBL* 108 (1989) 207–23.

10. I use the term "theodicy" in a nontechnical sense to indicate simply a religious concern to vindicate apparently unjust actions of a deity, in this case YHWH's decision to destroy the Northern Kingdom and to send Judah into exile. Cf. J. L. Crenshaw, "Theodicy," *ABD* (1992) 6.444–47.

11. Clements, "Patterns."

12. "The main theme of Habakkuk is theodicy" (D. E. Gowan, "Habakkuk and Wisdom," *Perspective* 9 [1968] 159). Several of Gowan's arguments on wisdom are criticized by G. Tuttle, "Wisdom and Habakkuk," *Studia Biblica et Theologica* 3 (1973) 3–14. But Tuttle acknowledges wisdom affinities for Habakkuk (p. 14).

13. "The quest to interpret Torah is actually playing a central role in the very formation of the Hebrew Bible" (Dozeman, "Inner-Biblical Interpretation," 223).

14. Clements, "Prophecy as Literature," 59–60, 63, 68–71. Clements's observations throughout are fundamental to the present essay.

Several final, introductory observations must be made. First, the use of Exod 34:6–7 in the Twelve is only one of many factors in its editing, though its literary, hermeneutical, and theological roles in the final redaction of Hosea-Micah are fundamental. Second, the base text, especially in Joel and Jonah, sets up a dialectic with regard to the Day of the Lord in Amos as a day of divine judgment (its varied permutations into a day/days of judgment/salvation are not of primary concern here). Finally, as C. F. Keil observed long ago, the first six books (in the MT order) alternately place their *primary* (not exclusive) focus on the Northern or Southern kingdoms (Hosea–N, Joel–S, Amos–N, Obadiah–S, Jonah–N [here the modified book "title" is crucial, see below], Micah–S).[15] While the pattern breaks with Nahum, the first book of the second half of the Twelve, his focus on Assyria (the agent of the North's demise as well as trouble for Hezekiah's Judah)[16] is certainly to be contrasted with Habakkuk's turn to Babylon. These geographic patterns are not adventitious or decorative in the final ordering of the Twelve, but serve to reinforce the grave postexilic theological concern to provide a theodicy for the conquest and exile that struck first North and then South, at the hand of Assyria and Babylon, respectively. The interaction of these three factors (base text, Day of the Lord, and geography/nations) will be crucial to my argument.

EXODUS 34:6–7 IN THE TWELVE

Hosea

The first use of the base text (or its tradition) is in the first two chapters of Hosea, where it is sometimes overlooked.[17] The naming of

15. Cited in House, *Unity,* 64.

16. See J. J. M. Roberts, *Nahum, Habakkuk, and Zephaniah* (Louisville, Ky.: Westminster/John Knox Press, 1991) 40–41.

17. Fishbane (*Biblical Interpretation,* 335–50), for example, overlooks Hosea's use of Exod 34:6–7, as does Dozeman, "Inner-Biblical Interpretation," 207–23. H. Spieckermann ("Barmherzig und gnädig ist der Herr . . . ," *ZAW* 102 [1990] 1–18) correctly sees an allusion here to the *tradition* of Exod 34:6. However, Spieckermann considers that the full form of the *Gnadenformel* (universally acknowledged to be Exod 34:6 in its earliest occurrence) is exilic at the earliest (p. 3). Hence Hos 1:9 would be an independent attestation of a tradition that goes back to Canaanite El. However, Hosea's use of the name "Not-My-People" appears to presuppose some form of the golden calf narrative as do his references to calves (8:4–5; 13:2; cf. 14:4). While the connections of Hosea to the golden calf pericopes do not necessarily establish an original intertextuality, in the larger context of the redaction of the Twelve, these connections *become* a matter of intertextuality, which begs analysis. Thus, the prominence given the Exod 34:6 tradition at

Hosea's children is an ironic undoing of YHWH's compassion or love (*rḥwm*, Exod 34:6) toward the covenant people (*'m*, Exod 32:1–34:10 passim): "Call her name 'Not-Loved' [*l' rḥmh*], for no longer will I love [*'rḥm*] the family of Israel" (Hos 1:6, my trans.; cf. 2:6 [Eng. 2:4]; Exod 33:19); "Call his name 'Not-My-People' [*l' 'my*], for you are not my people [*l' 'my*] and I-WILL-BE no longer yours [*w'nky l' 'hyh lkm*]" (Hos 1:9, my trans.).[18] The name "Not-My-People" appears to play on the argument between Moses and God, as each attempts to ascribe "ownership" of the people to the other (Exod 32:7, 11, 12; 33:13, 16).[19] But it is the remarkable punning negation of the divine name YHWH that signals the radical character of God's refusal to be Israel's compassionate God.[20] The pun in v. 8 may be paraphrased, "I will no longer be YHWH for you."[21]

But Hosea quickly moves from the undoing of the divine name and attributes to their restoration, with the attendant mercy and salvation for his (restored) people (2:1, 3, 25 [Eng. 1:10; 2:1, 23]).[22] These plays on the names of YHWH and Hosea's children foreground the problem of YHWH's character vis-à-vis Israel at the very beginning of the Twelve.

The naming of Hosea's children also sets in motion another central theme in the Twelve, that of the Day of the Lord. While Hosea does not use the phrase *ywm yhwh*, the name Jezreel is set in contexts that anticipate the development of the Day of the Lord in Joel, Amos, and elsewhere. Hosea 1:5 uses the common prophetic phrase "on that day" (*wyhy bywm hhw'*) to refer to the Assyrian destruction of Israel (cf. Amos

---

the very onset of the Book of the Twelve has important repercussions for the theological shape and agenda of the Twelve *as developed by its redactors*. Thus for our purposes, it is not necessary to know the exact form of the exodus and golden calf traditions employed by Hosea. Cf. G. M. Tucker, "The Law in the Eighth-Century Prophets," *Canon, Theology, and Old Testament Interpretation: Essays in Honor of Brevard S. Childs* (ed. G. M. Tucker, D. L. Petersen, and R. R. Wilson; Philadelphia: Fortress Press, 1988) 201–16, esp. 209–11.

18. Unless marked otherwise, biblical quotations are from the RSV.

19. S. E. Balentine, "Prayers for Justice in the Old Testament: Theodicy and Theology," *CBQ* 51 (1989) 597–616, esp. 608–10.

20. The general importance of the name YHWH in the Hosea book appears, for example, from the formula "to know YHWH" (5:4; 6:3; cf. 13:4), from the hymnic refrain "YHWH is his name" (12:5), and from the rejection of the name Baal (2:16–17).

21. See the LXX of Hos 1:9 and W. Rudolph, *Hosea* (KAT 13; Gütersloh: Gerd Mohn, 1966) 38, 54–55. Cf. the punning on the divine name (*'hyh* or *yhwh*, Exod 3:12, 14–15) in the burning bush passage, which Hosea need not have known.

22. Rudolph (*Hosea,* 56) considers the reversal in Hos 2:1–3 original; Clements ("Patterns," 52–53), as secondary. If redactional, these reversals are evidence for the larger "pattern" of redactional shaping that gives the Twelve a unified message in which mercy triumphs over judgment (so Clements, "Patterns"; cf. Sir 49:10). Cf. also the vocabulary of Hos 2:21–22 (cf. 4:1) to Exod 34:6.

5:1–20; 8:3, 9–10, 13).[23] Hosea 2:2 (Eng. 1:11) speaks of the "*great . . . day* of Jezreel" (cf. Joel 2:11) to prophesy the *undoing* of the original judgment on Jezreel in 1:4–5.

The dialectic of God's wrath and mercy here set in motion will find further echoes in the Twelve, echoes that employ Exod 34:6–7 and its context to develop a wisdom theodicy in relation to the Day of the Lord. This theodicy is in the first instance a response to the northern exile of 722 BCE, but also, ultimately, to the southern exile of 587 BCE.

The first explicit redactional sign of the theodicy is the well-known wisdom admonition that concludes Hosea:

> Whoever is wise, let him understand these things;
> whoever is discerning, let him know them;
> for the ways of the Lord are right,
> and the upright walk in them,
> but transgressors stumble in them. (14:10 [Eng. 14:9])

Gerald Sheppard has discussed the final redaction, wisdom character of this passage.[24] But the literary and interpretive significance of Sheppard's observations for the shaping of the Twelve has not been pursued. A final redactor works with a synoptic overview of the varied materials he wishes to bring together. Since both MT and LXX reveal Nahum-Malachi as a consistently ordered block of books, our attention is directed to the first six, where LXX and MT diverge. What factors led to the particular order of Hosea-Micah in the MT? And what are the clues that reveal the redactor's intentions?

The redactor's creation of Hos 14:10 is inexplicable apart from the use of Exodus 32–34 (especially 34:6–7) in Joel and Jonah. Nor can Hos 14:10 be understood apart from the doxology that concludes the first half of the Twelve (Mic 7:18–20), a text that again uses Exod 34:6.

After the debacle of the golden calf, and after much intercession, Moses requests of the Lord, "Let me *know* your *ways*, that I may *know* you" (Exod 33:13, my trans.). This request, as the narrative sequence indicates (33:17–19; 34:5–9), occasions the revelation of YHWH's name

23. The phrase may be redactional in Hos 1:5; so Rudolph (*Hosea*, 52), who sees the content of the verse as original, nonetheless.

24. Sheppard, *Wisdom*, 129–36. Cf. Ps 107:40–43; Jer 9:11. The conclusion of Psalm 107 bears evidence of the same redactional hand, strategy, and themes as Hos 14:10. The psalm opens the last "book" of the Psalter just as Hosea opens the Twelve. Wilson ("The Shape," 134) considers that "the strategic placement of 'wisdom' psalms provides a structuring framework in the last two books (Pss. 90 + 91; 106; 145)." Wilson overlooks Psalm 107, but see L. C. Allen (*Psalms 101–150* [WBC 21; Waco, Tex.: Word, 1983] 61), citing F. Crüsemann.

and bipolar attributes that are the "ways" of YHWH in dealing with sinful humans. This "knowing" of YHWH's "ways" appears in Mic 4:1–5 (par. to Isa 2:1–5), a late addition to Micah. In itself the language is ambiguous, referring either to YHWH's behavior toward humans or to the behavior he requires of humans. (Torah, as "law" or "instruction," is similarly ambiguous [Mic 4:2].) But in Micah 4, this ambiguity is weighted, in connection with the eschatological *judgments* of YHWH (4:3–4), to refer primarily to *YHWH's* attributes ("name") as the context for human existence:[25]

> For all the peoples walk
> each in the name of its god,
> but we will walk in the name of the Lord our God
> for ever and ever. (Mic 4:5)

Most significantly, this verse is a redactionally expanded variant of its Isaianic parallel. It stems from the wisdom redactor of Hos 14:10 (Eng. 14:9):

> the ways of the Lord are right,
> and the upright walk in them,
> but transgressors stumble in them. (cf. Mic 6:7–17; Prov 10:29)

This redactional line connecting Hos 14:10 to Mic 7:18–20 via Mic 4:5 is confirmed by the logic of Psalm 25, an acrostic psalm so filled with wisdom themes and motifs that one is tempted to include it among the wisdom psalms.[26] Psalm 25 brings together the scattered vocabulary, concepts, and logic of the Twelve's redactor into one clear literary unit. Particularly noteworthy is the parallelism that renders equivalent YHWH's "ways," his "name," and his attributes according to Exod 34:6. The psalmist as "sinner" prays,

> Make me to know *thy ways* [*drkyk . . . hwdyʿny*], O Lord; . . .
> *Lead me* in thy *truth* [*hdrykny*].
> Be mindful of thy *mercy* [*rḥmyk*], O Lord,
> and of thy steadfast love [*ḥsdyk*]. . . .

25. While the ambiguity is *weighted* by Mic 4:5, it is not dissolved. For walking "in the presence" of YHWH's character has ethical consequences (Mic 6:8).

26. See the uncertainty regarding genre and the comments on wisdom in Psalm 25 by H.-J. Kraus, *Psalms 1–59: A Commentary* (Minneapolis: Augsburg Publishing House, 1988); P. C. Craigie, *Psalms 1–50* (WBC 19; Waco, Tex.: Word, 1983) 218. For Craigie, the acrostic and the "preponderance of language typical of the Wisdom Literature" suggest the psalm is literary and late. R. E. Murphy's classic study notes the psalm's wisdom elements ("A Consideration of the Classification, 'Wisdom Psalms,'" VTSup 9 [1963] 156–57, 165–66).

Good and upright [*yšr*] is the Lord;
therefore he instructs sinners in *the way.*
He leads the humble through the judgment,[27]
and teaches the humble *his way.*
All the paths of the Lord are
steadfast love and faithfulness [*ḥsd w'mt*]....
For thy *name's* sake, O Lord,
pardon my guilt. (Ps 25:4–13)

In Psalm 25, as in the end-redaction of the Twelve, the ambiguity of the key-word "way" is exploited. It is, on the one hand, the right way for humans to live. On the other hand, it is equally the way (or ways) in which YHWH acts toward sinners in mercy or judgment. Wise sinners know their lot is deserving of judgment and so appeal to the *positive* attributes of YHWH ("for your name's sake"), as revealed in Exod 34:6. It is the character of YHWH that Moses (Exod 33:18), the psalmist, and the redactor of the Twelve wish to "know" and understand (cf. Ps 103:3–13). It is this "way," this "name," that they wish to walk in (Mic 4:5), believing it to be judgment for incorrigible rebels, but mercy and forgiveness for the repentant. This prayer applies not only to the individual but to the nation (Ps 25:22; Exod 33:16; cf. Mic 7:7–10, 18–20).

The wisdom admonition ending Hosea also has a striking double connection with the attribute formula in Joel and Jonah. Immediately after an admonition appealing to the name formula, Joel 2:14 asks, "*Who knows* whether he [YHWH] will not turn and repent?" And in Jonah, immediately before God relents of the evil he is about to visit upon Nineveh, and just before Jonah's bitter complaint about God's merciful attributes (3:10–4:2), the repentant king of Nineveh asks, "*Who knows,* God may yet repent and turn?" (Jonah 3:9; cf. 1:6). The connections with Hos 14:10 are two. First, theologically, the wise, those instructed by the Book of the Twelve, are those who *know* the *ways* of God, that he does forgive those who repent; they have moved beyond the stereotypical expression of uncertainty, "*Who knows*...?"[28] to the knowledge of YHWH's bipolar ways of mercy and justice.

Second, this theological observation is buttressed by a brilliant wordplay connecting not only Hosea to Joel and Jonah, but all three to

27. RSV modified, *ydrk*...*bmšpṭ*. MT points with the article; cf. Ps 1:5, where RSV translates "in the judgment." Craigie (*Psalms 1–50,* 222) notes that the wisdom of Psalms 1 and 25 is complementary, but he does not explore the insight in detail.

28. J. L. Crenshaw, "The Expression *Mî Yôdea* in the Hebrew Bible," *VT* 36 (1986) 274–88.

the doxological ending of Micah. The pun has to do with the collocated words "Who/ever" and "know" (*my . . . yd'*) in each of the first three passages (Hos 14:10; Joel 2:14; Jonah 3:9). The Micah doxology, like the other three, begins with "who" (*my*). But, as noted by many commentators, the opening of the Micah passage is already a pun on the prophet's name, "Micah," a theophoric name referring to the incomparability of YHWH ("Who is like YH/WH?"). Micah 7:18 asks, "Who is a God like thee," and goes on to praise God for the familiar attributes of mercy, compassion, and forgiveness from Exod 34:6 (see below). The Micah doxology ends the collection of the first six books of the Twelve with a description of the one whose name the wise have learned to know through God's ways as revealed by the prophets.

Joel

Joel contains the first explicit use in the Twelve of Exod 34:6 in connection with the Day of the Lord. While Hosea is clearly eighth-century in its origins, Joel shows all the signs of exilic or postexilic "anthological" composition. It extensively alludes to earlier scripture to convey its message.[29] Joel may be divided into essentially two parts. Joel 1:1–2:27 presents an inner-historical threat of a Day (or Days) of the Lord (locusts, drought, invasion) against Zion, which is averted. Joel 3:1–4:21 (Eng. 2:28–3:21) presents an eschatological, perhaps proto-apocalyptic day (or days) in which Judah's enemies are defeated and Judah is restored both spiritually and materially. As Hosea has a negative and positive "day of Jezreel," so Joel has negative and positive Days of the Lord. This is in keeping with the general movement in the prophets from judgment to salvation.[30]

The difficulty of finding a concrete *Sitz im Leben* for Joel is notorious. To find specific historical referents for the Days of the Lord in Joel is equally difficult. Thus Ferdinand Deist suggests that Joel is primarily a *literary* theology of the Day of the Lord.[31] This general point seems

29. It is generally more apt to use the term "inner-biblical allusion" than "inner-biblical exegesis" to describe this intertextual phenomenon. See the discussion of Fishbane in L. Eslinger, "Inner-Biblical Exegesis and Inner-Biblical Allusion: The Question of Category," *VT* 42 (1992) 47–58.

30. See Clements, "Patterns."

31. F. E. Deist, "Parallels and Reinterpretation in the Book of Joel: A Theology of the Yom Yahweh?" *Text and Context: Old Testament and Semitic Studies for F. C. Fensham* (ed. W. Claasen; JSOTSup 48; Sheffield: Sheffield Academic Press, 1988) 63–79.

correct.[32] Moreover, Dale Schneider's analysis, that Joel is a late insertion into an original cluster of preexilic prophets (Hosea, Amos, Micah, so the LXX), is also valid.[33] Thus its placement in the Twelve is crucial for an understanding of the literary theo-logic that governed the final compilation of the Twelve. Consequently, our concern is not the original historical setting of the book, but its present literary and theological function in the Twelve.

Joel's use of the positive attribute formula from Exod 34:6 takes place in connection with the possibility of averting a threatened Day of the Lord (2:11) through repentance and fasting (2:12, 15–16; cf. 1:14; Jonah 3:5, 7–8):

> "Yet even now," says the Lord,
> "return to me with all your heart. . . . "
> Return to the Lord, your God,
> for he is gracious and merciful,
> slow to anger, and abounding in steadfast love,
> and repents of evil.[34]
> Who knows whether he will not turn and repent.
> (Joel 2:12–14a; cf. Jonah 3:9)

Joel has the priests appearing in the position of Moses, who had interceded for "thy people" (*'mk*, Exod 32:11–12):

> "Spare thy people, O Lord,
> and make not thy heritage a reproach. . . .
> Why should they say[35] among the peoples,
> 'Where is their God?' " (Joel 2:17; cf. Mic 7:10)

In response, YHWH "became jealous [*wyqn' yhwh*, cf. Exod 34:14] . . . and had pity on his people" (2:18), and promises to restore the land's fertility (in language from Hos 2:8) and remove Israel's "reproach among the nations" (Joel 2:19). Thus the first half of Joel (1:1–2:22) por-

32. Though contrary to Deist, Joel need not therefore be nonreferential, but is multireferential in its typicality vis-à-vis history; cf. Amos 4:6–11.

33. Schneider, "Unity," 72–89. Schneider makes good observations on the literary relations connecting Joel to Hosea and Amos, though he is disinclined to see all of these as redactional. He dates Joel in the late seventh century. The most extensive demonstration of Joel's anthological character is S. Bergler, *Joel als Schriftinterpret* (Beiträge zur Erforschung des Alten Testaments und des Antiken Judentums 16; Frankfurt am Main: Lang, 1988). See also Deist, "Parallels."

34. This last phrase is from Exod 32:12, 14.

35. *Lmh y'mrw,* so also Exod 32:12. Moses' prayer in Num 14:13–19 uses similar logic in connection with the divine attribute formula, with similar positive results (v. 20). Cf. Nehemiah's prayer (Neh 9:16–37).

trays an imminent Day of the Lord that is averted by repentance and fasting and through an appeal to YHWH's merciful attributes.

The attributes of the Day of the Lord in Joel have obvious affinities with the Day and related phenomena in Amos. For our purposes, we need note only that the impending Day is averted by the people's repentance. This is in marked contrast to the failure of repentance in response to the preexilic preaching of Amos. The ending of Joel confirms that Amos and subsequent books are to be read in the light of Joel. Joel or his redactors offer verbatim citations that anticipate (not chronologically but literarily) later texts in the Twelve. Joel 4:16 (Eng. 3:16) anticipates the *opening* of Amos (1:2) as Joel 4:18 (Eng. 3:18) anticipates the *end* of Amos (9:13).[36] The purpose of these intertextual repetitions is to link the reading and thus the dialectic message communicated by the two books.[37]

To these well-known links between the books must be added the puzzling last verse of Joel:

> And I shall certainly not hold innocent their [the nations', cf. v. 19] bloodshed,
> for the Lord dwells in Zion. (Joel 4:21 [Eng. 3:21])[38]

This crux belongs to the final redaction of the Twelve and functions as a pivot between Joel and Amos. It is oddly located after Joel 4:20 (Eng. 3:20), which otherwise makes a good ending for the book. It attaches through wordplay to the statement regarding "innocent blood" (*dm nqy'*) in v. 19 and to the utterances of vv. 16–17 concerning Zion. Its status as final redaction in the Twelve is clear because it has no real function other than to link Joel and Amos in a manner that contrasts

36. The long controversy concerning the authenticity or (preexisting) redactional character of these verses does not affect our argument, which concerns the end-redaction of the Twelve.

37. For an analysis of verbatim repetition as the most powerful literary means of linking noncontiguous passages, see D. Pardee, *Ugaritic and Hebrew Poetic Parallelism: A Trial Cut* (VTSup 39; Leiden: E. J. Brill, 1988). Cf. A. Berlin, *The Dynamics of Biblical Parallelism* (Bloomington: Indiana University Press, 1985) 17.

38. *Wnqyty dmm l' nqyty.* This rendering seeks to convey the allusive reference of v. 21a to the judgment formula of Exod 34:7. It assumes the grammatical function of the first finite verb has been contaminated by the infinitive absolute of the base text (*wnqh l' ynqh*). For the placement of the negative, see B. K. Waltke and M. O'Connor, *An Introduction to Biblical Hebrew Syntax* (Winona Lake, Ind.: Eisenbrauns, 1990) 583. Others interpret v. 21a as a question and answer after the model of Jer 25:29, "Shall I leave their bloodshed unpunished? I will not" (Allen). In either case, the allusion to Exod 34:7 and the basic sense remain unaffected. See L. C. Allen, *The Books of Joel, Obadiah, Jonah and Micah* (NICOT; Grand Rapids, Mich.: Wm. B. Eerdmans Publishing Co., 1976) 117 n. 47; and D. Stuart, *Hosea-Jonah* (WBC 31; Waco, Tex.: Word Books, 1987) 264.

Judah (4:16–20) and Israel, the primary topic of Amos.[39] It does this by alluding to the punishment formula of Exod 34:7: "He will by no means hold innocent [the guilty]." By these links Joel 4:21 reinforces and focuses the anticipation of Amos 1:2 found in Joel 4:16 (Eng. 3:16). The "Lion" who roars from Zion (Amos 1:2) is YHWH who, via his prophet (Amos 3:1–8), announces the Day of YHWH from which there is no escape (5:18–20). The postexilic concluding verses of Joel suggest that the true locus for the hope of YHWH's people is Judah, not Israel. While Judah ultimately receives God's mercy and compassion, the North, which the prophecy of Amos is about to address, is a nation subject to the contrary dictum, "He will by no means clear the guilty." Specifically, Israel will be subject to a Day of the Lord that entails death for the body politic through exile, *without* the restoration experienced by postexilic Judah. In this the North is like Assyria and Babylon, who disappear from history (Nahum and Habakkuk).

Amos and Obadiah

Amos, earliest of the writing prophets, provides the first *chronological* instance of a Day of the Lord (Amos 5:18–20; cf. 8:2–3, 9–10). All subsequent developments of the day are derivative of the concept first adumbrated by Amos.[40] Significantly, there is no allusion in Amos to the golden calf story or to the attributes of YHWH from Exod 34:6–7.[41] This fact is to be explained simply by the early and independent character of the bulk of Amos. For the end-redactors of the Twelve, Amos (with Hosea) and the northern exile — which Amos and Hosea prophesied — were problematic data to be explained (cf. the Deuteronomist in 2 Kings 17). How can a merciful God, speaking through Amos (3:1–8; 7:15), prophesy the Day of the Lord as the "death" of the northern "body politic" (Amos 5:1, 16–20; 8:2–3, 9–10) without any apparent opportunity for repentance and renewal?[42]

39. See on Nah 1:3, below.

40. The *original* ambiguity of the day should be noted. Amos's audience was expecting a *salvific* day (Amos 5:18; cf. 6:3).

41. Though cf. Amos 5:14–15 (*'wly yḥnk yhwh*) and 7:3, 6 with Exod 32:12, 14; Joel 2:14; Jonah 3:9 (*nḥm yhwh ʿl z't*).

42. But note Amos 5:4–5, 14–15 and Amos's initial Moses-like intercessions in 7:1–6. Note also the series of past plagues, unsuccessful in their purpose to get Israel to "return" to YHWH (*wl' šbtm*, 4:6–11; cf. Joel 2:12, *šby ʿdy*), which leads to the anacoluthic threat of Amos 4:12, to the first hymn fragment (4:13), and finally to the extended "encounter" with YHWH on the deadly Day of the Lord (5:1–20). The logic of this literary macromovement in Amos 4 and 5 was the subject of my unpublished M.A.

Part of the answer to this question is provided by the placement of Joel immediately prior to Amos. As shown above, Joel presents a way of escape from the prophesied Day of the Lord through "return" or repentance. The juxtaposition of the two books forces the conclusion that the Northern Kingdom did not repent in response to the preaching of Amos. Thus Joel vindicates in advance the justice and integrity of YHWH's judgment, announced by Amos and consummated by Assyria.

As shown by James L. Crenshaw, the famous hymn fragments in Amos (4:13; 5:8; 9:5–6; cf. 8:8) also function in wisdom fashion to vindicate the integrity of YHWH's *name* (*yhwh . . . šmw*, cf. 2:7) in judgment.[43] While the authenticity of the hymn fragments has recently been defended, most scholars take them as redactional. About their function as theodicy, however, there can be no doubt.

To fully treat Obadiah and its position in the Twelve would lead too far afield. It is sufficient to note several points. As regards the book, Obadiah has clear affinities with Joel (e.g., Obad 17 || Joel 3:5 [Eng. 2:32]; Obad 15 || Joel 4:4, 7, 14).[44] Moreover, Obadiah's views of the Day of the Lord are similar to Joel's in two key respects (cf. the LXX sequence of Joel, Obadiah, Jonah). First, for both Joel and Obadiah, it is the Day of Judah's calamity and distress, threatened or realized (Joel 1–2; Obad 10–14); second, it is the eschatological Day of Judgment upon the nations (represented by Edom in Obad 15–18). In the judgment against Edom, its wise men will come to naught (Obad 7–8). Furthermore, Amos and Obadiah are to be read together, since Obadiah functions "as a virtual commentary on Amos 9:12."[45] Finally, Obadiah anticipates Jonah, because the Assyrians are among the nations on whom YHWH's judg-

---

thesis, "The Day of Yahweh: Theme and Form in Amos 4 and 5" (Toronto: University of Saint Michael's College, 1975). On the composite literary unity of Amos 5:1–17, which introduces the Day of the Lord in 5:18–20, see also N. J. Tromp, "Amos 5:1–17: Toward a Stylistic and Rhetorical Analysis," *OTS* 23 (1984) 56–84, and J. de Waard, "The Chiastic Structure of Amos v. 1–17," *VT* 27 (1977) 170–77.

43. See the works of J. L. Crenshaw, "*YHWH Ṣᵉbaʾôt šᵉmô:* A Form-Critical Analysis," *ZAW* 81 (1969) 156–75; idem, "Popular Questioning of the Justice of God in Ancient Israel," *ZAW* 82 (1970) 380–95, esp. 390–92; idem, *Hymnic Affirmation of Divine Justice* (Missoula, Mont.: Scholars Press, 1975); idem, "Prolegomenon," *Studies in Ancient Israelite Wisdom* (ed. J. L. Crenshaw; New York: KTAV Publishing House, 1976) 1–60, esp. 22–35.

44. See especially Bergler, *Joel*, 295–333, on *Joels Edom-typologie* and the manifold connections with Obadiah.

45. L. C. Allen, *The Books of Joel, Obadiah, Jonah, and Micah* (Grand Rapids, Mich.: Wm. B. Eerdmans Publishing Co., 1976) 129.

ment must come. Obadiah is thus part of the canonical, literary logic of the Twelve that broadens the concern of the preexilic prophets beyond the Northern Kingdom to include Judah and the eschatological future.

Jonah

This reading together of Joel, Amos, and Obadiah is confirmed by the book of Jonah, which, like Joel, appears to be a late, anthological composition inserted into the Twelve. If Joel anticipates the problem of the Day of the Lord in Amos and Obadiah, Jonah functions as an afterword, particularly to Amos.[46] And, as Thomas Dozeman has shown, the use of the Exod 34:6 base text in Joel and Jonah is powerfully cross-referential.[47]

The genre of Jonah is disputed. It is perhaps best taken as an early midrashic homily on Exod 34:6 (not on 2 Kgs 14:25).[48] It may even be an ad hoc literary composition designed for insertion in the Twelve, and stemming from the scribal sages praised by Sirach, who were

46. Cf. H. W. Wolff, *Hosea* (Philadelphia: Fortress Press, 1974) 3–4, cited in House, *Unity*, 67.

47. Dozeman, "Inner-Biblical Interpretation," passim. Dozeman argues that "the repetition of YHWH's gracious and compassionate character in Joel and in Jonah functions as an instance of anthological exegesis not only of each other but also of the central account of covenant renewal in the Torah" (p. 209). Two caveats are in order. First, as noted above, we have here "inner-biblical allusion" or intertextuality rather than "inner-biblical interpretation," something that Dozeman himself anticipates (p. 209 n. 7). Second, Dozeman's argument, that Joel and Jonah are "anthological exegesis . . . of each other," needs comment, for it does not clearly distinguish the order of *writing* from the order of what is *written* (as arranged by the editors of the Twelve), or from the order of *reading*, which may be arbitrary. In the diachronic order of writing, only one of the prophets can allude to another, and in the case of Joel and Jonah, priority of composition is disputed. But in the order of what is written and read, it is clear that Jonah is to be read in the light of Joel, which it echoes. Only when the literary work of the Twelve is finally complete can cross-referentiality become fully functional (editor and reader aware of *both* Joel and Jonah together in the Twelve). But this sort of "simultaneity" does not nullify priority and posteriority in a literary work. Thus I differ with Dozeman's comment, "A set order for analyzing these quotations does not appear to be dictated by the texts themselves — either by their tradition history or by their present literary structure. Thus, we could just as well reverse the order of the inner-biblical interpretation" (p. 216; cf. n. 22). Dozeman's own exegesis, where he intends to read Joel in the light of Jonah, actually runs counter to this argument (p. 217, last paragraph).

48. Cf. D. Simonsen, "Ein Midrasch im IV. Buch Esra," *Festschrift I. Lewy* (ed. M. Brann and J. Elbogen; Breslau: M. and H. Marcus, 1911) 270–78. Simonsen treats 4 Ezra 7:132–140 as a midrash on Exod 34:6. The larger context of the Ezra passage is wisdom and theodicy. The Prologue to John's Gospel, a passage whose wisdom aspects are well known, is another instance of a midrashic reading of Exodus, this combining tabernacle, Moses' incomplete vision of YHWH's glory (Exod 33:18), and the attribute formula (John 1:14–18). The non-Septuagintal rendering "full of grace and truth" (*plērēs xaritos kai alētheias*, John 1:14) is unique to John.

"devoted . . . to the study of the law . . . and . . . concerned with prophecies" (Sir 38:24; 39:1).[49] But the story's attachment to Jonah ben Amitai, like Amos a prophet to the north in the reign of Jeroboam II (2 Kgs 14:25), is most telling.[50] This synchrony sets up a retrospective theological contrast: Israel had forty years before the massive negative prophecy of Amos was fulfilled in the Day of the Lord of 722 BCE. But Assyrian Nineveh, the scourge of the ancient Near East and Israel's destroyer, has a mere forty days from Jonah's negative prophecy (Jonah 3:4) to its doom. Yet in Nineveh's case, repentance averts the threatened prophetic judgment. Dozeman has shown that the pattern of repentance and the use of the Yahwistic attribute formula in Joel and Jonah are parallel.[51] But Dozeman did not analyze the role of these literary patterns in developing a theodicy of divine judgment, especially concerning the Day of the Lord and the two exiles affecting the North and the South.

Joel serves as a paradigm for the Day of the Lord that shows by way of anticipation that Israel could have averted the Assyrian "Day" through repentance and appeal to the compassionate name of YHWH. But Jonah goes further. It shows that even the most wicked Assyrians (and by implication Obadiah's Edomites) are able to receive forgiveness and respite from prophetic judgment through repentance and appeal to YHWH's mercy (Jonah 3:5–10). Jonah is a bitterly ironic indictment of Israel's presumption of divine grace and mercy that it wishes to possess for itself only (Jonah 4:1–2), and without concomitant obedience to the word and purposes of YHWH (Jonah 1:1–3; 4:3–11). In this Jonah reflects those in Amos who presumed upon their election (Amos 3:1–2; 9:7), upon YHWH's automatic favor (6:1, 3–6), and upon the beneficent character of the Day of the Lord (Amos 5:18–20; 8:9–10) without obedience to YHWH's requirements of justice and righteousness.

49. Sirach's assessment of the Twelve is also noteworthy: "They comforted the people of Jacob and delivered them with confident hope." Sirach also employs Exod 34:6 in an instructional theodicy (2:7–18).

50. G. M. Landes, "Jonah: A Masal?" *Israelite Wisdom: Theological and Literary Essays in Honor of Samuel Terrien* (ed. J. G. Gammie et al.; Missoula, Mont.: Scholars Press, 1978) 137–38, esp. 137, 158 n. 82.

51. Dozeman, "Inner-Biblical Interpretation." Dozeman correctly sees that Joel presents a more exclusive and Jonah a more universal reading of the divine attributes of Exod 34:6. This is in keeping with the macromovement in the Twelve from a primary concern with Israel/Judah to a more comprehensive, cosmic concern also for the nations.

Micah

As noted above in the section on Hosea, the doxology that concludes Micah is the most significant use in this book of Exod 34:6, especially in its redactional relation to Hos 14:10 and Mic 4:5. The significance of the intermediate term here (Mic 4:5) is reinforced by Mic 2:7, which also alludes, by way of negation, to Exod 34:6[52] and to the wisdom redaction that ends Hosea (14:10). The Micah passage is notoriously difficult, but some significant points of clarity exist. The rhetorical question, "Is the Lord's patience shortened?" (*ḥqṣr rwḥ yhwh,* Mic 2:7, my trans.; cf. Prov 14:29), inverts the attribute "slow to anger/patient" from Exod 34:6 (*ʾrk ʾpym,* cf. Prov 14:17, and *ʾrk rwḥ,* Qoh 7:8; Sir 5:11).[53] The passage also picks up vocabulary and themes from Hos 14:10:

> House of Jacob, can one ask,
> "Is the Lord's patience truly at an end?
> Are these his deeds?
> Does good not come of his words?
> Is he not with those who are upright?"[54]
> But you are not my people;
> you rise up as my enemy to my face.
> (Mic 2:7–8a, REV)[55]

Micah 4:12 is a further redactional comment, employing typical wisdom vocabulary, which takes up the concern of theodicy first adumbrated in Hos 14:10. The nations, presumably in contrast to chastened Judah,

> do not know the thoughts of the Lord,
> they do not understand his plan,
> that he has gathered them as sheaves. . . .

These connections bring us to the liturgical ending of Micah (7:18–20), which is the book's most weighty allusion to Exod 34:6–7. It may be seen as a doxological response of the "wise" to the admonition of Hos 14:10.[56] The ways of YHWH that the wise need to know are seen in his

52. So D. R. Hillers, *Micah* (Hermeneia; Philadelphia: Fortress Press, 1984) 36.

53. Dentan ("Literary Affinities") has correctly situated this semantic cluster in wisdom.

54. *ʿm hyšr hwlk;* cf. *yšrym drky yhwh wṣdqym ylkw bm* (Hos 14:10).

55. For philological details and proposed solutions, see especially the commentaries of Rudolph and Hillers. "You are not my people" is based on emendation, but something of this sort must be understood. If correct, the allusive connections to the golden calf story and to Hosea are reinforced.

56. The allusion to Exod 34:6 is discussed by Fishbane, *Biblical Interpretation,* 349–50, and by Allen, *Joel,* 402–3. The commentaries of W. Rudolph, H. W. Wolff, R. L. Smith, and D. Hillers overlook the allusion.

prophetic judgments, but most profoundly in the merciful attributes of YHWH as revealed in Exod 34:6, repeatedly cited in Hosea-Micah, and finally hymned in Mic 7:18–20. This doxology thus makes a fitting end to the composite redactional unit, Hosea-Micah. Moreover, this doxology on YHWH's mercy moves these often gloomy prophets toward hope for the future. In the end, God's mercy triumphs over his works of judgment as announced by the prophets.[57]

Nahum-Malachi

The hopeful ending of Micah is also striking in its juxtaposition to Nahum, a book famous for its portrayal of the divine wrath on Nineveh. In Nah 1:2b–3a, we find a two-line redactional expansion of the letter aleph in the eleven-unit acrostic (half of the alphabet!) that opens the book with the epithet, "a jealous God" (cf. Josh 24:19; Exod 34:14). The redactor's hand is patent since every other letter of the acrostic consists only of one poetic line. That this redactional plus stems from the hand of the Twelve's final, scribal editor is now clear. First of all, it uses his base text, Exod 34:6–7. Second, this gloss functions primarily to stitch together the two major composite clusters in the Twelve (Hosea-Micah and Nahum-Malachi).[58] That is, it serves the end-redactional purpose of combining the two great subquilts into a greater, more complex quilt. This purpose is effectively realized because the base texts in Mic 7:18–20 and in Nah 1:3a are a double thread, mutually reinforcing the join at the seam.

In Nah 1:3a the bipolar aspects of the attribute formula both appear, slightly modified:

> The Lord is slow to anger and of great might,
> and the Lord will by no means clear the guilty.[59]

57. H. Gunkel's famous essay is still essential, "The Close of Micah: A Prophetic Liturgy," *What Remains of the Old Testament* (New York: Macmillan Co., 1928) 115–40. Gunkel argues that Mic 7:7–20 is a psalmic unit. Thus, the confession of sin in 7:8–10 is especially important in the theodicy. See also J. T. Willis, "A Reapplied Prophetic Hope Oracle," VTSup 26 (Leiden: E. J. Brill, 1974) 64–76. While it cannot be argued here, Micah 6–7 as a whole may be seen as a dialogical, miniature theodicy, concluding the collection (with the additions of Joel, Obadiah, and Jonah) of the three eighth-century prophets. Cf. J. L. Mays, "The Theological Purpose of the Book of Micah," *Beiträge zur alttestamentlichen Theologie: Festschrift für Walther Zimmerli zum 70. Geburtstag* (ed. H. Donner, R. Hanhart, and R. Smend; Göttingen: Vandenhoeck & Ruprecht, 1977) 276–87, esp. 283–87.

58. Compare the similar function of Joel 4:21, which stitches the seam between Joel and Amos (see above).

59. Rudolph (*Micha — Nahum,* 154) sees "slow to anger" here as "eine Art Theodizee ('Gottes Mühlen mahlen langsam')." Rudolph correctly insists on retaining

Several further literary and theological purposes are served by this redactional stitching. The linkage of Micah and Nahum emphasizes the dialectic of God's mercy and justice in history. It is also crucial to the logic by which the redactors move from the first six books of the Twelve to the second six, in which Nahum and Habakkuk have an important transitional function. On the microlevel, the redacted prophetic books regularly move from judgment to salvation, even, as in Amos, where the basic message is overwhelmingly judgment. On the macrolevel (as in Isaiah), the Twelve also move from judgment to salvation.[60] On this macrolevel, Nahum and Habakkuk must be read together, for they "justify" YHWH's use of wicked Assyria and Babylon to judge his own people.[61] The transition from Habakkuk to Zephaniah is then a natural one. The primary *historical* referent of Zephaniah's Day of the Lord is the fall of Jerusalem. Only via this tortured route do the Twelve arrive at postexilic promises of salvation in Haggai and Zechariah. The present book of Zechariah opens with explicit reference to the prophetic history that precedes it:

> The Lord was very angry with your fathers.... Be not like your fathers, to whom the former prophets cried out, "Thus says the Lord of hosts, Return from your evil ways and from your evil deeds." But they did not hear or heed me, says the Lord. Your fathers, where are they? And the prophets, do they live for ever? But my words and my statutes, which I commanded my servants the prophets, did they not overtake your fathers? So they repented and said, As the Lord of hosts purposed to deal with us for our ways and deeds, so he has dealt with us. (Zech 1:2–6)

Finally, Malachi, like Trito-Isaiah, concludes the Twelve with warnings not to repeat the folly of the past, for the new age has not yet fully come.

But the main focus in the present essay is on the redactional logic that governs the scribal employment of Exod 34:6–7 to create a comprehensive prophetic theodicy. The quotation in Nah 1:3a sets up a theologically crucial connection with the attribute formula in Jonah 4:2. Jonah and Nahum are, on the face of it, theologically contradictory

"great in strength," which combats the notion that the delay of justice indicates YHWH's weakness vis-à-vis the great nations. Cf. the theological analysis of Roberts, *Nahum*, 39, 48–50. Roberts considers Nah 1:3a an insertion "from a different source" (p. 50). The use of "great" also strengthens the connection with Jonah. As noted by many, "great" (*gdwl*) is a key-word in Jonah, appearing 14/15 (as root) times. Jonah refers to Nineveh as "great" in 1:2; 3:2, 3; 4:11. The character Jonah considers the sparing of Nineveh a "great evil" (4:1), which leads to his angry citation of Exod 34:6 (Jonah 4:2).

60. See again, Clements, "Patterns."

61. Cf. the composite text, Isa 10:5–27, for similar logic.

books. In the former, contrary to the prophet's wishes, YHWH grants his mercy and compassion to the wicked Ninevites. But Nahum is the book of God's wrath against the great Assyrian capital. By using the full, bipolar contrast of mercy and justice from Exod 34:6–7, the redactor affirms, on the one hand, that YHWH is free to exercise his forgiveness and mercy toward *any* who repent and, on the other, that he will not be held forever hostage to the evil of the wicked.[62] In the divine dispensation concerning nations there appears to be a "time to kill and a time to heal" (Qoh 3:3; cf. Exod 33:19). It is this fearsome divine mystery that governs the wisdom redaction of the Twelve as a whole, that creates its logic of theodicy, and that seeks to answer the wisdom admonition that ends Hosea: "Whoever is wise, let him understand these things."

CONCLUSIONS

I have argued that the end-redaction of the Book of the Twelve is sapiential in character and that throughout Hosea-Micah this redaction employs the bipolar attribute formula on YHWH's name from Exod 34:6–7 as a base text in developing an overarching theodicy vis-à-vis the divine judgments of 722 and 587 BCE. This concern for historical theodicy corresponds to the wisdom theodicy that Wilson discerns in the final editing of the Psalter, and to the concern for prophecy and historical theodicy evident in Ben Sira.

My analysis assumes that the end-redaction of the *Tanakh* as a whole was the work of scribal sages who were forerunners of Ben Sira. This larger assumption, while having an adequate evidential base, still awaits a comprehensive study. The present work is intended as a contribution to the hermeneutical circle of that larger project. The Book of the Twelve itself still awaits an adequate full-scale treatment of its final form.

62. Abraham Heschel's classic work on the pathos of YHWH remains perhaps the best account of wrath as an inverse function of God's love at work in justice and righteousness (*The Prophets* [New York: Harper & Row, 1962] vol. 2).

4

WISDOM IN THE PSALTER

Samuel Terrien

Determining the place and importance of wisdom in the Psalter requires special caution. Are there "sapiential psalms"? If so, were these composed by sages? In spite of many monographs and articles that have been published on this topic, the answer to these questions is not obvious.

I

The wisdom literature and the sacred songs now preserved in the Psalter most probably remained in a stage of oral poetry before they became written books. In other words, they did not originally belong to the realm of literature. Most of the sayings and poems of the wise as well as the hymns and prayers — individual or national — were meant to be chanted or sung, with instrumental accompaniment.

Far more than prose, even with its often rhythmic sentences of the tribal or national traditions, wisdom and psalmody belong to the category of the fine arts. A study of their interrelationship demands hermeneutical methods that are peculiar to the styles of musical poetry.[1]

Times have changed since wisdom was supposed to reflect the teaching prevalent in the schools for the youth of the Jewish bour-

1. See, for another mode of discourse, the comments of G. W. Anderson, "Israel's Creed: Sung, Not Signed," *SJT* 16 (1963) 277–85; cf. B. O. Long, "Recent Field Studies in Oral Literature," *VT* 26 (1976) 187–98.

geoisie in the Persian era. It is now recognized that sapiential poems had their roots among the folk sages of early Israel[2] as well as in the courts of the United and Divided monarchies.[3] The scribes of Solomon, Hezekiah, and other kings of Judah frequently served as diplomats who traveled to the capitals of neighboring nations and entertained foreign ambassadors in Samaria or Jerusalem. Like international tradesmen, they must have become acquainted with the wisdom not only of Canaan-Phoenicia but also of Egypt, Edom, Syria, and Mesopotamia.[4]

This does not mean that royal scribes were also sages or teachers of wisdom. Moreover, it was not before the time of Ezra (7:6–12) and Nehemiah (8:1–13; 12:26–36) that the *Sopherim* acquired an official status and modeled, with the priests, the constitution of the provincial government according to the Torah of Moses, with the statutes and ordinances of the completed Pentateuch (Ezra 7:10).

In preexilic times, the royal scribes were high functionaries who sometimes played a part in the administration of the kingdom.[5] Their association with priests and cultic diviners or prophets indicates that one should not press too far either an identification or a differentiation between them and the sages. Jeremiah's attacks against the lying pen of the scribes ridiculed the sages as well as those who claimed to be wise and who also boasted that the law of Yahweh was on their side or belonged to them (note the ambiguity of the phrase in Jer 8:8–9). Thus, in the late Judahite monarchy, priests as well as scribes and sages lived in a tight circle of acquaintanceship. It may be surmised that their

2. A. Drubbel, "Le conflit entre la sagesse profane et la sagesse religieuse," *Bib* 17 (1936) 48, 407–8.

3. A. Alt, "Die Weisheit Salomos," *TLZ* 76 (1951) 139–44; R. B. Y. Scott, "Solomon and the Beginning of Wisdom in Israel," VTSup 3 (1955) 262–79; C. Westermann, *Wurzeln der Weisheit: Die ältesten Sprüche Israels und anderer Völker* (Göttingen: Vandenhoeck & Ruprecht, 1990) 9–10.

4. A. Lods, "Le monothéisme israélite a-t-il eu des précurseurs parmi les 'sages' de l'Ancien Orient?" *RHPR* 14 (1934) 197–98; W. F. Albright, "Some Canaanite-Phoenician Sources of Hebrew Wisdom," VTSup 3 (1955) 1–15; E. Würthwein, "Die Weisheit Ägyptens und das Alte Testament," *Schriften der Philips-Universität Marburg* 6 (1960), also in *Wort und Existenz, Studien zum Alten Testament* (Göttingen: Vandenhoeck & Ruprecht, 1970) 197–216; R. B. Y. Scott, "Folk Proverbs of the Ancient Near East," *Transactions of the Royal Society of Canada* 55 (1961) 47–56; H. H. Schmid, *Wesen und Geschichte der Weisheit: Eine Untersuchung zur altorientalischen und israelitischen Weisheitsliteratur* (Berlin: Töpelmann, 1966) 9–16, 85–129; A. Caquot, "Israelite Perceptions of Wisdom and Strength in the Light of the Ras Shamra Texts," *Israelite Wisdom* (ed. J. G. Gammie, et al.; Festschrift S. Terrien; Missoula, Mont.: Scholars Press, 1978) 25–33.

5. For example, Seraiah and Sheva, at the time of David (2 Sam 8:17; 20:25), Shebnah, under Hezekiah (2 Kgs 18:18–19; Isa 36:3; cf. 22:15), and Shaphan, secretary of Josiah (2 Kgs 22:8–10).

social exchanges were friendly, even intimate. There may also have been rivalries or conflicting opinions and beliefs.

It is now recognized that the sages of Israel and Judah were no strangers to the great prophets in preexilic times,[6] and that they were also in contact with the scribes who codified the traditions of jurisprudence, both civil and religious.[7] Is it therefore not likely that they were also acquainted with the sacred musicians who composed most of the psalms? While the exact dates at which the hymns and prayers now preserved in the Psalter were originally composed cannot be determined, it clearly appears that the great majority of them, like the proverbs and hymnic poems later collected in the wisdom literature, surfaced orally and were then chanted or even sung before the fall of Jerusalem under Babylon. Some of them have come perhaps from David himself.[8]

Hebrew scribes, priests, prophets, and sages were likely to socialize with musicians.[9] Samaria and Jerusalem were relatively small cities.

6. J. Fichtner, "Jesajah unter den Weisen," *TLZ* 74 (1949) 75–80; J. Lindblom, "Wisdom in the Old Testament Prophets," VTSup 3 (1955) 192–204; S. Terrien, "Amos and Wisdom," *Israel's Prophetic Heritage* (ed. B. W. Anderson and W. Harrelson; Festschrift J. Muilenburg; New York: Harper & Row, 1962) 108–15; H. W. Wolff, *Amos' geistige Heimat* (Neukirchen-Vluyn: Neukirchener Verlag, 1964); W. McKane, *Prophets and Wisdom* (London: 1965) 65–66; J. W. Whedbee, *Isaiah and Wisdom* (Nashville: Abingdon Press, 1971); J. Vermeylen, "Le Proto-Isaïe et la sagesse d'Israël," *La sagesse de l'Ancien Testament* (ed. M. Gilbert; Louvain: Louvain University Press, 1979) 39–58.

7. J. Malfroy, "Sagesse et la Loi dans le Deutéronome," *VT* 15 (1965) 46–65; J. L. Crenshaw, "Method in Determining Wisdom Influence upon 'Historical' Literature," *JBL* 88 (1969) 129–42; F. R. McCurley, Jr., "The Home of Deuteronomy Revisited," *A Light Unto My Path* (ed. H. N. Bream et al.; Festschrift J. M. Meyers; Philadelphia: Temple University Press, 1974) 295–315; C. Brekelmans, "Wisdom Influence in Deuteronomy," in Gilbert, *La Sagesse*, 28–38; D. F. Morgan, *Wisdom in the Old Testament Traditions* (Atlanta: John Knox Press, 1981).

8. For example, the psalms of Korah (Psalms 84–85; 87–88) may well have originated at the ancient sanctuary of Dan, near the ravines and torrents in the foothills of Mount Hermon (cf. Psalms 42–43; 44; 49; 88); M. D. Goulder, "A Sequence of Festal Psalms," *The Psalms of Korah* (JSOTSup 20; Sheffield: Sheffield Academic Press, 1982) 122; idem, *The Prayers of David (Psalms 51–72)* (JSOTSup 102; Sheffield: Sheffield Academic Press, 1990) 24–30; G. A. Rendsburg, *Linguistic Evidence for the Northern Origin of Selected Psalms* (Atlanta: Scholars Press, 1990).

9. The legendary memories of Solomon's wisdom and musical artistry point to a relationship, but also to a distinction, between the enunciation of proverbs and the composing of new songs (note the ambiguity of the Hebrew phrase "one thousand and five songs were his" [1 Kgs 4:32 = H 5:12]). There may have been long traditions of musical training among some of the ancient Near Eastern scribes. Already in the proto-Babylonian period II, it was recorded that Sumerian scribes learned to play musical instruments (B. Landsberger, "Scribal Concepts of Education," *City Invisible: A Symposium on Urbanization and Cultural Development in the Ancient Near East* [Chicago: University of Chicago Press, 1958] 94–123; cited by L. G. Perdue, *Wisdom and Cult* [Missoula, Mont.: Scholars Press, 1977] 326 n. 11).

An intellectual as well as an artistic osmosis inevitably accompanied conversations in a fruitful sharing of ideas and artistic endeavors. It is thus understandable that some of the musical poets who composed hymns and prayers were friends of the sages and the scribes, the intelligentsia of Israel and Judah.[10] There is no evidence, however, that these psalmists were scribes themselves.[11]

II

Several psalms of exhortation, prayer, meditation, and even of praise have been called didactic or sapiential and may have been composed by sages or their friends. In addition, a number of words, expressions, phrases, and sentences, as well as themes, appear in other canticles of the Psalter. Many scholars have attempted to formulate a methodology through which such pieces or fragments may be identified.[12] There is no consensus, as yet, on the validity of the criteria so far proposed.[13] The oral form of both wisdom and psalmody before these became two bodies of literature may explain in part the main difficulty in evaluating the nature of their relationship and the direction of their eventual interdependence.[14]

Sapiential words and expressions abound in numerous psalms,[15] but similarities in terminology and phraseology indicate only that the

10. S. Mowinckel, "Psalms and Wisdom," VTSup 3 (1955) 205–24.

11. In Ps 45:2, where the eulogist of a king and his bride at the occasion of their wedding wishes that his tongue might be as the pen of a tachygrapher, he indicates thereby that he is a singer and not a writer. Contra Mowinckel, "Psalms and Wisdom," 207.

12. H. Gunkel and J. Begrich, "Weisheitsdichtung in den Psalmen," *Einleitung in die Psalmen* (Göttingen: Vandenhoeck & Ruprecht, 1933) 381–97; S. Mowinckel, "The Learned Psalmography," *The Psalms in Israel's Worship* (New York: Abingdon Press, 1962) 2.104–14; R. E. Murphy, "A Consideration of the Classification 'Wisdom Psalm,'" VTSup 9 (1963) 156–67; J. K. Kuntz, "The Canonical Wisdom Psalms of Ancient Israel — Their Rhetorical, Thematic, and Formal Dimensions," *Rhetorical Criticism* (ed. J. J. Jackson and M. Kessler; Festschrift J. Muilenburg; Pittsburgh: Pickwick Press, 1974) 186–222; idem, "The Retribution Motif in Psalmic Wisdom," *ZAW* 83 (1977) 223–33; A. R. Ceresko, "The Sage in the Psalms," *The Sage in Israel and the Ancient Near East* (ed. J. G. Gammie and L. G. Perdue; Winona Lake, Ind.: Eisenbrauns, 1990) 216–30; R. Davidson, *Wisdom and Worship* (Philadelphia: Trinity Press International, 1990) 17–30.

13. J. Luyten, "Psalm 73 and Wisdom," in Gilbert, *La sagesse*, 61–64; R. N. Whybray, *The Intellectual Tradition in the Old Testament* (BZAW 135; Berlin: Walter de Gruyter, 1979) 75–76, 78–79, 93–98.

14. B. O. Long, "Recent Field Studies in Oral Literature," *VT* 26 (1976) 187–98.

15. A. Hurvitz, "Wisdom Vocabulary in the Hebrew Psalter: A Contribution to the Study of 'Wisdom Psalms,'" *VT* 30 (1981) 41–53; J. Trublet, "Le corpus sapiential et le Psautier: Approche informatique du lexique," VTSup 43 (1991) 187–98.

wise and some sacred musicians moved in the same social circles. This becomes evident when one observes that each of the so-called wisdom psalms belongs in fact to several *Gattungen* and includes a great variety of theological motifs, which in turn are expressed in diverse styles.

For example, the macarism *ʾašrê* ("Oh! The happiness of . . . ")[16] is undoubtedly a sapiential keyword.[17] It does not constitute only a bouquet of congratulations and of bon voyage wishes, but also exhortations, admonitions, and warnings; that is, the macarism takes several forms and mixes a surprisingly large number of themes.[18]

Thus, the same macarism introduces, punctuates, and sometimes accentuates the apex of a psalm or even terminates its movement from topic to disparate topic, all of which are found in Proverbs or in Job:

> The law of Yahweh (Psalms 1:1, 2; 40:5, 9; 94:12; 106:3; 112:1; 119:1, 2, 55, 61; etc.);
>
> Trust in his eventual forgiveness (Psalms 2:12; 33:1, 2; 34:9; 40:5);
>
> Pleasure in his word (Psalms 34:4; 112:1);
>
> Expectation of his just retribution (Psalms 89:16; 31–33; 94:20–23; 106:40–43);
>
> A clear distinction between the righteous and the evildoers (Psalms 1:4–6; 32:10–11; 94:20–23);
>
> Compassion for the poor and hope of deliverance from enemies (Ps 41:4);

16. This is an interjection of dynamic movement that may derive from the nomadic image of transhumance or of going on a journey (cf. the warning against marching or even traveling with evildoers as guides, stopping on the way with good-for-nothings, and halting with cynics, Ps 1:1). This interjection is not to be confused with the blessing, a passive participle, which implies a ritual transfer of power to a static recipient.

17. Contra Crenshaw, "Wisdom Influence," 132; Whybray, *Intellectual Tradition*, 125–26; Hurvitz, "Wisdom Vocabulary," 43. The word *ʾašrê* appears often in Proverbs, Job, and Qoheleth, and in psalms that precisely exhibit sapiential style and concern. The few other uses are found exclusively in contexts that reflect a wisdom connotation (Deut 33:29; 1 Kgs 10:8 =2 Chr 9:7; Isa 30:15; 32:20; 56:2; Dan 12:12).

18. H. Schmidt, "Grüsse und Glückwünsche im Psalter," *TSK* 103 (1931) 141–50; A. George, "La forme des béatitudes jusqu à Jésus," *Mélanges bibliques . . . A. Robert* (Paris: Bloud & Gay, 1958) 398–403; C. Keller, "Les béatitudes de l'Ancien Testament," *Hommage à Wilhelm Fischer* (Montpellier, 1960) 88–100; F. C. Fensham, "Malediction and Benediction in Ancient Near Eastern Treatises and the Old Testament," *ZAW* 74 (1962) 1–9; E. Gerstenberger, "Woe-Oracles of the Prophets," *JBL* 81 (1962) 261; H. W. Wolff, *Amos geistige Heimat*, 165–66; W. Janzen, "ʾAshrê in the Old Testament," *HTR* 58 (1965) 215–26; J. Dupont, "Béatitudes égyptiennes," *Bib* 47 (1966) 185–222; E. Lipiński, "Macarismes et psaumes de congratulation," *RB* 70 (1968) 321–67; W. Käser, "Beobachtungen zum alttestamentlichen Makarismus," *ZAW* 82 (1970) 225–50; C. Westermann, "Der Gebrauch von אשרי im Alten Testament," *Forschung im Alten Testament: Gesammelte Studien* (Munich: C. Kaiser, 1974) 2.194.

Thanksgiving for fertility (Psalms 65:6–14; 144:12–15);

Prosperity and honest work (Ps 128:1–2);

Terror of nothingness (Ps 89:47–49);

Marvels and stability of the cosmos (Psalms 33:6–7; 65:6–9; 89:10–16; 146:5–6, 16–18).

Occasionally, the exclamation of wishing happiness precedes the sapiential theme par excellence. "Happy is the man who seeks in [Yahweh] his refuge" (Ps 33:9) is the key to the most typical exhortation of a teacher to his sons or disciples:

Come, my sons! Listen to me!
  I shall teach you the fear of Yahweh:
Who is the man that finds delight in life
  And desires to prolong his days and enjoy happiness?
Preserve thy tongue from evil
And thy lips from words of deceit!
Depart from evil and do what is good! (Ps 34:12–15)

Is the author of this psalm one of the sages who chanted their prayers in the presence of their disciples and also addressed them directly? Or was he, rather, a temple musician, highly trained in psalmodic art, who combined his artistic talents with an academic responsibility? The answer to these questions is not obvious, for his poem is highly structured, integrating three strophes on a concentric pattern and articulating three different themes into a unified and sequential whole: praise for deliverance (vv. 2–7); the happiness of good behavior (vv. 8–11); and a strict distinctiveness between the righteous and the evildoers (vv. 12–15).[19]

Likewise, the exordium of Psalm 78 to a review of the ancestral misdeeds borrows sapiential terminology:

My people, listen to my instructions!
  Lend your ears to the words of my mouth!
I shall open my mouth for a gnomic discourse;
  Let me reveal the riddles of ancient times! (Ps 78:1–2)

19. J.-N. Aletti and J. Trublet, *Approche poétique et théologique des Psaumes* (Paris: Cerf, 1983) 72; cf. M. Girard, *Les Psaumes: Analyse structurelle et interprétation* (Montreal: Bellarmin, 1984) 267; A. R. Ceresko, "The ABCs of Wisdom in Psalm XXXIV," *VT* 35 (1985) 99–104; E. S. Gerstenberger, *Psalms, Part I* (Grand Rapids, Mich.: Wm. B. Eerdmans Publishing Co., 1988) 146–49.

This appeal, however, differs from those found in Proverbs, for it is directed not to a single disciple (cf. Prov 2:1; 3:1; etc., which are presumably addressed to a young student in a college), but to a community of worshipers assembled in a sanctuary.[20] Was its poet a sage who offered in the course of a festival ceremony a versified homily shaped like an epic ballad, even a national lament, or, on the contrary, a temple musician who borrowed for his opening strophe a sapiential mode of discourse? If the body of the long rehearsal (vv. 3–4, 5–59) is ancient, the culmination of the psalm with the election of David (vv. 70–72) suggests a "rereading" by a sage of the court of Judah.[21]

Thus, the macarism permeates the whole gamut of psalmodic poetry. This observation alone tends to show that sages and sacred musicians, while fulfilling diverse functions, did not live apart in esoteric circles devoid of communication. To the contrary, they shared similar talents, although they received different training, and their aspirations often met as they both affirmed their faith in Yahweh and his righteousness.

III

The so-called Torah-Psalms, especially Psalms 1, 19, and 119, are examples of sapiential instruction. At the end of its semantic evolution, the word *torah* came to designate the written Law par excellence, namely, the Pentateuch. It was in this sense that the final editors of the Psalter understood it.[22]

20. H. Junker, "Die Entstehungszeit des Ps 78 und des Deuteronomiums," *Bib* 34 (1953) 487–500; O. Eissfeldt, *Das Lied Moses* (Berlin: Akademic Verlag, 1958); J. Schildenberger, "Psalm 78 (77) und die Pentateuchquellen," *Lux Tua Veritas* (ed. H. Gross and F. Mussner; Festschrift H. Junker; Trier: Paulinus Verlag, 1961) 231–56; R. P. Carroll, "Psalm LXXVIII: Vestiges of Tribal Polemic," *VT* 21 (1971) 133–50; A. F. Campbell, "Psalm 78: A Contribution to the Theology of Tenth-Century Israel," *CBQ* 41 (1979) 51–79; H. Spieckermann, *Heilsgegenwart: Eine Theologie der Psalmen* (Göttingen: Vandenhoeck & Ruprecht, 1989) 132–49.

21. The title of this psalm, *maskîl*, "artistic and didactic song," perhaps "instruction," confirms this conjecture. Cf. V. Maag, "Zur Übersetzung von *maskil* in Amos 5:12; Ps 47:7 und in den Überschriften einiger Psalmen," *Schweiz. Theolog. Rundschau* (1943) 105–15. Note also the affinities in Ps 78:2 with those in Ps 49:4–5. Cf. L. G. Perdue, "The Riddles of Psalm 49," *JBL* 93 (1974) 533–47.

22. The history of the term is long and complex. See B. de Pinto, "The Torah and the Psalms," *JBL* 86 (1967) 154–74; H.-J. Kraus, "Zum Gesetzverständnis der nachprophetischen Zeit," *Kairos* 11 (1969) 122–33; J. A. Sanders, "Torah and Christ," *Int* 29 (1975) 25–34; G. Wallis, "Torah and Nomos," *TLZ* 105 (1980) 321–32; cf. A. Robert, "Le sens du mot loi dans le Ps. CXIX," *RB* 46 (1937) 182–206; J. D. Levenson, "The Source of Torah: Psalm 119 and the Modes of Revelation in Second Temple Judaism," *Ancient*

The sapiential origin of Psalm 1 does not preclude in any way the probability of its early date. The comparison of the tree planted near streams of water (Ps 1:5) with its development by Jeremiah (17:7–8), who also expands the malediction of a human being relying solely upon humans (vv. 5–6), clearly indicates, among other features, that it belongs to the period of the monarchy.[23]

In preexilic times, the word *torah* designated not the written Law but the instructions of the wise. To be sure, it already included decalogues in their pithy form, most likely oral, as well as lists of prohibitions and casuistic prescriptions. However, it had not lost its power, flexible but constraining, of divine pedagogy. It meant principally the moral and religious nurture that Yahweh dispensed to his children through the intermediary of his servants, the early prophets and sages.

At the core of a confidence comparable to familial intimacy and clan loyalty (or even to the marital mutuality of responsibility [Prov 31:25]), the *torah* was understood for centuries to be the words of a pueri-culture, maternal (Prov 1:8; 6:20, 23) as well as paternal (Prov 3:1; 4:2; 7:2). In this relational sense, the *torah* was a notion familiar to the circles of the sages rather than to those of the priests, since these latter acted chiefly as the keepers of shrines and the preservers of ritual acts performed by laity (Deut 26:3–4).

Moreover, because it was expressed by the word *torah,* the divine teaching on how to live inevitably created an association of ideas with a garden (Ps 1:3). Real or popular etymology related *torah* to *moreh* (Prov 5:13), which designates at once a tutor, an educator, and even the autumn rain that revived the vegetation of the soil after the torrid heat of summer (Joel 2:23; Ps 84:7; cf. Deut 11:14; etc.).

For the great prophets, the *torah* comprehended the whole of divine self-disclosure, together with the revelation of God's standards for human behavior (Jer 9:12; 16:11; Isa 42:21). It penetrates the heart of

---

Hebrew Religion (ed. P. D. Miller, Jr., et al.; Philadelphia: Fortress Press, 1987) 559–74, esp. 570; J. L. Mays, "The Place of the Torah-Psalms in the Psalter," *JBL* 106 (1987) 3–12; J. C. McCann, Jr., "The Psalms as Instruction," *Int* 46 (1992) 117–28.

23. I. Engnell, "Planted by the Streams of Water: Some Remarks on the Interpretation of the Psalms as Illuminated by a Detail of Ps. 1," *Studia Orientalia* (Festschrift J. Pedersen; Haunaie: E. Munksgaard, 1953) 92; cf. R. Davidson, "The Interpretation of Jeremiah XVII 5–8," *VT* 9 (1959) 202–3; P. E. Bonnard, *Le Psautier selon Jérémie...* (Paris: Cerf, 1960) 27–31; S. Mowinckel, *Psalmen-Studien* (reprint, Amsterdam: P. Schippers, 1961) 5.123–24; J. Krasovec, "Jeremiah 17, 5–8 and Psalm 1," *Antithetic Structure in Biblical Hebrew Poetry,* VTSup 35 (1984) 108–12; W. C. Holladay, *Jeremiah* (Philadelphia: Fortress Press, 1986) 1.489–90.

humankind; it reaches the emotions, the intelligence, and the volition. It blends into a complex psychology open to the ultimate purpose of Yahweh for humanity (Isa 51:7; cf. Psalms 27:31; 50:9).

Even during the torment and the humiliation of the exile in Babylon, the *torah* — which was preserved among the disciples of Ezekiel, the prophet-priest, and the sages who had survived the fall of the monarchy — maintained the dynamism of its dialogue with Yahweh.

The creator of the world and animator of nature was also the anxious parent of all living beings. Friend of Abraham and liberator of Israel from self-centered as well as foreign slavery, his initiatives precede and embrace all commandments, statutes, maxims, remonstrances, warnings, and interdicts that eventually were published in the written Law.

Torah is veritably *gospel,* for it comforts as it judges, and it rehearses acts of grace as it invites human beings to fulfill on earth the grand design.

For the poet of Psalm 1 the delights of the would-be righteous man consist in attuning himself to the delights of God (Ps 1:2; cf. Isa 44:28). Meditation on the *torah* was primitively not an audible, "mouthed," and chanted reading of a written text, such as one of the five scrolls that ultimately formed the "Penta-teuch" (five scroll-jars) around the time of Ezra and Nehemiah. The verb *hāgâ,* "to meditate," expressed originally an inarticulate and restrained sobbing or the murmured assent to the dawning of an inner truth. Its groaning could be compared to the distant roaring of a lion (Ps 31:4) or the cooing of a dove (Isa 38:14). Meditation on the salvation-history, anchored upon the desolation of Cain's brood, indeed begins with a moan before it turns into a sigh of joy or a cry of love.

The verb *hāgâ* may even suggest flights of imagination, ready to inspire intelligible expressions of purpose in a new kind of activity (Josh 1:8; Isa 33:18; Psalms 63:7; 77:13; 143:5; etc.). Its cognate, *higgāyôn,*[24] refers probably to a sung soliloquy, the susurration of a melody whose words exteriorize an intimate thought (Psalms 9:17; 19:15; 92:4). If the *torah* implies a mode of divine compassion, the musicians of the temple and the sages of the schools who meditate upon its demands or its warnings do not submit to an obligation of obedience. They overflow with gratitude. Meditation on the *torah* is comparable to the reverie

24. Cf. Ps 1:2 with 37:30 and see *hegyôn* in Ps 19:15.

of a lover who, when awake, thinks of his beloved, and when asleep, dreams of further ecstasies. His diurnal or nocturnal responses alike are transfigured into transports of love (Ps 119:24, 77, 92, 97, 143, 165, 176).

The psalmists who meditate upon the instructions of Yahweh resemble the children of personified Wisdom; their delights mirror her own delights (*ša'ăšû'îm*). In turn, she exults with a macarism, wishing for them happiness and the fullness of life (Prov 8:30–31, 32–36).

Eventually, Lady Wisdom becomes identified with the Torah, "the Law," written on five scrolls. In turn, both of them — Wisdom and Torah — approached the stage of hypostatization (Sir 24:18–23; etc.).

The image of the fruit tree, not only planted but also rooted on the bank of running waters, haunts to this day the minds of nomads, for whom the oasis connotes mystical as well as physical delights.[25] Happy people resemble trees whose sap is constantly renewed (Ps 92:13–15; cf. Jer 11:19; 17:5–8; Ezek 17:5–8). Consequently, they give their fruit in its season (Ps 1:3). Wisdom, which is *torah* in the original, all-embracing sense of the nurture of Yahweh, coalesces with happiness to introduce a dramatic contrast between the righteous, who listen, and the evildoers, who rebel (vv. 4–6).

IV

In other sapiential psalms, the word *torah* implies a similar amplitude of meanings, with their flexibility and diversity.[26]

Psalm 19, whose unity of composition, long denied, is now increas-

25. The image of the green tree already appeared among the sages of the ancient Near East — for example, the Sumerian king Chulgi, of the First Dynasty of Ur, or the Egyptian sage Amen-em-Opet. See Engnell, "Planted by the Streams of Water," 92; *ANET*, 421–25; G. E. Bryce, *A Legacy of Wisdom: The Egyptian Contribution to the Wisdom of Israel* (Lewisburg, Pa.: Bucknell University Press, 1979) 121.

26. Cf. H.-J. Kraus, "Freude an Gottes Gesetz," *EvT* 11 (1951) 337–51; idem, "Zum Gesetzverständnis der nachprophetischen Zeit," *Biblische Aufsätze* (Neukirchen-Vluyn: Neukirchener Verlag, 1972) 179–94; A. Deissler, "Zur Datierung und Situierung der 'kosmischen' Hymnen, Psalms. 8, 19, 29," in Gross and Mussner, *Lux Tua Veritas*, 57–58; J. Milgrom, "The Cultic *segaga* and Its Influence in Psalms and Job," *JQR* 58 (1967) 115–25; H. A. van Zyl, "Psalm 19," *Studia biblica et semitica* (Festschrift Th. H. Vriezen; Wageningen: H. Veenman, 1967) 142–57; D. J. A. Clines, "The Tree of Knowledge and the Law of Yahweh (Psalm XIX)," *VT* 24 (1974) 8–14; A. Meinhold, "Überlegungen zur Theologie des 19. Psalms," *ZTK* 79 (1982) cols. 119–36; I. Fischer, "Psalm 19 — Ursprüngliche Einheit oder Komposition?" *Biblische Notizen* 20 (1983) 16–25; M. Oesch, "Zur Übersetzung und Auslegung von Psalm 19," *Biblische Notizen* 26 (1985) 71–89; G. T. Glass, "Some Observations on Psalm 19," *The Listening Heart* (ed. K. G. Hoglund et al.; Festschrift R. E. Murphy; JSOTSup 58; Sheffield: Sheffield Academic Press, 1987) 147–59.

ingly recognized, applies the symbolism of Yahweh's marvels in the cosmos (first strophe, vv. 2–7) to the equally wondrous aspects of the education that he tirelessly bestows upon his children (second strophe, vv. 8–10). The silent melodies of the heavens together with the reliability of the sun's daily rounds are echoed in the multifaceted beneficence of his nurture.

While the sun, perfect in shape, revives the earth, Yahweh's instructions, perfect in their intent, reanimate humans in the depth of their being. His promises are dependable as the sunrise, for they transform ignorance into wisdom, just as dawn dissipates darkness. The purity of his precepts and the permanent effect of his judgments promote an enduring enlightenment and endow humankind with a happiness more precious than gold for security, and than honey for enjoyment.

The sensual aspect of these delights leads in the third strophe (vv. 13–14) to a new sensitivity: a severe reappraisal of human righteousness. The psalm begins as a lyrical vision of harmony in nature (first strophe), promotes satisfaction in human selfhood (second strophe), and ends in a continuous searching that betrays a profound anxiety about life (third strophe). Thus the meditation inevitably bursts into a prayer (v. 14).

Here is a wise man whose anthropological optimism and self-centeredness are shaken by doubts when he takes time to reflect upon his situation. The sage becomes a psalmist who begs for the forgiveness of his secret failures. The pride inherent in success spoils the achievements of his wisdom. Not unlike the great prophets, especially Hosea, Isaiah, Micah, Habakkuk, and Jeremiah, he trembles when he discovers that moral virtue may lead to ego-sufficiency, which is the source of ultimate sinfulness: theological hubris. His only recourse is now to throw himself upon the mercy of his God. The radiance of his sapiential trust is marred by the pathos of his prophetic lucidity. Yet the firmness of his faith does not invalidate his hope.

As a consummate artist, he does not forget the thematic coherence of the entire poem. The reliability of the creator and the patience of the divine teacher lead to the magnanimity of the God who loves to pardon. Hence, the final plea is addressed both to his "Rock," symbol of permanence, and to his "Redeemer," that is to say, the liberator of his own enslavement (v. 15).

Likewise, the poet of Psalm 119 is not a scribe of the Persian era but a musician (v. 54) and close disciple of the author of Psalm 19. The longest poem of the Psalter, Psalm 119 is articulated according to an acrostic of the twenty-two letters of the Hebrew alphabet,[27] the complex spacing of eight words for instruction (the word *torah* and its seven synonyms). The whole forms an elaborate structure of eight strophes.[28]

The affinities of Psalm 119 with Psalm 19, with Jeremiah,[29] with the Deuteronomic school and its dogma of retribution so eloquently presented by the friends of Job, together with an ignorance of the agonies of the exile in Babylon and the priestly legislation,[30] combine to indicate not a postexilic but a late seventh-century date.

Like Psalm 19, Psalm 119 displays an ambiguous attitude toward the moralism of success, typical of the book of Proverbs, as the poet constantly prays for Yahweh's sustained nurture:

> "Do not abandon me entirely!" (v. 8).
>
> "Teach me thy statutes!" (vv. 12, 23, 26, 64, 68, 124, 135).
>
> "Do good to thy servant, that I may live!" (v. 17).
>
> "Open my eyes!" (v. 18).
>
> "Make me understand!" (v. 27).
>
> "Make me live in thy way!" (v. 37).
>
> "Give me intelligence!" (v. 73).
>
> "Turn thy face toward me!" (v. 132).
>
> "Let my true being live!" (v. 175).

The psalmist was not a superficially benign follower of orthodox wisdom. The many allusions to the plight of his situation reveal a tormented spirit, profoundly stirred by the grandeur of God and the

27. Imperfections that may be observed in this programmatic framework should not be attributed to the carelessness of the poet or to his inability to carry out a flawless plan. Rather, they suggest mnemonic errors of oral transmission, over a long period of time, before this lengthy psalm was finally fixed in a written text. This consideration confirms the validity of a seventh-century date, proposed above.

28. D. M. Miller, "Strophenbau und Responsion," *Biblische Studien* 2 (1898) 54–55, according to B. Bonkamp, *Die Psalmen* (Freiburg: Visarius, 1949) 534; cf. Ch. and E. G. Briggs, *The Book of Psalms* (ICC; New York: Scribners, 1906), 409–18; A. Deissler, *Psalm 119 (118) und seine Theologie* (Munich: Zink, 1955) 55; S. Bergler, "Die längste Psalm-Anthologie oder Liturgie? (Ps 119)," *VT* 29 (1979) 257–88; J. P. M. van der Ploeg, "Le Psaume 119 et la sagesse," in Gilbert, *La Sagesse,* 82–87; W. Soll, *Psalm 119: Matrix, Form and Setting* (CBQMS 23; Washington, 1990).

29. Cf. Ps 119:23 with Jer 36:1–2; v. 84 with Jer 15:15; v. 85 with Jer 18:20; v. 154 with Jer 50:34.

30. Psalm 119, in particular, omits any allusion to the ritual of the atonement.

human inability to fulfill the hopes that Yahweh entertains for humankind. He confides: "My flesh shivers from the terror of thee!" (v. 120). Like the great prophets in their solitude, he felt alienated from the decaying society that surrounded him, and he complained: "I am a stranger on the earth" (v. 19). The awareness of his ostracism pursues him throughout the tortuous unfolding of his *mélopée.* At last, his existential pathos catapults an *in-extremis* call for an ultimate succor: "Like a sheep I am a wanderer: seek thy servant!" (v. 176). A dutiful observer of all the precepts revealed by the supreme teacher of wisdom, he remains suspicious of a secret failure. Like the poet of Psalm 19, he is torn between obedience and the fear of displeasing the supreme Master of wisdom.

Thus, at the apex of his concentric structure, which stands precisely at the halfway point of his thematic tapestry (vv. 81–86) and provides the key to his theology of crisis, the psalmist has no other recourse than the double cry: "I am thine! Save me!" (v. 94). Yahweh, the *Moreh* of an as-yet-unwritten Torah, compels this lonely and highly scrupulous perfectionist to expostulate passionately. The psalmist then responds to the feeling of his own emptiness, the overwhelming devotion of his love, and the need for his existential salvation. Although this disciple of the wise boasts of his sense of superiority over his teachers and over the elders of his school (vv. 99–100), he is aware that he may be lost. His begging for salvation denies the worth of his highest achievements.

Numerous exegetes have dismissed Psalm 119 as a contribution to nascent legalism and as a somewhat pedantic exercise in anthological artifice. They might not have been led to this conclusion if the LXX and most traditional translators had not rendered the dynamic Hebrew word *torah* by the Greek word *nomos,* with its eventual connotation of staticity. A scrutiny of the poet's repeated pleas for mercy discloses a never-fulfilled lover of divinity.

V

Several hymns, laments, and prayers of supplication have been called sapiential psalms because they subscribed at one point or another to the views of orthodox wisdom. For example, Psalms 111 and 112 proclaim that "the fear of Yahweh," which is "the beginning of wisdom" (cf. Prov 1:7; 9:10; Job 28:28), together with the observance of his precepts (Ps 111:10), not only produces "a sane reason" but also brings success, wealth, and a large posterity:

> Oh! The happiness of the man who fears Yahweh,
> And finds a supreme pleasure in his commandments!
> His descendants will be powerful in the earth. (Ps 112:1–2)

A contrary trend also appears in sapiential poetry. Wisdom is not always a recipe for prosperity. Some sages vigorously challenged the doctrine of individual retribution. Like the prophets Habakkuk and Jeremiah during the agony of the kingdom of Judah, at the end of the seventh century, they were bewildered by the scandal of innocent suffering. One of these sages, acquainted with the dialogues of the ancient Near East, composed the poem of Job. Using the well-known oral folktale of an Edomite hero, he created a multidialogue on the meaning of pure religion.[31] His purpose was not to solve the problem of innocent suffering. It was to take the story of Job's downfall as a setting for the discussion of divine irony, of human doubt and nevertheless of faith.[32] He intended to comfort the first exiles in Babylon with a sacred drama as a substitute for the ritual celebration of the New Year festival, when, deprived of a temple ceremony, they were desolate in a foreign land.[33]

Although the poem of Job has been called "A Masque of Revolt,"[34] and even "Wisdom in Revolt,"[35] its eventual theophany with Yahweh's speeches and the hero's refusal to fight with the creator of the cosmos might justify a different description. The poet, who knew orthodox wisdom, was a protagonist of heterodox wisdom. Yet his prolonged and tormented search for meaning, despite the chaotic horrors of his time, led him to temper his rebelliousness because the evocation of evil in nature, through the myths of Behemoth and Leviathan, brought to him a new perspective on divine omnipotence.[36] Moreover, the personal at-

31. S. Terrien, *Job* (Commentaires de l'Ancien Testament 13; Neuchâtel: Delachaux et Niestlé, 1963) 46–49, 269–71.

32. Idem, *Job: Poet of Existence* (Indianapolis: Bobbs-Merrill Co., 1957) 218–49; idem, "The Yahweh Speeches and Job's Responses," *RevExp* 68 (1971) 497–509.

33. S. Terrien, "Le poème de Job: Drame para-rituel du Nouvel-An?" VTSup 17 (1969) 220–35.

34. Idem, "A Masque of Revolt," *The Elusive Presence: Toward a New Biblical Theology* (San Francisco and New York: Harper & Row, 1978) 361–62.

35. L. G. Perdue, *Wisdom in Revolt: Metaphorical Theology in the Book of Job* (JSOTSup 112; Sheffield: Almond Press, 1991).

36. J. G. Gammie, "Behemoth and Leviathan: On the Didactic and Theological Significance of Job 40:15–41:5," in Gammie, *Israelite Wisdom*, 217–31; Perdue, *Wisdom in Revolt*, 196–238.

tention granted him by the faithful creator restored and then deepened his trust. The awareness of divine injustice toward him was displaced by the wonder of a mystical vision. He discovered the sufficiency of grace.

In addition to many parallels of vocabulary and theme that have been observed between the laments of the Psalter and the discourses of Job,[37] at least three psalms present striking affinities with the mood, the style, or the theological outbursts of the Joban poem. They may well have emerged from the same sapiential circles.

Psalm 49 is generally considered to be a didactic meditation.[38] Yet its initial appeal to the whole of humanity sounds like the hyperbole of a buffoon, who wants to be heard by

> all nations, the inhabitants of the universe,
> the low-born as well as the high-born,
> the poor as well as the rich. (vv. 2–3)

The solemnity of tone surprises. Is the singer's persiflage different from the rather vulgar comedy with which Elihu began his harangue after Job and his three visitors had completed their sterile debate (Job 32:1–33:33)? Just as Elihu had concluded his preposterous exordium with this unexpected exhortation,

> Sages! Listen to my discourses!
> You, bright ones! Give me your ears (34:2),

so also the psalmist wishes to command an equally preposterous attention. He seems to parody sapiential solemnity and also sacred music, for he adds, immodestly:

> My mouth speaks wisdom;
> My heart exudes intelligence!
> I attune my ears to a proverb:
> Upon the lyre, I lay open a riddle! (Ps 49:4–5)

Similar to the poet of Psalm 119 (cf. v. 54), this sage is a musician. However, whereas his colleague conformed to the traditional catechism of divine justice, but hinted at his own uncertainties, the author of Psalm

37. C. Westermann, *The Structure of the Book of Job: A Form-Critical Analysis* (Philadelphia: Fortress Press, 1981) 31–36.

38. P. Volz, "Psalm 49," *ZAW* (1937) 235–64; Ch. Barth, *Die Erretung vom Tode in den individuellen Klage-und Dankliedern des Alten Testaments* (Zollikon: Evangelischer Verlag, 1947) 158–61; J. P. M. van der Ploeg, "Note sur le Psaume XLIX," *OTS* 13 (1963) 137–72; R. Pautrel, "La mort est leur pasteur," *RSR* 54 (1966) 531–36; N. Tromp, "Psalm 49," *Ons Geestelijk Leven* 45 (1968–69) 239–51; Perdue, "Riddles of Psalm 49," 533–42; J. J. Slotki, "Psalm XLIX, 13, 21," *VT* 28 (1978) 361–62.

49 pretends to sing a song in order to unravel the riddle of existence only to gloat, and also to moan, that such an existence ends in death.

Years and perhaps centuries before Qoheleth, this wise man, who plays the lyre, finds life is not worthwhile, since the righteous as well as the evildoers eventually will inhabit a tomb, and "death will be their pastor" (v. 15).

Should then the spectacle of iniquitous success disturb the equilibrium of the sage? Not in the least, for the reiterated refrain of this sad jester offers the key to the riddle:

> A man loaded with honors does not last,
> He is like beasts going to the slaughter. (v. 13; cf. v. 21)

The melancholy theme on which both Job and his adversaries agreed is: "Death, the great leveller! The righteous and the good-for-nothing are alike, for they soon 'will lie down in the dust, and worms will devour them'" (Job 21:26).

Wealth is of little use, for nobody is able to offer a ransom to God (Ps 49:8–9). The psalmist may well have recalled at this point Elihu's hope that an angel will say to God, on behalf of a person, "I have found a ransom!" (Job 33:24). Because the psalmist has suffered from the oppression of the rich, he knows their guilt. It is they who need a ransom, not he! Yet at this very moment he departs from his mood of despondency and reveals himself to be, after all, a sacred musician, trained for the vocation of prayer and praise. He exults with assurance:

> God will redeem my life from the power of Sheol,
> For he will take me. (v. 1)

The use of the verb "redeem" shows that the thought of a ransom lingers in his mind. This thought refers not just to the angel-motif to which Elihu alluded but also to the theme of the mediator invoked by Job himself, who was probably the first to break through the Hebraic negativism concerning an afterlife, when he lifted his head and deliberately proclaimed, "I know that my Redeemer is alive" (Job 19:25). After his death, but "from a [new] flesh," he will come face-to-face with the Almighty (vv. 26–27).[39]

Still obsessed by the perspective of an eternal sleep, has he now discovered, like the author of Psalm 73, that communion with his divine lover means a translation "into glory" (Ps 73:23–24)?

39. Terrien, *Job*, 44–45, 149–54; this interpretation was adopted by W. R. Irwin, "Job's Redeemer," *JBL* 81 (1962) 217–29, cited by Perdue, "Riddles of Psalm 49," 541.

The sentence of Ps 49:16 preserves the mystery of the enigma.[40]

The poet of Ps 73 also belonged to sapiential circles, although some scholars regard his work as a song of thanksgiving.[41] Like the authors of Psalms 119 and 49, he was a cultic musician. He shows his concern for the purity of Israel (v. 1) and "the sanctuaries of God" (v. 17).[42] His work is less a didactic psalm than the autobiographic report of his spiritual odyssey.[43]

Stylistic features and the use of rare words link this poem with the sapiential modes of thinking in an exceptional way.[44] Like Job, the psalmist cannot understand the happiness of evildoers (vv. 1–9; cf. Job 21:34). He concludes that it was vain for him to purify his heart and to wash his hands in innocence (v. 13; cf. Job 9:30; 13:18; 16:17; 31:1–40). His language may have derived from the priestly rites of purification, but he has not performed them. He refers to them indirectly as metaphors of psychological stages of behavior. Like many sages, however, he practiced piety and its morality as a technique to improve his character, to find comfort in time of misery, and to obtain assurance of success in society. Tempted to deny that the Almighty intervenes in human affairs (vv. 11, 15), he regained just in time a sense of responsibility toward the members of his community. After prolonged reflection, in an effort to soothe his perplexity (v. 16), he received a mystical apprehension of divine presence; he penetrated within the sanctuaries of God (v. 17).[45] Imbued with this unexpected knowledge, he regained his belief in divine justice and power (vv. 18–20; cf. Prov 24:19–20).

40. Cf. J. Lindblom, "Die Eschatologie des 49 Psalms," *Horae Soederblomianae* 1 (1944) 21–27, with Perdue, "Riddles of Psalm 49," 541 n. 41 and H.-J. Kraus, *Theology of the Psalms* (Minneapolis: Augsburg Publishing House, 1986) 174.

41. Cf. J. K. Kuntz, "The Canonical Wisdom Psalms," in Jackson and Kessler, *Rhetorical Criticism*, 186–87, with J. Luyten, "Psalm 73 and Wisdom," in Gilbert, *La Sagesse*, 59–81.

42. H. Birkeland, "The Chief Problems of Ps 73, 17ss," *ZAW* 67 (1955) 89–102.

43. M. Buber, "The Heart Determines: Psalm 73," *Right and Wrong: An Interpretation of Some Psalms* (London: SCM Press, 1952) 34–52; S. Blank, "The Nearness of God and Psalm Seventy-Three," *To Do and to Teach* (Festschrift C. L. Pyatt; Lexington, Ky.: College of the Bible, 1953) 1–13; H. Ringgren, "Bemerkungen zum LXXIII Psalm," *VT* 13 (1973) 265–72; A. Caquot, "Le Psaume LXXIII," *Semitica* 21 (1971) 31–53; Perdue, *Wisdom and Cult*, 286–97; F. G. Ross, "Psalm 73," in Gammie, *Israelite Wisdom*, 161–75; B. Renaud, "Le Psaume 73: Méditation individuelle ou prière collective?" *RHPR* 59 (1979) 541–50; J. L. Crenshaw, *A Whirlpool of Torment: Israelite Tradition of God as an Oppressive Presence* (Philadelphia: Fortress Press, 1984) 528–30; R. J. Tournay, "Le Psaume LXXIII: Relectures et interprétation," *RB* 92 (1985) 187–99.

44. Luyten, "Psalm 73 and Wisdom," 66–77.

45. The meaning of *miqdĕšê-'ēl*, "sanctuaries of God," is uncertain. The word may refer to an abstract but vivid reality, "secret and holy mysteries of God."

Thereafter, before his commitment to tell, diffuse, or preach all the works of God (v. 28), only a single, but climactic, reminiscence needs to be added: the exposure to an I-Thou, proximate, direct experience of communion with the infinite lover of humankind. The style is restrained, and the emotion is recalled in sobriety, but the certitude is as solid as a rock. This communion will last in such a way that death itself cannot interrupt its duration (vv. 21–26).[46]

Such a confession strikingly parallels Job's dramatic asseveration of his belief that within his new flesh he will see God (19:25–26; cf. Ps 73:26).[47] The passionate cry of expectation with which the man from Uz affirms this belief is echoed here, but its futurity has begun here and now and has already become a reality.

Several exegetes have suggested that Psalm 73 was used, if not specifically intended, for the celebration of the New Year festival.[48] Its date is uncertain, but the close relationship that unites this song with the poem of Job tends to confirm the validity of the hypothesis that this enigmatic drama, before it reached the written level of literature, was first enacted in the early days of the exile in Babylon.[49]

Although one could hardly maintain that Psalm 139 was composed by the Joban poet himself,[50] there is little doubt that it reflects the intellectual intimacy and spiritual congeniality that linked some wisdom circles and some psalmists,[51] probably during the last years of the kingdom of Judah or at the beginning of the exile in Babylon. The structure of the poem pleads for the integrity of its composition, including its sudden vituperation against the enemies (vv. 19–22).[52] The poem may

46. M. Mannati, "Sur le quadruple avec toi du Ps LXXXIII 21–26," *VT* 21 (1971) 59–67; cf. S. Terrien, *The Psalms and Their Meaning for Today* (Indianapolis: Bobbs-Merrill Co., 1952) 258.

47. Terrien, *Job*, 150–54.

48. E. Würthwein, "Erwägungen zu Psalm 73," *Festschrift für Alfred Bertholet* (ed. W. Baumgartner; Tübingen: J. C. B. Mohr, 1950) 532–49; H. Ringgren, "Bemerkungen zum LXXIII Psalm," 265–66; R. T. O'Callahan, "Echoes of Canaanite Literature in the Psalms," *VT* 4 (1954) 164–76; A. Caquot, "Israelite Perceptions," 35; M. Mannati, "Les adorateurs de Môt dans le Psaume LXXIII," *VT* 22 (1972) 420–25.

49. Terrien, "Le poème de Job," 221–22.

50. M. Buttenwieser, *The Psalms* (Chicago: University of Chicago, 1938) 541–42.

51. J. L. Koole, "The Sapiential Milieu of Ps. 139 and Job," *Studia biblica et semitica,* 176–80.

52. H. P. Müller, "Die Gattung des 139. Psalms," *ZDMG* 1 (1969) 345–55; J. Holman, "The Structure of Psalm CXXXIX," *VT* 21 (1971) 298–310; Terrien, *Elusive Presence,* 327–29; P. Auffret, *La sagesse a bâti sa maison: Études de structures littéraires dans l'Ancien Testament et spécialement les Psaumes* (Fribourg: Editions Universitaires, 1982) 323–82; Aletti and Trublet, *Approche poétique et théologique des Psaumes,* 102–3.

be a "protest of innocence," perhaps aimed at a judicial situation,[53] but the profundity of its theology sets it apart from the other examples of the genre. Such a piece deserves to be placed at the highest rank of sapiential psalmody.[54]

The cultural friendship of this musician with the sages of the Joban circle appears in the use of rare words, sometimes found nowhere else, and also in the similarity of themes: (1) The peculiar meaning of the verb *hiskantâ* in the *hiphil*, "thou penetratest my ways" (Ps 139:3), echoes *hasken-nā ʿimmô*, "be intimate with him" (Job 22:21). The only other occurrence is found in the oracle of Balaam (Num 22:30), with sapiential connections. (2) The phrase *wattāšet ʿālay kappekâ*, "thou layest the palm of thy hand upon me" (Ps 139:5), is close to Job's request for a conciliator who "would place his hand upon us both" (Job 33:33). (3) The sentence *peliyyâ* (Qerê) *daʿat mimmennî*, "such knowledge is too wonderful for me" (Ps 139:6), offers a thematic as well as a verbal equivalent in *pĕlaʾîm lĕtûšîyâ*, "too wonderful for intimate comprehension" (Job 11:6). (4) The verb *ʾaṣṣîʿâ*, "I should spread my bed [in Sheol]" (Ps 139:8), is a cognate of the noun *yaṣûaʿ*, "a love couch," a term that appears in Job in a similar context (Job 17:8). (5) The poetic metaphor "wings of dawn" (Ps 139:9) is similar to "the eyelids of dawn" (Job 3:9) and the contemplation of the early break of day in the discourse of Yahweh (Job 38:12–15). (6) The verb *tĕsukkēnî*, in the *piel*, "thou didst weave me" (Ps 139:13), is the same as *tĕsôkkēnî*, in the *polel*, "thou didst intertwine [my bones and muscles]" (Job 10:11). These verbs are found nowhere else, and both describe the phenomena of embryology.

The listing of these verbal parallels between Psalm 139 and the poem of Job supports likewise the argument for their thematic kinship. Even if the psalm was used ceremonially as a "protest of innocence" or as a "plea for self-disculpation" during the ritual of ordeal, it cannot be altogether understood as a prayer of appeal.[55] The evildoers are indeed attacked as "men of blood," whom the psalmist shuns (v. 19),

53. H. Schüngel-Straumann, "Zur Gattung und Theologie des 139 Psalms," *BZ* 17 (1973) 39–51; cf. E. Würthwein, "Erwägungen zu Ps. 139," *VT* 7 (1957) 165–82.

54. G. A. Danell, *Psalm 139* (Uppsala: Universitet Arsskript, 1951); S. B. Frost, "Psalm 139: An Exposition," *CJT* 6 (1960) 113–14; E. J. Young, *Psalm 139. A Study of the Omniscience of God* (London: Banner of Truth Trust, 1965); K.-H. Bernhardt, "Zur Gottes Vorstellung von Psalm 139," *Kirche, Theologie, Frömmigkeit* (Festschrift G. Holtz; Berlin: Evangelische Verlagsanstalt, 1965) 20–31; R. Kilian, "In Gott geborgen: Eine Auslegung des Psalms 139," *Bibel und Kirche* 26 (1971) 97–102; S. Wagner, "Zur Theologie des Psalms CXXXIX," VTSup 29 (1978–79) 337–76.

55. Contra Würthwein, "Erwägungen zu Ps. 139," 165–66.

but they are God's enemies (v. 20), not his own, and they become the poet's adversaries only because he assumes a personal association of commonality with the divinity. He hates them because they hate God (vv. 21–22), and he is a friend of that God. Thus, the poet is different from the hero of the Joban masterpiece. Moreover, he never explicitly questions divine justice. Job, on his part, maintains that he is persecuted unfairly by humans and God alike (19:22). The psalmist may have been unjustly pursued by human beings, but he does not feel that he has been haunted by a divine tyrant. He may have been pursued by a God who will not let him alone, but at the core of his consciousness, he knows that the intentions of this God were not hostile, but benevolent.

The poet of Psalm 139 does not sing his thankfulness for a presence that he equivocally accepts. Else, why should he attempt to flee and even dwell in Sheol (v. 7)? At the same time, he not only turns to the praise of a creator who marvelously intertwined his bones and muscles in his mother's womb (vv. 13–18), but he also shows his eagerness to be examined and scrutinized anew (cf. vv. 1 and 23–24). To conclude his meditation, he then dares to pray:

> Search me, O God, and know my heart,
>   Test me, and know my doubts,
> And see whether there is any idolatrous way in me,
>   And lead me to the everlasting road!

This last petition hints at the ambiguity of his attitude. This man is not an apostate; nor is he guilty of pagan syncretism. Faithful to the para-philosophical stance of heterodox wisdom, he entertains secret "doubts."[56] He seems to have known, with fearful appreciation, of the meandering torments of Job and also of Job's final vision.

Through such psalms the bold questioning of sapiential thinkers has inflamed and elevated to a sublime level the Hebraic theology of transcendence. They discerned at its core the paradox of an immediate and constant immanence.

VI

Not only did the psalmists receive from the wise a para-scientific urge to examine natural phenomena, like those of embryology, but they

56. The word *śar'appîm,* also spelled *śe'ippîm* (v. 23; cf. Ps 94:19; Job 4:13; 20:2), denotes the idea of divided and conflicting opinions.

also learned the faculty of contemplation from the sapiential school.[57] Psalm 19, as was noted above, and many other poems of the Psalter that belong to the didactic and various genres received from Egyptian wisdom the aesthetic impulse to describe the cosmic objects of this contemplation. But they freed themselves, perhaps at a painful emotional cost, from the mythical deification of these cosmic phenomena. It was possibly the thrust of syncretistic inclination that the poet of Psalm 139 implied when he referred to his idolatrous thoughts (v. 24).

The poet of Psalm 104[58] has sketched the creative acts (vv. 2–30) that assure the stability and growth of universal life. Its model, the hymn to the sun-god attributed to Amenhotep IV (Akhenaten), has not prevented the psalmist from exalting his contemplation of nature into a strict theology of transcendence: he began with praise of Yahweh concealing himself with light (v. 1), and he ended with a proclamation of Yahweh's glory (vv. 31–35).

Cosmic hymns were familiar to Hebrew sages. Personified Wisdom attends the maker of the universe and plays in his presence with the terrestrial globe (Prov 8:22–31). The creator suspends the earth above emptiness (Job 26:7). Meteorological events mark the seasons (Job 37:4–18), which lead to the theophany of the New Year (vv. 19–24).

Like the wise, the psalmists look at the sovereign of the cosmos and tirelessly anchor their theology of history and their eschatological hope on their contemplation of the faithful creator (Psalms 8:19; 89:12–13; 102:26; 113:1–3; 136:6). They even invite the marine monsters who inhabit "all the abysses" (Ps 148:7) to join in a universal symphony of praise.[59]

VII

The rubric "Wisdom in the Psalter" does not directly involve the question whether the sages played a part in the final editing of the book

57. J. Eaton, "Contemplation in the Psalms," *The Contemplative Face of Old Testament Wisdom in the Context of World Religions* (London: SCM Press, 1989) 92–123.

58. P. Humbert, "La relation de Genèse I et du Ps. CIV avec la liturgie du Nouvel-An israélite," *RHPR* 15 (1935) 24–25; A. van der Voort, "Genèse I à II, 4a et le psaume CIV," *RB* 58 (1951) 321–47; K. H. Bernhardt, "Amenophis IV und Ps 104," *Mitteilungen des Instituts für Orientforschung* 15 (1969) 193–206; P. Auffret, *Hymnes de l'Égypte et d'Israël: Études de structures littéraires* (Fribourg: Editions Universitaires, 1981) 279–95.

59. S. Terrien, "Creation, Cultus and Faith in the Psalter," *Theological Education* 2 (1966) 116–28; R. Albertz, *Weltschöpfung und Menschenschöpfung* (Stuttgart: Calwer Theologische Monographien, 1974); R. J. Clifford, "The Hebrew Scriptures and the Theology of Creation," *TS* 46 (1985) 512–20.

of Psalms. The probable date of this editing implies that the scribes who collected the sacred songs of Israel and published them on written scrolls were only distant heirs of the ancient sages. Furthermore, the distinction between sages and scribes has not been clearly established. Nevertheless, the scribes who brought out the Psalms on written scrolls not only produced a more or less fixed text for the hymnal of temple and synagogue but also provided a book of instruction.[60]

The order in which the hymns and prayers had been preserved in preliminary collections reveals concatenations of several groups of psalms. These were selected and assembled according to thematic parallels and repetitions of keywords destined to link the end of one psalm to the following psalm.[61]

Psalms 1 and 2 were placed at the head of the definitive collection in order to serve as the preface for a manual of education comparable to the law of Moses. This manual was divided into five parts (Psalms 3–41; 42–72; 73–89; 90–106; 107–50).

The organization of the preliminary collections may have also depended upon several concentric structures. For example, Psalm 19 seems to have attracted a cluster of preceding and subsequent units according to an alternating order: Psalms 18 and 20–21 (royal psalms); 17 and 22 (laments); 16 and 23 (prayers of trust); 15 and 24 (sapiential meditations). Again, depending on methods employed, either Psalm 73 or Psalm 90 may have constituted a mnemonic turning point for the understanding of the whole Psalter as instruction.

If these suggestions are correct, the editors of the final text have put a wisdom stamp upon the Psalter as scripture.

60. J. C. McCann, Jr., "The Psalms as Instruction," *Int* 46 (1992) 118–20.

61. Franz Delitsch had long ago shown in his *Symbolon ad Psalmos* (1846) the existence of such a conscious order (*The Psalms*, vol. 1 [Edinburgh: T. & T. Clark, 1871]); Ch. Barth, "Concatenatio im Ersten Buch des Psalters," *Wort und Wirklichkeit* (ed. R. Benzing et al.; Meisenheim am Glan: Hain, 1976) 1.30–40; J. Reindl, "Weisheitliche Bearbeitung von Psalmen: Ein Beitrag zum Verständnis der Sammlung des Psalters," VTSup 32 (1981) 333–36; G. T. Sheppard, *Wisdom as a Hermeneutic Construct: A Study in the Sapientializing of the Old Testament* (BZAW 151; Berlin: Walter de Gruyter, 1980) 136–44; G. H. Wilson, *The Editing of the Hebrew Psalter* (Chico, Calif.: Scholars Press, 1985); idem, "The Shape of the Book of Psalms," *Int* 46 (1992) 48–49; cf. idem, "The Use of the Royal Psalms as the 'Seams' of the Hebrew Psalter," *JSOT* 35 (1986) 85–94.

5

WISDOM IN THE BOOK OF JOB

Leo G. Perdue

THE SAGES' CONCEPTION OF WISDOM

While there are many nuances of the meaning of the term "wisdom" (*ḥkm*) in sapiential literature,[1] the sages of Israel and Judah primarily conceived of it in three ways: wisdom as an epistemology or way of knowing; wisdom as discipline (*mûsār*); and wisdom as world-construction.

Wisdom as Knowing

The sages' understanding of wisdom as knowledge involved three related features: (1) a body of knowledge (in other words, a tradition); (2) ways of obtaining and understanding this content (memory, sense perception, reason, experience, reflection); and (3) the process of teaching and learning by which the tradition is transmitted and received.

Wisdom literature embodies a body of knowledge, a tradition that was incorporated eventually into five main canonical and deuterocanonical writings: Proverbs, Job, Qoheleth, Ben Sira, and the Wisdom of Solomon. In addition, during the postexilic period, the sages played

1. The root *ḥkm* has the following derivatives: *ḥokmâ* (fem. noun, "wisdom"), *ḥākam* (verb, "to be wise"), and *ḥākām* (adj., "wise"; noun, "wise person/sage"). For a detailed study of *ḥkm*, see R. N. Whybray, *The Intellectual Tradition in the Old Testament* (BZAW 135; Berlin and New York: Walter de Gruyter, 1974).

an important part in the shaping and editing of nonsapiential traditions that came to form the canonical literature of the Hebrew Bible. The influence of Israelite and Jewish wisdom literature impacted in significant ways apocalyptic literature, early Christian writings, and rabbinic texts.[2]

This body of knowledge possessed literary, social, theological, and ethical features that are rather distinctive. Literary features of the tradition included various forms of expression: sayings (proverb, beatitude, riddle, question, numerical saying, prohibition, and admonition), instructions, poems (e.g., Prov 8:22–31), dialogues, and didactic narratives.[3] These forms and the tradition they shaped more than likely developed within both formal school settings associated with the royal court and the temple and informal teaching situations that included the family.[4] The sages were not only officials and scribes working in the major social institutions of the court and temple, but also parents concerned with the teaching of the young. Perhaps the common denominator for all sages was their involvement in teaching and passing on an evolving sapiential tradition.[5] Subsequently, wisdom involved the transmission of a body of knowledge and its reception through learning. Yet this accumulating body of knowledge was fluid and open to challenge, reformulation, and augmentation. Learning, at least at a sophisticated level, involved more than rote memorization and the unquestioning acceptance of what was taught. Critical engagement, including even the possibility of rejecting the teaching, and reformulation were required and indeed carried out. While the hoary tradition shaped by past generations was honored, new generations tested the teaching in the arena of their own experience and added their own insights.

The theological and ethical teachings of the sages were centered in the conviction that the orders of life for both creation and creature were sustained by divine and human activity. Each element of reality had its own time, place, and norms governing existence within the created

2. In addition to the essays in this volume, see *The Sage in Israel and the Ancient Near East* (ed. J. G. Gammie and L. G. Perdue; Winona Lake, Ind.: Eisenbrauns, 1990); and G. Shepherd, *Wisdom as a Hermeneutical Construct* (BZAW 151; Berlin: Walter de Gruyter, 1980).

3. See J. L. Crenshaw, "Wisdom," *Old Testament Form Criticism* (ed. J. H. Hayes; San Antonio: Trinity University Press, 1974) 225–64.

4. See A. Lemaire, "The Sage in School and Temple," in Gammie and Perdue, *Sage in Israel,* 165–81; and C. Fontaine, "The Sage in Family and Tribe," in ibid., 155–64.

5. See Gammie and Perdue, *Sage in Israel.*

order. Creatures, institutions, and individuals were expected to act and live within these life-giving structures of existence that were established by the creator. God's own justice permeated creation and was the divine force that sustained its life-giving structures. In addition, God as the creator of humanity provided individuals with the organs of perceiving and knowing and gave them the capacity to live wisely and righteously. While no one was born wise, humans were invited to follow wisdom's path to justice, knowledge, and well-being. Subsequently, the moral life, as conceived by the sages, took on both a communal and an individual character. The various components of society (institutions, roles, and values) were to encompass this righteous order of life at work in creation, for justice was a defining attribute of the nature and activity of God. Yet, equally important for the wise, the life and character of the sage were to embody this same justice that permeated creation, provided the *nomos* for human institutions, and derived from the nature and activity of God. Through wisdom the sage learned not only to live in harmony with God, the cosmos, and society, but also to engage in behavior and discourse that would enhance and even extend the structures of life in creation, society, and individual existence. Thus, ethical existence for the wise not only reflected but at the same time created justice as the life-giving force at work in reality.[6]

There were sages, most notably Qoheleth, who denied the existence of a moral order of justice within those elements of reality that were open to human observation. But Qoheleth's rejection of what was traditionally taught did not end the sages' theological affirmation of the justice of God at work in the world, as witnessed by the later writings of Ben Sira and the Wisdom of Solomon. And while there were sages who legalistically defined justice as an inflexible system of retribution, overseen by a stern and demanding deity, this dogmatic articulation misshaped and misrepresented the more astute understanding of justice as a divine and human force at work in reality to create and sustain life. Or, theologically expressed, the sages contended that the justice of God operated providentially in continuing creation and shaping human history. Humans had the same responsibility for embodying and actualizing justice in the world.

Unlike prophets who received the knowledge of God in revelatory

6. See my essay, "Cosmology and the Social Order in the Wisdom Tradition," in Gammie and Perdue, *Sage in Israel*, 457–78.

states (e.g., standing in the council of Yahweh) or priests whose religious experiences included theophanies in cultic settings, sages came to their understanding of God and the moral life through ways of knowing that included memory, sense perception, reason, experience, and reflection. Through memory that recalled the teachings of their ancestors, the sages engaged and transmitted their tradition by study, critical inquiry, and reflection. Furthermore, by using their powers of observation and the ability to think rationally, the sages sought to understand God, social institutions, and the moral life through their reflections on creation and human experiences, including their own. Yet they never deified their own powers of understanding, for they recognized the limits of their capacity to comprehend reality. This recognition of limits to human knowledge allowed the sages to deal with contingencies that defied efforts at rational explanation.

Charismatic states of revelation, theophanies, dreams, and visions were not the normal, sapiential ways of achieving understanding, though it is worthy of mention that the dream of Eliphaz (see Job 4:12–21) and the "voice from the whirlwind" (Job 38–42) are notable exceptions. More in character with the sages' quest to understand God, the world, and human existence is Qoheleth's mode of inquiry. Through his recall of what the sages had taught, he engaged sapiential tradition. Yet he assayed its veracity by his own investigation of life. In this investigation, he used his sense perceptions ("I have seen") and reasoned critical inquiry to assess a wide variety of activities or experiences, reflected on their meaning for human life, and then drew his conclusions. While many other sages would disagree with Qoheleth's conclusions, his methods of knowing, including the testing of sapiential teaching in the arena of his own experience, and the frank admission of limits to human understanding were endemic to the discovery and assaying of wisdom.

This fundamental understanding of wisdom as knowledge provided the foundation for the sages' understandings of wisdom in two other ways: wisdom as discipline (*mûsār*) and wisdom as world-building.

Wisdom as Discipline

Israel's and Judah's sages made no significant distinction between faith and reason, or belief and knowledge, or piety and ethics, for both ends of these dialectics converged into a single conduit of faithful knowing that fed into their shaping and embodiment of the moral life.[7] The traditional sages speak of this integration of public and personal faith, corporate and private piety, and traditional and individual understanding in their common confession: "The fear of the Lord is the beginning of knowledge" (e.g., Prov 1:7). Faith and piety, expressed in the affirmation and worship of the creator of heaven and earth as the one who cares for and sustains all life, are foundational components of wisdom as an intellectual tradition. The sages' search for wisdom, then, represents an intended or at least desired convergence of confession, piety, and knowledge.

The sages conceived of wisdom as *mûsār* or what might best be defined as discipline. *Mûsār* is the disciplined formation of character that both embodies virtue and leads to well-being. The formation of character took place through the discipline of study, reflection, and the practice of justice and piety. While wisdom literature points to a variety of virtues valued and actualized in the life of the sages, two of the most fundamental ones are justice and piety. For example, the introduction to the book of Proverbs (1:2–7) indicates that wisdom, identified as the discipline (*mûsār*) of insight, involves the "incorporation [lit.: 'taking'] of righteousness, justice, and equity" (v. 3). And at the introduction's close, the oft-repeated affirmation of the sages is made: "The fear of the Lord is the beginning of knowledge" (v. 7a), while "fools despise wisdom and discipline [= *mûsār*]" (v. 7b). Enclosed within the literary framework of these two defining virtues are those of "prudence," "knowledge," and "discretion." These are the virtues the sages sought to understand and then embody in both word and deed.

The embodiment of sapiential virtue, or wisdom as discipline, did not lead only to the moral transformation of the character of the sage. At the same time, *mûsār* enabled the sage to enter into a state of well-being or success. Well-being points to a mode of existence, of being and doing, that results from the process of becoming wise. Through discipline (*mûsār*) sapiential virtues were to be actualized in a life that continued to pursue a wisdom that, though continually sought, was never fully possessed (Prov 1:2–7). This sphere of well-being, or blessing, was a state of existence in which the sage lived in harmony with the world, other people, and, most importantly, the creator. Since the sages did not contrast material accoutrements with immaterial values, success in-

7. R. Murphy, "Wisdom and Creation," *JBL* 104 (1985) 3–11.

cluded both tangible and intangible elements: prosperity and long life, but also honor and happiness.

Wisdom as World-Construction

The wisdom tradition, or sapiential knowledge, is moral discourse, that is, instruction in a body of knowledge that taught one how to live rightly and uprightly. Yet the wisdom tradition also constructed, legitimated, and reflected a distinctive worldview as the framework for the moral life.[8] This sapiential construction of reality represented a level of reflective thought that provided the theoretical context for wisdom as knowledge and wisdom as *mûsār.*[9]

In their world-construction that originates in a type of reflective activity, perhaps best understood as sapiential imagination,[10] the sages believed that God was the creator of heaven and earth who, through wisdom, established the structures of life and continued to maintain them through providential guidance. This life-giving and life-sustaining order in the cosmos, along with its active undergirding by divine power, wisdom, and compassion, was conceived as justice, and not as some early scientific expression of natural law.

Through their imagination, the sages projected a worldview in which the social order was to be a microcosm of justice present both in creation and in the nature and character of God.[11] Social institutions that were the objects of sapiential reflection included especially governance, education, the cultus, and the family, along with their accompanying social roles: the king, royal officials, scribes, lawyers, judges, teachers, students, priests, parents, children, husbands, and wives. Each institution and social role was defined and governed by laws, customs, and expectations (i.e., a *nomos* for life or, simply put, justice) that ultimately were given legitimation and sustained by a righteous and caring God who established and oversaw their operations. Through their teachings, the sages socialized the "simple" into a symbolic universe, enabling them to live in conformity with its presentation of reality, and then

8. See my essays, "The Social Character of Paraenesis and Paraenetic Literature," *Paraenesis: Act and Form,* vol. 50 of *Semeia* (1990) 5–39; and "Cosmology," 457–78.

9. See P. Berger and T. Luckmann, *The Social Construction of Reality* (New York: Doubleday & Co., 1966).

10. See chap. 9, "From History to Imagination: Between Memory and Vision," in my book *The Collapse of History* (OBT; Minneapolis: Fortress Press, 1993).

11. H. H. Schmid, *Gerechtigkeit als Weltordnung* (BHT 40; Tübingen: J. C. B. Mohr [Paul Siebeck], 1968).

legitimated its defining features as true by means of persuasive argument and appeals to authoritative norms (God, tradition, reason, and experience). The components of the larger symbolic universe were to be actualized in social and individual life by those in quest for wisdom.

World-construction at times was construed by the personification and revelation of wisdom, understood as both an attribute of God and the sapiential tradition. Woman Wisdom as a cosmic power appears for the first time in Proverbs 1–9, where she was the first of God's creative acts. In Prov 8:22–31, she appears either as an architect whose skillful planning gives order and sustenance to the created order or as the little child in whom God takes delight and whose own rejoicing over the world of human habitation provides the bond between creation and the creator. Elsewhere in this collection, she constructs her temple (or palace), initiates her reign of overseeing the created order, and invites the untutored to come and eat of her banquet of life (Prov 9:1–6). She also is the teacher or sage who goes in search of the simple to come and take up her course of study that leads to life and well-being (Prov 1:20–33; 8:1–11). In Prov 8:12–21 she is the Queen of Heaven by whom kings and princes govern the earth and are blessed by her bounty. Taken as a whole, Wisdom is the voice of God who instructs humans in how to live their lives wisely and well.[12]

In their efforts at world-construction, the sages recognized that the mystery and otherness of God imposed limits and constraints. Thus, in their theological imagination, God was both the creator and sustainer of reality, but at the same time not equated with it. Transcendence was thus an important element of sapiential imagination that avoided the iconic heresy of equating God with the symbols and values of a tradition's construal of the world.[13] The mystery and otherness of God allowed for both the presence and interpretation of contingencies in life. In the face

12. See Sirach 24 for another important presentation of Woman Wisdom, who originates from the breath of God, exists within the divine council, goes in search of a dwelling place among the nations, and takes up residence in Israel. In this poem, she not only embodies the wisdom tradition, but also is identified with the Torah and the temple worship in Jerusalem. In the Wisdom of Solomon, Wisdom moves from the personification of a divine attribute to a hypostasis who is given an independent existence. As a divine hypostasis, Wisdom is involved in creating the world as a divine architect, provides immortality of the soul for those who seek and find her, and is the redeemer who leads the righteous (both individuals and the people of Israel) to salvation (see B. Mack, "Wisdom Myth and Mythology," *Int* 24 [1970] 46–60; and H. Ringgren, *Word and Wisdom* [Lund: Hakan Ohlssons Boktryckeri, 1947]).

13. See my *Wisdom and Creation: The Theology of Wisdom Literature* (Atlanta: Abingdon Press, forthcoming).

of the harsh contingencies of life, divine mystery and the frank recognition that a comprehensive knowledge of reality was beyond even the sages' grasp provided the twin bases not only for legitimating their construction of the world, but also for defending the justice of God.

WISDOM IN THE BOOK OF JOB

Historical Setting

Due to the lack of explicit or even implicit evidence in Job, one may only imagine the specific sociohistorical calamity that gave rise to the radical questioning of conventional faith and sapiential understanding in the poetic dialogues. However, there are a few intimations that would point to the Babylonian holocaust in 586 BCE as the most logical stimulus for this crisis of both intellect and faith. In Ezek 14:12–20, Yahweh's word to the prophet, living during the dark times of the Babylonian destruction of Judah and the exile, refers to three exceptional examples of moral character: Noah, Daniel, and Job. Even if they were present during the coming tribulation, Yahweh says, their righteousness would save only themselves and not others. The growing concerns with theodicy, represented in Job, are present in other late seventh- and early sixth-century texts: Jeremiah (especially the laments) and Habakkuk. Furthermore, Job 3 may have been patterned after Jeremiah's lament in 20:14–18. Of course, there are other possible dates for the poetry of Job, but the sixth century BCE seems plausible.

Literary Sources

To attempt an understanding of the meaning of wisdom in Job is in large measure to attempt an interpretation of the entire book. Yet very quickly into this investigation, one discovers that the search for wisdom, both by the characters involved in the literary drama and by the inquiring scholar, leads to a variety of meanings and nuances of understanding. This variety is due in part to the different literary sources that comprise the canonical book of Job. While it is important to attempt holistic readings of biblical books, including those whose literary history may involve several centuries of composition and redaction, one should not ignore major differences in style, themes, and understandings present in the same book. As we shall see later in this essay, these differences of understanding, or nuances of meaning, are present in the differing understandings of wisdom in the literary components of the book of Job.

Elsewhere I have presented my views of the literary development of the book of Job, and I shall not repeat them in detail here.[14] Suffice it to say that I consider the prose narrative, surviving in chaps. 1–2 and 42:7–17, to be an older story than the one contained in the poetry. One may suggest a monarchial dating for the prose narrative, though such dating is imprecise. The poetic dialogues (3–31; 38:1–42:6) may have been written soon after the Babylonian holocaust of 586 BCE. In any case, the poet rewrote the older tale in order to subvert its theology of suffering as divine testing. Sometime later, in the postexilic period, two additions were made to the now twice-told tale: the speeches of Elihu (32–37) and the poem on the inaccessibility of Wisdom (28).

Wisdom in the Narrative of Job

The canonical book of Job preserves two major parts of a narrative about a pious, righteous, and patient Job: chaps. 1–2 (the so-called prologue) and 42:7–17 (the epilogue). These two sections of a presumably older Joban story were taken by the poet who used them for the introduction and conclusion of the present book. The form of the Joban narrative is a didactic narrative in which the hero embodies a particular virtue or set of virtues.[15] An antagonist is also common to these stories. His or her opposition leads to the misfortune, at least for a time, of the hero. The action of the story proceeds by means of the conflict between the hero and antagonist until the climax is reached, usually in some form of judgment that confirms the integrity of the hero and then exalts him or her to a place of honor, while the antagonist experiences, directly or implied, some sort of humiliation or defeat. The story serves as a narrative world in which the virtues of the hero are exemplified and then affirmed. This narrative, then, provides a structure of reality, a symbolic world that makes sense of and legitimates the moral life.

While the terms "wisdom," "wise," and "to be wise" do not occur in the surviving parts of the prose narrative, one may legitimately argue that "wisdom" as moral behavior and discourse (i.e., ethics) and

14. L. G. Perdue, *Wisdom in Revolt: Metaphorical Theology in the Book of Job* (JSOTSup 112; Sheffield: Sheffield Academic Press, 1991) 75–85; and the introduction to *The Voice from the Whirlwind: Interpreting the Book of Job* (ed. L. G. Perdue and W. C. Gilpin; Nashville: Abingdon Press, 1992) 11–18.

15. See H.-P. Müller, "Die weisheitliche Lehrerzählung im Alten Testament und seiner Umwelt," *WO* 9 (1977) 77–98.

"wisdom" as piety (the worship of and faith in God) are brought to life in the literary character Job. In 1:1 the narrator describes the hero as a "blameless" (*tām*), "upright" (*yāšār*) person who "feared God" (*yārēʾ ʾĕlôhîm*) and "turned from evil" (*sār mērāʿ*). God mentions these very same virtues to describe Job to the accuser, Job's otherworldly antagonist, in the two heavenly scenes of judgment (1:8; 2:3).

Job's moral virtue and piety provide the basis for the dramatic movement in the story. "The satan" ("accuser in a trial," see Ps 109:6) is the adversary who, as a member of the divine council ("the sons of God"), is responsible for discovering evil on the earth and presenting a report to the divine judge. This report is given presumably on "the day" (New Year's?) when "the sons of God" gather in assembly to hear Yahweh's judgment. While not the demonic being of later apocalyptic literature who stands in opposition to God, "the satan" still questions the motivation behind Job's moral virtue and piety and succeeds in raising the specter of divine suspicion. His accusation is that Job's moral virtue and piety are inspired by self-interest: by currying divine favor Job experiences prosperity and is protected against misfortune.

Throughout the narrative, however, an almost superhuman Job continues to embody sapiential virtue. One notices his scrupulous attention to cultic piety in the prologue, even to the point of rising early in the morning, sanctifying his children, and then sacrificing burnt offerings for them just in case they may have sinned and "cursed God in their hearts." Cultic piety, including sacrifices, offerings, and prayers, was an important dimension of "wise" action in the sapiential tradition, as long as it was correlated with moral behavior (see Prov 3:9–10; 15:8, 29; 21:27; 28:9; Sir 34:18–35:26 [Gk.]).[16] Even when faced with enormous loss, Job continues to bless, not curse, the One who gives and takes away.

The two series of tests, sanctioned by divine judgment, demonstrate that Job's virtuous behavior and faithful praise are not motivated by the desire for success and protection against misfortune, but rather are the selfless expression of disinterested piety and virtue for its own reward. In the face of adversity, Job does not abandon *mûsār* by disavowing his faith, cursing God, and turning to evil.

Whatever occurred in the missing middle part of the original narrative, now replaced by the poetic dialogues, it appears that Job continued

16. L. G. Perdue, *Wisdom and Cult* (SBLDS 30; Missoula, Mont.: Scholars Press, 1977).

to maintain his integrity and piety in spite of his wife and friends. One may imagine that the friends, like Job's wife, counseled him to abandon his virtue because of the apparent faithlessness and caprice of God. In the "everyday" world of Job's existence, his wife and presumably the friends become his human antagonists. In any case, in the final judgment scene, the friends are condemned for not having "spoken correctly" (*nĕkônâ*) about God as has Job. Speaking "correctly" about God means in this context that Job continued to affirm divine sovereignty and did not follow his wife's (and friends'?) counsel to abandon moral virtue and piety, in the face of adversity attributed to a capricious and destructive deity. To speak "correctly" not only sustains personal integrity and faithful piety, but also upholds the moral order of the world and the veracity of religious belief (see Exod 8:22; Ps 5:10; Prov 4:26). This Job has done. In contrast to traditional wisdom in the book of Proverbs, sapiential discipline (*mûsār*) is not predicated on the promise of reward.

One final example of Job's actualization of *mûsār* — that is, morality and piety — is presented in his intercessory prayer on behalf of his friends. The value of the mediation of a righteous person is often noted in the Hebrew scriptures (e.g., see Moses in Exodus 32; and Noah, Daniel, and Job in Ezek 14:12–20). And when Job prays on behalf of his friends in order to appease divine wrath, his own fortunes are restored. But as was true for his earlier testimonies of faith and integrity, Job engaged in this act without the expectation of reward. This narrative world legitimates the value of maintaining moral integrity and faithful piety, even in the face of adversity. Sapiential *mûsār* forms the character of the sage, a character that does not fail even when well-being and success are lost.

The ability of Job to withstand the brutal assault on his life and family leads to more than his eventual restoration at the story's end. Indeed, the troubling depiction of a suspicious tyrant who would abuse and terrorize even his most faithful and virtuous servant is at least partially altered at the end by righteous judgment. In a very real sense, the restoration of Job leads to the redemption of God. In its theological imaginings that construct the world, the narrative has raised the specter of a divine judge who would not only allow unjust suffering, but also would be its cause. In spite of the restoration of Job, the reassuring theological world of the traditional sages, one in which God is the righteous judge nurturing life, has been thoroughly shaken, though it may not have disintegrated. Could a God who abandons justice, even for a time, be a worthy object of faithful devotion? The narrative is also a troubling tale for another reason: it takes an almost superhuman Job to endure these horrors. What about men and women of lesser strength of character and resolve?

The Dialogues: The Opponents and Job

What was at stake in the narrative, then, is the question of whether wisdom's traditional affirmation of divine justice could be sustained and then used as the basis for ethics and piety, if God, as judge, were to become, for whatever reason, a suspicious tyrant who turned even his most faithful and righteous servant over to an accuser's malicious abuse. Far more is at stake than the integrity of Job. Even more critical is the integrity of God. It is this issue that leads the poet to rewrite the narrative with dramatically different results.

Job's Opponents. Wisdom for the friends of Job and Elihu[17] was a *nomos* of meaning, that is, a structure of reality within which guidance for being and doing was actualized in communal and individual life. For them, as was true of traditional sages in general, wisdom is also knowledge that shapes character and leads to pragmatic ends, that is, well-being and success. Through the ways of knowing and the actualization of the teachings of wisdom in human existence, the wise learned to live a moral existence in harmony with the orders of cosmos and society so as to achieve success and well-being in life. In addition, there was also a creative element to sapiential living, that is, the just order in the cosmos and human society was sustained but also enhanced through wise language and behavior.

Yet there is a new feature in both the anthropology and the cosmology of the friends and Elihu. Traditional wisdom argued that, while no one was born wise, humans possessed the innate capacity to become sages through study, reflection, and the correlation of instruction with human experience. Subsequently, traditional wisdom offered an anthropology that suggested people had the capacity to take up the path to wisdom and to incorporate its teachings within their lives. However, for the opponents of Job, the possibilities of becoming wise and acting

17. While the speeches of Elihu are a later insertion, he primarily repeats the arguments of the three friends.

in accordance with sapiential instruction are severely limited because of an innate human sinfulness. To quote Eliphaz, "A mortal is born to mischief" (5:7).

In setting forth his understanding of human nature, Eliphaz mentions the revelatory words of a spirit who spoke to him in a vision of the night:

> Can a human being be righteous before God?
>   Can a person be pure before the creator?
> Behold, he puts no trust in his servants,
>   and he charges his messengers with error.
> How much more then those who dwell in houses of clay,
>   whose foundation is in the dust;
>   they are crushed before the moth.
> From morning to evening they are punished,
>   they perish forever without any notice.
> Their abundance is taken away,
>   they die, without wisdom. (Job 4:17–21)

Eliphaz contrasts the righteousness of God with the corruption of human mortals and even argues that those who comprise the divine council ("servants" and "messengers") possess a sinful nature. Thus, this sovereign Lord places no faith even in these who dwell in his presence and carry out his commands. Thus, sinful humans, evil by nature and by deed, are justifiably punished by the divine judge. And, even sages, whose abundance exceeds what they need, eventually lose their prosperity and die, "without wisdom." Ultimately, the guidance of wisdom fails and even the sages perish. This more pessimistic view of human nature, while not unique in the Hebrew Bible (cf. Psalm 51), was used to explain why even the righteous suffered: all are inclined to evil because of corruption. And even their wisdom fails to redeem them. For the friends, there are no superhuman Jobs whose character is upright and whose words and deeds are pure.

Later, Eliphaz argues that in their scheming the wicked, including at times even sages, led astray by their bent toward evil, attempt to behave and speak in ways that will promote their self-interest. However, because they misuse their wisdom to plot to gain success for themselves, their plans are sure to fail. They fail because the God of justice brings the wicked and foolish, along with their misbegotten plans, to quick destruction. For example, Eliphaz, in the midst of his doxology (5:8–16), sings in praise of the God of justice:

He makes ineffectual the plans of the crafty,
so that works of their hands do not achieve success.
He catches the sages in their craftiness,
and the scheme of the cunning ones is quickly finished.

"Plans" (*maḥšĕbôt*, Isa 55:7; 59:7; Prov 12:5; 19:21; Job 21:27) are those thoughts or perceptions, shaped by shrewd contrivance ("craftiness" = *ʿōrem*), that plot a course of action designed to lead to success. It is false wisdom, or wisdom that follows an evil intent, that leads to wicked behavior, that ultimately results in destruction.

Yet for Eliphaz and the other two friends, humanity's situation is not hopeless. While the pursuit of wisdom's ethical instruction and the actualization of righteousness within one's existence are counseled, faithful piety holds out the hope for redemption. All are corrupt by nature. Even wise and righteous acts are perverted by the sinfulness of the human condition. Thus, the only real recourse to redemption is to "seek God," that is, turn to the Almighty in submissive repentance, acknowledge one's sins, and pray for salvation. This counsel to "seek God" comprises the final part of the first speech of Eliphaz (5:8–27), which begins with a doxology that praises the justice of God, is followed by the acknowledgment of one's guilt, and then concludes with the expectation that a just and merciful God will deliver the penitent from destruction and restore him or her to a state of well-being and success. What is particularly worthy of note in the friends' understanding of wisdom is that, apart from piety, even ethical behavior ultimately fails. Even sages through wise and righteous existence cannot save themselves from destruction by meritorious living. All are sinners, including the wise. The true hope for redemption ultimately resides in God.

For the friends, God's understanding of wisdom is at work in his providential governance of creation and history. Through his comprehension of wisdom, a comprehension that is far beyond the limited capacity of humans to understand, God not only knows the structures of creation and what humans do and say in the world, but also is aware of the sinfulness of human creatures. God uses this knowledge in both acting to sustain life and pronouncing judgment. However, God's decrees of justice, in their view, are tempered with mercy. Without divine compassion, the meting out of judgment would bring sinners to swift destruction. Thus Zophar says to Job:

Would that God might speak,
and open his lips to you,

so that he would reveal the secrets of wisdom,
for there are two sides to understanding.
And know that God exacts of you
less than your guilt requires. (11:5–6)

In making his point about God's comprehension of wisdom, Zophar notes that there are two sides to wisdom, one that is open to human insight and one that is mysterious and known only to God.[18] If God would reveal this mysterious side to wisdom, known only to him, then Job might have the information necessary to understand his dilemma. In the larger context of this statement by Zophar, he appears to argue that Job's contention that he is righteous in God's eyes not only is based on unwarranted pride but also issues forth from ignorance. For the friends, Job does not recognize how corrupt humans really are, a sinfulness that limits the capacity to know and understand.

Eliphaz makes a similar case against Job in chap. 15. He begins by asking Job a rhetorical question that indicates a "sage" (*ḥākām*) should not answer with "windy knowledge" — that is, knowledge falsely called and uttered in a spirit of pomposity is destructive. Indeed, for Eliphaz, Job's assault on God's justice subverts piety, one of the major elements of sapiential *mûsār* (15:2–4) and for the friends the one and only hope for redemption. Job's speech reflects not true wisdom, but rather crafty deceit that results only in his own condemnation (15:5).

Eliphaz then questions whether Job believes he is the "first man," renowned for having access to divine wisdom, though condemned for allowing his pride to corrupt his understanding (see Ezekiel 28). The question may be a rhetorical one, but it serves to remind Job of the tragic fate of this primordial human. Eliphaz goes on to ask Job if he is claiming access to the divine council, where the secret decrees of God are made. Approaching the divine council to receive the revelation of God's will normally was limited in the Hebrew Bible to prophets (cf. Jer 23:18). Eliphaz does not deny that access to the revelation (or wisdom) of God may be obtained in the divine council, but he does question if Job has such access. While reiterating his doctrine of the corruption of human nature (15:14–16), Eliphaz points to the sapiential tradition ("what the sages have told and their ancestors have not hidden") that teaches that the wicked are those who experience great suffering for daring to defy and oppose the Almighty.

18. See M. Pope, *Job* (AB; Garden City, N.Y.: Doubleday & Co., 1965) 82; and N. Habel, *The Book of Job* (OTL; Philadelphia: Westminster Press, 1985) 203.

There also is, in the world constructed by the opponents, a shift away from the traditional sages' conception of the cosmos as a righteous order. One might say that, for the friends, even the cosmos sighs heavily under the weight of corruption. This is especially noted in the examples from nature that the opponents use in shaping their arguments against Job. In his first speech to Job, Eliphaz speaks of the swift retribution that God brings against the "plowers of iniquity," and then underscores that affirmation by reference to the strong lions who perish for lack of food while their helpless whelps are left to fend for themselves. Although a just, though compassionate God renews creation through such life-giving acts as the sending of rain, the world is not a righteous order containing the structures of life that of themselves enable life to endure. Only a sovereign deity works in and through creation and history to make life possible (Job 4:7–11).

In the world constructed by the opponents of Job, creation, itself corrupt, is the domain of sinful human beings, ruled over by a sovereign Lord of justice who brings the wicked to an ignoble end but also is willing to save the penitent who turn to him for mercy (5:8–16). This worldview is not completely grounded in a retributive theory of justice. It is true that the friends refer to the godless who forsake both God and wisdom and encounter swift destruction. However, the friends have a darker view than that. Humans, even sages, are weighed down by the sinfulness of their mortal nature. By extension, human institutions, from the family to government, even when shaped by righteousness and directed by prudence, partake in that corruption. Thus, Bildad offers the cruel conclusion that even Job's children must have sinned, and thus were delivered by God "into the power of their transgression" (8:4). Piety is the one true hope for salvation. There is an order of justice, but it exists within the character and activity of the ruler of heaven and earth, not in nature, not in human institutions, and certainly not in corrupt human beings.

Job. Job has attempted to live and act within the traditional worldview of the sages. And, at least in times past, he has tried through discipline (*mûsār*) to actualize this world and its virtues within his character and behavior (chap. 29) and thereby to legitimate its veracity. Yet, through reflecting on his own experiences of agonizing pain, including the loss of family and honor, he realizes that something must have gone awry. Job's angst reflects an obvious breakdown of traditional wisdom's symbolic universe in which the sages participated and carried out their work. The teachings of the sages, especially those that speak of the success and well-being of the wise-righteous, do not mesh with his own experiences. One may even legitimately propose that the loss of confidence in wisdom's epistemological certainties and religious convictions, so clearly reflected in the Joban disputations, resulted from a rather dramatic collapse of the larger social order that provided part of the symbolic framework for sapiential knowing and therefore doing.[19] This dissolution of a larger social order led some, including at least one school of sages, to question critically those cherished cultural traditions that projected and undergirded the socioreligious world of Judah for several centuries. At the same time, the cosmos was also affected by disruption, for creation was no longer perceived as a benign order that sustained the life of the righteous.

The book of Job, and the poetry in particular, then, issues from the shattered spectrum of an intellectual and confessional system of meaning. Nature and society no longer seemed to be permeated and guided by divine justice. An epistemological and religious crisis leads the poet of Job to a serious questioning of the worldview that traditional wisdom had constructed, a reality that was both just and benign and overseen by a God at work in creation and history to sustain the righteous and to bring the wicked to destruction.

As the poetic Job encounters this intellectual crisis of faith, his major contention with both his narrative counterpart and the friends in the dialogues is over the explanation given to the breakdown in epistemological understanding and the faithful expectations of the righteous: the narrative points to divine testing and offers a discipline of wisdom that expects no reward; the friends and the intruder Elihu blame a corrupt nature (cosmic and human) that restricts and even perverts the best efforts of the wise to actualize virtue and counsel piety as the proper recourse for redemption; the poetic Job, seeking to maintain a worldview in which justice is the hallmark of reality, rejects piety and indicts a God turned cruel.

Chapter 12 is one of the best examples of Job's views on cosmology, the social order, and divine rule. Positioned within a lengthy speech that encompasses three chapters (12–14), chap. 12 comprises three stro-

19. See R. Albertz, "The Sage and Pious Wisdom in the Book of Job: The Friends' Perspective," in Gammie and Perdue, *Sage in Israel*, 243–61.

phes, the last two outlining his view of the divine (mis)rule of creation and history. Each of these two strophes seeks to legitimate the assertion in v. 6 that the perpetrators of violence who shake the foundations of justice experience peace and dwell securely.

STROPHE II: THE REVELATION OF CREATION (VV. 7–12)

But ask the beasts, and they will instruct you,
 the birds of the heavens, and they will tell you;
Or speak to the earth, and it will teach you,
 and the fish of the sea will inform you.
Which among all these does not know that the hand
 of Yahweh has done this.
He who has the life of every living thing in his hand,
 and the breath of all human flesh.
Does not the ear test words, or the palate taste its food?
Among the aged is wisdom, and insight in the length of days.

Job's assertion draws on the sapiential view that wisdom as knowledge derives from an astute observation and understanding of creation. However, contrary to the friends' conviction that a just and merciful God sustains life and brings the wicked to destruction, Job contends that creation offers a startling and severe counter-revelation: it is the hand (a metaphor for power) of God that brings well-being to the violent. Since God for Job is the sovereign Lord who holds in his power the life of every mortal, he must be the responsible agent whose misrule of reality gives peace and security to the wicked.

In the following strophe, Job moves into the social arena to undergird his contention that God is a malicious tyrant.

STROPHE III: THE REVELATION OF CREATION AND THE SOCIAL ORDER (VV. 13–25)

With him (God) is wisdom and might;
 he has counsel and insight.
Behold, he tears down, and there is no rebuilding;
 he imprisons one, and there is no release.
Behold, he withholds the waters, and the lands dry up;
 when he sends waters forth, they engulf the land.
With him are strength and sound wisdom,
 the deceived and the deceiver belong to him.
He makes counselors walk naked,
 and makes fools of judges.

He loosens the discipline [*mûsār*] of kings,
and ties a waist cloth on their loins.
He makes priests walk about barefoot,
and ruins wise officials.
He takes away the speech of those who are trusted,
and deprives the aged of discernment.
He pours contempt upon princes,
and loosens the girdle of the strong.
He reveals deep mysteries from darkness,
and brings to light deep darkness.
He exalts nations and destroys them,
he expands them and then leaves them forsaken.
He removes reason from the leaders of the people of the earth,
and makes them wander in a pathless waste.
They grope about in the darkness with no light,
causing them to stagger like one who is drunk.

Job now turns to his observations not only of creation, but also of society. Job does not doubt that God possesses great wisdom and power, but what is significantly absent, he contends, is divine justice. Indeed, through caprice and malicious intent, God takes away wisdom and success from the very leaders who were to embody sapiential knowledge and thus lead their people intelligently and well. These leaders, who are responsible for maintaining justice within their society, are the victims of divine abuse. With this strophe, Job denies that God has any benign plan for nations or any norms of justice by which history is guided. The chaos wrought in creation is paralleled by what God has brought upon human nations.

Job abandons traditional wisdom's understandings of cosmology and society. God is responsible for perverting social institutions. The cosmos groans under the weight of an oppressive deity. History is misdirected by a God who leads nations to their destruction. The only solution for Job is that, by coming to trial, the divine tyrant would be removed from the throne and replaced by a benign and just humanity who no longer would be the slaves of God suffering under the oppressive heel of their creator. This is the intent of the "oath of innocence" in chap. 31: Job hopes to indict, convict, and then remove God from the throne of heaven. In this quest for justice, it is interesting to recall that the Job of the narrative tale is the one who without questioning accepts whatever lot he is given by God and continues to praise the deity in the face of great loss, even when divine justice appears to be absent. The Job of the dialogues, however, cannot praise and honor a divine sadist who afflicts his own creation with grievous evil and subverts the efforts of human communities to establish and maintain justice.

The crisis for Job is that the traditional sapiential understanding of God does not correlate with his own experience. He cannot accept the view of his narrative counterpart that even in the absence of justice God must be praised. And he cannot accept the dark views of the friends concerning the corruption of nature, both human and cosmic. Yet, at least until the conclusion of the poetry, it is not the cosmic and social world constructed and legitimated by traditional wisdom that is called into question; rather it is God. Justice, for Job, must be the order that holds together cosmos and society. God, in the poetic Job's experience, for reasons beyond his fathoming, has become a malicious and destructive tyrant who destroys not only the wicked, but the righteous as well. No longer meriting faithful devotion, this God must be removed from heaven's throne.

Wisdom in the Speeches from the Whirlwind

Thus far wisdom has been understood as knowledge, discipline that forms character, and world-construction. Each of these understandings of wisdom is operative in the various literary segments of Job, though at times with different nuances. Not surprisingly, the same three general understandings of wisdom, also differently nuanced, are present in the climax of the book of Job: the two speeches from the whirlwind and Job's two responses.

Wisdom as Knowledge: The First Divine Speech (38:1–40:2). The first speech of Yahweh begins with a question, soon to be followed by many other questions. But the first question is the key one on which the others turn: "Who is this who darkens counsel with words lacking in knowledge?" The initial part of the question, "Who is this," does not simply seek to identify the one who has dared to challenge divine rule, but also expresses Yahweh's contempt for the human opponent (Exod 5:2; Judg 9:28, 38; Isa 28:9). Further, "counsel" (*'ēṣâ*) in wisdom literature is a well-conceived plan that leads to success. Here, it is Yahweh's plan for creating and ruling the world (Prov 8:14; Isa 5:19; 46:10). Job's questioning of divine justice, left unchecked, seeks to subvert God's life-sustaining plan by returning creation to the darkness of chaos (cf. chap. 3). Thus, God has come not simply to instruct an ignorant Job in the mysteries of creation, but more importantly to defend divine providence.

What follows in the first speech of God is a lengthy list of questions directed to Job, questions that ask if Job has the wisdom to understand the workings of the cosmos and if he possesses the power to rule over it. Yet the questions are asked in such a way as to emphasize that while Job may lack the knowledge and power to direct the cosmos, he should know that God does not. Thus, the first speech not only attests to God's wisdom and power in creating and maintaining the structures of the cosmos and its orders of life, but it also demonstrates Job's own obvious limits as a finite human creature. Without the knowledge to understand the workings of the cosmos and without the power to sustain it, how can Job question divine justice? In this speech and the one following, justice is understood not as retribution for human deeds, but rather as an active agent within divine rule that creates and sustains life. God defends divine justice not by referencing it to individual human experience, but rather by placing it within the active sway of divine rule of the cosmos.

God points to illustrations of divine providence in providing and sustaining life. For example, in 38:39–39:30, five pairs of animals are the recipients of a divine nurturing that enables them to live. Most of these are wild, not domesticated, creatures, and several are even potentially harmful to human life. Even so, God sustains them, including the ostrich who is devoid of life-giving wisdom. Odd is the omission in this speech and the following one of any providential nurturing of human life, perhaps suggesting in a rather shocking way that reality is not anthropocentric, as Job's railings against God would imply. Even precious rain falls on a desert land "where no mortal is."[20] If Job were truly wise, God seems to say, then his observations of creation and the moral teachings he deduces from them would be far different from what they are. The certainties of Joban and traditional sapiential epistemology are even less secure than either Job or the sages of Proverbs had dared to allow.

Wisdom as World-Construction: The Second Divine Speech (40:6–41:26). At times the voice of personified wisdom was the revelatory instru-

20. See M. Tsevat, "The Meaning of the Book of Job," *HUCA* 37 (1966) 73–106.

ment used by the sages to speak of world-construction. However, in the conclusion to the poetic dialogues, it is now the voice of God, not a personified divine attribute, that speaks. The second speech from the whirlwind also presents a defense of divine creation, but by taking a somewhat different approach from that found in the first speech. The second speech begins with another seminal question, this one different from the primal question introducing the first speech. In 40:8 Yahweh asks Job:

> Will you negate my justice,
> will you pronounce me guilty that you might be declared innocent?

Job had thought that the defense of his own integrity required the disproving of God's. In his experiences of great suffering, certainly not deserved, Job had mistakenly indicted God for being the responsible agent.

What follows is something of a surprising revelation. God offers Job the throne, if he can remove the wicked from the face of the earth, and if he can defeat the two incarnations of chaos, Behemoth and Leviathan. In this world-construction, God is the one who comes to do battle with these mythical personifications of evil. No human, including Job, has the wisdom and power to defeat them and thus to remove evil from reality. The implication is that Yahweh is actively at work in combating the power of evil, but even divine wisdom and power do not once and for all vanquish chaos from the world. This active striving against chaos presents an understanding of divine justice that is at variance with the anthropocentric one with which Job had operated in his disputations. However, the affirmation of Job's integrity, his embodiment of justice (cf. esp. chap. 31), does not depend on proving God is unjust.

In 40:15 God admits he has created Behemoth, even as he made Job. Does this mean that God is responsible for creating chaos? The logical answer seems to be yes, if Behemoth, and presumably Leviathan, are mythical creatures of God's own making. Second Isaiah portrays a God who is responsible for evil (45:7), and it could be that this is what the poet implies. But even more important to the poet, Behemoth and Leviathan are mythical creatures who threaten divine rule and the creation that God has established. Like Prince Yam and Lotan in Canaanite myth, they have not stayed within their allotted boundaries of the mythical sea, but rather seek in their own arrogant pride to overwhelm the created order (cf. 38:8–11). Thus, God in Job battles them both, to keep them in their place, thereby preserving a cosmic order that makes the continuation of life possible. This is justice.

Wisdom as Mûsār: *Job's Responses (40:3–5; 42:1–6).* Job's two responses, while brief and enigmatic, may best be understood as a return to the unquestioning piety of his narrative counterpart (and that of the poem on Wisdom in chap. 28). Of course, it is possible to argue that this turning back to wisdom as discipline or *mûsār* that does not expect reward may be "tongue in cheek," but that is more easy to assert than to argue.[21] On the surface, at least, Job admits there is more to creation, justice, and divine rule than he understands. The element of mystery, indigenous to sapiential epistemology, returns. Job also returns to the *mûsār* of his narrative counterpart, but it is a second naiveté, a faithful praise that has emerged from the caldrons of a human desperation expressed in the pathos and words of one who could no longer keep quiet. Job had experienced the darkness of human suffering and uttered out of the agony of his own torment an indictment of God. While never abandoning his own actualization of justice — indeed it was his insistence that this virtue be a defining feature of both God's and his own character — Job could not praise a deity he believed had become perverse. Now, chastened by the revelation that humans are not at the center of the universe, that retributive justice is a false teaching, and that God does act to sustain life (another understanding of justice), Job once again is able to open his lips in faithful praise.

It is important to note that the repentant Job's virtue is now grounded in both a different worldview and a different understanding of God than those of traditional wisdom. It is grounded in the understanding that the creator engages in a life and death struggle with a chaos, embodied in two mythological monsters, intent on bringing creation to an end. Justice as a life-giving power is not a guaranteed given in the nature and operation of the cosmos, but rather an agent at work in the character and active rule of God. And this God, though powerful and wise, is not omnipotent. While evil may not have gained the upper hand, it still infringes on the world and causes great suffering. The descriptions of Behemoth and Leviathan focus mainly on their fearsome power and the inability of humans to control them. Job learns

21. D. Robertson, "The Book of Job: A Literary Study," *Soundings* 56 (1973) 446–69; and J. G. Williams, "'You Have Not Spoken Truth of Me': Mystery and Irony in Job," *ZAW* 83 (1971) 231–55.

that the ongoingness of life is ultimately dependent on Yahweh's power and wisdom in bringing mighty chaos and its mythical incarnations to their knees. This active struggle for the continuation of threatened life is divine justice. But it is an ever-recurring battle, made all the more suspenseful by the sober realization that Yahweh could lose.[22]

Wisdom in Job 28

The poem on the inaccessibility of Wisdom appears to have been appended by a later editor to the last speech of Job in the dialogues with the three friends. Wisdom in this poem is Woman Wisdom, a personification of a divine attribute active in the creating and sustaining of the cosmos. The poem represents the use of theological imagination by an unknown sage who attempts to construct another world than those of the narrative and poetic dialogues as the context for sapiential discipline.

Job 28 is a poem about Woman Wisdom, though here she is beyond human reach. In spite of the best efforts of humans and personified elements of the world (e.g., Sheol and Abaddon in v. 22) to find and know her, she cannot be grasped. Only God knows her, for he created her and knows the path to her dwelling. Now Wisdom is a mysterious cosmic being, not accessible to human beings. Instead of seeking to find her and to learn the secrets of the divine and human worlds, the poem teaches instead that humans should learn to embody the virtues of *mûsār:* "the fear of the Lord" and "departing from evil" (v. 28). Thus, this poem counsels humans to give up the quest for cosmic wisdom that is denied to them and instead to study the sapiential tradition in which wisdom, defined as piety and ethics (i.e., *mûsār*), may be appropriated and actualized within human existence. In many ways, this poem returns to the narrative's understanding of wisdom as *mûsār,* with one notable exception. The narrative has allowed its readers to observe the heavenly divine council where the decrees of God are formulated for activation in the human world. The poem denies that troubling look at the divine world. Instead, the poem concludes that cosmic wisdom is beyond human comprehension.

22. See J. D. Levenson, *Creation and the Persistence of Evil: The Jewish Drama of Divine Omnipotence* (San Francisco: Harper & Row, 1988).

CONCLUSION

Each of the segments of Job contains various views of wisdom as knowledge, as discipline, and as world-construction. For the narrative, wisdom is primarily discipline, a discipline that is sorely tested by a theological world in which a normally just God turns over his most faithful and righteous servant to undeserved horror. While suffering is seen as divine testing, the portrait of a suspicious God, turned cruel even for a time, was a troubling one.

The poet presents in the friends of Job and Elihu an understanding of wisdom as knowledge: the tradition of the ancestors, its recall by the powers of human memory, and its examination in the realm of their own experience. In their own critical engagement of the teachings of the earlier sages, they add the pessimistic view that humans and the cosmos are corrupt. The cosmos, society, and humans do not embody justice, but rather are weighed down by corruption. Even sages cannot save themselves by meritorious actions. Thus, they understand wisdom to be a discipline in which ultimately piety, not even righteous works, offers the one real hope for redemption. Their counsel to Job is to repent and turn to God in the hope that the Almighty will redeem him. The world they construct is one in which the creator and sustainer of life is the God of justice and compassion who brings punishment to the wicked, though it is less than they deserve.

Job understands that wisdom is not simply bowing the knee to the teachings by the sages, but rather it involves the testing of the tradition by experience. Wisdom as an epistemology allows for the authentic, critical engagement of the past in the light of new understanding. Job also understands wisdom to be discipline, the embodiment of virtue, especially justice and piety. But his experience leads him to abandon not justice, but rather piety. If God is indeed a malicious tyrant who brings destruction even to the righteous, then this deity is no longer worthy of praise. In the world of Job's own making, justice is an anthropological category by which the wise-righteous should enter into well-being and success. Yet in the glaring absence of this anthropological reference point of justice, it must be that God has turned cruel. The transformation of Job at the end can only be based on his recognition, if not complete understanding, that God is just. Thus the justice of God allows for Job to open once again his lips in praise. He returns to *mûsār*, wisdom as moral virtue and piety.

God's speeches view wisdom as knowledge, particularly knowledge about the operations of creation. This is a wisdom that God has, but that Job does not. In the world constructed by the voice from the whirlwind, justice is an active agent in the rule of God to sustain the orders of life and to defeat the powers of chaos that threaten the cosmos. Though not omnipotent, God continues to struggle against the threats to life posed by the two mythical beasts of chaos.

Finally, in the poem in Job 28, the quest to understand cosmic wisdom is given up. Efforts at world-construction, other than those that posit mystery, are abandoned. Indeed, true wisdom, so the poem asserts, is discipline: the embodiment of righteousness and piety.

6

WISDOM IN PROVERBS

Carole R. Fontaine

The book of Proverbs, the oldest of the canonical wisdom books, offers an excellent starting point for the consideration of the meaning of wisdom in all its aspects: as a distinctive tradition of language and literature, as a social movement within ancient Israel, and as a world-view held by members of that movement and communicated through their special vocabulary and literary forms.

Answering the questions posed in the quest for an understanding of the meaning of wisdom in Proverbs is not so simple a matter as one might expect, because the history of that book is itself complicated. It is clear to critics that the book consists of several different parts, some of which are poetic compositions that explore the excellence of wisdom, while other sections include what seem to be independent collections of proverbs tied together loosely by theme or literary devices, such as "catchwords," mnemonics, and wordplay. Each of these subsections has its own literary prehistory and no doubt was the focus of complex editing strategies, so that it becomes difficult to identify a single time, place, or social stratum that might serve as a reference point for the whole book. Further, the date and life setting for each of the subsections occasion much debate among scholars who study them. For my purposes here, I will simply refer to those portions of the book that can be placed with some certainty during the life of monarchies of Israel and Judah as "early" (10:1–29:27) and those that are judged by a consensus of scholars to reflect exilic and postexilic society as "late" (Proverbs 1–9; 31:10–31). But as always, questions with dating remain. For example, when is it most likely to assume that Egyptian influence, such as that found in the forms and content of Proverbs 1–9, would have been prevalent — during the time of the monarchy when international exchange might have been frequent, or after the exile when the hated rival power of Egypt was no longer a major issue for the intellectual elite, now under home rule? Similarly, one's assessment of the astonishing figure of personified Wisdom will certainly affect one's judgments about dates for Proverbs 1–9. Those who see her as a saving remnant of a Hebrew goddess, based on models from Egypt, Mesopotamia, or Canaan, will be more likely to date these passages to the early period, where others who view Woman Wisdom as a mediating figure who gains in importance based on real-life role models of human women in the Jewish community may find a postexilic date more congenial for their reconstructions.[1]

SOCIAL MOVEMENTS AND THEIR WORLDVIEWS

As we begin our reconstructions during the early period (tenth to early sixth centuries, BCE), there immediately appear to be several distinct settings that give rise to the materials in the so-called Solomonic collections (10:1–22:16). While scholars have concluded that Solomon was not, in fact, the author of the bulk of these materials, nevertheless, the world of the royal court in Jerusalem is taken as the most probable context in which these materials emerged and were first collected.[2] However, this reconstruction, which emphasizes the role of the elite in the composition and redaction of the proverb collections, has long been

1. Cf., for example, the views on dating in B. Lang, *Wisdom and the Book of Proverbs: An Israelite Goddess Redefined* (New York: Pilgrim Press, 1986) 4–5, with those of C. Camp, *Wisdom and the Feminine in the Book of Proverbs* (Sheffield: Almond Press, 1985) 233–54. Certainly, the date of the redaction of the book is postexilic, but this, of course, still leaves open the possibility of early composition dates for some material that received editing in the later period. In the same vein, if the figure of Woman Wisdom is viewed as a repressed archetype, she might erupt into consciousness during any period, and would be especially likely do so in times of social disintegration and reorganization, such as postexilic Israel. Obviously, playing the dating game is hazardous and frustrating at best.

2. For discussion of this setting for wisdom tradents, see W. A. Brueggemann, "The Social Significance of Solomon as a Patron of Wisdom," *The Sage in Israel and the Ancient Near East* (ed. J. G. Gammie and L. G. Perdue; Winona Lake, Ind.: Eisenbrauns, 1990) 117–32; R. N. Whybray, "The Sage in the Israelite Royal Court," in ibid., 133–40; and A. Lemaire, "The Sage in School and Temple," in ibid., 165–84.

challenged by others who have attended to the role of the family, clan, and tribe in the origins of wisdom as a social movement.[3] A third way of approaching the question of the authors behind these texts explores the possibility of the existence of schools whose teachers used the texts of Proverbs as didactic material for students.[4] In fact, there is very little direct textual evidence for the reconstruction of any of these proposed groups as the natural locus in which wisdom thinking and texts developed. In the absence of any one theory that clearly wins allegiance over the others, this essay will examine each of the potential settings for wisdom in Proverbs in an attempt to suggest the kinds of pragmatic and intellectual motivations that may have structured the concept of wisdom as we find it in our texts. In all likelihood, each of the contexts so disputed — family and tribe, court, and school — probably made overlapping contributions to the composition, use, and understanding of the meaning of wisdom.[5]

The Family and Tribe

To begin with the earliest group, that of family and tribe, Proverbs contains many "instructions"[6] that retain a flavor of the family. These lengthy compositions give examples to be followed and pointed

3. E. Gerstenberger, *Wesen und Herkunft des sogennanten 'apodiktischen Rechts' im Alten Testament* (WMANT 20: Neukirchen-Vluyn: Neukirchener Verlag, 1965); C. R. Fontaine, *Traditional Sayings in the Old Testament: A Contextual Study* (Bible and Literature 5; Sheffield: Almond Press, 1982); and idem, "The Sage in Family and Tribe," in Gammie and Perdue, *Sage in Israel,* 155–64; C. Westermann, "Weisheit im Sprichwort," *Schalom: Studien zu Glaube und Geschichte Israels* (ed. K. H. Bernhardt; Festschrift Alfred Jepsen; Stuttgart: Calwer, 1971) 73–85; and most recently, idem, *Wurzeln der Weisheit: Die ältesten Sprüche Israels und anderer Völker* (Göttingen: Vandenhoeck & Ruprecht, 1990).

4. H. J. Hermisson, *Studien zur israelitischen Spruchweisheit* (WMANT 28; Neukirchen-Vluyn: Neukirchener Verlag, 1968) 97–136; B. Lang, "Schule und Unterricht im alten Israel," *La sagesse de l'Ancien Testament* (ed. M. Gilbert; BETL 51; Gembloux: Duculot, 1979) 186–201; N. Shupak, "The 'Sitz im Leben' of the Book of Proverbs in the Light of a Comparison of Biblical and Egyptian Wisdom Literature," *RB* 94 (1987) 98–119; A. Lemaire, *Les Écoles et la formation de la Bible dans l'ancien Israel* (OBO 39; Göttingen: Vandenhoeck & Ruprecht, 1981), and idem, "The Sage in School and Temple," 165–81. For a more cautious assessment of the existence of schools, at least for the early period, see R. N. Whybray, *The Intellectual Tradition in the Old Testament* (BZAW 135; Berlin: Walter de Gruyter 1974); J. L. Crenshaw, "Education in Ancient Israel," *JBL* 104 (1985) 601–15; idem, "The Acquisition of Knowledge in Israelite Wisdom Literature," *Word and World* 7 (1987) 245–52.

5. This is nicely summarized in chart 10, "Institutional Settings of Israelite Wisdom," in N. K. Gottwald, *The Hebrew Bible: A Socio-Literary Introduction* (Philadelphia: Fortress Press, 1985) 569.

6. Prov 1:1–19; 2:1–22; 3:1–12, 21–35; 4:1–9, 10–19, 20–27; 5:1–23; 6:20–35; 7:1–27; 22:17–24:22; 31:1–9.

motivations to the young. In them students are directly addressed as "my son."[7] While the Egyptian influence on the instruction form is well understood, it is interesting to see the familial aspects of imparting wisdom, enjoined by the Torah (Exod 10:2; 12:26; Deut 4:9; 6:7; 20:21; etc.), surface in these materials despite their possible courtly origins and use:

> Listen, O sons, to a father's instruction;
> pay attention, so as to know insight;
> for good precepts I give to you;
> my teaching do not forsake!
> For I was a son to my father,
> tender and unique in my mother's sight,
> and he used to teach me, and told me,
> "Let your heart grasp my words,
> keep my commandments and live." (4:1–4)

It is also worth noting that while most instructions preserved have as their ostensible composer the figure of the father/sage, Prov 31:1–9 preserves an example attributed to a woman — and a foreigner, no less! — the queen mother of Lemuel, king of Massa.

The imprint of the father's and mother's authority as sources of wisdom is found throughout the book: in motivations for heeding the wisdom found in the instructions (1:8; 6:20), in the occurrence of the two together as a traditional word-pair in the proverbial sayings (10:1; 15:20; 20:20; 23:22, 25; 28:24; 30:11, 17), and in the concerns and activities these verses attribute to the parents. The wisdom or folly of one's children brings gladness or grief (10:1; 15:20; 23:25); a curse against one's parents extinguishes one's "lamp," invoking the inevitable correspondence between evil acts and wretched consequences so believed in by wisdom thinkers (20:20). The "capable wife" of 31:10–31 "opens her mouth with wisdom, and the teaching of kindness is on her tongue" (v. 26), in the midst of her myriad of home-building activities. Given the basic importance of the family as the primary economic unit in agrarian societies, it is not surprising that a book such as Proverbs, which is so identified with the teachings of the parents, should concern itself with matters of importance to the survival of the family: finding a good wife (12:4; 14:1; 18:22; 19:13, 14; 21:9, 19); the discipline of children and slaves (19:18; 20:20; 22:6, 15); care for one's family and land, the usual source of one's

7. This form of address occurs twenty-two times, with only two occurrences in the saying form (19:27; 27:11). In instructions, it is found in Prov 1:8, 10, 15; 2:1; 3:1, 11, 21; 4:10, 20; 6:1, 3, 20; 7:1; 23:15, 19, 26; 24:13, 21.

economic livelihood (5:10; 6:31; 12:11; 14:4; 15:6; 21:20; 24:27; 28:19); regulating one's relationships with neighbors (3:29; 6:3, 29; 14:20–21; 24:28; 25:8, 9, 17, 18; 26:19; 27:10, 14; 29:5). We may locate, then, at least one of the social movements that gave rise to the concept of wisdom in Proverbs within the everyday world of the extended family,[8] for as the sayings tell us

> By wisdom a home is built,
> and by understanding it is established;
> by knowledge the rooms are filled
> with choice and pleasant riches. (24:3–4)

Since the male heads of Israel's "father's house" (*bêt ʾāb*) automatically acted as "elders" (*zĕqēnîm*) of the clan (*mišpāḥâ* = familial groups of related fathers' houses) and the tribe, it may be presumed that the "family-gone-public" character of the wisdom traditions of this group may also have fed into Proverbs. Whereas wisdom within the family primarily centered upon the teaching functions of the parents and the management of family resources, tribal or clan wisdom probably paid less attention to educational aspects and placed more emphasis on enacting judicial decisions between persons and groups, concerned itself with allocation of resources on a larger scale than that of the single family, and advised tribal leaders in moments of political crisis.[9] Wisdom is found particularly associated with such elders in Num 11:16; Ps 105:21–22; Job 12:12, 20; Ezek 7:26. Before the monarchy is well established, we see elders taking part in counseling and planning in a variety of contexts in Num 22:4–7; Judg 8:5–6, 14, 16; 11:5–11; 1 Sam 8:4; 2 Sam 3:17. Later, they appear as the counselors of kings in 1 Kgs 12:6–11 and 1 Kgs 20:7–12, and at all periods seem to render legal decisions at lower levels where the later nation-state might well choose not to concern itself (Deut 19:12; 21:19; 22:13–21; 25:7–8; Josh 20:4; Ruth 4; Jer 26:17–19). One intriguing text in Judges 8 shows Gideon, a tribal leader and "judge," using "proverb performance" (the purposeful transmission of a saying in a social context in order to evaluate or influence outcomes) skillfully to settle a dispute between his own group and another concerning the distribution of spoil.[10] Even more tantalizing for our reconstruc-

8. For further discussion, see Fontaine, "The Sage in Family and Tribe," 155–63; and idem, "Proverbs," *The Women's Bible Commentary* (ed. C. A. Newsom and S. H. Ringe; Louisville, Ky.: Westminster/John Knox Press, 1992) 145–52.

9. See Fontaine, "The Sage in Family and Tribe," 163–64.

10. See Fontaine, *Traditional Sayings*, 76–86.

tions of the widespread authority of tribal wisdom is the passage that follows, in Judg 8:21. Here, the captive Midianite leaders Zebah and Zalmunna use a traditional saying directed at Gideon to obtain their goals.[11] This is striking because the two groups are quite foreign to one another and stand in the position of enemies, yet the simple wisdom of a folk saying is portrayed by the author as a universally recognized and efficacious method of evaluating events and calculating appropriate actions. Clan wisdom, then, operates not just *within* groups, but *between* them as well, and so paves the way for the international, diplomatic functions attributed to court sages and bureaucrats.

The Court and the School

Given the fact that scholars inevitably turn to a discussion of the royal court and scribal school when examining the origins and use of wisdom in Israel, it is surprising how little textual information for these actually exists. In Prov 25:1, the "men of Hezekiah" are connected with the collecting or editing of the proverb collection that follows, thus providing our only direct link between the text of Proverbs and the work of the court. In Eccl 12:9, we hear that Qoheleth, a *ḥākām*, "taught the people," but we are not told in precisely what context this took place, so that it is possible to regard the phrase as a less than concrete reference to work of a hypothetical social class of "sages." Our first indisputable reference to a wisdom school is found in the apocryphal book of Sirach (ca. 180 CE), where Ben Sira speaks of his school (*bêt midrāš*, 51:23).

Despite the slender basis for reconstruction that such textual notices provide, scholars — with varying degrees of comfort and certainty — generally accept the notion that a group of scribes, teachers, and counselors existed at court, and perhaps taught in small schools (though not "schools" as modern persons might think of them) in home, court, and temple.[12] As it happens, such organs of state bureaucracy are well attested in surrounding cultures (though often not as explicitly as one would like), and growing evidence of literacy in ancient Israel prompts one to reexamine the question of schooling during the monarchy.

It is usually assumed that with the move from tribal organization to statehood, which took place during the reigns of David and Solomon, there grew a basic institutional need to handle the accumulating in-

11. Ibid., 86–95.
12. See notes 2 and 4, above, for the most recent round of discussions on this topic.

formation required to run a country from a centralized power base. Perhaps using Egyptian models, these rulers went about the task of setting up an efficient bureaucracy and filled its ranks with those who supported the new ideal of statehood under a king. While we have no designated class of "sages" in Proverbs (or anywhere else, for that matter) whose activities, qualifications, and goals have been spelled out in detail, a close reading of the materials having to do with court life, especially those found in the Succession Narrative (2 Samuel 11–1 Kings 2), reveals several groups who perform sagelike tasks.[13] These experts are the counselor (*yôʿēṣ*), the "king's friend" (*rēʿēh hammelek*), and the scribe (*sôpēr*),[14] and we find the concerns of these courtiers echoed in the materials in Proverbs.

While it is by no means clear what distinction, if any, should be made between the position of counselor and king's friend, the actions performed by these court functionaries are straightforward enough: they offer advice to their king (2 Sam 16:15–17:14). In an ancient world where writing was a specialty craft, scribes served as secretaries to court and individuals alike, and were engaged in the composing and keeping of records of all kinds (Jer 36:4–18; 2 Kgs 12:10; Ezekiel 9; 1 Chr 27:32).[15] We must assume that all of these persons received training of some sort in order to fulfill their duties: some may have served in apprenticeships at home for hereditary positions; others may have been taught privately in small groups by accomplished professionals attached to the court or temple.[16]

The proverb collections found in Prov 16:1–22:16, 25:1–29:27 and the instructions of 22:17–24:22, which freely adapt the Egyptian Instruction of Amenemope, reflect the concerns, needs, and worldview of these sparsely documented court figures. These sections ponder the roles and talents of kings; the demands of justice; the necessity of wily behavior in the presence of the powerful; the dangers of character flaws such as greed, drunkenness, sloth, and imprudent speech; and the perils of

13. R. N. Whybray, *The Succession Narrative: A Study of II Samuel 8–20; I Kings 1 and 2* (SBT 2/9; London: SCM Press, 1968).

14. Whybray, "The Sage in the Israelite Royal Court," 134–37. We might also note the presence of "wise women," at least one of whom spoke with kings (2 Samuel 14), but I would place them and their concerns among the representatives of tribal/clan wisdom. So, too, C. Camp, "The Female Sage in the Biblical Wisdom Literature," in Gammie and Perdue, *Sage in Israel,* 188–190; and idem, "The Wise Women of 2 Samuel: A Role Model for Women in Early Israel," *CBQ* 43 (1981) 14–29.

15. Whybray, "The Sage in the Israelite Royal Court," 136–37.

16. Lemaire, "The Sage in School and Temple," 168–78.

the company of women.[17] Two points of interest emerge as one peruses Proverbs with its possibly courtly origins in mind. First, while it is assumed that the worldview of a professional elite is in evidence here, it is not so divorced from the everyday world of family and clan wisdom as might be expected. "King" is mentioned only eighteen times throughout the book, whereas there are thirty-three references to children. In this book that supposedly reflects the secularized consciousness of pragmatic professionals, we find the deity mentioned ninety-five times (eighty-seven occurrences as Yahweh; eight references to Elohim), but counselors and advisers are found only on four occasions (11:14; 12:20; 15:22; 24:6). While we may sometimes infer a "class ethic" of the royal sages who know very well *whose* social order they are paid to support, in fact the proverbs concerning the plight of the poor and the wealth of the rich often point out the greed and cruelty of the very class to which we assume our sages must have belonged.[18]

After the fall of Judah in 587/86 BCE, many of the specific social matrices that produced the wisdom traditions of the "early" portions of Proverbs experienced profound change. As the elite class went into exile in Babylon, one can well imagine that family and clan wisdom was rediscovered as a source of guidance in changing times. Likewise, the wisdom of the political sages that had proved so useless against the great historical upheavals of their day might have been dramatically rejected, or at least severely curtailed in its daily sphere of influence (cf. Ezek 7:26). Without the institution of kingship, a class of royal advisers was unnecessary, but new social needs arose, such as the preservation of the legal and narrative traditions of Israel and Judah, and the ongoing reinterpretation of those traditions. In the experience of the exile, wisdom provided a concrete tie with the past and plan for the future, as scribes and their teachers turned their attention first to the tasks of

17. For more detailed analysis, see C. R. Fontaine, "Proverbs," *HBC* (ed. J. L. Mays; San Francisco: Harper & Row, 1988) 510–14. It should be clear by this point that the sages addressed most of their reflections on life to a male audience.

18. Gottwald, *Hebrew Bible*, 570, 573; see also B. W. Kovacs, "Is There a Class-Ethic in Proverbs?" *Essays in Old Testament Ethics: J. P. Hyatt, In Memoriam* (ed. J. Crenshaw and J. T. Willis; New York: KTAV Publishing House, 1974) 171–89. See also R. van Leeuwen, "Wealth and Poverty: System and Contradiction in Proverbs," *Hebrew Studies* 33 (1992) 25–36; and R. N. Whybray, *Wealth and Poverty in the Book of Proverbs* (JSOTSup 99; Sheffield: Sheffield Academic Press, 1990), where he concludes that 10:1–22:16 and 25–29 are by farmers of modest means who are extremely aware of the precariousness of life, while 22:17–24:22 and 1–9 derive from "the world of educated, well-to-do, acquisitive urban society."

compilation, editing, and composition of a literary heritage brought by the exiles, and later to the tasks of preserving themselves as a discrete people in a new political context. Scholars speculate that during this time, Proverbs received its final editing, and so assumed the shape it has today. While it incorporated materials from a different past, it was compiled in such a way as to meet the needs of a community in radically different circumstances. Because wisdom in Proverbs grew out of a diversity of rich settings, its appeal to a newly resettled community of exiles remained fresh: laziness, good land management, the greed of the wealthy, and the difficulties of family life amid foreign influences continued to be timely topics during this second "pioneer" period of later times. Some scholars feel the "theological introduction" of Proverbs 1–9 is addressed to this time and worldview, though, to be sure, some have posited other settings as well.[19]

Proverbs 1–9, with its lengthy instructions and beautifully constructed "wisdom poems," offers the reader a far different experience than is found in the proverb collections. In these elegant chapters, the traditional themes that will be replayed in the subsequent proverb lists are introduced and interpreted in narrative-like examples created by the sages' expressive language: wisdom and folly, rich and poor, diligent and lazy, male and female, humanity and deity, family values and the lure of the Strange Woman, the primal world of creation and the sphere of the everyday. Whether these compositions are didactic in use — some speculate that they may have formed the basis for copybook exercises for students — their effect is to prepare the reader for the collections by sustained consideration of wisdom's typical topics. Certainly, the introduction to the book as a whole, found in 1:2–6, emphasizes the teaching goals of the sages:

> For learning about wisdom and instruction,
> for understanding words of insight,
> for gaining instruction in wise dealing,
> righteousness, justice, and equity;
> to teach shrewdness to the simple,
> knowledge and prudence to the young —
> Let the wise also hear and gain in learning,
> and the discerning acquire skill,

19. See especially Claudia Camp's reconstruction of this period as a major impetus for the inclusion of the enigmatic figure of Woman Wisdom (*Wisdom and the Feminine*, 233–82). See also L. G. Perdue, "Liminality as a Social Setting for Wisdom Instruction," *ZAW* 93 (1981) 114–26.

> to understand a proverb and a figure,
> the words of the wise and their riddles. (NRSV)

The curriculum of wisdom teaching is well presented here, with the piling up of many synonyms, all of which revolve around the rather optimistic view that education *does* make a difference in the way people live their lives. That the sages emphasize here that the teaching they are about to convey is couched in special forms of language — proverbs, figures, riddles — leads us to a consideration of the language and style of the book of Proverbs.

THE WORDS OF THE WISE

Wisdom Genres

Scholars have rightly spoken of "an aesthetic of words" when discussing the distinctive language of the sages,[20] for it is clear that when we first hear the voices of the wise in Proverbs, we are hearing the speech of the artistic elite. Further, as Gerhard von Rad has pointed out, it is no coincidence that the insights of the sages are cast in poetic form, for their way of considering the world of experience required of them special forms to contain their content.[21] The holistic perception of an insight expressed in parallelism, along with the rhythmic and mnemonic enhancement provided by various literary devices such as paronomasia, alliteration, and the use of sharply drawn metaphors, all combine to render the diction of the sages elegant and erudite.

The most basic form used by the sages in Proverbs is the *māšāl* or saying. This term is actually used quite broadly within the Hebrew Bible, covering a variety of genres that to the modern interpreter sometimes seem quite unrelated. However, the linkage between the various forms may be found in the basic meaning of the verbal root, which carries two meanings. These are "to rule over" and "to be similar," and understanding them together enhances appreciation of the "ethnic" genre designation used by the sages themselves (and which ought to be preserved, if for no other reason than that).[22] The purposeful *māšāl* form both presents a figure that is *similar* to what it is observing, and by

20. R. E. Murphy, *The Tree of Life: An Exploration of Biblical Wisdom Literature* (Anchor Bible Reference Library; New York: Doubleday, 1990) 6.

21. G. von Rad, *Wisdom in Israel* (Nashville: Abingdon Press, 1972) 24–25.

22. O. Eissfeldt, *Der Maschal im Alten Testament* (BZAW 24; Giessen: Töpelmann, 1913) 43.

doing so, allows the audience to identify, classify, and respond appropriately to all other like happenings. Thus, the *māšāl* invites one to rule over and take charge of events once they are properly understood. As such, it is no wonder that it is a favorite with the sages.

We may distinguish here between the one-line folk or traditional saying found reported in some of the historical books and the two-line proverb or artistic saying that predominates in Proverbs. While both are noted for their abbreviated syntax and penchant for juxtapositions, generally the proverb shows greater signs of artistic shaping and completed parallelism and makes greater use of metaphor, thus enhancing its usability in a broader variety of contexts. In content, the same kinds of topics are likely to be found in both types of saying, but the proverb often goes beyond simple observation to didactic recommendation.[23] Given that these forms are used in teaching, it comes as no surprise that antithetic parallelism (second line contrasts with the first) is a favorite among the wise, for it allows them a graceful use of form to highlight their oppositional content. Presented with proverb after proverb in antithetic parallelism, as in 10:1–15:33, the audience can hardly fail to notice that one "way" or set of choices is clearly superior to the other — exactly the conclusion the sages had in mind.

Within the classification of proverbs, there are several subdivisions: "good/not good" sayings, "better" sayings, "numerical" sayings, "abomination" sayings, and "blessed" sayings.[24] When proverbs move from the indicative mood to the imperative, they are then classified as "admonitions," another favorite form with teachers. The "command" is the positive form; the "prohibition" is the negative, and both may be found either as free-standing parallel sayings within the collections (20:13, 22), or more frequently woven into the longer compositions of the instruction (3:1, etc.). Although the introduction to Proverbs mentions the riddles of the wise, no intact riddles survive in the book, although some posit disintegrated forms underlying 5:1–6, 15–23; 6:16–19, 23–24; 16:15; 20:27; 23:27, 29–35; 25:2–3; 27:20; and 30:15–33.[25]

The two other distinctive genres found in Proverbs are the instruction and the wisdom poem, both of which are lengthy compositions but may include various types of sayings or admonitions. The instruction has been traced to the Egyptian *sebayit*, where courtiers or pharaoh

23. See Fontaine, *Traditional Sayings*, 1–27, 63–71.
24. Murphy, *Tree of Life*, 8–9.
25. Fontaine, "Proverbs," *HBC*, 496–97.

himself write a sort of testament to their experience for their successors. Naturally, good and timely advice abounds, sometimes in proverb or admonition form, along with rhetorical questions, compelling examples, and value judgments. Instructions are found throughout Proverbs 1–9, in 22:17–24:22, and 31:1–9.[26]

The wisdom poem most often celebrates the excellence of wisdom, often in self-praising speeches by Woman Wisdom that are reminiscent of Hellenistic Isis aretologies. These compositions (1:20–33; 8:1–36; 9:1–6) may include any of the other shorter forms, and often include hymnic elements familiar from the Psalter. Wisdom poems contain some of the most strikingly positive female imagery in the book — or in the entire Hebrew Bible, with the exception of Song of Songs, for that matter — and give important clues to the sages' view of the concept of wisdom (see next section). Certainly, their extended use of the device of literary personification for the figures of Woman Wisdom and her evil twin, Woman Stranger/Folly, is one of the most distinctive features of the sages' style. In their lush and yet stark depictions of the paths of life and death through the metaphorical use of these two female figures, the poems of the sages make total use of the erotic power of language, as well as signaling the traditional preoccupations of the patriarchal male. Proverbs 3:13–20 may also be considered a wisdom poem, since Woman Wisdom is the topic, although it is the sage who speaks. One might also consider 2:16–19; 5:1–6; 6:20–35; 7:6–27; and 9:13–18 as antiwisdom poems since they concern Wisdom's wicked rival for men's attentions, the strange, foolish woman, who can also be characterized as adulteress and prostitute.

While not confined solely to wisdom discourse, the alphabetizing or acrostic poem is also found in Proverbs (31:10–31 and 2:1–22). In these compositions, each verse begins with a successive letter of the Hebrew alphabet (as in 31:10–31), or important letters serve as organizing principles for the structure of the poem (2:1–22). This may reflect the didactic interests of the sages, and may have served as exercises for pupils.

Given the sages' extraordinary care in shaping their literary work into pleasing forms and their pragmatic roles as counselors and teachers, it should occasion no surprise that such topics play an important

26. For an interesting analysis of the sages' linguistic strategies in this form, see C. A. Newsom, "Woman and the Discourse of Patriarchal Wisdom: A Study of Proverbs 1–9," *Gender and Difference in Ancient Israel* (ed. P. L. Day; Philadelphia: Fortress Press, 1989) 142–60.

part in the book. The wise are much concerned with words — their pleasurable aspects, their probity, their uses, their strength.[27] They are speaking of their own experience when they give us the proverbs of 18:20–21:

> From the fruit of the mouth one's stomach is satisfied;
> the yield of the lips brings satisfaction.
> Death and life are in the power of the tongue,
> and those who love it will eat its fruits. (NRSV)

IN SEARCH OF WISDOM IN PROVERBS

What then can be said about the concept of wisdom in Proverbs? First, we need not be troubled if we find *many* meanings for wisdom in this book, because we have seen how the concerns of different groups, times, and places came together to form the work as we now have it. The social groups responsible for the writing of the wisdom traditions span epochs and class settings, and if they vary in the particular nuances that they give to wisdom, this should not surprise modern readers. It is this diversity of origins of wisdom in Proverbs, as much as the international and bureaucratic character of some of its tradents, that contributes to the ecumenicity of wisdom's worldview. Many of the groups responsible for Proverbs may well be placed among the intellectual elite of their day, but the world of the family and farm is represented there too.

In my view, the worldview of wisdom in Proverbs does not represent a sharp break with the rest of ancient Israel's society, but only reflects a difference in emphases and interests. It has been rightly noted that, in the absence of traditions about covenant and election, wisdom theology is creation theology,[28] but this is not the only place in the Hebrew Bible where such theology is found. Likewise, the "act-consequence" relationship (*Tun-Ergehen Zusammenhang*) that undergirds so many of the proverbs in the collections and warnings in the instructions may be traced throughout the biblical corpus, and is especially prevalent in the Prophets. This view that the outcome of any

27. W. Bühlmann, *Vom Rechten Reden und Schweigen* (OBO 12; Fribourg: Universitätsverlag, 1976), cited in Murphy, *Tree of Life,* 22.

28. W. Zimmerli, "Concerning the Structure of Old Testament Wisdom," *Studies in Ancient Israelite Wisdom* (ed. J. L. Crenshaw; New York: KTAV Publishing House, 1976) 175–207; idem, "The Place and Limit of the Wisdom in the Framework of the Old Testament Theology," in ibid., 314–28; and von Rad, *Wisdom in Israel,* 144–65.

act is contained within the deed itself, so that good trees can only produce good fruit, and desirable ends can never proceed from undesirable means, is the linchpin of the ancients' understanding of cause and effect and is not exclusive to wisdom thinking, however much it may be outlined and explored there (cf. 22:8; 26:27; 28:10). One might even argue that the emphasis in Proverbs on the value of human experience as a starting place for reflection on life and the ways of the divine is no less present in Genesis or Exodus, although there it goes hand in glove with the dramatic activity of the covenant Lord. Woman Wisdom may locate much of her authority in her relationship to God and her role/presence at creation, but the sages are clear in subordinating this authority to the radical possibilities contained within the classic characterizations of Israel's God. Not only is "fear of the Lord" the proper relationship of creature to creator that orients all subsequent action and knowledge, but such fear is also the "beginning of wisdom" (1:7; 9:10; 15:33a); further, the sages warn sternly against trusting in one's own wisdom (2:5–7), for "no wisdom, no understanding, no counsel, can avail against the Lord" (21:30). While wisdom's worldview *does* concern itself with a search for order in the world and human activities, wisdom is itself *more* than the voice of that order, and that order is both flexible and provisional. Wisdom's world order can never *be* static, because neither Israel's God nor its people are static — Hebrew *ḥokmâ* is not Egyptian *ma'at,* for all that they share important characteristics. As the people used to say in Israel, "The horse is made ready for the day of battle, but the victory is from the Lord" (21:31). All causation is negated when Israel's God wills it so.

What, then — or *who* — is wisdom to the sages of Proverbs? The most basic meaning of wisdom as know-how, the native intelligence and craft to be effective in whatever activity one takes up, often obtains in the proverb collections (13:2, 15; 14:8; 15:21–24; 19:8; 24:5–6; 27:12, etc.), while the more unified compositions of Proverbs 1–9 strike a highly theological note. There, wisdom is directly related to God in many ways: As Woman Wisdom, she is present at creation, playing before God and delighting in humanity, and she is also the plan by which creation is made (Prov 3:19–20; 8:1–32). Indeed, Camp has argued, in light of the inclusio of female imagery that encircles the collections, that Woman Wisdom is herself the "root metaphor" that organizes the book as a whole.[29] In fact, as a "character" Woman Wisdom receives more

29. C. Camp, "Woman Wisdom as Root Metaphor: A Theological Consideration,"

treatment than any other female in the Hebrew Bible, and ranks fifth among both male and female characters behind God, Job, Moses, and David.[30]

So we may say immediately that Wisdom in Proverbs is both concrete and abstract, intensely personal and cosmically grounded. While the sages often make abstract statements about Wisdom (3:19; 4:7; 19:8; 24:7), they more often turn to the rich, lyric language of erotic poetry to describe this most desired entity. They speak of "watching" and "waiting" for her (8:34), seeking and searching (2:4), laying hold (3:15), prizing, loving, and embracing (4:6–8) this female who should not be forsaken (4:6). As a partner, she is "precious" (3:15), "better than jewels" (8:11), gold, silver, or anything one might desire (8:19). She is a "tree of life" (3:18), a "gushing stream" (18:4), a "crown" (14:24), and "a fountain of life" (16:22). When she comes into the heart of a follower, she brings pleasure, peace, and security (2:6–15). To those who find and keep her, she brings "long life" and "riches" (3:16), "life for the soul" and "adornment for your neck" (3:22), a "fair garland" and a "beautiful crown" (4:9). No wonder the sages adopt the language of erotic discovery and commitment when they tell their audience, "Say to Wisdom, 'You are my sister!' and call Insight your intimate friend!" (7:4). In their description of Woman Wisdom, they turn aside from the language of pragmatics and didacticism and enter fully into the realm of love and encounter.

Are the sages, then, "mystical" writers? It is hard to imagine our scribes and bureaucrats, clan elders or court teachers in such a role. But as poets, the sages found their muse in *ḥokmâ,* and in Proverbs 1–9 they have clearly given themselves up to her adoration. Who is she to them? An abstract inspiration, a memory of a scribal goddess known to them from neighboring wisdom traditions, or a trope formed in the familiar outline of a beloved woman's work-worn face and hands? Is she the voice of creation — if our authors even had such an intangible concept for the sensory-rich environment that cradled them and knit itself through and through their daily experience — turned in didactic love to a frail but potentially brilliant humanity? She seems to be more than that in the poets' tributes to her, more than concept, more than

---

The Listening Heart: Essays in Wisdom and the Psalms in Honor of Roland E. Murphy, O. Carm. (ed. K. G. Hoglund et al.; JSOTSup 58; Sheffield: Sheffield Academic Press, 1987) 45–76.

30. S. Cady, M. Ronan, and H. Taussig, *Wisdom's Feast: Sophia in Study and Celebration* (San Francisco: Harper & Row, 1989) 15.

nature, more than the archetypal homemaker or delightful daughter, though she is all of these things too. The text says it best: she is more like some primal energy acquired by Yahweh before creation and seeded into every part of it (8:22–31) — a sort of cosmic will-to-harmony. She is knowable; she is near; and she is willing to love those who love her (8:17). Unlike *ma'at*, she has stories; unlike Inanna, Ishtar, Inara, Anat, and their human counterpart, Woman Stranger/Folly, she brings life to her human lovers and champions justice and moderation. From the foundation of the throne to the busy courtyard markets, her presence is everywhere manifested in the book of Proverbs, and her speech is as authentic as any deity's when she proclaims: "He who finds me finds life!" (8:35a). A striking anomaly within Israel's patriarchal worldview, the figure of Woman Wisdom is the most unique and expressive answer to the question of the meaning of wisdom in the book of Proverbs.

7

WISDOM IN QOHELETH

Michael V. Fox

Israelite wisdom is the only self-conscious wisdom literature from the Near East.[1] It looks at itself and is aware that it is wisdom and is teaching wisdom — not only wise behavior, but wisdom itself. Proverbs (especially chaps. 1–9) sets wisdom as both the goal and the reward of human effort. Qoheleth too places wisdom in the center of focus, but he understands it differently.

The deepest innovation in Qoheleth's teaching is not his complaint against life's injustices and absurdities. This has parallels in various Psalms, in Job, and in several skeptical and pessimistic works from elsewhere in the ancient Near East. Qoheleth is most radical in his concept of human wisdom, not so much in recognizing its limits as in extending its scope.

WHAT WISDOM IS

The word *ḥokmâ* is different from English "wisdom."[2] "Wisdom" denotes the good sense to take the long view and judge things by moral

1. The present essay is a development of ideas presented in my *Qohelet,* chap. 3, going beyond the earlier study particularly in refining the semantic range of *ḥokmâ* and distinguishing more clearly the various aspects of wisdom (see M. V. Fox, *Qohelet and His Contradictions* [JSOTSup 71; Sheffield: Almond Press, 1989]). All translations in this article are my own.

2. In describing the aspects of wisdom, we can take into account the noun *ḥākām* ("wise man") and the verb *ḥākam* ("become wise"), since they imply the possession of *ḥokmâ.*

as well as practical criteria and the sagacity to discern the best ends as well as the best means. Within the broadest relevant framework, wisdom is always an ethical use of intellect. Wisdom also entails the will to pursue those ends, for we would not call one wise who knew the right course but did not take it. In short, wisdom requires having the good sense to take seriously the unquestionable truth of truisms.[3]

Wisdom of this sort is certainly included in the semantic range of *ḥokmâ*, but *ḥokmâ* embraces other aspects of intelligence and knowledge as well, such as the craftsman's skill, the magician's arts, the statesman's savvy, the merchant's know-how, the sly person's wiles. Conversely, a scholar's (or magician's) intellect and amassed knowledge would be called *ḥokmâ*,[4] but not, in the usual English usage, "wisdom." "Wisdom" is the appropriate rendering of *ḥokmâ* when that is its contextual sense, but the *lexical* sense of the word does not bear the same connotations as English "wisdom," and we should avoid transferring these to the all that is called *ḥokmâ* in the Bible.

Wisdom in all domains (artistry, politics, social behavior, etc.) can exist in two modes, as a faculty and as knowledge. As a faculty, *ḥokmâ* is an intellectual potential close to our concept of intelligence in the uses to which it can be put. It is realized as common sense, practical skills, learning ability, and in a great many other ways. *Ḥokmâ* can be exercised as the faculty of reason, that is, the capacity for orderly thinking whereby one derives true conclusions from premises. *Ḥokmâ* also exists as knowledge, that is, that which is known, the communicable content of knowledge. Thus the successful imparting of the teacher's *ḥokmâ* (as knowledge) to pupils also imbues them with the *ḥokmâ* (as faculty) needed to make the right decisions and act correctly in new situations.

The sages treat this complex of faculties and knowledge as a unity, though the language was able to distinguish different facets thereof: good sense (*tĕbunâ*), analytic understanding (*bînâ*), cunning (*ʿormâ*), the ability for private thinking (*mĕzimmâ*), maneuvering skills (*taḥbûlôt*), and more.[5] These all belong to *ḥokmâ*, and the wise person has them

3. In this regard, see the penetrating philosophical examination of the concept of wisdom by S. Godlovich ("On Wisdom," *Canadian Journal of Philosophy* 11 [1981] 148).

4. E.g., Dan 1:4 (scholarship); Gen 41:8 and Isa 44:25 (magic).

5. Several words in the semantic field of wisdom are near-hyponyms of *ḥokmâ*. In an article ("Words for Wisdom") scheduled to appear in *ZAH*, I seek to differentiate among some of them (*tĕbûnâ*, *bînâ*, *ʿēṣâ*, *tûšiyyah*, *ʿormâ*, and *mĕzimmâ*).

all. The single best gloss for *ḥokmâ* may be "intelligence," with the proviso that in the ancient view intelligence can be learned (in the absence of a spiritual blockage), and recognizing that *ḥokmâ* (like, occasionally, English "intelligence") includes knowledge as well as ability.

Ḥokmâ (again like "intelligence" but unlike "wisdom") is ethically neutral. Wicked persons and nations may have *ḥokmâ* (e.g., 2 Sam 13:3; Isa 29:14; 47:10; Ezek 28:5), and this *ḥokmâ* is genuine, even when abused.[6] (Like strength, *ḥokmâ* can be used ethically or not; it can be overcome or not; but it is still strength.) Hence, when Proverbs insists that *ḥokmâ* starts with piety and inevitably yields ethical behavior, it is making new and bold assertions about the validity of human intelligence, not merely spinning tautologies out of a meaning already built into the language.

It is noteworthy that Qoheleth does *not* make use of the rich vocabulary for wisdom that Proverbs employs. Proverbs heaps up synonyms for cognitive powers and knowledge in an attempt to place them all, even those of questionable virtue (such as *mĕzimmâ* and *taḥbûlôt*), under the aegis of wisdom. Qoheleth rarely uses any terms besides *ḥokmâ* and *da'at*. The latter is employed as a pendant to *ḥokmâ* in a way that resists the drawing of distinctions between the two (they are virtually indistinguishable in Proverbs as well). Qoheleth calls all the knowledge he acquired, including the sort that caused him discomfort, both *ḥokmâ* and *da'at* (1:16, 18). He occasionally also uses two terms absent from Proverbs, *kišrôn* ("skill") and *ḥešbôn* ("calculation"), which cover a more restricted range in the same general semantic field.

WISDOM'S POWERS

Ḥokmâ in Qoheleth is manifest in three basic aspects: ingenuity, good sense, and intellect.

Ingenuity

Ingenuity enables one to attain practical goals. A person with this kind of *ḥokmâ* is smart, though not necessarily wise.

Ingenuity provides power. It enables one to devise clever stratagems capable even of delivering a city from siege (9:13–15). Hence it is

6. God destroys and confounds the wisdom of hostile parties (e.g., Isa 29:14; 44:25), which would be unnecessary if this were not actual, effective wisdom.

more powerful than a warrior's might (9:16) and weapons of war (9:18). It can even enable a poor youth to rise from prison to kingship (4:13–14).

Ingenuity brings wealth. Qoheleth believes that one who toils "in *ḥokmâ*" will probably grow rich, as he himself did (2:9, 19, 21). Wealth accompanies *ḥokmâ* (7:12).

Ingenuity facilitates understanding of obscurities. "Who is so wise, and who knows the meaning of anything?" (8:1a)[7] is a wry exclamation of despair at the possibility of ever understanding women (7:27–29). Though Qoheleth considers understanding impossible in this particular matter, the exclamation shows that it is usually employed in finding the explanation (*pēšer*) of puzzling matters. Moreover, the exclamation indicates that *ḥokmâ* usually succeeds in this function; otherwise it would not be surprising that no one is wise enough to penetrate this particular mystery.

Good Sense

Ḥokmâ is also good sense — sound judgment in personal behavior and practical affairs. One aspect of good sense is prudence, the ability to recognize and pursue the behavior that will promote one's interests and avoid harm to oneself. (This is not denoted by the word *ḥokmâ,* but it does belong to the kind of behavior that Proverbs advocates.) Good sense is a practical intelligence insofar as its goal is effective action rather than knowledge as such. Good sense requires no unusual insight beneath the surface of reality, no special learning, and not even a particular cleverness in maneuvering through life. Good sense, rather than practical ingenuity or intellectual penetration (or even, necessarily, sagacity), is the type of *ḥokmâ* usually in view in Proverbs' counsels.[8]

When Qoheleth praises and recommends *ḥokmâ,* he is usually referring to good sense, with a particular emphasis on its prudential function. He affirms the value of such wisdom emphatically. He too possessed it. It enabled him to keep his wits about him (*welibbî nōhēg baḥokmâ;* 2:3) and to monitor his own experiences even while immersed in pleasures.

Such wisdom is unquestionably beneficial. The *ḥākām*'s speech is

7. Reading *mî kōh ḥākām* with Aq, Sym, and probably OG. Verse 1b begins a new unit.

8. This is the aspect of *ḥokmâ* closest to English "wisdom," though "wisdom" usually implies sagacity beyond everyday good sense and may even allow for violation of prudential calculations.

pleasant and careful (10:12), his face cheerful (8:lb). He senses the right time and form of behavior, particularly in the presence of authorities (8:5). Thus the sensible man's softly spoken speech is more effective than a ruler's shout among fools (9:17).

When things take a turn for the worse, it is not prudent to ask why this is so (7:10).[9] The wisdom to refrain from such questions spares one the frustrations of futile inquiry. (Yet it is precisely *bĕḥokmâ* — "by intellect" — that one inquires into such matters.)

Ḥokmâ as prudence keeps its possessors alive (7:12).[10] In sum, the mind of the sensible man is his blessing, the fool's is his bane (10:1).

Intellect

For Qoheleth, wisdom includes intellect, the rational-analytical faculty that enables one to investigate the world and infer new truths about life. This type of intelligence aims at understanding itself, apart from its practical or prudential value, though decisions about behavior may be based on the understanding it produces. Intellect naturally overlaps with ingenuity, yet there is a difference. Ingenuity aims at problem solving and reaches its resolution when the solution is found, whereas intellect is used in an open-ended search for new understanding.

Strangely, no other biblical author associates this faculty with *ḥokmâ,* or, for that matter, even describes its operation. *Ḥokmâ* occasionally means speculative *knowledge,* as in Prov 30:3[11] and perhaps a few times in Job, and *da'at* refers to an understanding of the mysteries

9. The issue in 7:10 is (as Yaḥyah ibn Yaḥyah recognized) a change of fortunes in someone's life. When things get worse, it is wise not to inquire into the reason why, but simply to recognize that God has made it so (7:14). In 7:10 we should probably read *bḥkmh* with the Greek and Syriac.

10. Qoheleth 7:19 seems to be displaced and to belong after v. 12 (H. L. Ginsberg, *Qohelet* [Jerusalem: M. Newman] 1961). I would paraphrase 7:11–12, 19 thus: (11) Good sense (*ḥokmâ*) is every bit as beneficial as a rich inheritance; in fact, it is even better. (12) For the protection [lit.: "shade"] good sense provides is as great as that provided by silver. And a further advantage of possessing understanding (*da'at*) is that good sense (*ḥokmâ = da'at*) keeps its possessors alive. (19) Indeed, good sense benefits its possessor more than all the wealth of a city's magnates (reading *'ōšer haššalîṭîm*).

11. Agur, as I understand this difficult passage, is contrasting *ḥokmâ/bînâ,* which he did not learn, with *da'at 'ĕlōhîm,* which he *does* possess. The former is *studied* or *learned,* which must be something like "theology" — a knowledge of doctrines and theories derived from human investigation and speculation. This *ḥokmâ* is the sort of knowledge repudiated in the rhetorical questions of v. 4. *Da'at qĕdōsîm* is probably synonymous with *da'at 'elōhîm* (compare Prov 9:10 with 2:5), and "knowledge of God" is an awareness of God's will, an ethical-religious attitude (Hos 4:1; 6:6); this type of knowledge is affirmed in vv. 5–6.

of God's ways in Ps 139:6. Job 28 is aware of the notional existence of the knowledge (*ḥokmâ* || *bînâ*) produced by that faculty, but he denies its existence.

Outside Qoheleth, *ḥokmâ* is never an instrument in open-ended exploration. Proverbs teaches us to seek wisdom, not to seek something else *by* wisdom. The truths that wisdom literature would have us grasp are already given. If you call to wisdom and go forth to meet it, you will find it (2:4–5; 8:17; etc.). Once you have found wisdom, you need only embrace it. Wisdom is and always has been out there, waiting for your embrace. (There will always be *more* knowledge, but in essence it is given.) The uninitiated may have to invest some effort in understanding and applying these truths, but there is no notion that they are at any stage unknown to all.

Qoheleth employs wisdom in his investigation, but wisdom is also his starting point. In preparation for the task he has taken upon himself, he accumulates wisdom and knowledge surpassing that of his predecessors (1:16). This *ḥokmâ-da'at* must be knowledge, not a faculty, because it is something increased and amassed. It was presumably learned from traditional teachings, since he says that he carried it beyond his predecessors, meaning that they too possessed it. Qoheleth does not indicate what the specific content of this learning was. We should not assume that it was coextensive with the genre we call wisdom literature, but the wisdom of Qoheleth's predecessors that he surpassed presumably included the genre he himself worked within. The knowledge gained from didactic wisdom literature would be a good point of departure for explorations such as Qoheleth undertakes, for it affirms the validity and profit of wisdom, promises wealth and happiness to wisdom's adherents, and insists on the universal working of justice.

Once the investigation is under way, the wisdom used is not the wisdom learned. Qoheleth does not employ learned wisdom in his investigation, but only his own faculties of observation, analysis, and reason. He never invokes (though he may quote) the teachings of other sages to support his conclusions. Nevertheless, he identifies both learned knowledge and the faculty of reason as wisdom. Hence he assumes that absorbing the former should enhance the latter, making him better able to investigate life. The sages of Proverbs believed this as well. If you take in the father's *ḥokmâ*, you gain *ḥokmâ*.

Qoheleth draws on wisdom terminology to describe his quest for truth and does not distinguish his approach from that of the other sages. We should not imagine him as an outsider or revolutionary attacking wisdom. He calls what he is doing "wisdom" and considers it an extension of the wisdom he studied. In 8:17, Qoheleth calls a man "wise" who does exactly what he says he himself did. Nevertheless, the idea of using one's independent intellect to discover new knowledge and interpret data drawn from individual experience is radical and, I think, unparalleled in extant wisdom literature.

Qoheleth's instrument of investigation is his rational intellect — his "wisdom." He proceeds in his inquiry "by wisdom"[12] into "all that happens under the heavens" (1:13).[13] Likewise in 7:23 he says that he tested "all this" (sc. "that which happens," see v. 24) "by wisdom."

Qoheleth has a clearly conceived methodology. It is grounded in individual experience. He seeks experience, observes it, judges it, then reports his perceptions or reactions. He also employs experience in argumentation, referring to what he has "seen" as evidence for the validity of his conclusions. This methodology may be termed empirical, insofar as it seeks to infer knowledge from individual experience. Qoheleth does not follow this procedure consistently, but he does regard it as pertaining to his entire book. He describes the investigation first in 1:12–18, mentions it again in 7:23, 25, 27, and 8:16, and maintains its continuity by reporting how he "turned" (*panâ, šûb,* or *sābab*) from one thing to another or urged his heart to experience something new. All his teachings are encompassed within the framework of this report, and thus, it is implied, were discovered during the investigation introduced in 1:12–18. The investigation starts from wisdom (1:16), proceeds by wisdom (1:12), and aims at wisdom (1:17; 7:23b).

Qoheleth's argumentation, though sporadic, is likewise experiential. One form of experiential argumentation is *testimony.* In testimony, one claims to have observed the fact that is being asserted or the data from which the conclusion is drawn. Qoheleth uses testimony most prominently in 2:1–10, where he infers and then asserts the value of

12. J. L. Crenshaw (*Ecclesiastes* [OTL; Philadelphia: Westminster Press, 1987] 68) appropriately translates "by rational means."

13. Words from the root *ʿśh* often signify "happening," as Ginsberg (*Qohelet,* 15–16) recognized. In particular, the phrase *hammaʿăśeh ʾăšer naʿăśâ taḥat haššemeš* (and variants) means "the events that occur under the sun," and *maʿăśeh haʾĕlōhîm* means "the work of God in the sense of the events that he brings to pass." Likewise *hāyâ* usually means "happen" or "happened." See the discussion in Fox, *Qohelet,* 151–52 and chap. 5 passim.

pleasure on the basis of his own experience with it.[14] A second form of experiential argumentation is *validation*, employing publicly observable facts as premises. In 2:21–23, for example, Qoheleth bases his contention that toil is absurd on the undisputable fact that at death (if not before) a toiler must leave his wealth to someone who did not weary himself in pursuit of it (see also 2:3–9 and 5:7–8).

I have elsewhere distinguished the epistemological presuppositions of Qoheleth's methods from those of other wisdom literature, which are often misconstrued as empirical.[15] Although their teachings certainly derive in part from experience, the other sages do not present their experience as the source of new knowledge, and, outside theodicy,[16] rarely adduce specific, individual perceptions as the source of a doctrine. At most, a sage may make general reference to his life-experiences in order to strengthen his ethos (e.g., Sir 34:9–12). In brief, if one could ask a sage, "How do you know this?" he would probably, I believe, answer: "Because I learned it," while Qoheleth would reply: "Because I saw it." The difference is profound.

It seems reasonable to look for external factors conducive to such a fundamental innovation, one that could fairly be called a paradigm shift, if it had not remained peculiar to its initiator. Qoheleth's epistemology is, as far as I can tell, foreign to the ancient Near East, but it is paralleled in his Hellenistic environment. R. Braun's thorough and partly convincing study of Qoheleth's Hellenistic background raises in passing the possibility that Qoheleth was influenced by Greek popular philosophy and the literary culture of early Hellenism. He finds evidence of this influence in Qoheleth's empirical methods, his unbiased questioning, his individualistic and cosmopolitan self-questioning, and his attitudes toward rhetoric and motifs.[17] Qoheleth's thought does not show affinity to a particular Greek philosopher or school, and not even

14. See also the appeals to experience in the following: 4:1–2, 15; 5:12–13; 6:1–2; 7:15–16; 8:9 and 10.

15. See my *Qohelet*, chap. 3. Wisdom empiricism has recently been asserted by D. Michel, *Untersuchungen zur Eigenart des Buches Qohelet* (BZAW 183; Berlin: Walter de Gruyter, 1989) 27. The example Michel gives, Job 4:7–8, comes from theodicy, which, unlike didactic wisdom, does appeal to experiential argumentation to support its tenets. These tenets, however, are not *derived* from experience or dependent on it.

16. E.g., Ps 37:25, 35–36; Job 4:8; Sir 16:5–14 (the latter is theodicy in the sense of arguing for the inevitability of God's justice; note that what Ben Sira has "seen" is a series of ancient events).

17. R. Braun, *Kohelet und die frühhellenistische Popularphilosophie* (BZAW 130, Berlin: Walter de Gruyter, 1973) 178.

to the Greek empiricists generally. I do not imagine that the author had read the Greek philosophy or aligned himself with a particular viewpoint. He does, however, incorporate the fundamental tenet of Greek philosophy — the autonomy of individual reason, which is to say, the belief that individuals can and should proceed with their own observations and reasoning powers on a quest for knowledge and that this may lead to discovery of truths previously unknown.

HOW WISDOM FAILS

Although wisdom is largely effective in carrying out practical undertakings, in making one's way through life with minimal harm, and in attaining knowledge, it fails to accomplish what it should.

Wisdom Does Not Provide Enough Knowledge

Qoheleth's methods and conclusions *are* wisdom, yet they do not lead to or constitute an understanding of the rationale of life's events. That kind of knowledge ever eludes him, because God obstructs human wisdom.

To "discover" or "comprehend" (*māṣa'*)[18] events of life is wisdom's purpose, as Qoheleth sees it (7:24–26; 8:17). This undertaking is foredoomed, because God "has also put <the toil>[19] in their hearts, without one being able to comprehend [*mṣ'*] in any way whatsoever that which God has brought to pass" (3:11). Yet God has created the world in such a way as to make it impossible to "discover what may happen afterwards" (7:14b), and thus to ascertain the consequences of an action.

18. *Māṣā'* and *yāda'* can both mean "understand." More precisely, *māṣā'* signifies attaining the understanding designated by *yāda'*. The near synonymity of *māṣā'* and *yāda'* is seen in 8:17b: even if the wise man intends to "know" (*yd'*), he cannot "attain understanding" (*mṣ'*). Examples of *māṣā'* in this sense are Judg 14:18b; Job 11:7; and 37:23. Appropriate renderings of *māṣā'* are "discover," "come to an understanding of," "grasp," as well as "find." These are all expansions of the root-meaning "reach," "overtake," "catch" (see S. Iwry, "*Whnmṣ'* — A Striking Variant Reading in *1QIs^a*," *Textus* 5 [1966] 35–39). Note esp. Sir 31:22, in which *tmṣ' 'mry*, "understand my words," is rephrased as *tśyg 'mry*, "attain/grasp my words," in the doublet.

19. Reading *h'ml* for *h'lwm*, as suggested by D. B. MacDonald (*JBL* 18 [1899] 212–213) and affirmed by H. L. Ginsberg (*Qohelet*, ad loc.), I find the numerous identifications of the "world" or the "eternity" that God put in humanity's heart intriguing but farfetched. Comparison with 8:16–17 shows that the futile intellectual effort to "find" "all that happens under the sun" is *'āmāl*. To be sure, *'āmāl* is not elsewhere said to be "in" the heart. Yet the *nepes* can possess *'āmāl* (Isa 53:11), which shows (as does Qoh 8:16–17) that *'āmāl* can be mental or emotional. This is also shown by the way that Qoheleth pairs *ra'yôn libbô* with *'ămālô* and makes both the direct object of the verb *'āmāl* (2:22).

Qoheleth himself strove for wisdom day and night (8:16), but he learned that "one cannot comprehend [*mṣ'*] anything that God brings to pass, that is, the events that occur under the sun, for however arduously a person may seek, he will not comprehend [*mṣ'*] it. And *even if the wise man* intends[20] to understand" — though he is best equipped and most worthy to do so — "he is not able to comprehend [*mṣ'*] it" (8:17).

At one point Qoheleth says that he failed to become wise: "All this I tested by wisdom. I said, 'I will gain wisdom [*'eḥkāmâ*],' but it was remote from me. Remote indeed is that which happens, and very deep: who can comprehend [*mṣ'*] it?" (7:23–24). The wisdom Qoheleth failed to obtain must be wisdom of a particular type or of a certain degree, not wisdom in its entirety. After all, he had some wisdom — more, in fact, than anyone else (1:16); even in 7:23, where he denies that he became wise, he claims to have used wisdom in testing "all this." The kind of wisdom he lacks according to 7:23 is defined by its object as the comprehension of "that which happens" (7:24), that is to say, of life.[21]

Wisdom Is Overwhelmed by Fickle Fortune

Wisdom is too vulnerable to human folly and life's vicissitudes to guarantee the results it *should* produce.

Intelligence is more powerful than weapons, but stupidity is, in a sense, even more powerful, because one offender (9:18), one bit of folly (10:1), can foul up what much intelligence achieved.

A shrewd businessman may prosper, but he may also lose his wealth in an unfortunate incident (5:13). Not only can an intelligent man lose what he earned, but one who did not work for those earnings may obtain them (2:18–19). Indeed, the fortunate recipient may even be an idler or a dullard. In that case, he must, paradoxically, be reckoned as having received wisdom from God (2:26). After all, the

20. *Yō'mar* here means "intends," not "claims"; cf. the use of *'āmar* in 7:23. Note that *yō'mar* in 8:17 rephrases "gave my heart," "determined," in 8:16. It describes what the wise man (Qoheleth, for example) *resolves* to do rather than what he believes or asserts he has accomplished.

21. Earlier (*Qohelet*, 240) I followed Ginsberg in pointing *'eḥkāmehâ*, "I will understand it," an Aramaism equivalent to *'eda'eha*. I do not now think it necessary to suppose an otherwise unattested sense of the Hebrew verb *ḥkm* to avoid a contradiction. We can compare the analogous use of *yd'* in Qoh 8:17, where *wĕgam 'imyo'mar heḥākām lāda'at* shows that *yd'* can refer to a certain kind of understanding that is beyond the wise man's grasp, though he undeniably has *da'at* of some sort. In both cases the unattainable types or degrees of wisdom can be designated *ḥokmâ* and *da'at* and are defined by specifying what was *not* attained.

industrious man had labored in "wisdom and knowledge and skill" (*bĕḥokmâ ûbĕda'at ûbĕkišrôn;* 2:21). Therefore — in this paradox — the recipient of the toiler's wealth must have also received *ḥokmâ wĕda'at*. The really smart man turns out to be the one who sits around and enjoys himself until someone's hard-earned fortune falls into his lap. Wisdom reveals itself as foolish and folly as wise.

Even when intelligence makes a man rich, it cannot *secure* his sustenance, let alone wealth and public favor (9:11), because all efforts and talents may flounder on the shoals of happenstance (v. 12). "The race does not belong to the swift," and so on (9:11–12), does not mean that the swift never win the race or that the mighty never prevail in the war or that the ingenious never earn their bread, for they usually do. Rather, what burdens Qoheleth is the realization that such talents do not secure their rightful rewards, because chance misfortunes can obviate genuine advantages.

The wise surely merit high esteem; nevertheless, people respect wealth more, holding the wisdom of poor persons in contempt (9:16b) and quickly forgetting them, even if they saved their city from capture (9:13–15). Though intelligence may carry a poor person from prison to throne, he too is inevitably supplanted, and the fickle public soon turns away and forgets him (4:14–16).

Wisdom Is Overwhelmed by Death

Most exasperating is the way *God* treats the wise, for God shows them no favor in the most crucial matter of all — life and death. Wise and fool alike die and quickly slip into oblivion (2:16). The crude egalitarianism of death makes Qoheleth disgusted with life itself (2:17).[22] Death ignores the distinctions that seem to make individuals significant. As R. E. Murphy observes,[23] 2:15–16 is not a rejection of wisdom but a complaint about its failure to deliver. Qoheleth's protest against the wrong done *to* wisdom presumes its intrinsic value. The inequities do not obliterate the qualitative difference between wisdom and folly; rather, the difference exacerbates the inequity.

22. He does not cling to this despair. All of 1:13–2:26 is an account of an earlier experience. The conclusions he arrived at remain valid, but the hatred he reports having felt toward life and wealth (here called *'āmāl*) is an extreme reaction that did not stay with him. Whatever their flaws, life and wealth remain "good things" in Qoheleth's store of values.

23. R. E. Murphy, "Qohelet's 'Quarrel' with the Fathers," *From Faith to Faith* (ed. D. Y. Hadidian; D. G. Miller Festschrift; Pittsburgh: Pickwick Press, 1979) 237.

Qoheleth is indignant that the wise person is denied the full rewards of wisdom, in the same way that he is rankled by such inequities as a toiler not securing the full benefits of earnings (6:1–6) or the rich having to "sit in lowly places" (10:6). Life's insults to the wise do not make Qoheleth repudiate wisdom, any more than death's indifference to righteousness makes him discard moral virtue (7:14; 9:2–3).

Wisdom fails to reach the grand goals that Qoheleth (sharing the attitudes of the other sages) sets for it. This failure is due not so much to the inherent feebleness of human intellect as to the cussedness of life. An absurd world thwarts understanding. Qoheleth's complaints are not a polemic against wisdom,[24] but a protest against life — and God — on wisdom's behalf.

Wisdom Hurts

To the degree that wisdom — that is, intellect — succeeds in gaining knowledge, it causes pain. Wisdom should, of course, create and enhance happiness, but Qoheleth learned otherwise. He applied his heart "to gaining wisdom and knowledge" (1:17a),[25] and he succeeded, but he soon realized "that this too is a vexation, for in much wisdom there is much irritation, and whoever increases knowledge increases pain" (1:17b–18). For wisdom reveals life's absurdity, an absurdity exacerbated by the intractability of events. Hence (to paraphrase 7:16), you should not become extremely righteous or perceptive, lest you see things that will shock you, such as the wicked living long and the righteous dying young (7:15). Wisdom is a "miserable business" (1:13). The wise man — Qoheleth is projecting his own experience — uses wisdom (reason) in examining life, and this leads him to the conclusion that all is absurd and irreparable.

We Should Still Choose Wisdom

Qoheleth possessed wealth, pleasure, and wisdom, but his satisfaction in his achievement is marred by a sense of injustice. He is aggrieved

24. Many scholars have read Qoheleth as a polemic against wisdom or the wisdom school, e.g., W. Zimmerli, *Prediger* Salomo (ATD 16; Göttingen: Vandenhoeck & Ruprecht, 1962) 132–35; J. Fichtner, *Die altorientalische Weisheit in ihrer israelitisch-judischen Ausprägung* (BZAW 62; Giessen: Töpelmann, 1933) 8; and G. von Rad, *Weisheit in Israel* (Neukirchen-Vluyn: Neukirchener Verlag, 1970) 301; see Fox, *Qohelet*, 101 n. 28.

25. Delete "inanity and folly," as a gloss providing an acceptable target for the *hebel*-judgment. The judgment "this too is a vexation" has a singular pronoun as its subject, and v. 18 gives the reason only for an evaluation of wisdom and knowledge (a hendiadys).

that work does not secure wealth, that pleasure does not produce happiness, and that wisdom does not receive its due. Nevertheless, he advocates work (9:10; 11:6), affirms pleasure (3:12, 22; 5:18; 8:15; 9:7–10; 11:9–10),[26] and praises wisdom (see above). Most important, he chooses wisdom for himself and commends it to others.

Though fully aware of wisdom's fragility, Qoheleth seems to revel in the mind's power to grasp widely and deeply. He sees in wisdom a superiority over stupidity as great as that of light over darkness (2:13).[27] Sight (knowledge) is better than blindness (ignorance), even if what we see is a world of absurdities and injustices, for the darkness awaits us in any case.[28]

Human intellect does attain knowledge, some of it useful, some of it discomforting. The possession of knowledge in and of itself gives the living, however unhappy, at least one advantage over the dead: "The living know that they will die, while the dead know nothing" (9:5). Though this disturbing truth is painful, the living should keep it ever in mind (7:2); hence the thoughts of the wise man dwell ever in the "house of mourning" (7:4). Qoheleth does not tell us just what good this knowledge will do. Some truths have slipped through the barriers God placed before human knowledge. The fact of death is one, and we should not avert our eyes from it.

We must embrace "activity and calculation and knowledge and wisdom" while we can, because in Sheol there are none of these (9:10). The limit death sets to all human powers and endeavors makes them precious whatever their inadequacies.

Qoheleth's affirmation of wisdom is not absolute or consistent. In

26. *Śimḥâ* in Qoheleth (and often elsewhere) means "pleasure," not "happiness"; see Fox, *Qohelet*, 63–64. Qoheleth lists the components of his *śimḥâ* — wine, food, women, etc. These are pleasures, and he had many of them, but "happiness" and "joy" eluded him. It is pleasure, not happiness, that he finds meaningless and absurd (2:1–2).

27. Michel (*Untersuchungen zur Eigenart des Buches Qohelet*, 25–30) argues that *rā'â* in 2:13 (as in 1:14, 16; 2:12) means *(prüfendes) betrachten* (i.e., scrutinize, examine) rather than "see." He understands 1:13 as citing an opinion Qoheleth examines rather than a conclusion he affirms. (Gordis too understands the verse as a quotation.) However, *rā'â* with a "that"-clause always introduces a proposition the speaker accepts. *Rā'â* governing a noun as object, on the other hand, means "see," "look at," "consider"; and since the object of observation has no propositional content, there is no implication of truth or falsity.

28. Thus E. H. Plumptre (*Ecclesiastes* [Cambridge: Cambridge University Press, 1881]) interprets 2:13–14: "A man is conscious of being more truly man when he looks before and after, and knows how to observe." He compares the *Iliad* 17.647: "And if our fate be death, give light, and let us die" (similarly G. A. Barton, *The Book of Ecclesiastes* [ICC; New York: Scribner's, 1908]).

7:16 he warns us against becoming too wise, lest we become dumbfounded. The wisdom he is warning against here can only be the awareness of facts such as the injustice he describes in v. 15. In 4:3 he says that it is better never to have been born than to have to see life's evils. He once even recommends dulling the ache of consciousness by means of pleasure: a man allowed to steep himself in pleasure "will not much call to mind the days of his life, since God is keeping him occupied[29] with his heart's pleasure" (5:19). This anodyne did not, however, work for Qoheleth (2:1–2; 11), who, by persisting in his search for knowledge, proves that he really considers it more important to strive for enlightenment than to eliminate the attendant soreness. Qoheleth ferrets out and reports maddening absurdities and injustices because he feels that it is imperative that he — and we — know these truths, a knowledge that belongs to wisdom.

The motive of this imperative is not a moral equation between wisdom and righteousness. In sharp contrast to Proverbs, but not to most of the Bible, Qoheleth does not regard wisdom as an ethical or religious virtue. A central principle of Proverbs — that to be smart is to be righteous and being righteous makes you smart — is not a truism. It is a new doctrine being expounded programmatically by the authors of Proverbs or, more likely, one layer of proverbial material. It is a teaching that Ben Sira absorbed better than Qoheleth. Qoheleth never says that wisdom entails or ensues from righteousness or fear of God, though he certainly affirms these virtues. There is no suggestion, for example, that the "wise" youth of 4:13 has any moral superiority over the old king, or that amassing wealth "in wisdom" (i.e., by intelligence) is an inherently honest process, or that Qoheleth himself was pursuing some moral imperative in seeking wisdom (1:12–17). He does pair righteousness and wisdom in 7:16 and 9:1, but he is bracketing the categories as positive values, not equating them.

Yet even without its moral valence, and quite apart from its utility, wisdom in Qoheleth's view has autonomous, irreducible value. Whatever his disappointment with wisdom, he is still convinced that wisdom is vastly better than stupidity. He seems to have carried over from con-

29. Reading *ma'ănēhû* (MT *ma'ăneh*). Possibly the direct object is implicit even without the emendation; thus R. E. Murphy, "On Translating Ecclesiastes," *CBQ* 53 (1991) 591. Murphy grasps the pathos of this verse: "Humans can be induced to forget their pitiable condition. God tranquilizes them, as it were, by the (erratic) pleasures given to them, holding out nostrums as a distraction from the misery of the short lives of human beings."

ventional wisdom a feeling for the moral valuation of wisdom without the ethical or religious substance it has there. He praises wisdom and advocates it, whatever its irritations and defects, and he is convinced that the wise, however they manifest their wisdom, deserve a better fate than the foolish. He does not, however, explain the reason for wisdom's excellence and special merit, which seem independent of benefits.

There is an affinity between Qoheleth's eagerness for wisdom and Albert Camus' embrace of *clairvoyance,* "lucidity," in the *Myth of Sisyphus.* Both thinkers stare intently at life, rake up its absurdities, and spurn easy comforts. They realize that knowledge is constricted, achievements are undone by chance, and merits are overridden by death. Lucidity (as Camus states and Qoheleth demonstrates by his choices) allows humans to rise above their helplessness, to look at the world with an unflinching gaze, and to judge it by human measures. Lucidity is not pleasant or necessarily advantageous, but it is quintessentially human. It is the moment of Sisyphus's triumph and the realm of his freedom.

THE UNITY OF WISDOM

Wisdom, as noted, manifests itself in different aspects: practical ingenuity, good sense, intellect, and more. These aspects can exist in different modes: as faculties, as mental activity, and as knowledge.

Such distinctions are useful in describing Qoheleth's thought, but they are extrinsic to it. For Qoheleth, wisdom is a unity, whatever its applications. He could have drawn distinctions by, for example, consistently referring to practical ingenuity as *kišrôn* or *tĕbûnâ* and to speculative wisdom as *ḥesbôn* or *bînâ.* Instead, he chooses to apply the concept of *ḥokmâ* (and, synonymously, *da'at*) to all the different kinds of wisdom and knowledge he is evaluating. He treats smartness, knowledge, judiciousness, common sense, and intellect as manifestations of a single human faculty and holds that they must be inspected and judged together. Qoheleth is a hedgehog.

"Hedgehogs" (in the terminology that the cognitive psychologist Howard Gardner borrows from the Greek poet Archilochus) are the opposites of "foxes."[30] Foxes (such as Gardner himself) split the mental powers into components and emphasize the relative autonomy of the

30. H. Gardner, *Frames of Mind* (New York: Basic Books, 1983) 7.

various functions of the mind. Hedgehogs hold to a unitary conception of intelligence, the idea that there is a single mental capacity that operates in numerous ways. The latter is Qoheleth's attitude. The choice is not a matter of truth and falsity, but rather of descriptive efficiency. A commentator analyzing Qoheleth's ideas on wisdom must draw distinctions Qoheleth did not make; indeed, this is inherent in the very act of analysis. But at the end we must return to Qoheleth's unitary view.

Had Qoheleth distinguished different kinds of wisdom, he might have achieved greater clarity and consistency. He might have praised practical good sense (*tĕbûnâ*) while repudiating the value of intellect (*bînâ*, perhaps). He might have distinguished some failures of "wisdom" (the fact that a smart businessman can go broke, for example) from wisdom's power to probe reality. He might have realized there is not necessarily an ethical incongruity in the fact that the astute merchant suffers the same mortality as the commercially incompetent, though the former is called a *ḥākām* and the latter a *kĕsîl*. In drawing such distinctions, however, Qoheleth would have sacrificed his perception of the unity of mind. This is an important insight that can, after all, appeal to the evidence of introspection. Can we really distinguish, say, the mental act operating in a decision to purchase promising pharmaceutical stocks from the intellect used in textual analysis? Qoheleth would not say so. For him, human intelligence — wisdom — is a unity, whether it is used in making money, in pleasing a ruler, or in probing the meaning of life. A failure of any use of intelligence exposes the fragility and vulnerability of the human mind in its entirety.

ANOTHER VIEW OF WISDOM

The book of Qoheleth advances a second view of wisdom, namely, that of the epilogist (12:9–14), who describes Qoheleth as a sage, a teacher, and a composer of wisdom. The epilogue, I have argued elsewhere,[31] is probably the concluding comment of a frame-narrator rather than a later addition by an editor. This narrator speaks as one who has transmitted the teachings of Qoheleth and now looks back on Qoheleth, who is surely a fictional persona, though certainly a projection of the author's actual views. But whether author or editor, the epilogist speaks

31. Fox, *Qohelet*, 311–21, and, more fully, idem, "Frame-Narrative and Composition in the Book of Qohelet," *HUCA* 48 (1977) 83–106.

as a conservative sage. Nevertheless, he praises Qoheleth as a *ḥākām* and calls his teachings *da'at*.

The epilogue provides a buffer to the words of Qoheleth, which are as sharp as goads, and reassures the reader of their legitimacy. It does not do this defensively, as if forestalling an objection to the legitimacy of Qoheleth's teachings. It does so affirmatively, by identifying Qoheleth's words with wisdom and praising them as lovely and true. But it then subordinates wisdom to the religious values of piety and obedience: "The last thing to be said, when everything has been heard, is: fear God and keep his commandments, for this (applies to) everyone" (12:13).

The epilogist's caution is directed not toward Qoheleth's words alone, but toward wisdom as such, to which Qoheleth's teaching belongs. By giving piety the final word, the epilogue blunts the danger inherent in the roamings of human intellect yet allows Qoheleth — and other intellectuals — the freedom to pursue their inquiries. All wisdom may be heard and considered, so long as it is finally subordinated to the proper religious attitude and behavior.

8

THE MEANING OF WISDOM IN BEN SIRA

Alexander A. Di Lella, O.F.M.

Everyone who has read the Wisdom of Ben Sira would agree that wisdom is, if not the principal concern, certainly a major theme of the author[1] as well as his grandson who made the Greek translation. In the book, including the grandson's Prologue, the number of occurrences of the words "wisdom" and "wise" is instructive. In Greek I, which is one of the extant, complete, pre-Christian forms of the book (Greek II is the other), the root *soph-*, as the noun "wisdom," the adjective "wise," the noun "the wise," and the verb "to be wise," occurs a total of 91 times.[2] In the NAB, which was based on the Cairo Geniza mss. and other Hebrew fragments of the book, the word "wisdom" occurs 66 times, and "wise"

1. Scholars have argued about the primary theme of Ben Sira. J. Haspecker (*Gottesfurcht bei Jesus Sirach: Ihre religiöse Structur und Ihre literarische und doktrinäre Bedeutung* [AnBib 30; Rome: Biblical Institute, 1967] 87–105) is of the opinion that fear of God is the total theme. But G. von Rad (*Wisdom in Israel* [Nashville: Abingdon Press, 1972] 242) and J. Marböck (*Weisheit im Wandel: Untersuchungen zur Weisheitstheologie bei Ben Sira* [BBB 37; Bonn: Hanstein, 1971]) insist that wisdom is the fundamental theme. My own view is that Ben Sira's primary theme is wisdom as fear of God. See P. W. Skehan and A. A. Di Lella, *The Wisdom of Ben Sira* (AB 39; New York: Doubleday, 1987) 75–76.

2. Using Pandora 2.5, the search engine designed for the Thesaurus Linguae Graecae (TLG) CD-ROM and the AppleCD SC Plus drive, I did the concordance work for this root. The TLG contains only Greek I of Rahlfs's less-than-perfect edition of the LXX. For critical study, I used J. Ziegler's critical edition, *Sapientia Iesu Filii Sirach* (Septuaginta 12/2; Göttingen: Vandenhoeck & Ruprecht, 1965), which gives Greek II in smaller typeface. Greek II has a few more occurrences of the root *soph-*. About 68 percent of the Hebrew of Ben Sira is extant in fragments from Cairo Geniza mss. A, B, C, D, E, F; 2Q18; 11QPs[a]; and Masada; see Skehan and Di Lella, *Wisdom of Ben Sira*, 51–56.

or "the wise" 38 times for a total of 104 times. In the NRSV, which was based primarily on the Greek translation, "wisdom" occurs 66 times, and "wise" or "the wise" 36 times for a total of 102 times.[3] The purpose of this study is to determine as exactly as possible what Ben Sira meant by wisdom.

INTRODUCTION

As in the other parts of the Bible, so also in the Wisdom of Ben Sira, the word "wisdom" has many meanings. The subscription to the book provides some clue as to what Ben Sira meant by wisdom:[4]

> Instruction in understanding and knowledge
> I have written in this book,
> Jesus son of Eleazar son of Sirach of Jerusalem,[5]
> whose mind poured forth wisdom.
> Happy are those who concern themselves with these things,
> and those who lay them to heart will become wise.
> For if they put them into practice, they will be equal to anything,
> for the fear of the Lord is their path. (50:27–29)

Wisdom comes from instruction, understanding, and knowledge. One becomes wise by being concerned with these things. When one puts them into practice, one has a successful and meaningful life. Significantly, Ben Sira adds a further note: fear of the Lord is the way to wisdom.

Ben Sira employs the words "wisdom" and "wise" and cognates in many other ways, some of which are hardly complimentary. I shall attempt a careful examination of the contexts where Ben Sira uses this vocabulary in order to obtain some idea of the varied meanings he attached to these words.

3. In the book of Proverbs, by way of contrast, the Hebrew root *ḥkm* occurs 97 times in 94 verses. For the concordance work of the MT, NAB, and NRSV, I used the respective *MacBible* computer programs (Grand Rapids, Mich.: Zondervan Publishing House, 1991); regarding these powerful and fast tools, see *OTA* 14 (1991) 235–36.

4. Generally, the scripture quotations contained herein are from the NRSV. I was the primary reviser of Sirach for the NRSV. Since the RSV was based primarily on the grandson's Greek version, the NRSV translation committee followed suit. But in the revision, I made extensive use of the Hebrew fragments from the Cairo Geniza, Qumran, and Masada as well as the Syriac and Latin versions. I shall provide, when necessary, text-critical notes to the passages cited. When, however, the thought of Ben Sira seems better represented by the translation found in Skehan and Di Lella, *Wisdom of Ben Sira,* I shall quote from that source.

5. The phrase "of Jerusalem" is found only in the Greek and of course Latin, but not in Geniza ms. B.

THE KINDS OF WISDOM IN BEN SIRA

Like the authors of the other Old Testament wisdom books, Ben Sira uses the term "wisdom" and cognates in two basic senses: (1) theoretical wisdom, and (2) practical wisdom. Theoretical or speculative wisdom has as its goal the education or perfection of the intellect by study and reflection, by reading and travel, and by listening to the elders and avoiding the foolish. Practical or pretheoretical wisdom has as its goal the discipline and perfection of the will by which the devout believer makes the proper choices in the spiritual and secular, social and economic, and moral and ethical issues of daily life. In Ben Sira, it is chiefly practical wisdom that enables a person to be in a right relationship with God and with other human beings.

Ben Sira, however, adds a new, important note regarding wisdom: wisdom resides in Jacob/Israel and is to be identified with the law of Moses. In the following passage, personified Wisdom is the speaker:

"Over waves of the sea, over all the earth,
and over every people and nation I have held sway.
Among all these I sought a resting place;
in whose territory should I abide?
Then the Creator of all things gave me a command,
and my Creator chose the place for my tent.
He said, 'Make your dwelling in Jacob,
and in Israel receive your inheritance.' (24:6–8)

"Thus in the beloved city he gave me a resting place,
and in Jerusalem was my domain.[6]
I took root in an honored people,
in the portion of the Lord, his heritage. (24:11–12)

"Come to me, you who desire me,
and eat your fill of my fruits. (24:19)

"Whoever obeys me will not be put to shame,
and those who work with me will not sin."
All this is the book of the covenant of the Most High God,
the law that Moses commanded us
as an inheritance for the congregations of Jacob. (24:22–23)[7]

6. Regarding the significance of Jerusalem in the thought of Ben Sira, see R. Hayward, "The New Jerusalem in the Wisdom of Jesus Ben Sira," *SJT* 6 (1992) 123–38.

7. The Greek of 24:23bc is a word-for-word quotation of LXX Deut 33:4. For fuller studies of the magnificent poem in Sirach 24, see M. Gilbert, "L'Éloge de la Sagesse (Siracide 24)," *RTL* 5 (1974) 326–48; and G. T. Sheppard, *Wisdom as a Hermeneutical*

J. Blenkinsopp writes that Wisdom here may be "modelled on the goddess Isis [or Egyptian Maat, who stood for cosmic order], or perhaps a Syro-Palestinian counterpart like Astarte." He then states that this poem was "Ben Sira's way of attributing universal significance to Torah as the divine principle of order which has been made available to Israel."[8] I believe, however, that R. E. Murphy puts the matter more accurately when he observes:

> The very symbol of Lady Wisdom suggests that order is not the correct correlation. Rather, she is somehow identified with the Lord, as indicated by her very origins and her authority. The call of Lady Wisdom is the voice of the Lord. She is, then, the revelation of God, not merely the self-revelation of creation. She is the divine summons issued in and through creation.[9]

The clear implication of Sirach 24 is that real wisdom is to be found in Jerusalem, and not elsewhere, and this wisdom is to be found in "the book of the covenant," the law of Moses. This passage is one of several where Ben Sira reminds his students to resist the allure of Greek ways and culture.[10] One need not turn to Athens to become wise, for knowledge and culture alone do not make a person wise. Indeed, one can be considered truly wise only if one has observed the covenant stipulations given to Moses. Ben Sira's identification of wisdom with the law of Moses was not an entirely new idea. The idea is alluded to in Deut 4:5–8.[11] Following the lead of Ben Sira, the author of the poem in Bar 3:9–4:4 also identifies wisdom with "the law that endures forever" (Bar 4:1).

THEORETICAL WISDOM

In the opening couplet of his book, Ben Sira states unambiguously that wisdom of every sort comes from God alone and remains with him

---

Construct: A Study in the Sapientializing of the Old Testament (BZAW 151; Berlin: Walter de Gruyter, 1980) 19–71.

8. J. Blenkinsopp, *Wisdom and Law in the Old Testament* (Oxford Bible Series; Oxford: Oxford University Press, 1983) 143–44.

9. R. E. Murphy, "Wisdom and Creation," *JBL* 104 (1985) 9–10. See also idem, *The Tree of Life: An Exploration of Biblical Wisdom Literature* (ABRL; New York: Doubleday, 1990) 115–18.

10. See also 2:12–14; 19:20, 22–25; and 41:8–10, which are discussed below.

11. Sheppard (*Wisdom as a Hermeneutical Construct*, 63–71) argues that Deuteronomy 4, 30, and 32 provide the basis for Ben Sira's conclusion that "the book of the covenant of the Most High" is wisdom.

forever (1:1). Because God is the source of wisdom, he alone is all wise; and because of his mighty power, he can do all things (1:2–6).

> There is but one who is wise, greatly to be feared,
> seated upon his throne — the Lord.
> It is he who created her;
> he saw her and took her measure;
> he poured her out upon all his works,
> upon all the living according to his gift;
> he lavished her upon those who love him.[12] (1:8–10)

Right at the outset, Ben Sira insists that wisdom is a gift that God bestows only on those who love him. Wisdom in this passage is theoretical wisdom, as is clear from the references to God's omniscience in ordering and understanding the enormous complexities and impenetrable mysteries of creation. The implication is that even though one must exert great efforts to possess theoretical wisdom, as Ben Sira himself admits (in 39:1–4; see below), ultimately it is God who gives the requisite knowledge for one to comprehend the manifold wonders of the universe.

Ben Sira had a superior education, probably the best available in his day. From earliest youth he associated with the wise and learned, and he did not "suffer fools gladly."[13] Many autobiographical details indicate that he read widely and traveled extensively. This is why he did not hesitate to remind his readers that he had a high degree of theoretical wisdom.

> An educated person knows many things,
> and one with much experience knows what he is talking about.
> An inexperienced person knows few things,
> but he that has traveled acquires much cleverness.
> I have seen many things in my travels,
> and I understand more than I can express. (34:9–12)

Ben Sira, therefore, felt competent to teach. It was his own commitment to learning and discipline that motivated him to share his wisdom and experience with others.

> Consider that I have not labored for myself alone,
> but for all who seek instruction. (33:18)

12. See also Prov 2:6; 8:22–23, 30; Job 12:13; Wis 7:26–27; 9:4, 6. Significantly, a few Greek mss. and Syriac read "those who fear him" rather than "those who love him."

13. This proverbial expression comes from the KJV of 2 Cor 11:19.

Draw near to me, you who are uneducated,
and lodge in the house of instruction. (51:23)

Though wisdom is a gift that comes from the Lord, Ben Sira reminds his students that they must do their part to acquire the learning that is necessary.

Where the pupil of the eye is missing, there is no light,
and where there is no knowledge, there is no wisdom. (3:25, AB)

Those who are lazy, therefore, will never come to wisdom because they refuse to submit to the direction and discipline involved in education.

The idler is like a filthy stone,[14]
and every one hisses at his disgrace.
The idler is like the filth of dunghills;
anyone that picks it up will shake it off his hand.
It is a disgrace to be the father of an undisciplined son. (22:1–3a)

Ben Sira's coarse imagery conveys his utter disgust for those who are lazy or unprincipled, for such as these can never become wise. Shakespeare expresses in his own elegant way much of Ben Sira's thought: "Wisdom and goodness to the vile seem vile: / Filths savour but themselves" (*King Lear,* 4.2.39–40).

At times Ben Sira does not distinguish clearly between theoretical and practical wisdom or else implies both meanings. A good example is 38:24–39:11, the long poem on the vocations of skilled workers, who of course have the theoretical wisdom of their respective crafts,[15] and the righteous scribe, who has the theoretical wisdom of study and learning as well as the practical wisdom of a living faith that comes from fear of the Lord. Ben Sira acknowledges that skilled workers are essential to the well-being of a people and city:

Without them no city could be lived in,
and wherever they stay, they do not hunger. (38:32, AB)

Ben Sira, however, extols to the skies "the person who devotes himself to the fear of God[16] and to the study of the Law of the Most High" (38:34cd, AB). It is not difficult to understand the reason why.

14. This is a (presumably smooth) stone used by the ancients, and by some Bedouin even today, for wiping themselves after a bowel movement.

15. Exodus 36:1 states that Yahweh had given "wisdom" and "understanding" to the artisans who made the liturgical furnishings; the wisdom is theoretical.

16. The phrase "to the fear of God" comes from the Syriac; Greek omits it.

He seeks out the wisdom of all the ancients,
    and is concerned with prophecies;
he preserves the sayings of the famous
    and penetrates the subtleties of parables;
he seeks out the hidden meanings of proverbs
    and is at home with the obscurities of parables.
He serves among the great
    and appears before rulers;
he travels in foreign lands
    and learns what is good and evil in the human lot.
He sets his heart to rise early
    to seek the Lord who made him,
    and to petition the Most High;
he opens his mouth in prayer
    and asks pardon for his sins.
If the great Lord is willing,
    he will be filled with the spirit of understanding;
he will pour forth words of wisdom of his own
    and give thanks to the Lord in prayer.
The Lord will direct his counsel and knowledge,
    as he meditates on his mysteries.
He will show the wisdom of what he has learned,
    and will glory in the law of the Lord's covenant. (39:1–8)

In this exuberant poem,[17] which is apparently autobiographical, Ben Sira describes what is involved in getting an education like his. Such an education enables the scribe to acquire theoretical wisdom. But more importantly, the scribe has studied the law of the Most High and freely chooses to remain faithful to the covenant; that is to say, he possesses practical wisdom. Ben Sira not only traveled a great deal but also read many books. His reading was not restricted to the sacred literature of Israel; it also included Greek and even Egyptian authors. Chief among these were the Greek elegiac poems of Theognis and the Egyptian gnomic work attributed to Phibis.[18] From these authors and others Ben Sira took the insights that were compatible with Jewish belief and practice and incorporated them into his own thought,[19] for as he states in the opening couplet of his book, "All wisdom is from the Lord." At the same time, however, Ben Sira cautions his students about potential

17. For a fuller study of this poem, see J. Marböck, "Sir. 38,24–39,11: Der schriftgelehrte Weise. Ein Beitrag zu Gestalt und Werk Ben Siras," *La Sagesse de l'Ancien Testament* (ed. M. Gilbert; BETL 51; Louvain: Louvain University Press, 1979) 293–316.

18. For a discussion of Ben Sira's use of these materials, see J. T. Sanders, *Ben Sira and Demotic Wisdom* (SBLMS 28; Chico, Calif.: Scholars Press, 1983).

19. See Skehan and Di Lella, *Wisdom of Ben Sira*, 48–50.

dangers, for many people were tempted to compromise their faith for the allurements of Greek philosophy, customs, and culture.

Woe to timid[20] hearts and to slack hands,
  and to the sinner who walks a double path!
Woe to the fainthearted who have no trust!
  Therefore they will have no shelter.
Woe to you who have lost your nerve!
  What will you do when the Lord's reckoning comes? (2:12–14)

The "double path" refers to the traditional path of Jewish faith and practice, and the new path of Hellenism and its life-style.[21]

Ben Sira's most extended statement regarding the work involved in theoretical wisdom is the twenty-two-line poem in 6:18–37.[22] The limits of this poem are marked out clearly by an *inclusio: ḥokmâ,* "wisdom," in the first bicolon, and *yĕḥakkĕmekâ,* "he will make you wise," in the last bicolon.

My child, from your youth choose discipline,
  and when you have gray hair you will still find wisdom.
Come to her like one who plows and sows,
  and wait for her good harvest.
For when you cultivate her you will toil but little,
  and soon you will eat of her produce.
She seems very harsh to the undisciplined;
  fools cannot remain with her.
She will be like a heavy stone to test them,
  and they will not delay in casting her aside.
For wisdom is like her name;[23]
  she is not readily perceived by many. (6:18–22)

Without discipline (Heb. *mûsār,* Gk. *paideia*) one would never be disposed to expend the time or the effort to attain theoretical wisdom. Study is hard work, which Ben Sira compares to the toil of the farmer. Those who lack discipline are called fools, for they refuse to exert themselves. The other striking images emphasize the determination and will power one must have.

20. Three Greek mss., Syrohexapla, and some versions read "double."

21. In 41:8–10, Ben Sira has even harsher words for those who compromise their faith.

22. Ben Sira often wrote poems of twenty-two and twenty-three lines to match the letters of the Hebrew alphabet; see Skehan and Di Lella, *Wisdom of Ben Sira,* 74.

23. Ben Sira plays on the homonym *mûsār,* "discipline," making it also mean "withdrawn," for *mûsār* is the hophal masculine singular participle of the verb *sûr,* "to turn aside, depart, withdraw." See Skehan and Di Lella, *Wisdom of Ben Sira,* 193.

Put your feet into her fetters,
    and your neck into her collar.
Bend your shoulders and carry her,
    and do not fret under her bonds.
Come to her with all your soul,
    and keep her ways with all your might.
Search out and seek, and she will become known to you;
    and when you get hold of her, do not let her go. (6:24–27)

Wisdom, like everything else that is worthwhile, will never come easily or cheaply. But the rewards are worth all the effort.

Ben Sira stresses repeatedly, though somewhat naively, that the education required for theoretical wisdom is available to anyone who has the will power and the energy to work at it without stint.

If you are willing, my child, you can be disciplined,
    and if you apply yourself you will become clever.
If you love to listen you will gain knowledge,
    and if you pay attention you will become wise.
Stand in the company of the elders.
    Who is wise? Attach yourself to such a one.
Be ready to listen to every godly[24] discourse,
    and let no wise proverbs escape you.
If you see an intelligent person, rise early to visit him;
    let your foot wear out his doorstep. (6:32–36)[25]

Yet even here Ben Sira insists that fidelity to the law, which is at the heart of practical wisdom, must come first, for the Lord alone can bestow theoretical wisdom.

Reflect on the law[26] of the Most High,
    and on his commandments meditate constantly;
then he will give understanding to your mind,
    and he will make you wise as you desire. (6:37, my trans.)[27]

One must first desire wisdom and then do all that is necessary to acquire it before the Lord will grant it.[28] Wishful thinking will not do.

Whoever wants to become wise, however, must be humble and docile, as befits one who fears the Lord. One must also be ready to

24. The word "godly" is omitted in Geniza ms. A and also in Greek ms. 575.

25. See also 3:25, 29; 8:8–9; 9:14; 16:24–25; 18:28–29; 21:21; 34:9.

26. Read *bĕtôrat ʿelyôn,* as in 41:4, 8; 42:2 of the Masada ms., and 49:4 in ms. B; ms. A has *bĕyirʾat* (so also Syriac).

27. See also 1:9–10; 9:15–16; 38:6; 43:33; 51:17.

28. In a splendid poem, 15:11–20, the limits of which are marked off by an *inclusio,* Ben Sira spells out his teaching on freedom of the will.

learn from the experience and training of others, especially the elders of the community.

> Do not slight the discourse of the sages,
> but busy yourself with their maxims;
> because from them you will learn discipline
> and how to serve princes.
> Do not ignore the discourse of the aged,
> for they themselves learned from their parents;
> from them you learn how to understand
> and to give an answer when the need arises. (8:8–9)[29]

Wisdom is viewed as something that is handed down by the parents and elders of one generation to the youth of another generation.[30] Such wisdom legitimates the values of the community and is in turn validated by the religious and social controls of the community.

Ben Sira teaches that speculative wisdom is superior to wealth or social standing.

> It is not right to despise one who is intelligent but poor,
> and it is not proper to honor one who is sinful. (10:23)

> The poor are honored for their knowledge,
> while the rich are honored for their wealth. (10:31)[31]

What Ben Sira writes here is noteworthy, for he lived in a social and religious world that valued legitimately acquired wealth as a sign of God's blessing or a reward for fidelity.[32]

PRACTICAL WISDOM

Following the lead of the book of Proverbs, his favorite and most often used source, Ben Sira writes:

> To fear the Lord is the beginning of wisdom;
> she is created with the faithful in the womb. (1:14)[33]

Wisdom here is practical wisdom, for it manifests itself in loyalty to the Lord. Ben Sira explains why practical wisdom is essentially fear of the Lord:

29. See also 16:24–25; 18:27–29; 21:21.
30. See 6:18, 34 as well as 25:3–6, discussed below.
31. See also 11:1 and 40:19ab.
32. See, for example, Job 1:1–3; 42:10–15; and Sir 31:8–11.
33. See Prov 1:7 and 9:10; also Ps 111:10.

> To fear the Lord is fullness of wisdom;
> she inebriates mortals with her fruits.
> The fear of the Lord is the crown of wisdom,
> making peace and perfect health to flourish.
> To fear the Lord is the root of wisdom,
> and her branches are long life. (1:16, 18, 20)[34]

All the blessings of wisdom result from fidelity to the covenant, which, according to the Deuteronomistic theology of Ben Sira, assures the believer of long life, prosperity, and physical and psychological well-being.[35] From these poems at the beginning of the book, it is apparent that above all else Ben Sira cherished practical wisdom as fear of the Lord.[36]

It is not surprising, therefore, that most of the Wisdom of Ben Sira is concerned with practical wisdom. According to Ben Sira, you could have all the theoretical wisdom in the world; but if you lacked practical wisdom, you would not fear the Lord or fulfill the demands of the law, and as a result you would ultimately be a fool, and your life would have no meaning.

> How great is the one who finds wisdom!
> But none is superior to the one who fears the Lord.
> Fear of the Lord surpasses everything;
> to whom can we compare the one who has it? (25:10–11)[37]

Often, however, in a single poem Ben Sira writes of the work that goes into acquiring theoretical wisdom and of the fear of the Lord that is the essence of practical wisdom.

> If you gathered nothing in your youth,
> how can you find anything in your old age?
> Rich experience is the crown of the aged,
> and their boast is the fear of the Lord. (25:3, 6)

In the society of that day, as noted above, wisdom was thought to be the domain primarily of the elders in the community.[38]

34. See also 21:11.

35. See Deut 28:1–14. For a discussion of this theology, see O. S. Rankin, *Israel's Wisdom Literature: Its Bearing on Theology and the History of Religion* (Edinburgh: T. & T. Clark, 1936) 77–80. Regarding retribution in Ben Sira, see A. A. Di Lella, "Conservative and Progressive Theology: Sirach and Wisdom," *CBQ* 28 (1966) 143–46.

36. According to Haspecker (*Gottesfurcht bei Jesus Sirach*, 82), the expression "fear of the Lord" or its equivalent occurs some fifty-five to sixty times in Ben Sira, a number that is exceeded only in Psalms, where the expression occurs seventy-nine times.

37. See also 1:11–30; 6:32–37; 24:23–29.

38. See also 6:18, 34; 8:8–9; 32:3.

The two-stanza poem in 14:20–15:10 combines theoretical and practical wisdom in a masterful synthesis.[39] The first stanza, 14:20–27, describes with colorful and daring images the zest and the zeal Ben Sira encourages his students to have in their pursuit of theoretical wisdom.

Happy is the person who meditates on wisdom
  and reasons intelligently,
who reflects in his heart on her ways
  and ponders her secrets,
pursuing her like a hunter,
  and lying in wait on her paths;
who peers through her windows
  and listens at her doors;
who camps near her house
  and fastens his tent peg to her walls;
who pitches his tent near her,
  and so occupies an excellent lodging place;
who places his children under her shelter,
  and lodges under her boughs;
who is sheltered by her from the heat,
  and dwells in the midst of her glory. (14:20–27)

The extraordinary images of hunting and stalking, of eavesdropping and pitching the tent near Wisdom's house, punctuate the single-minded effort involved in the quest for wisdom. The image of the person "peer[ing] through her windows" and "listen[ing] at her doors" (14:23) contrasts pointedly with a similar image describing the conduct of the person who lacks social graces that are integral ingredients of theoretical wisdom.

A boor peers into the house from the door,
  but a cultivated person remains outside.
It is ill-mannered for a person to listen at a door;
  the discreet would be grieved by the disgrace. (21:23–24)

Those who refuse to accept discipline and training even in basic civility will never attain wisdom.[40]

The second stanza affirms that it is precisely practical wisdom as fear of the Lord that alone can enable one to obtain theoretical wisdom. The imagery again is striking.

Whoever fears the Lord will do this,
  and whoever holds to the law will obtain wisdom.

39. Here again Ben Sira borrowed ideas from his favorite book; see Prov 2:1–16.
40. See 21:14–16, 18–19, 20, 25–26; 22:1–2, 6, 9–18.

> She will come to meet him like a mother,
> and like a young bride she will welcome him.
> She will feed him with the bread of learning,
> and give him the water of wisdom to drink.
> He will lean on her and not fall,
> and he will rely on her and not be put to shame.
> She will exalt him above his neighbors,
> and will open his mouth in the midst of the assembly.
> He will find gladness and a crown of rejoicing,
> and will inherit an everlasting name.
> The foolish will not obtain her,
> and sinners will not see her.
> She is far from arrogance,
> and liars will never think of her.
> Praise is unseemly on the lips of a sinner,
> for it has not been sent from the Lord.
> For in wisdom must praise be uttered,
> and the Lord will make it prosper. (15:1–10)

Ben Sira emphasizes that the foolish can never come to practical wisdom for the simple reason that they are sinners. Sin and folly are synonyms in Ben Sira's lexicon. Lady Wisdom, however, will come to the righteous as mother[41] and bride — two images that would particularly attract notice in the male-oriented world of Ben Sira. The blessings of wisdom are what the faithful were taught to expect from their loyalty to the covenant: a life of honor and respect (15:5)[42] without shame (15:4);[43] great happiness and joy in the present life;[44] surrogate immortality through children who will ensure a lasting good name (15:6);[45] and a prayer life of praise that only wisdom can make possible (15:9–10).[46]

41. Cf. Mephistopheles's words to the student (in J. W. von Goethe, *Faust* [rev. ed.; New York: Bantam Books, 1985]):

> Just as a child does not at first
> accept its mother's breast quite willingly,
> but soon imbibes its nourishment with zest,
> you will feel a growing lust
> when clinging to high wisdom's bosom. (pt. 1.2)

42. See also 21:17 as well as Job 29:7–25; Prov 22:11; and Qoh 10:12.
43. See Pss 22:6; 25:2–3, 20; 119:6, 46.
44. See Deut 28:1–14; Isa 51:3; 56:1–7.
45. See also 37:26; 39:9–11; 41:11–13; 44:14; 46:11d; 49:1, as well as Prov 10:7.
46. See also 17:9–10 and Pss 33:1–5; 148:11–14. As G. von Rad observes (*Old Testament Theology* [New York: Harper & Row, 1962–65] 1.369–70), "Praise is man's most characteristic mode of existence: praising and not praising stand over against one another like life and death."

TRUE AND FALSE WISDOM

Though Ben Sira places a high value on theoretical and practical wisdom, he nonetheless warns his students that not all wisdom is true wisdom. Without fear of the Lord and keeping the commandments there can be no true wisdom; or as Ben Sira puts it:

> The whole of wisdom is fear of the Lord,
> and in all wisdom there is the fulfillment of the law. (19:20)

The mere accumulation of knowledge or cleverness alone or even great skill is not true wisdom. Indeed, Israel's history has had its share of "wise" individuals who were unrepentant scoundrels.[47] Knowing that history so well, Ben Sira writes:

> The knowledge of wickedness is not wisdom,
> nor is there prudence in the counsel of sinners.
> There is a cleverness that is detestable,
> and there is a fool who is free of sins.[48]
> Better are the God-fearing who lack understanding
> than the highly intelligent who transgress the law.
> There is a cleverness that is exact but unjust,
> and there are people who abuse favors to gain a verdict. (19:22–25)

It is probable that in this passage Ben Sira had in mind the Jews who were tempted to compromise their faith for the blandishments of Hellenistic learning and culture. The Greeks prided themselves on their achievements in philosophy and art, science and technology — all of which may be described as theoretical wisdom. Ben Sira, who had certainly read pagan authors, as we noted above, would indeed praise such wisdom, provided that it was bound together with fear of the Lord or practical wisdom. Often, however, that was not the case. So Ben Sira reminds his fellow Jews that knowledge alone, divorced from ethical conduct, is worse than ignorance. In fact, the less intelligent who fear God and even fools who are without sin are better off than the intelligentsia who bend or break the law. This passage goes right to the heart of Ben Sira's teaching: wisdom is fundamentally a practical matter of

47. Jonadab, who advises Amnon in the rape of his half-sister Tamar, is described as *ḥākām mĕʾōd,* "very wise/clever" (2 Sam 13:3). For other examples of how the Deuteronomic History demonstrates a negative assessment of wisdom, see K. I. Parker, "Solomon as Philosopher King? The Nexus of Law and Wisdom in 1 Kings 1–11," *JSOT* 53 (1992) 75–91, esp. 86–87. Parker writes (p. 89), "Wisdom that is not bound to Torah, as the story of Solomon shows, is almost the same as folly." For Ben Sira's evaluation of Solomon's early wisdom and final folly, see 47:12–21.

48. So the Syriac; the NRSV, following the Greek, has "who merely lacks wisdom."

fearing the Lord (vv. 20a, 24a) and observing the law (v. 20b), and not simply a theoretical matter of training the mind and acquiring skills (vv. 22–24).[49]

In Ben Sira's view, education is indeed worthwhile, but it must go hand in hand with righteous living if one is to reap the benefits and enduring blessings of wisdom.

> If a person is wise to his own advantage,
> the fruits of his good sense will be praiseworthy.
> A wise person instructs his own people,
> and the fruits of his good sense will endure.
> A wise person will have praise heaped upon him,
> and all who see him will call him happy.
> The days of a person's life are numbered,
> but the days of Israel are without number.
> One who is wise among his people will inherit honor,
> and his name will live forever. (37:22–26)

The wise not only do good for the community but also enjoy the material rewards that accrue from their training. But the lasting merit of their wisdom is the honor they will inherit and the good reputation that will endure among the people of Israel.[50]

CONCLUSION

It is without question that Ben Sira held theoretical wisdom in high esteem. Having a superb education himself, he was anxious to share his knowledge and experience with others in the community. That is why he speaks so frequently and eloquently of the objective value and subjective utility of theoretical wisdom. The effort, training, and discipline to which Ben Sira refers are a small price to pay in order to educate the mind. It is equally clear, however, that in Ben Sira practical wisdom as fear of the Lord is above everything else, for it is what enables the believer to be truly human according to the coordinates and legitimations of Jewish society and religion.

Socrates once said, "The unexamined life is not worth living."[51] Ben Sira would say, "The life without wisdom has no meaning." What Ben Sira means by wisdom may be summarized in the following points:

49. For a view similar to Ben Sira's, see Jas 3:13–18.
50. See 39:8–11 and Prov 3:35.
51. Plato *Apology* (Stephanus) 38a, ll. 5–6.

1. *Wisdom is fear of the Lord:*
Whoever keeps the law controls his thoughts,
   and the fulfillment of the fear of the Lord is wisdom. (21:11)

2. *Fear of the Lord means love of the Lord:*
Those who fear the Lord do not disobey his words,
   and those who love him keep his ways. (2:15)

3. *Wisdom means faithfully observing the commandments:*
If you desire wisdom, keep the commandments,
   and the Lord will lavish her upon you. (1:26)

4. *Fear of the Lord involves discipline:*
For the fear of the Lord is wisdom and discipline,
   fidelity and humility are his delight. (1:27)

5. *Wisdom is the source of the greatest blessings in life:*
Whoever loves her [Wisdom] loves life,
   and those who seek her from early morning are filled with joy.
Whoever holds her fast inherits glory,
   and the Lord blesses the place she enters.
Those who serve her minister to the Holy One;
   the Lord loves those who love her.
Those who obey her will judge the nations,
   and all who listen to her will live secure.
If they remain faithful, they will inherit her;
   their descendants will also obtain her. (4:12–16)[52]

52. Geniza ms. A has personified wisdom as speaker in vv. 15–18. For a detailed study of this poem, see N. Calduch Benages, "La Sabiduría y la prueba en Sir 4,11–19," *EstBib* 49 (1991) 25–48.

9

WISDOM IN THE WISDOM OF SOLOMON

David Winston

The quest for ultimate wisdom is deeply rooted in the human psyche, but views have widely differed as to both its legitimacy and its potential for actual attainment. The author of Job 28 entertains no hopes for the success of such an enterprise, and Qoheleth is sorely aggrieved at the fact that divinity has planted such a futile urge in the human heart (3:11). To plumb the mysteries of the cosmos presupposes an ability to comprehend deity, but as the author of the Babylonian poem *Ludlul Bel Nemeqi* (I will praise the Lord of Wisdom) had already put it, "Where have mortals learnt the way of a god?"[1] The author of the Wisdom of Solomon, however, disdainfully dismissing every trace of pessimism, exasperation, rage, or a placid contentment to remain within narrow bounds, summons his fellow mortals to espouse a bold and confident commitment to follow his lead and explore the uttermost limits of divine Wisdom.

WOMAN WISDOM: LITERARY PERSONIFICATION OR DIVINE HYPOSTASIS?

In his description of wisdom, the author invokes a female figure of cosmic beauty and grandeur, and employs a magnificent fivefold metaphor in which she is conceived as an eternal emanation of God's power

1. W. G. Lambert, *Babylonian Wisdom Literature* (Oxford: Clarendon Press, 1960) 41.

and glory (7:25–26). She is no figment of his own imagination, having already made her appearance as a cosmic force in Proverbs 8 under the guise of a charming female playing always before Yahweh, after having been created by him at the beginning of his work, and having obvious roots in ancient Near Eastern myth. It appears she can be defined as a hypostasis if one follows the very broad definition of that term offered by W. O. E. Oesterly and G. H. Box: "a quasi-personification of certain attributes proper to God, occupying an intermediate position between personalities and abstract beings."[2] *Hu* and *Sia*, for example, are in Egyptian tradition the creative word and understanding of the high god Re-Atum, personified and separated from their originator. Mythologically expressed, they are, as Helmer Ringgren suggests, "the first begotten children of Re-Amun and his assistants in the creation of the world."[3] Similarly, Egyptian Maat is a personification of the concept *maat*, right order in nature and society (Hebrew *yošer*, "straightness" or "uprightness," is precisely equivalent), who became the daughter of Re and was vouchsafed a cult of her own. According to one text, "Re has created Maat, he rejoices over her, he delights in her, his heart is joyful when he sees her."[4] Examples from the Akkadian sphere are *Mešaru* and *Kettu*, "Righteousness" and "Right," who were conceived sometimes only as qualities of the sun-god or as gifts granted by him, and sometimes in a more concrete way as personal beings, even independent deities.[5]

Although R. B. Y. Scott has argued that, according to Prov 8:22, Yahweh "possessed" (*qānānî*) wisdom as an attribute or faculty integral to his being from the very first, and "in or with his wisdom founded the earth,"[6] the Hebrew text is much too ambiguous to bear this interpretation with any degree of certainty. It is therefore fair to conclude that it is only in the book of Wisdom and in Philo, where Sophia is conceived of as an eternal divine emanation, that she appears for the first time in Hellenistic Jewish writings as a hypostasis in the sense defined above. Indeed, the most remarkable feature about the author of Wis-

2. W. O. E. Oesterly and G. H. Box, *The Religion and Worship of the Synagogue* (London: Pitman, 1911) 169.

3. H. Ringgren, *Word and Wisdom* (Lund: H. Ohlssons, 1947) 27.

4. C. Bauer-Kayatz, *Studien zu Proverbien 1–9* (Neukirchen-Vluyn: Neukirchener Verlag, 1966) 98.

5. See Ringgren, *Word and Wisdom*, 53–58.

6. R. B. Y. Scott, *Proverbs and Ecclesiastes* (AB 18; Garden City, N.Y.: Doubleday & Co., 1965) 72.

dom's description of Sophia is that she is depicted as an effluence or emanation of God's glory, a notion that even the more philosophically ambitious Philo was loathe to express explicitly, preferring instead to use locutions that implied it. Although Philo does not apply the term *aporroia*, "effluence," to Logos/Sophia, he does employ the verbs *ombreō* and *plēmmyrō* in this connection. In *Som.* 2.221, paraphrasing Exod 17:6, he has God say, "I stand ever the same immutable, before thou or aught that exists came into being, established on the topmost and most ancient source of power, whence showers forth the birth of all that is, whence streams the tide of wisdom."[7] Wisdom 7:25 is the earliest attestation of the term *aporroia* applied to Logos/Sophia as an emanation from God. It is very likely, however, that the notion of an outflow from God was already used by adherents of the Middle Stoa, perhaps by Posidonius, since Cicero writes: "And if humankind possesses intelligence, faith, virtue, and concord, whence can these things have flowed down [*defluere*] upon the earth if not from the powers above?" (*Nat. D.* 2.79; cf. *Sen.* 78; *Div.* 1.110; Seneca *Ep.* 120.14). In any case, here the author finally makes good his promise in 6:22 to tell us how Wisdom came into being. Unlike Ben Sira (1:4; 24:9), who asserts that God has created Wisdom, he says not a word about her creation, but instead describes her in the present tense as a divine effulgence. The answer to *pōs egeneto*, how she came into being, thus turns out to be that she is in reality an eternal emanation of which one would have to say more precisely that she is *aei gignomenē kai gegēnemenē*, ever being produced and in a state of having been produced (Proclus's formula in his *In Ti.* 290.3–25).[8]

7. Cf. Philo *Post.* 69; *Fug.* 198. At *Spec.* 1.40, the simile employed would seem to imply that the logos is an emanation from God.

8. Some commentators (such as J. Schulthess, H. Ewald, and H. Bois) would supply *emoi* before *egeneto* in Wis 6:22 and translate "how I got her," since the author of Wisdom apparently nowhere tells us how Sophia actually came into being. Moreover, it is sometimes argued (most recently by Offerhaus) that if Wisdom is an eternal logos, we should require the verb form *gegone* rather than *egeneto*. Grimm and Goodrick understand *egeneto* after the manner of Wisdom's creation according to Prov 8:24; Job 28:26; and Sir 1:24. I agree with Grimm that it is quite arbitrary to supply *emoi*, since the author would hardly have omitted such an important modification if that were really his intent. On the other hand, it is not difficult to suppose that in introducing his boldly new conception of Wisdom as an eternal divine hypostasis, he would in his introductory remarks promising to expose Wisdom's origins use the usual expression *pōs egeneto*, not yet committing himself to this new conception, and then at the right moment launch into an overpowering literary effusion that does not speak explicitly either of Wisdom's creation or of her eternal emanation, but that leaves the reflective reader with the irresistible conclusion that the author wishes him to draw. See C. L. W. Grimm, *Das Buch der Weisheit* (Leipzig: S. Hirzel, 1860) 133–34; A. T. S. Goodrick, *The*

Wisdom Described

In 7:22–24 the author proceeds to describe Wisdom by a series of twenty-one epithets (7 x 3, a triple perfection):

> For in her is a spirit intelligent [*pneuma noeron*] and holy,
> unique of its kind yet manifold, subtle [*lepton*], agile, lucid, unsullied,
> clear, inviolable, loving goodness, keen,
> unhindered [*akōlyton*], beneficent [*euergetikon*], humane [*philanthrōpon*],
> steadfast, unfailing, untouched by care, all-powerful, all-surveying,
> and pervading all spirits, intelligent, pure, and most subtle.
> For wisdom is more mobile than any motion,
> she pervades and permeates all things by reason of her pureness.

There are numerous parallels for such serial lists in the ancient world. In the representation of the initiation into immortality delivered in the so-called Mithras Liturgy, part of the great Paris Magical Codex (presumably compiled in the early fourth century CE), Aion is similarly invoked with twenty-one epithets that consistently refer to him as god of light and fire.[9] Similarly, in its twenty-one words, the Ahuna Vairya, "the most sacred and probably the most ancient of the Zoroastrian formulas of devotion," contained in germ the whole revelation of the Good Religion and the twenty-one *nasks* of which it was composed.[10]

Wisdom's twenty-one epithets are borrowed largely from Greek philosophy, especially that of the Stoa. Posidonius defined God as "intelligent breath [*pneuma noeron]* pervading the whole of substance" (F100, Kidd), and Stoics described the soul as a "subtle [*leptomeres*], self-moving body" (*SVF* 2.780). Moreover, according to Chrysippus, "since the universal nature extends to all things, everything that comes about in any way whatever in the whole universe . . . will necessarily have come about conformably with that nature and its reason in due and unimpeded [*akōlutōs*] sequence" (*SVF* 2.937). Chrysippus also referred to the gods as beneficent (*euergetikoi*) and humane (*philanthrōpoi,* lit.: lovers of humanity) (*SVF* 2.1115). What characterizes the

---

Book of Wisdom (London: Rivingtons, 1913) 178–79; U. Offerhaus, *Komposition und Intention der Sapientia Salomonis* (Bonn: Self-published, 1981) 108–12; C. Larcher, *Le Livre de la Sagesse* (Paris: Gabalda, 1984) 2.434–35.

9. See H. Lewy, *Chaldean Oracles and Theurgy,* rev. ed. by M. Tardieu (Paris: Etudes Augustiniennes, 1978) 405.

10. *Greater Bundahishn* 1.15. The twenty-one *nasks* were divided into three groups of seven each. See R. G. Zaehner, *The Dawn and Twilight of Zoroastrianism* (New York: G. P. Putnam's Sons, 1961) 261; idem, *Zurvan: A Zoroastrian Dilemma* (New York: Biblo and Tannen, 1972) 314, 415.

Stoic pneuma above all, however, is that it pervades (*diēkei*) and permeates (*chōrei*) all things (*SVF* 2.416, 1021, 1033). According to Stoic cosmology, an active principle (the divine Logos) totally pervaded a passive principle (qualityless matter) as the passage of body through body. The pneuma's extension through matter is described as tensional motion (*tonikē kinēsis*), characterized as a form of oscillation in which the pneuma "moves itself from itself and into itself" or backwards and forwards, a simultaneous motion in opposite directions.[11] This scientific theory appealed so strongly both to Philo and to the author of the Wisdom of Solomon that they were willing to take up this stark corporealism and adapt it to their own Platonist way of thinking, an adaptation undoubtedly made possible by their transposition of the materialist Stoic terminology into literary metaphor.

The author's emphasis on Wisdom's pervasiveness throughout the cosmos is balanced by his countervailing insistence that she nonetheless enjoys a symbiotic relationship with God, a condition of unbroken intimacy with the divine (8:3). It may therefore be said that there is an aspect of God's essence in everything (and in the human mind preeminently); yet for all that, this essence remains inseparable from God. The only comparable concept in ancient Jewish thought is Philo's similar notion of an all-penetrating divine Logos that reaches into each individual's mind, thereby converting it into an extension of the divine mind, albeit a very fragmentary one (*Det.* 90; *Gig.* 27; *Leg. All.* 1.37–38; cf. M. Aurelius 8.57; *Corp. Herm.* 12.1).

Like Philo, the author of Wisdom evidently teaches that God created the world by means of Wisdom. Although his statement that "God made all things by his 'word' [*logō*], and through his 'wisdom' [*sophia*] framed man" (9:1–2) is in itself ambiguous,[12] since it is by no means clear that "word" and "wisdom" here refer to Logos/Sophia, the matter is, I think, settled by his description of Wisdom as "chooser of God's works" (8:4), which clearly implies that Wisdom is identical with the divine mind through which the deity acts. In light of this, the assertion that "with you is Wisdom who knows your works and was present when you created the world" (9:9) undoubtedly signifies that Wisdom contains the paradigmatic patterns of all things (cf. 9:8) and serves as the instrument of their creation.

11. See R. B. Todd, *Alexander of Aphrodisias on Stoic Physics* (Leiden: E. J. Brill, 1976) 34–37.

12. Wis 8:5–6 is also somewhat ambiguous, and has been variously translated.

But if Wisdom is pervasively present in all things, and above all in the operations of human reason, what is the significance of humanity's hot pursuit of her and the need for special supplication to the Lord that he dispatch her from his heavenly throne (9:10)? The issue here is one of perspective. Since Wisdom is both immanent and transcendent, these modes of description are easily interchangeable, depending on the focus of the writer. To explain this double aspect, the platonizing Roman Stoic philosopher Seneca employs a vivid simile, which probably derives from the Middle Stoa, and, incidentally, recurs much later in the writings of Schneur Zalman of Liadi, founder of Habad Hasidism, who cites it from the Cabalistic tract *Pardes Rimmonim* (1548) of Moses Cordovero of Safed. Seneca states:

> Just as the rays of the sun do indeed touch the earth, but still abide at the source from which they are sent [cf. Wis 7:27], even so the great and hallowed soul, which has come down in order that we may have a nearer knowledge of divinity, does indeed associate with us, but still cleaves to its origin; on that source it depends, thither it turns its gaze and strives to go, and it concerns itself with our doings only as a being superior to ourselves. (*Ep.* 41.5)[13]

The Neoplatonist Proclus (fifth century CE) later provides a concise expression of this bifocal perspective:

> The gods are present alike to all things; not all things, however, are present alike to the gods, but each order has a share in their presence proportioned to its station and capacity, some things receiving them as unities and others as manifolds, some perpetually and others for a time, some incorporeally and others through the body. (*The Elements of Theology* 142, trans. Dodds)

From the human viewpoint, the divine Wisdom enters the human being and departs; from the eternal perspective of God, however, it is ever present to us, though its consummation in any particular case is conditioned by the fitness of the recipient. Hence our author speaks in no uncertain terms of "desire for instruction" (6:17), "training in Wisdom's society" (8:18), and the need for predawn vigilance on her behalf (6:14–15).

Wisdom's Salvific Power

The greatest boon bestowed by Wisdom is the gift of immortality, a gift made possible by the fact that human beings enjoy kinship with her:

13. Cf. Philo *QG* 2.40; *Det.* 90; M. Aurelius *Med.* 8.57; Justin *Dial.* 128.3–4; Tertullian *Apol.* 21.10–13; Lactantius *Div. Inst.* 4.29.4–5.

> After thinking this over in my mind, and pondering in my heart that there is immortality in kinship with Wisdom, and in her friendship sheer delight, and in the labors of her hands unfailing wealth, and in training in her society understanding, and great renown in the sharing of her words, I went about in search of how I might make her my own. (Wis 8:17–18)

The theme of human kinship with God occurs in Plato and is a characteristic teaching of the Stoa. Plato writes: "We declare that God has given to each of us, as his daemon, the kind of soul that is housed in the top of our body and that raises us — seeing that we are not an earthly but a heavenly plant — up from earth towards our kindred in the heaven" (*Ti.* 90A). In the pseudo-Platonic *Alcibiades I,* Socrates says that the part of the soul that is the seat of knowledge and thought resembles God, and those who look at this will gain thereby the best knowledge of themselves (133B–C; cf. *Phd.* 79D; *Resp.* 490B; 611E; *Laws* 899D; Posidonius F187, Edelstein and Kidd). Philo takes up the theme with equal vigor: "It is the human [being's] lot to occupy the place of the highest excellence among living creatures because his stock is near akin to God, sprung from the same source in virtue of his participation in reason, which gives him immortality, mortal though he seems to be" (*Spec.* 4.14; cf. *Opif.* 145–46; *QG* 2.60; *Decal.* 41).

In a fine ode to Wisdom's saving power in history (10:1–21), the author assimilates the old covenantal salvation-history with its miraculous and sudden divine irruptions to the immanent divine ordering of human events as mediated by the continuous activity of Wisdom. It is her generation-by-generation election of holy servants (7:27) that structures the life of Israel. Her saving and punishing power is illustrated by the enumeration of seven righteous heroes and their wicked counterparts: Adam and Cain; Noah and the Flood generation; Abraham and the confounded nations; Lot and the Sodomites; Jacob and Esau; Joseph and his critics; Israel led by Moses and the Egyptians led by pharaoh. The ode is marked by the use of anaphora, repetition of the same word at the beginning of successive verses. Wisdom is thus introduced throughout the chapter with the emphatic pronoun "she" (*hautē*), which marks off six sections each of which contains the word "righteous" once. E. Norden pointed out that this is one form of the encomia of the gods in Greek literature.[14] A particularly good illustration of this kind of encomium is Cicero's well-known hymn to Philosophy:

14. See E. Norden, *Agnostos Theos* (5th ed.; Darmstadt: Wissenschaftliche Buchgesellschaft, 1971) 163–65, 223–24. Cf. Acts 7:35–38; Heb 11; CD 2.17–3.12; Lucretius *De*

> O Philosophy, thou guide of life, O thou explorer of virtue and expeller of vice! Without thee what could have become not only of me but of the life of man altogether? Thou hast given birth to cities, thou hast called scattered human beings into the bond of social life, thou hast united them first of all in joint habitations, next in wedlock, then in the ties of common literature and speech, thou hast discovered law, thou hast been the teacher of morality and order: to thee I fly for refuge, from thee I look for aid, to thee I entrust myself, as once in ample measure, so now wholly and entirely. (*Tusc.* 5.5, trans. King)

Wisdom's Efficacy

In light of the tradition of speculation on Wisdom, with its strong individualistic, humanistic, and universalistic orientation, and above all its linkage of divine revelation with the natural order rather than with Sinai, it is easy to understand why our author chose the figure of Wisdom as the ideal mediator of his message to his contemporaries. She was the perfect bridge between the exclusive nationalist tradition of Israel and the universalistic philosophical tradition that appealed so strongly to the Jewish youth of Roman Alexandria. Moreover, for his own use in describing Sophia, the author very skillfully adapted the Isis aretalogies, a literature that held great appeal for him in view of his profound empathy with the passionate religious intensity and mystical intimacy that characterized the Isis mysteries. The cult of Isis and Sarapis was one of the most popular Oriental religions in the Roman world from the fourth century BCE to the fourth century CE, though its peak of popularity was reached in the second century CE. It should also be noted that the emperor Gaius, who had decorated a room, the *aula Isiaca,* in his palace on the Palatine with paintings depicting numerous Egyptian religious symbols, had also built a special temple to Isis and had instituted Isiac mysteries in which he is said to have participated himself while dressed in female garb (Josephus *Ant.* 19 §30). In the eyes of our author it was only fitting that he reclaim what in his view were falsely appropriated *aretai* for "her" to whom they truly belonged.

As the divine mind immanent within the universe and guiding and controlling all its dynamic operations, Wisdom represents the entire range of the natural sciences: cosmology, physics, astronomy, biology, botany, in addition to all esoteric knowledge (7:17–21). She is also the teacher of all human arts and crafts, including shipbuilding and the

---

Rer. Nat. 1.1–9; Seneca *Ad Marc.* 20.2; Philo *Praem.* 11; *Mut.* 149–50; and the Hellenistic aretalogies or hymns of praise discovered in Egypt.

art of navigation (7:16; 14:2). She is skilled in ontology ("the unerring knowledge of existent being" [7:17]) and in the intricacies of logic and rhetoric. Having unsurpassed experience of both past and present, she also infers the future and possesses the key to all the divinatory arts (8:8). Moreover, she is the source of all moral knowledge (8:7), is each individual's counselor and comforter, bringing rest, cheer, and joy, and bestowing riches and glory on her own, though her greatest gift is that of immortality (8:9–13). Above all, as we have already seen, she is synonymous with divine providence, controlling historical events and in each generation guiding the friends of God and inspiring his prophets (7:27; 14:3). It is significant that the author, unlike Ben Sira, nowhere explicitly identifies Wisdom with Torah, and with the exception of a brief historical reference in 18:9 makes virtually no mention of the sacrificial cult. His statement that "love for Wisdom means the keeping of her laws" (6:18) is ambiguous and probably refers to the statutes of natural law. All we have from him in this regard is but a passing allusion to Israel's mission of bringing the imperishable light of the law to the world (18:4).[15] Very likely he believed with Philo that the teachings of the Torah were tokens of divine Wisdom, and that they were in harmony with the law of the universe and as such implant all the virtues in the human psyche,[16] but when he focuses his attention on Wisdom, it is philosophy, science, and the arts that are uppermost in his mind. He conceives of Wisdom as a direct bearer of revelation, functioning through the workings of the human mind, and supreme arbiter of all values. She is clearly the archetypal Torah, of which the Mosaic law is but an image. When he insists that unless God send his Wisdom down from on high humanity would not comprehend God's will (9:17), he is certainly implying that the Torah is in need of further interpretation for the disclosure of its true meaning, interpretation that Wisdom alone is able to provide. The author here closely approximates the position of Philo of Alexandria, in whose view, even before the Sinaitic revelation, the Patriarchs were already constituted *nomoi empsychoi*, living embodiments of divine Wisdom. Similarly, in Wisdom 10, Sophia had already served as a personal guide to six righteous heroes who lived before the Sinaitic revelation. An echo of this notion is later found in the statement

15. Cf. *Bib. Ant.* 11.1–2; 51.3; *T. Levi* 14:4; *T. Orph.* 3; 2 *Apoc. Bar.* 48:40; 4 Ezra 7:20–24; Philo *QE* 2.41; *Mos.* 2.36, 44; *Abr.* 98.

16. Cf. Josephus *Ant.* 1. Proem 4.24; Pseudo-Aristeas 161; 4 Macc 1:16–17; 5:25; Philo *Opif.* 3; *Mos.* 2.52.

of R. Avin (fourth century) that the Torah is an incomplete form (*nobelet*, lit.: the fruit falling prematurely off the tree) or image of the supernal Wisdom (*Gen. Rab.* 17.5; 44.12, Theodor-Albeck 157, 237).

Wisdom and Love of Humanity

Although the substantive *philanthrōpia* never occurs in the book of Wisdom, the adjective *philanthrōpos,* humane or benevolent, appears thrice. Wisdom is described twice as *philanthropōs* (1:6; 7:23), and in 12:19 we are told that God's mercy is a model-lesson for the Israelites, teaching them that the righteous person must be humane. God loves all that exists, loathing nothing that he has created (11:24), and as the lover of all that lives, he spares all, for his imperishable spirit is in all things (11:26; 12:1). We have here a faint intimation of the Middle Stoic doctrine of *philanthrōpia,* which is fully elaborated in the writings of Philo. The special kinship between God and humankind, based on the notion of a divine logos at once immanent and transcendent, led inevitably to the concept of the unity of humanity. The Stoics spoke of the common community of gods and human beings, since they alone make use of reason and live according to right and law (Cicero *ND* 2.154; *SVF* 2.527–28). The early Stoics, however, still emphasized the dichotomy between the wise and the foolish, and Zeno insisted that only the wise are capable of concord and unity (Diog. Laert. 7.32.3). The Cynics had gone so far as to say that the nonwise are not human beings (Diog. Laert. 6.41, 60). It was only in the Middle Stoa, in the writings of Panaetius and in those of the stoicizing Antiochus of Ascalon (who professed to be both an Old Academic and a Stoic), that an all-embracing doctrine of human unity took shape.[17] Panaetius focused his attention on the ordinary human being and thus produced an ethical ideal suited to the capacity of all (Seneca *Ep.* 116.5; Cicero *On Duties* 1.46, 99). Going beyond the negative formulation of justice that forbids injury to another, he advances the positive definition of it as an active beneficence that forms the bond of society (Cicero *On Duties* 1.20–22). The fundamental principles on which this is based are elucidated as follows:

> We must go more deeply into the basic principles of fellowship and association set up by nature among men. The first is to be found in the association that links together the entire human race, and the bond that creates this is reason and speech, which by teaching and learning, by communication,

17. See H. C. Baldry, *The Unity of Mankind in Greek Thought* (Cambridge: Cambridge University Press, 1965) 177–203.

> discussion, and decision brings men into agreement with each other and joins them in a kind of natural fellowship. (Cicero *On Duties* 1.50, trans. Baldry; cf. Philo *QG* 2.60; *Decal.* 41, 132–34)

Following Panaetius, Philo too emphasizes the positive aspect of justice as an active beneficence (*Virt.* 166–70). This quality is epitomized by him in the word *philanthrōpia,* a term that apparently came into philosophical prominence in the writings of Panaetius and Antiochus, and later in those of Musonius Rufus, and with special emphasis in those of Plutarch. In a section of his treatise *On the Virtues* devoted to *philanthrōpia* (51–174), Philo points out that it has *eusebeia,* "piety," as its sister and twin, for the love of God involves the love of human beings, inasmuch as the human being, "the best of living creatures, through that higher part of his being, the soul, is most nearly akin to heaven . . . and also to the Father of the world, possessing in his mind a closer likeness and copy than anything else on earth of the eternal and blessed Archetype" (*Decal.* 134). Moreover, in practicing *philanthrōpia,* the human being is imitating God (*Spec.* 1.294; 4.73). Here we touch upon the formula that constitutes for Philo the best way to describe the *telos* of human life, *homoiōsis theō,* "imitation of God," and in adopting this Platonic goal, his teaching here fully converged with that of the Jewish tradition.[18]

The Divine-Human Equation in Wisdom and Qumran

The splitting of humanity into two opposing camps constitutes a central teaching in both the Wisdom of Solomon and the Dead Sea Scrolls. An analysis of this theme as it appears in these texts will illuminate the divergent ways in which they describe through subtle shifts of emphasis the nature of the relative autonomy allowed to "dwellers in clay whose origin is dust" (Job 4:19). We read in 1QH 15:12–21:

> I know through the understanding which comes from Thee
> that righteousness is not in a hand of flesh,
> that man is not master of his way
> and that it is not in mortals to direct their step.
> I know that the inclination of every spirit is in Thy hand;
> Thou didst establish all its ways before creating it,
> and how can any man change Thy words?
> Thou alone didst create the just

18. For a fuller discussion, see D. Winston, *Wisdom of Solomon* (AB; Garden City, N.Y.: Doubleday & Co., 1979) 43–46.

and establish him from the womb
for the time of goodwill. . . .
But the wicked Thou didst create
for the time of Thy wrath,
Thou didst vow them from the womb
to the Day of Massacre,
for they walk in the way that is not good. (trans. Vermes)

Similarly, in the book of Wisdom the idea of being worthy either of Death or of Wisdom occurs more than once. In 1:16 we are told that "godless men have summoned Death through word and deed; thinking him a friend they pined for him, and made a pact with him, for they are worthy to be members of his party" (cf. 1QM 13:12; 15:9–10; 17:4, where, as Amir has correctly noted, it is stated that the wicked are attached to Belial because "their desire is for him"). We are further told that "it was through the devil's envy that Death entered into the cosmic order, and they who are his own experience him" (2:24). Wisdom, on the other hand, goes about seeking those who are worthy of her (6:16), and grace and mercy, we are informed, belong to God's chosen (3:9).[19]

As for the question of the origin of this fateful division of humanity, however, the position of Qumran is seen by some to differ radically from that of the book of Wisdom. The scrolls explicitly state that it was God who "has appointed for man two spirits in which to walk until the time of his visitation; the spirits of truth and falsehood" (1QS 3.18, 25). The Wisdom of Solomon, however, according to Yehoshua Amir, locates the source of the split in the free choice of the wicked:

Do not court death through a deviant way of life
nor draw down destruction by your own actions.
For God did not make death,
nor does he take delight in the destruction of the living;
he created all things that they might endure.
All that has come into existence preserves its being,
and there is no deadly poison in it.
Death's rulership is not on earth, for justice is immortal.
(Wis 1:12–15)

But if God did not create Death, where did he come from? He was invited by his confederates (1:16), and it was through the devil's envy that Death came about (2:24). Amir says that the devil, who is mentioned in

19. The theme of the predestinarian splitting of humankind into two rival camps of the just and the wicked is also found in rabbinic literature. See *Mek. Pisha* 16; *Gen. Rab.* 3.8; Theodor-Albeck, 23. See Winston, *Wisdom of Solomon*, 56, 113–14, 121–23.

this verse of Wisdom alone, must be identical with Death, who at the moment of creation stands outside like an exiled monarch who is envious of this happy world being established before his very eyes, but in which he has no share. He cannot by brute force work his way into it, for God has firmly barred his entry; and if no one from within opens up a secret pathway for him, he will forever have to remain on the outside. In fact, however, it turns out that he has his own fifth column within, who through their words and deeds ensure his eventual infiltration. Why such a fifth column exists in the first place is a question that remains outside the author's purview.

Amir thus places the onus for the coming of Death squarely on the shoulders of humanity, who have circumvented God's original intent to exclude that sinister figure from his blissful world. The human creature is no empty tool impotently subordinate to heavenly forces. The world is indeed split into the camps of the righteous and the wicked; the latter belong to the portion of Death, but only those who are worthy of Death are given over to him. This explains the emphasis in the book of Wisdom that God loves all his creatures, for if he had hated anything he would never have fashioned it (11:24); this contrasts with the Dead Sea Scrolls, where it is said that the wicked are hated by the Lord (1QS 3:26). But what of the author's assertion that the Canaanites' "seed was evil and their viciousness innate, and that their mode of thought would in no way vary to the end of time" (12:10–11)? The Canaanites are a special case, claims Amir, since the author is clearly referring to their condition of being accursed from the very first as specified in Gen 9:25. As for the Egyptians at the sea, where we are told that a "condign fate drew them on to this denouement and made them forget what had happened, so that they might fill in the one penalty still lacking to their torments, and that your people might accomplish an incredible journey, while their enemies might bring upon themselves a bizarre death" (19:4–5), here again, says Amir, we have a special case, since scripture specifies that God "had hardened pharaoh's heart in order to display his signs among them" (Exod 10:1). Indeed the author of the Wisdom of Solomon may have anticipated the interpretation known to us from later times from R. Simeon b. Lakish's comment on Exod 10:1 that "when God warns a man once, twice, and even a third time, and he still does not repent, then does God close his heart against repentance so that he shall exact vengeance from him for his sins" (*Exod. Rab.* 13.3). It is apparently to this that Wisdom refers when it speaks of a "condign fate" (*axia anangkē*), that is, a fate that they deserved. We must therefore fully appreciate the book of Wisdom's bold independence in defending humanity's autonomous freedom in spite of the dualistic view common to both it and the scrolls.[20]

The seductive appeal of Amir's interpretation is great, yet in spite of its neatness it seems to me to be considerably forced and to read into the text of Wisdom later concepts of which the author was probably completely unaware. Thus the term "worthy" in the literature of the ancient world often simply refers to those whom God in his infinite wisdom has chosen in advance for their respective roles of righteousness or wickedness. So Philo, for example, can write of Melchizedek: "God has not fashioned beforehand any deed of his, but produces him to begin with as such a king, peaceable and worthy of his own priesthood" (*Leg. All.* 3.79). It is easy to find inconsistencies in these ancient writings where none exists. Helmer Ringgren, for example, sees an inconsistency in 1QH 15:13–20 (cited above) inasmuch as this passage gives the impression "that the righteous have indeed been predetermined to a life according to God's will, whereas punishment befalls the wicked because they themselves have done what is evil."[21] The clause "for they walk in a way that is not good," however, is only meant to indicate that the punishment they face is appropriate to their wickedness. The question of why they were chosen for this role in the first place is not here being addressed, and when it is addressed elsewhere, the only answer given is that it is in order to demonstrate God's illimitable might and glory. From the point of view of modern style, there is undoubtedly an unclarity of expression in the passage referred to, but we must not impose modern standards on ancient writings, especially one written in the hymnic style. A similar inconsistency might be seen to exist between Wis 1:4, which implies that the recipients of Wisdom must already be righteous, and 7:27, which suggests that it is Wisdom that makes them righteous; John J. Collins, however, is undoubtedly correct when he suggests that the presence of Wisdom is simply an identifying mark of the righteous.[22] Once again these verses do not address the question of why the righteous and the wicked were chosen for their respective roles, but

20. See Y. Amir, "The Wisdom of Solomon and the Literature of Qumran," *Proceedings of the 6th World Congress of Jewish Studies* 3 (Jerusalem, 1977) 329–35 (in Hebrew); idem, "The Figure of Death in the Book of Wisdom," *JJS* 30 (1979) 154–78.

21. H. Ringgren, *The Faith of Qumran* (Philadelphia: Fortress Press, 1963) 73–74.

22. J. J. Collins, *Between Athens and Jerusalem* (New York: Crossroad, 1983) 183.

only indicate that the active presence of Wisdom in any individual is a guarantee of friendship with God and is incompatible with fraudulence and wickedness.[23] It should be clear, then, that for the author of the Wisdom of Solomon the Canaanites and the Egyptians are not special cases cited in deference to scripture. When, for example, he wishes to idealize certain biblical incidents because their straightforward presentation would mar the effect of his encomiastic account of the Israelites he has no scruples in doing so;[24] and when in 12:19–22 he seeks to derive from God's mercy toward the Egyptians and the Canaanites a model-lesson for Israel, he nonchalantly omits any reference to the Lord's hardening of pharaoh's heart, which had robbed him in that instance even of his relative freedom of choice.[25]

There is, nevertheless, in Qumran a somewhat different approach to the human condition relative to that of the book of Wisdom. As I have indicated elsewhere,[26] the sectarians of Qumran, like the Stoic philosophers, accepted the all-regulating hand of an omnipotent providence and tended to view all things from the divine perspective, thus virtually collapsing the human pole. Neither wished thereby to deny relative human freedom, but their sharp focus on the divine rather than the human pole made a harsh impression on their contemporaries. The Qumranites were prone to see human spiritual capacities as the sheer gift of divine grace. Thus, even when emphasizing a voluntary human decision, they coupled it with the notion of its complete assimilation to the will of God. The author of Wisdom, in contrast, who wished to give due emphasis to the human part of the divine-human equation, insisted on our active participation in the divine plan and the relative freedom that characterizes our ethical action. He therefore prominently displayed the human role, limited though it be, and our personal responsibility, relative as it is, in introducing Death into the cosmic order.[27]

23. Cf. Philo *Deus* 3: "For while the soul is illumined by the bright and pure rays of wisdom, through which the sage sees God and his potencies, none of the messengers of falsehood has access to the reason, but all are barred from passing the bounds which the lustral water has consecrated" (trans. Colson).

24. See Winston, *Wisdom of Solomon,* on Wis 11:4 and 16:3.

25. Ibid., 46–58, 243–44.

26. See ibid., 57.

27. As for Wisdom's extraordinarily blunt statement that God did not make Death, we may surmise that it undoubtedly signifies (as do Philo's analogous statements that God has no direct contact with the disordered primordial matter, and that we may not ascribe evil human acts to him; *Spec.* 1.329; *Opif.* 72–75) that we may not impute to him any interest in Death as a part of his primary intentionality. Evil is an indirect

For both him and the Dead Sea Scrolls, however, the ultimate mystery in which the divine scheme for humanity is shrouded remains impervious to any open challenge. What peculiarly distinguishes the position of Qumran is that according to it, the active human partnership with God involves above all the privileged position of a creature fully self-conscious and aware of the role in which it has been cast by the supreme and mysterious divine fiat. D. Dimant put it well when she wrote that in Qumran

> the emphasis has shifted from freedom of action to the mystery of knowledge. The freedom given to man is not to choose where to go but to discover where he is. This can be done only with the aid of divinely-inspired knowledge of the true meaning of the world, of man and of history. This is why the starting point is ignorance, while the final election is marked by a gift of knowledge.[28]

There appears to be an open break, however, between Qumran and the book of Wisdom with regard to the divine attitude toward the righteous and the wicked: according to Qumran, God loves the former while hating the latter; according to the Wisdom of Solomon, God loves all equally. This divergence is nonetheless more apparent than real, for it must be noted that while God has placed eternal hatred between the sons of righteousness and the sons of deceit, and while he is said to love the former, when it comes to the latter, it is only asserted that their "counsel [*sōdah*] he loathes, and all [their] ways he hates forever."[29] We may conclude, then, by saying that although the scrolls do not hypostatize Wisdom, they do, like the author of the book of Wisdom, conceive of it as both immanent and transcendent, thus following a line of thought that induces a sense of mystical intimacy with the divine. Unlike the Wisdom of Solomon, however, which emphasizes the relative autonomy of the human intellect, the scrolls tend to assimilate it fully to the divine mind.

---

consequence of God's creative activity and must therefore not be ascribed directly to him, even though he alone is its ultimate source. See D. Winston, *Logos and Mystical Theology in Philo of Alexandria* (Cincinnati: Hebrew Union College, 1985) 50.

28. D. Dimant, "Qumran Sectarian Literature," *Jewish Writings of the Second Temple Period* (ed. M. E. Stone; Assen: Van Gorcum, 1984) 538.

29. Note how carefully he avoids saying, as one would have expected, "the one he loves, the other he loathes." Moreover, even if we were to translate *sōd* as "assembly," all the text would be saying is that God hates the coming together of the wicked to plan evil.

10

WISDOM, APOCALYPTICISM, AND GENERIC COMPATIBILITY

John J. Collins

The relationship between wisdom and apocalypticism has been the subject of at least two distinct debates in recent biblical scholarship. In Hebrew Bible/Old Testament scholarship, on the one hand, the debate is associated especially with the proposal of Gerhard von Rad that "the real matrix from which apocalyptic literature originates" is wisdom.[1] While that thesis has not won acceptance, it has contributed to a tendency in the discussion to view apocalypticism as a kind of wisdom.[2] In New Testament circles, on the other hand, the focus has been on the tension between sapiential forms and apocalyptic expectations in the teaching attributed to Jesus. This debate has recently been focused on the sayings source, Q. In a paper originally published in 1964, James Robinson identified the *Gattung* of Q as *Logoi Sophon.* He commented, presumably with von Rad in mind, that the presence of apocalyptic sayings in Q was "all the more comprehensible in view of the emerging scholarly awareness that apocalypticism and wisdom, rather than being at almost mutually exclusive extremes within the spectrum of Jewish alternatives, share certain affinities and congruencies that encourage a transition from one to the other."[3] Helmut Koester, however, argued that

1. G. von Rad, *Old Testament Theology* (New York: Harper & Row, 1965) 2.306.

2. Cf. the section on "Die Weisheit der Apokalyptiker" in M. Küchler, *Frühjüdische Weisheitstraditionen* (OBO 26; Göttingen: Vandenhoeck & Ruprecht, 1979) 62–87.

3. J. M. Robinson, "LOGOI SOPHON: On the Gattung of Q," *Trajectories Through Early Christianity* (ed. J. M. Robinson and H. Koester; Philadelphia: Fortress Press, 1971) 112.

apocalyptic predictions were not part of the primitive collection and that "Q domesticated the *logoi* through a kind of apocalypticism which identified Jesus with the future Son of Man."[4] Recently John Kloppenborg has taken up these issues in his thorough redactional study of Q and argued that "the formative component in Q consisted of a group of six 'wisdom speeches' which were hortatory in nature and sapiential in their mode of argumentation."[5] The announcement of judgment and apocalyptic sayings constitute a secondary stage in the formation of Q. Kloppenborg cautiously refrained from any claims about the ultimate origin of any of the sayings,[6] but Burton Mack has drawn a controversial inference: "To notice the aphoristic quality of the sayings of Jesus and isolate an early 'sapiential' layer in their collection is to define a particular style of speech of great significance for the quest of the historical Jesus."[7] Specifically, "this turns the table on older views of Jesus as an apocalyptic preacher and brings the message of Jesus around to another style of speech altogether."[8] For Mack, evidently, wisdom and apocalypticism are, again, "almost mutually exclusive extremes," the position from which Robinson thought scholarship had moved away in 1964.

I do not propose to resolve here such complex questions as the nature of Q or the teaching of the historical Jesus, but to fill in part of the background of the discussion by sketching the relationships between sapiential and apocalyptic traditions in Jewish materials around the turn of the era, and thereby try to clarify some of the issues in the New Testament debate.

THE OLD TESTAMENT DEBATE

The view that apocalypticism was derived from wisdom had been proposed by others before von Rad, but had never won much support.[9]

4. H. Koester, "GNOMAI DIAPHOROI: The Origin and Nature of Diversification in the History of Early Christianity," in Robinson and Koester, *Trajectories through Early Christianity*, 138.

5. J. S. Kloppenborg, *The Formation of Q: Trajectories in Ancient Wisdom Collections* (Philadelphia: Fortress Press, 1987) 317.

6. Ibid, 244.

7. B. Mack, *A Myth of Innocence: Mark and Christian Origins* (Philadelphia: Fortress Press, 1988) 60.

8. Ibid., 59.

9. It was proposed already in the nineteenth century by L. Noack and H. Ewald, and in the early twentieth century by G. Hölscher. See J. M. Schmidt, *Die jüdische Apokalyptik* (Neukirchen-Vluyn: Neukirchener Verlag, 1969) 13–14, 20–21, 258–59.

Von Rad's argument was based on the discontinuity he perceived between the apocalyptic view of history and that of the prophets, but he also noted the enormous erudition of Enoch and Daniel, the interest in nature exemplified in the "Astronomical Book" of Enoch, and the fact that the putative apocalyptists were described as wise men and scribes.[10] In all of this, he drew attention to aspects of the apocalyptic literature that had been neglected, and contributed to its subsequent reassessment. So H.-P. Müller traced the roots of apocalypticism to "mantic wisdom," which was concerned with dreams and omens, but which leaves little trace in the biblical wisdom books.[11] Michael Stone studied the "lists of revealed things" in the apocalypses and concluded that such speculative concerns most probably derived from wisdom sources.[12] Again, however, he found very few parallels in the biblical wisdom books. John Gammie discussed the different kinds of dualism in the two bodies of literature.[13] Others have pointed to examples of "wisdom thinking" in 4 Ezra and *2 Baruch,* which wrestle at length with the problem of theodicy,[14] and there is demonstrable apocalyptic influence in the Wisdom of Solomon, in its formulation of the judgment of the dead.[15] Yet the differences between the apocalypses and the biblical wisdom books remain overwhelming. It would be hard to think of two books more dissimilar than Ecclesiastes and *1 Enoch.*

A fundamental flaw in von Rad's proposal lay in his failure to define his terms, or to discriminate between the different kinds of material covered by the terms "wisdom" and "apocalyptic." In the subsequent quarter of a century much ink has been spilt on the ambiguity of "apocalyptic." We have learned to distinguish between apocalypse as a literary genre and apocalypticism as a worldview, to recognize the different strands of tradition in Jewish apocalypticism, and to beware of facile inferences from literary works to social movements.[16] While there have

10. Von Rad expanded his arguments in the fourth edition of his *Theologie* (Munich: Kaiser, 1965) 316–38.

11. H.-P. Müller, "Mantische Weisheit und Apokalyptik," VTSup 22 (1972) 268–93.

12. M. E. Stone, "Lists of Revealed Things in the Apocalyptic Literature," *Magnalia Dei: The Mighty Acts of God* (ed. F. M. Cross, W. Lemke, and P. D. Miller; Garden City, N.Y.: Doubleday & Co., 1976) 414–51.

13. J. G. Gammie, "Spatial and Ethical Dualism in Jewish Wisdom and Apocalyptic Literature," *JBL* 93 (1974) 356–85.

14. M. A. Knibb, "Apocalyptic and Wisdom in 4 Ezra," *JSJ* 13 (1982) 56–74; F. J. Murphy, "Sapiential Elements in the Syriac Apocalypse of Baruch," *JQR* 77 (1986) 311–27.

15. J. J. Collins, "Cosmos and Salvation: Jewish Wisdom and Apocalyptic in the Hellenistic Age," *HR* 17 (1977) 121–42.

16. See my essay "Genre, Ideology and Social Movements in Jewish Apocalypti-

also been important studies of wisdom in this period, not least by von Rad himself,[17] there has been less attention to the problems of ambiguity and definition. A volume edited by John Gammie and Leo Perdue ranges from Egypt and Mesopotamia in the second millennium to the Hellenistic period and beyond.[18] It provides the most compendious view of "wisdom" yet available. Thereby it also poses the question of coherence and variation within this vast corpus and highlights the need for a typology.

For our present purposes, it will be helpful to distinguish five broad types of sapiential material:[19]

1. wisdom sayings (*Spruchweisheit*, including aphorisms and more developed instructions and admonitions) such as we find in Proverbs 10–30;[20]

2. theological wisdom, including both speculative passages such as Proverbs 8 and reflections on theodicy (such as the entire book of Job);

3. nature wisdom, exemplified in Job 28, 38–41;

4. mantic wisdom (divination and dream interpretation); and

5. higher wisdom through revelation, including apocalyptic revelations.[21]

While these types are not mutually exclusive, and the first three are intermingled in the biblical wisdom books, they are, nonetheless, distinct. To say that apocalypticism is an example of wisdom by revelation (type 5) or is influenced by mantic wisdom (type 4) does not imply any neces-

---

cism," *Mysteries and Revelations: Apocalyptic Studies Since the Uppsala Colloquium* (ed. J. J. Collins and J. H. Charlesworth; JSPSup 9; Sheffield: JSOT Press, 1991) 11–32.

17. G. von Rad, *Wisdom in Israel* (Nashville: Abingdon Press, 1972).

18. J. Gammie and L. Perdue, eds., *The Sage in Israel and the Ancient Near East* (Winona Lake, Ind.: Eisenbrauns, 1990).

19. I am building here on the threefold typology of nature wisdom, practical wisdom, and theological wisdom proposed by J. Crenshaw ("Method in Determining Wisdom Influence Upon 'Historical' Literature," *JBL* 88 [1969] 132).

20. On this material see C. R. Fontaine, *Traditional Sayings in the Old Testament: A Contextual Study* (Bible and Literature 5; Sheffield: Almond Press, 1982); C. Westermann, *Wurzeln der Weisheit* (Göttingen: Vandenhoeck & Ruprecht, 1990).

21. For this category see M. Hengel, *Judaism and Hellenism* (Philadelphia: Fortress Press, 1974) 1.202–18.

sary connection between apocalypticism and the experiential wisdom of Proverbs.

It is also necessary to distinguish between the literary forms of wisdom and a sapiential worldview, if such a thing there be.

In his excellent introduction to Old Testament wisdom, James Crenshaw suggests that wisdom involves "a marriage between form and content." He argues: "Formally wisdom consists of proverbial sentence or instruction, debate, intellectual reflection; thematically, wisdom comprises self-evident intuitions about mastering life for human betterment, gropings after life's secrets with regard to innocent suffering, grappling with finitude, and quest for truth concealed in the created order and manifested in Dame Wisdom." He suggests that "wisdom is a particular attitude toward reality, a world view." The worldview consists in a way of looking at things that "begins with humans as the fundamental point of orientation. It asks what is good for men and women. And it believes that all essential answers can be learned in experience, pregnant with signs about reality itself."[22] It is, I think, apparent that Crenshaw has only the biblical wisdom books in mind in all of this and is not reckoning with mantic wisdom or with the higher wisdom through revelation of the Hellenistic period. His usage, however, is typical of Old Testament scholarship, and he is certainly right that the wisdom books of the Hebrew Bible share a worldview as well as particular literary forms. This worldview involves more than a point of orientation. It also involves a set of assumptions about the universe. It affirms a world where there is an organic connection between cause and effect; where human fulfillment, such as it is, is to be found in this life; and where wisdom can be attained from accumulated experience without recourse to special revelations. (The relationship of the book of Job to this worldview is complex, but that need not detain us here.)

Whether this worldview was distinctive in ancient Israel is open to question. Roland Murphy maintains that "the sapiential understanding of reality was shared by all Israelites; it was not a mode of thinking that belonged to only one class."[23] So, "it should come as no surprise that Isaiah, or any other prophet should use a parable. But Isaiah is not

22. J. L. Crenshaw, *Old Testament Wisdom: An Introduction* (Atlanta: John Knox Press, 1981) 19, 17, 18.

23. R. E. Murphy, *The Wisdom Literature: Job, Proverbs, Ruth, Canticles, Ecclesiastes and Esther* (Forms of Old Testament Literature 13; Grand Rapids, Mich.: Wm. B. Eerdmans Publishing Co., 1981) 3.

to be classified among the sages." Two observations about the wisdom tradition may help shed light on this situation. First, in the context of the Hebrew Bible, wisdom is often defined negatively: it is marked by its lack of explicit appeal to the specific revelatory traditions of Israel. Nonetheless, the sapiential worldview is also shared by other traditions, as Murphy observes, because they all draw on the common fund of human experience. Second, while the sages occasionally appeal to personal experience, the wisdom books are, for the most part, compendia of traditional opinions. The strategy of the sages is well articulated by Bildad, in Job 8:8–10:

> For inquire, I pray you, of bygone ages,
> and consider what the fathers have found;
> for we are but of yesterday, and know nothing,
> for our days on earth are a shadow.[24]

The sages do not aspire to originality. Rather they reflect the consensus of their culture and pass on the commonly accepted assumptions about reality. The biblical wisdom books do not give us the full range of ancient Israelite ideas about reality. They pay little attention to mythological beliefs, although the author of Job, at least, was familiar with them. It is reasonable to believe, however, that what they give us was widely shared in Israelite society.

The question arises, however, whether the characteristic forms of wisdom literature were necessarily wedded to that worldview, and this question is crucial for the relation between biblical wisdom and apocalypticism. The apocalyptic literature that first appears in the Hellenistic period introduces a view of the world that is sharply at variance not only with the biblical wisdom books, but with the Hebrew Bible as a whole.[25] This new worldview is distinguished primarily by the increased importance attached to supernatural agents and a world beyond this one, and by the hope for judgment and vindication beyond death. Of course, belief in the supernatural world was commonplace in antiquity. What was novel was the degree to which this world was thought to impinge on human affairs and to which human beings were viewed as having access to it.

24. Bible translations throughout this essay are from the RSV.

25. See J. J. Collins, "The Place of Apocalypticism in the Religion of Israel," *Ancient Israelite Religion: Essays in Honor of Frank Moore Cross* (ed. P. D. Miller, P. D. Hanson, and S. D. McBride; Philadelphia: Fortress Press, 1987) 539–58.

The new worldview is depicted most vividly in *1 Enoch.* Here we find that (1) the earth is corrupt and in need of cleansing; (2) the corruption is due, not just to human sin, but to the irruption of fallen angels; (3) we are assured that this condition is not final, because Enoch has had access to the divine throne and seen the heavenly tablets; and (4) his revelations include the final judgment both of this world and of the fallen Watchers, and also the abodes of the dead where individuals await justice.[26]

The book of Daniel, too, though written in a more traditional biblical idiom, has a similar view of the world. The earth is overrun by the beasts from the sea or is governed by the rebellious angelic princes of Persia and Greece. Daniel too sees the divine throne and is assured of coming judgment and of the resurrection of the dead.

The worldview of these early apocalypses may be contrasted with that of the biblical wisdom books in three crucial respects: (1) the increased importance of the supernatural world and supernatural agents in human affairs; this is reflected even in the literary form of the apocalypses, where angelic mediators play an essential role; (2) the expectation of eschatological judgment and reward or punishment beyond death; and (3) the perception that something is fundamentally wrong with this world. The latter is often described in modern scholarship as a sense of anomie, and such a description is well justified in the case of *1 Enoch* or Daniel, or in the Qumran texts that speak of a reign of Belial. Two qualifications are in order, however. First, the anomie is never total: *1 Enoch* in fact devotes considerable space to affirming the order of the cosmos (e.g., the "Astronomical Book," chaps. 72–82, and the "Book of the Watchers," chaps. 2–5). Second, the problem is not always portrayed in extreme cosmic imagery. In works like 4 Ezra and *2 Baruch* the fundamental problem is the fate of Israel. Of course the sages too could find this world less than satisfactory on occasion — witness the pessimism of Qoheleth. In apocalypticism, however, the sense that something is wrong with this world is sharpened by the expectation of eschatological judgment.

The contrast in worldview between apocalypticism and traditional wisdom is most sharply drawn in the wisdom books from about the time when apocalypticism was emerging. The ironic question of Agur,

26. On the worldview of *1 Enoch,* see further G. W. Nickelsburg, "The Apocalyptic Construction of Reality in 1 Enoch," in Collins and Charlesworth, *Mysteries and Revelations,* 51–64.

"Who has ascended to heaven and come down?" (Prov 30:4), was probably too early to constitute a polemic against the claims made for Enoch. On the other hand, when Qoheleth asks, "Who knows whether the spirit of man goes upward and the spirit of the beast goes down to the earth?" (Qoh 3:21), it is quite possible that he is polemicizing against the apocalyptic claims of life beyond death. Ben Sira, who was surely familiar with early apocalyptic speculation, unequivocally rejected it:[27]

> A man of no understanding has vain and false hopes,
> and dreams give wings to fools.
> As one who catches at a shadow and pursues the wind,
> so is he who gives heed to dreams. . . .
> Unless they are sent from the Most High as a visitation,
> do not give your mind to them.
> For dreams have deceived many,
> and those who put their hope in them have failed.
> Without such deceptions the law will be fulfilled,
> and wisdom is made perfect from truthful lips. (34:1–8)

Granted the escape clause, that dreams may be sent from the Most High on occasion, it is clear that Sirach is not favorably disposed to apocalyptic revelations. He is equally blunt on the question of afterlife: "Whether life is for ten or a hundred or a thousand years, there is no inquiry about it in Hades" (41:4).

Yet Sirach is a transitional figure in the history of Jewish wisdom. He is the first sage to find room for the biblical history, and the special place of Israel, in his worldview.[28] The fathers whom he praises are the patriarchs and heroes of biblical history. Even Enoch finds a place, though not as a source of revelation. Moreover, "the wisdom of all the ancients" includes prophecies, and preeminently the law of the Most High (39:1–2). Even the prayer in chap. 36, which is without parallel in the wisdom books of the Hebrew Bible in its nationalistic fervor and expectation of divine intervention, is not inconceivable on the lips of Sirach, steeped as he is in the biblical tradition, although it is also without

27. J. D. Martin ("Ben Sira — Child of His Time," *A Word in Season: Essays in Honour of William McKane* [ed. J. D. Martin and P. R. Davies; JSOTSup 42; Sheffield: JSOT Press, 1986] 141–61) labors to establish affinities between Sirach and apocalyptic literature with regard to the order of the cosmos and the use of history, but he lacks any criteria to assess the significance of the very general similarities he finds. Also D. E. Orton (*The Understanding Scribe: Matthew and the Apocalyptic Ideal* [JSNTSup 25; Sheffield: JSOT Press, 1989] 101, 224) overlooks the differences between Sirach and the apocalypses.

28. B. L. Mack, *Wisdom and the Hebrew Epic* (Chicago: University of Chicago Press, 1985).

parallel in his book.[29] In short, while Sirach was skeptical of ideas that were novel in his day, he illustrates the fact that the wisdom tradition could expand to take account of a wide range of traditional material.

In the period after the Maccabean revolt, apocalyptic literature won increasing acceptance in Judaism. Daniel is cited as authoritative scripture at Qumran,[30] and its authority is assumed in the New Testament and in Josephus. The belief in resurrection, one of the trademarks of the apocalypses, was taken up by the Pharisees. It is not surprising, then, that we find various combinations and permutations of sapiential and apocalyptic material in the so-called intertestamental literature. Leaving aside the mantic and revelatory kinds of wisdom that are intrinsically related to apocalypticism, we note that both nature wisdom and theological wisdom are used in apocalyptic contexts in various ways.[31] So the readers of *1 Enoch* are invited to contemplate the regularity of heaven and earth (chaps. 2–5). One of the earliest Enoch books, the "Astronomical Book," is an extended treatise on the regularity of the heavenly bodies, and such nature wisdom seems to have been a primary interest of the early Enoch movement. It is characteristic of apocalyptic literature, however, that the order of nature is flawed. In *1 Enoch* 5 the regularity of nature is a foil for human rebellion, while the "Astronomical Book" concludes with a prediction of how "in the days of the sinners the years will become shorter." The natural wisdom does not finally determine the worldview. The most important wisdom imparted by Enoch is derived from what he has seen on the heavenly tablets and is shown by angels. Even the order of the heavens is revealed by an angel.[32]

Again, the dialogues in 4 Ezra might be viewed as examples of deliberative theological wisdom, pondering the problem of theodicy. The solution to that problem, however, is given in the apocalyptic visions in the second half of the book. The sapiential elements are put in the new context of the apocalyptic worldview.

Sapiential sayings can also find a place in an apocalyptic context,

29. The authenticity of the prayer is disputed. It is assumed by some commentators (most recently A. A. Di Lella, *The Wisdom of Ben Sira* [AB 39; Garden City, N.Y.: Doubleday, 1987] 420), but rejected by T. Middendorp, *Die Stellung Jesu ben Siras zwischen Judentum und Hellenismus* (Leiden: E. J. Brill, 1973) 113, 125; and Mack, *Wisdom*, 200.

30. 4QFlor 2:3: "as is written in the book of Daniel the prophet."

31. See Collins, "Cosmos and Salvation," 121–42.

32. So also in *2 Enoch*, where Enoch is given extensive cosmological revelations in chaps. 23–33.

and it is on this material that I wish to focus here, both because this material is most commonly associated with the worldview of biblical wisdom, and because it is the kind of wisdom at issue in the New Testament debate about wisdom and apocalypticism.

SAPIENTIAL SAYINGS AND APOCALYPTICISM

Wisdom sayings are of various kinds. What they have in common is the attempt to express a general truth in a concise way. At the most fundamental level we can distinguish between declarative sayings, in the indicative, and commands and prohibitions, in the imperative.[33] On a more developed level there is a corresponding distinction between sayings collections (e.g., Proverbs 10–21), on the one hand, and instructions or admonitions, on the other. Collections of declarative sayings are never found in the apocalypses. There is an apparent ideological reason for this. Sayings, as we find them in Proverbs, draw on human experience and observation as their source of wisdom. Apocalypses are oriented toward supernatural revelation. It would be rash to conclude that declarative sayings could not be adapted to an apocalyptic worldview, but the apocalypse as a literary genre has a different way of presenting reality. Insofar as it purports to describe the unique experiences of the visionary it does not lend itself to the formulation of general proverbial truths.

There is, however, a place for instructions and admonitions in the apocalypses, and these sometimes have a sapiential character.[34] Both apocalyptic and wisdom literature aim to influence the behavior of the readers by instilling a view of the world. In the wisdom literature the implications are regularly filled out in instructions that freely use imperatives and prohibitions. In the apocalyptic literature the instruction is often left implicit. (E.g., when the wise in Daniel 11 instruct the *rabbîm*, the instruction is not narrated but can be inferred from the context.) There are, however, a few instances where the instruction is spelled out.

33. Murphy, *Wisdom Literature*, 4–6. See also Crenshaw, "Wisdom," *Old Testament Form Criticism* (ed. J. H. Hayes; San Antonio: Trinity University Press, 1974) 225–64.

34. This point has been noted on occasion, e.g., U. Wilckens, "Sophia," *TDNT* (1971) 7.503; Küchler, *Frühjüdische Weisheitstraditionen*, 81–84; and J. S. Kloppenborg, "Symbolic Eschatology and the Apocalypticism of Q," *HTR* 80 (1987) 290. Robinson lists "The Words of Enoch the Righteous" (*1 Enoch*) and the *Testaments of the Twelve Patriarchs* as examples of *Logoi Sophon* ("LOGOI SOPHON," 106–9). Also R. A. Piper, *Wisdom in the Q-tradition* (SNTSMS 61; Cambridge: Cambridge University Press, 1989) 8, who dismisses the apocalyptic material too quickly.

Perhaps the clearest use of a sapiential instruction in an apocalyptic context is found in the second Sibylline Oracle.[35] This is a Christian adaptation of a Jewish oracle, probably from the second century CE. The Jewish oracle was organized around the familiar Sibylline schema of ten generations. At the end of the description of the tenth generation, the Christian redactor inserted a passage about "a great contest for entry to the heavenly city. It will be universal for all men, holding the glory of immortality" (2:39–55). At this point there is inserted a lengthy extract from the sayings of Pseudo-Phocylides. This is known independently as a Hellenistic Jewish gnomologion, in the tradition of Greek gnomologia but very similar in theme to traditional Jewish wisdom.[36] At the end of the extract the Sibyllist resumes, "This is the contest, these are the prizes, these the awards..." (2:149). The extract from Pseudo-Phocylides is evidently meant to supply the rules for the contest, the criteria for the apocalyptic judgment.

This Sibylline Oracle is exceptional in several respects. It is the only case where we find an extensive quotation from a known sapiential text in an apocalyptic context. The usage, then, is blatantly secondary. Moreover, the sentences are inserted intact and not redacted. (There are a few omissions.) There is none of the eschatological urgency here that scholars usually identify in the sayings of Jesus. Rather we find the typical sapiential ethic of moderation: "Do not gain wealth unjustly, but live from legitimate things" (v. 56); "do not damage your mind with wine or drink to excess" (v. 95). There are echoes of biblical texts, including the Ten Commandments (vv. 58, 60, 64, 73). The sayings represent everyday wisdom and are not materially altered by their new context. While this text is exceptional in many respects, it may serve as a warning that ancient writers could sometimes juxtapose materials that seem ideologically incompatible to us.

Our second example is more in the mainstream of Jewish apocalypticism. The "Epistle of Enoch" (*1 Enoch* 91–104) is the last major section of the collection we know as *1 Enoch*. This document was customarily dated to the early first century BCE, but opinion has recently shifted in favor of a date before the Maccabean revolt.[37] A major factor in the dispute about the date concerns the unity of the composition. Those

35. J. J. Collins, "The Sibylline Oracles," *OTP* 1.345–53.

36. P. W. van der Horst, *The Sentences of Pseudo-Phocylides* (SVTP 4; Leiden: E. J. Brill, 1978).

37. See J. J. Collins, *The Apocalyptic Imagination* (New York: Crossroad, 1984) 52–53.

who favor the later date assume that the "Apocalypse of Weeks" is an independent composition, secondarily imbedded in the epistle. This assumption has been challenged in light of the Aramaic fragments from Qumran. While the apocalypse is formally distinct, there is no good evidence that it ever circulated independently, outside of its present context.

The affinity of the epistle with wisdom instructions is apparent from the exordium: "Hear, my children, all the words of your father, and listen properly to the voice of my mouth" (91:3). The ensuing instruction distinguishes repeatedly between the wise and the foolish. The typical form consists of an exhortation or admonition, followed by a short motivation clause (e.g., 94:1: "And now I say to you, my children, love righteousness and walk in it; for the paths of righteousness are worthy of acceptance, but the paths of iniquity will quickly be destroyed and vanish"). The most typical form of admonition is the woe (e.g., 96:8: "Woe to you, you powerful, who through power oppress the righteous, for the day of your destruction will come").[38] In the context of the Hebrew Bible, such woes are more typical of prophetic than of sapiential literature, but it has been argued that this form of expression (like the corresponding beatitude) was originally developed in wisdom settings.[39] The woe-form is attested in Sir 2:12–14; 41:8–9.[40]

The subject matter of Enoch's instruction is quite traditional and is primarily concerned with the exploitation of the poor by the rich. It differs from other sapiential instructions in two respects. First, the authority to which he lays claim derives from his knowledge of the heavenly tablets. His utterances, therefore, have the quality of revelation and give his instruction a prophetic as well as a sapiential tone. Second, the primary motivating factor is the expectation of judgment and the assurance for the righteous that they "will shine like the lights of heaven and will be seen, and the gate of heaven will be opened to you" (104:2). As a corollary of this, it is a premise of the apocalyptic worldview that earthly wealth is fleeting, and this conviction strengthens the woes against the wicked. Unlike the sayings of Pseudo-Phocylides

38. See the form-critical analysis by G. W. Nickelsburg, "The Apocalyptic Message of 1 Enoch 92–105," *CBQ* 39 (1977) 309–43.

39. E. Gerstenberger, "The Woe-Oracles of the Prophets," *JBL* 81 (1962) 249–64; J. W. Whedbee, *Isaiah and Wisdom* (Nashville: Abingdon Press, 1971) 80–110.

40. Nickelsburg ("Apocalyptic Message," 327) notes that the "Say not . . ." refutation form also occurs both in the epistle and in Ben Sira.

in the second Sibylline Oracle, the words of Enoch are thoroughly permeated with an apocalyptic worldview.

A third example of a sapiential instruction in an apocalyptic text is found in *2 Enoch,* a work of disputed origin that is most often ascribed to the Egyptian diaspora in the first century CE.[41] After his tour of the heavens, Enoch is given thirty days to instruct his sons, before he is finally taken from them. His instruction is found in chaps. 39–66. It begins in typical sapiential style: "Give heed my children to the admonition of your father. . . ." The instruction includes an account of what Enoch has learned in the heavens, but is chiefly given over to ethical exhortation. Especially notable is the use of macarisms and curses (42:6–14; 52:1–15). These are often reminiscent of traditional wisdom: "Happy is he who turns aside from the path of change and walks in the right paths!" (42:10; cf. Prov 4:11); "happy is he who sows right seed, for he shall harvest it sevenfold" (42:11; cf. Job 4:8; Prov 22:8). Moreover, they show the kind of universal humanist ethic usually associated with Near Eastern wisdom: "[Happy is he who] clothes the naked with a garment and to the hungry gives his bread! Happy is he who judges righteous judgment for orphan and widow" (42:8–9); "whoever insults a person's face insults the face of the Lord; whoever treats a person's face with repugnance treats the face of the Lord with repugnance" (44:2; cf. Prov 14:31); "happy is he who glorifies all the works of the Lord. Cursed is he who insults the creatures of the Lord" (52:5–6; cf. Sir 39:14–16); "happy is he who preserves the foundations of the fathers where they have been made sure. Cursed is he who destroys the rules and restrictions of the fathers" (52:9–10).

Unlike the sayings of Pseudo-Phocylides in the second Sibylline Oracle, however, the instructions of Enoch are integrally related to their context. In his heavenly journey, Enoch was shown the order of creation, and this is the basis of his ethical teaching: "The Lord with his own two hands created mankind; and in a facsimile of his own face. Small and great the Lord created" (44:1). But it is also reinforced by the prospect of a final judgment: "Because on the day of the great judgment every deed of mankind will be restored by means of the written record. Happy is he whose measure will prove to be just and whose weight just and scales just! Because on the day of the great judgment every measure

41. See Collins, *Apocalyptic Imagination,* 195–98; F. I. Andersen, "2 (Slavonic Apocalypse of) Enoch," *OTP* 1.91–221. Quotations here are from Andersen's translation.

and every weight and every scale will be exposed as in the market; and each one will recognize his measure and, according to measure, each shall receive his reward" (44:5). And again: "All this will make itself known in the scales in the book on the great judgment day" (52:15). The apocalyptic revelation provides a framework for the sapiential ethics, but does not materially change them in any obvious way.

Both the "Epistle of Enoch" and the instructions in *2 Enoch* have something of the character of testaments insofar as they are presented as deathbed addresses by Enoch to his sons. The testament as a literary form was most fully developed in the *Testaments of the Twelve Patriarchs.* The provenance of this document is notoriously difficult.[42] Our present interest is in the way in which the testaments, in their extant form, are structured. While the structure is not fully consistent in all twelve testaments, the following pattern is typical: (1) the patriarch addresses his sons; (2) he recalls an episode from his life; (3) he delivers an extended ethical exhortation; (4) there is a prediction, with an eschatological dimension; and (5) the testament concludes with the death and burial of the patriarch.[43]

The area of affinity between these testaments and the wisdom literature is obviously the ethical exhortation. As H. W. Hollander and M. de Jonge have shown, "The scholar who studies the ethical passages of the Testaments and looks for parallels will find them in the Septuagint, particularly in Eccl, Prov and Sir, and to a lesser extent, in WisSol and 4Mac."[44] Eckhard von Nordheim has even argued that the genre should be understood as an adaptation of the Near Eastern wisdom instruction/admonition.[45] The context of a father instructing his sons and the appeal to his own experience are typical sapiential motifs. Yet here again we find rather typical sapiential material embedded in a worldview that is typically apocalyptic.

The point may be illustrated from the *Testament of Dan.* In the opening chapter Dan recalls an episode from his youth, confessing that "in

42. See my review of the debate, "Testaments," *Jewish Writings of the Second Temple Period* (ed. M. E. Stone; CRINT 2/2; Philadelphia: Fortress Press, 1984) 325–55.

43. Compare E. von Nordheim, *Die Lehre der Alten,* vol. 1: *Das Testament als Literaturgattung im Judentum der Hellenistisch-Römischen Zeit* (Leiden: E. J. Brill, 1980) 228.

44. H. W. Hollander and M. de Jonge, *The Testaments of the Twelve Patriarchs: A Commentary* (SVTP 8; Leiden: E. J. Brill, 1985) 43.

45. Von Nordheim, *Die Lehre der Alten,* 1.239–40; and idem, *Die Lehre der Alten,* vol. 2: *Das Testament als Literaturgattung im Alten Testament und im Alten Vorderen Orient* (Leiden: E. J. Brill, 1985).

my heart I rejoiced concerning the death of Joseph, a true and good man, and that I took pleasure in the selling of Joseph, because father loved him more than us. For the spirit of jealousy and vainglory said to me: you also are his son" (1:4–6). While he does not evade responsibility for his crime, there was another factor at work: "One of the spirits of Beliar conspired with me." Dan proceeds to warn his children against the blinding force of anger and against lying. Such a warning is commonplace in the wisdom tradition, but here it is given with a metaphysical backdrop: "A twofold mischief is anger with lying, and they assist one another in order to disturb the mind; and when the soul is disturbed continually, the Lord departs from it and Beliar rules over it" (4:7). Finally Dan turns to predict the future: "In the last days you will depart from the Lord and be wroth with Levi and fight against Judah." The reason for their rebellion: "I have read in the book of Enoch, the righteous one, that your prince is Satan." So they will be led into captivity, but "when you return to the Lord you will obtain mercy." Then "there will arise unto you from the tribe of Judah and Levi the salvation of the Lord, and he will make war against Beliar and he will give a victorious vengeance to our fathers."

Whether the testament in its extant form is of Jewish or Christian origin, the manner in which sapiential and apocalyptic elements are combined is of interest. The ethical teaching of the testament is sapiential, undergirded by the experience of the patriarch. That experience, however, is understood in the light of the apocalyptic worldview. So sin is not solely of human making, but results from the prompting of Beliar. Moreover, the exhortation is strengthened by the eschatological prediction. There is a goal in view (the restoration of Israel) and an assurance that a savior will defeat Beliar. The wisdom tradition provides the ethical focus of the testament; the apocalyptic tradition provides the explanatory frame, the larger context of meaning.

APOCALYPTIC INFLUENCE IN WISDOM TEXTS

Our examples thus far have concerned the use of sapiential instructions in apocalyptic texts. We must also ask whether the wisdom instruction, as a free-standing genre, was at all affected by the apocalyptic worldview. In fact, there are very few examples of free-standing Jewish wisdom instructions from the period between Ben Sira and the Mishna. The fragmentary examples that have been published from

Qumran are quite traditional and may in any case be older compositions.[46] The lengthy admonition in the Damascus Document is thoroughly apocalyptic in perspective, but this of course is part of a larger, covenantal document.[47] The sayings of Pseudo-Phocylides and Pseudo-Menander, from the Egyptian diaspora, are also unaffected by apocalypticism.[48] (Pseudo-Phocylides expresses a belief in afterlife [vv. 103–4] but does so in Hellenistic terms without reference to a judgment.)[49]

Recently, however, Klaus Berger has resurrected a Hebrew wisdom text from the Cairo Geniza, which was originally published at the beginning of the century and is of considerable interest for our purposes.[50] Berger has argued for a date about the end of the first century CE. His arguments on this point have been sharply and effectively criticized by Hans-Peter Rüger, who makes a more plausible case for a medieval date.[51] The interest of the text, however, is to some extent independent of its date, as it raises the question of the relationship between worldview and genre in a Jewish wisdom text.

In many ways this text resembles Ben Sira, with frequent exhortations to love wisdom and avoid folly. The exhortation is rather general

46. 4Q 184, 185. Küchler, *Frühjüdische Weisheitstraditionen,* 102–5; H. Lichtenberger, "Eine weisheitliche Mahnrede in den Qumranfunden (4Q 185)," *Qumran: Sa piete, sa theologie et son milieu* (ed. M. Delcor; Louvain: Louvain University Press, 1978) 151–62; T. H. Tobin, "4Q185 and Jewish Wisdom Literature," *Of Scribes and Scrolls: Studies on the Hebrew Bible, Intertestamental Judaism and Christian Origins Presented to John Strugnell* (ed. H. W. Attridge et al.; Lanham, Md.: University Press of America, 1990) 145–52. For a wisdom admonition with possible eschatological overtones, see C. A. Newsom, "4Q370: An Admonition Based on the Flood," *RevQ* 49–52 (1988) 23–43. In view of the fragmentary nature of this document, however, it is difficult to discern its genre. After this article had gone to press, important new wisdom texts from Qumran became available, which shed new light on the interrelationship between wisdom and apocalypticism in the Hellenistic period. See Torlief Elgoin, "Admonition Texts from Qumran Cave Four," forthcoming in the Proceedings of the New York Conference on the Dead Sea Scrolls, in the *Annals of the New York Academy of Sciences.*

47. On the genre of the Damascus Document see P. R. Davies, *The Damascus Covenant* (JSOTSup 25; Sheffield: JSOT, 1983) 48–55. On its apocalyptic perspective, J. J. Collins, "Was the Dead Sea Sect an Apocalyptic Community?" *Archeology and History in the Dead Sea Scrolls* (ed. L. H. Schiffmann; JSPSup 8; Sheffield: JSOT, 1990) 25–51.

48. Küchler, *Frühjüdische Weisheitstraditionen,* 303–18.

49. Van der Horst, *Sentences of Pseudo-Phocylides,* 185–88.

50. K. Berger, *Die Weisheitsschrift aus der Kairoer Geniza: Erstedition, Kommentar und Übersetzung* (Tübingen: Franke, 1989). Cf. S. Schechter, "Genizah Fragments," *JQR* 16 (1904) 425–42.

51. H.-P. Rüger, *Die Weisheitsschrift aus der Kairoer Geniza* (WUNT 53; Tübingen: J. C. B. Mohr [Paul Siebeck], 1991) 1–19. While Berger had only collected early parallels, Rüger shows that later ones can also be found, and that some linguistic forms also point to a medieval date.

and abstract. Many traditional sapiential themes, such as wealth and poverty and family relations, are lacking. There are, however, admonitions against wine and strong drink, and a general disparagement of bodily satisfaction. The text is informed by a strong dualism in two senses. On the one hand, there is an antithesis of body and spirit: those who occupy themselves with building up their bodies will destroy their spirits and souls (1:8). On the other hand, this world stands over against the world to come. The skepticism of Ecclesiastes is accepted as valid for this world, but is corrected in light of the eschatological future. This world is folly; the next world is gain (1:4). Whoever seeks the world to come despises this world (3:5–6). No one can enjoy both. Those who satisfy their desires for food and drink and unchastity and deny the world to come are fools, while those who fear God do not love this world (4:11–13). Berger maintains that this document provides the closest extant parallel to the Instruction of the Two Spirits at Qumran, but it pays little attention to metaphysical powers. It does, however, outline two sharply conflicting ways, in a manner reminiscent of 1QS or of the Johannine literature. The way of folly is marked by pride and pleasure in this world; the way of the wise by humility and grief over the destruction of Jerusalem (4:1–2, 6; cf. 6:7–13). Life is under the shadow of an impending judgment: "Those who despise wisdom and the fear of God — what will they do on the last day?" (6:13).

The importance of this text for our purpose is that it shows that the traditional form of the wisdom instruction could be adapted to an apocalyptic worldview, similar to what we find at Qumran, although examples of such adaptation are rare. The form of sapiential sayings is not necessarily tied to a this-worldly ideology such as we find in Proverbs. The forms of wisdom speech are adaptable and may be used in the service of more than one worldview.

THE NEW TESTAMENT DEBATE

I return now to John Kloppenborg's thesis that "the formative component in Q consisted of a group of six 'wisdom speeches' which were hortatory in nature and sapiential in their mode of argumentation."[52] Kloppenborg's position rests on extensive redaction-critical argumentation, which is of necessity hypothetical. Such arguments are seldom

52. Kloppenborg, *Formation of Q*, 317.

definitive, and I doubt that Kloppenborg has had the last word on Q,[53] but for the present we can take his reconstruction to focus the discussion and to ask whether this view of the Jesus tradition necessarily "turns the table on older views of Jesus as an apocalyptic preacher" to the degree that Burton Mack suggests.

It should be clear from our discussion thus far that there is no necessary antithesis between "apocalyptic" and "sapiential." For the significance of the distinction, two questions are crucial: (1) What kind of wisdom is involved? and (2) What determines the worldview in the speeches in question?

Kloppenborg's formal analysis of the speeches makes clear that the dominant form is the admonition, usually in the imperative with a motivating clause.[54] The inaugural sermon begins with a series of beatitudes. Only once, in 6:43–45, do we find a cluster of declarative wisdom sayings ("For each tree is known by its own fruit. For figs are not gathered from thorns, nor are grapes picked from a bramble bush"). Such aphorisms, based on the observation of nature, are conspicuously lacking in the apocalypses, but they have a minor role here too. In contrast, there are good apocalyptic parallels for the beatitudes (e.g., *2 Enoch* 42:6–14; 52:1–15) and especially for the curses that follow them in Luke 6 (cf. the "Epistle of Enoch").[55] Admonitions, as such, are quite compatible with an apocalyptic context.

It is not easy to determine the worldview of the speeches as reconstructed by Kloppenborg. On the one hand, he defines these speeches by the lack of explicit apocalyptic elements (even the promise of reward in heaven in 6:22–23 is excised as secondary). On the other hand, several sayings can easily be taken to imply an apocalyptic context, and indeed are so taken in the tradition. These include the opening beatitudes, which surely imply a scenario of eschatological reversal. Kloppenborg contrasts the Q beatitudes with both sapiential beatitudes and the majority of those found in apocalyptic books because they do not function

53. See the review by A. Yarbro Collins in *CBQ* 50 (1988) 720–22. Also her article, "The Son of Man Sayings in the Sayings Source," *To Touch the Text: Biblical and Related Studies in Honor of Joseph A. Fitzmyer* (ed. P. Kobelski and M. Horgan; New York: Crossroad, 1989) 369–89.

54. Kloppenborg, *Formation of Q*, 342–45.

55. H. D. Betz, *Essays on the Sermon on the Mount* (Philadelphia: Fortress Press, 1985) 28: "In the field of Jewish literature, the type of religious macarism is encountered chiefly in apocalyptic writings." For use of beatitudes in a wisdom text see now 4QBeat and E. Puech, "Un Hymne Essénien en partie retrouvé et les Béatitudes," *RevQ* 49–52 (1988) 59–88.

as conditions of salvation or admonitions as to how one should act, but "pronounce blessing on a group defined by social and economic circumstances."[56] The "woes" in the "Epistle of Enoch," however, function in a precisely corresponding way: they pronounce woe on a group defined by social and economic circumstances (*1 Enoch* 94:8: "Woe to you, you rich . . . "). In both cases an impending reversal is presupposed. While Luke 17:33/Matt 10:39 ("Whoever loses his life will preserve it"), which Kloppenborg places at the end of the sapiential speeches, is open to more than one interpretation, it makes excellent sense in an apocalyptic context. In sum, the worldview of these wisdom speeches depends on the wider context in which they are read, and so it does not appear to me that Kloppenborg's stratification of the Q tradition necessarily "turns the tables" on the view that Jesus was an apocalyptic prophet.

The context provided by the Q document as a whole has, at the least, considerable apocalyptic features. To quote Kloppenborg:

> Q's perspective is framed both spatially by transcendent realities — heaven (6:23; 12:33), hell or Hades (10:5; 12:5), Sophia (7:35; 11:49), the Son of Man (12:8–9, 10, 40 etc.), angels (12:8–9), demons (11:14–26), and the devil (4:1–13) — and temporally by the coming judgment (3:7–9; 10:13–15; 11:31–32; 22:29–30), the destruction of the impenitent at the Parousia (3:17; 17:26–30) and the eschatological meal in the kingdom (13:28–29; cf. 14:16–24). Consistent with apocalyptic idiom, the Parousia marks an abrupt termination of the present age.[57]

In view of this description, it is not surprising that Norman Perrin could take Q as a prime illustration of early Christian apocalypticism.[58]

Kloppenborg, however, resists this conclusion. He admits that "it is difficult to miss the pervasive eschatological tenor" of the wisdom elements in Q, but questions whether the term "apocalyptic" is an accurate characterization of them.[59] He claims that two observations are crucial: "First, much of the specialized vocabulary of apocalypticism and even some of its central presuppositions are absent from large portions of Q. And second, in those sections which do reflect apocalyptic idiom, the restraint and high degree of selectivity in Q's use of apocalyptic language and assumptions are striking, and require some explanation."[60]

56. Kloppenborg, *Formation of Q*, 188.
57. Kloppenborg, "Symbolic Eschatology," 296.
58. N. Perrin and D. C. Duling, *The New Testament: An Introduction* (2d ed.; New York: Harcourt Brace Jovanovich, 1982) 100–107.
59. Kloppenborg, "Symbolic Eschatology," 291.
60. Ibid., 293.

The first of these observations seems to me specious. No individual apocalyptic work reflects the full repertoire of the genre. The "central presupposition" of apocalypticism that Kloppenborg finds lacking in Q is a "sense of anomie, of devastating and inescapable pollution, of demonic domination." Now it is fair to say that apocalypticism differs from other strands of biblical thought, and from Hebrew wisdom in particular, by the sense that the world is out of joint, but the forms and degree of anomie differ considerably. While the popular perception of apocalypticism is shaped to a great degree by such powerful images of chaos as the beasts of Daniel 7 or the dragon of Revelation, such images are not found in all apocalypses. On the other hand, Q hardly portrays a world where all is well. It is a world where the blessed are poor, hungry, and subject to some measure of persecution (6:20–23); a world inhabited by an "evil generation" and subject to impending judgment (11:29–32). Q lacks the powerful imagery of Daniel or Revelation, but its world is nonetheless disrupted by evil and is more reminiscent of the apocalypses than of Proverbs or Ecclesiastes.

It also seems specious to argue that the apocalyptic language does not function in the same way in Q as it does in other apocalyptic writings. Again, apocalyptic language has a range of functions, and all need not be exemplified in every pericope. Kloppenborg finds that the message of Q 17:23–37, that eschatological destruction will occur without any warning, is neither consoling nor comforting, but the moment of consolation in Q is found in the beatitudes, and the apocalyptic judgment is always a two-edged sword.[61] When New Testament scholars distinguish between apocalypticism and the "symbolic eschatology" found in the teaching of Jesus, or of Q, as if apocalyptic eschatology were not symbolic, it is difficult to avoid the impression that apologetic interests are at work.[62]

Kloppenborg's second observation, however, that Q's use of apocalyptic language is relatively restrained, seems to me valid and significant. Q, even in its final form, is certainly not an apocalypse, and consequently it lacks the kind of narrative descriptions that are typi-

61. In fact, in a footnote Kloppenborg acknowledges the affinity between the function of the judgment in Q and in the apocalypses ("Symbolic Eschatology," 306), but he does not modify his main argument in light of this concession.

62. Kloppenborg is neither the first nor the most flagrant example. See N. Perrin, "Eschatology and Hermeneutics: Reflections on Method in the Interpretation of the New Testament," *JBL* 93 (1974) 3–14; and my critique, "The Symbolism of Transcendence in Jewish Apocalyptic," *BR* 19 (1974) 5–22.

cal of that genre. Kloppenborg is surely right that a major component of Q can be appropriately categorized as "wisdom speeches." There is no generic incompatibility, however, between these speeches and an apocalyptic worldview. Accordingly the sharp redaction-critical separation of the sapiential speeches from the announcement of judgment should be viewed with some suspicion and will need to be evaluated critically. Q must be seen as a creative adaptation of both sapiential/instructional and apocalyptic traditions, and we should beware of imposing our ideals of generic purity. In the context of Judaism at the turn of the era, wisdom was polymorphous and was justified in many children.

11

WISDOM IN Q AND *THOMAS*

Stephen J. Patterson

Two of the oldest Christian documents that survived antiquity (directly or indirectly) are cast in the form of one of wisdom's favored genres, the sayings collection. They are the sayings gospel known as Q and the *Gospel of Thomas*. Their presence at the very beginning of early Christian literary activity raises acutely the question of the role played by wisdom in Christian origins.[1] This essay addresses this question through a tradition-historical study of these two documents. First, the overlapping of traditions in Q and *Thomas* is used to establish a minimal core of material, a cross section if you will, of the early Chris-

1. For the most part scholars have treated this question from the standpoint of Q and/or the Synoptic tradition in general (seldom, however, with *Thomas* in view). Recent contributions include: A. P. Winton, *The Proverbs of Jesus: Issues of History and Rhetoric* (JSNTSup 35; Sheffield: JSOT Press, 1990); R. A. Piper, *Wisdom in the Q-Tradition: The Aphoristic Teaching of Jesus* (Cambridge: Cambridge University Press, 1989); J. G. Williams, *Those Who Ponder Proverbs: Aphoristic Thinking and Biblical Literature* (Sheffield: Almond Press, 1981); C. E. Carlston, "Proverbs, Maxims, and the Historical Jesus," *JBL* 99 (1980) 87–105; D. Zeller, *Die weisheitliche Mahnsprüche bei den Synoptikern* (Würzburg: Echter Verlag, 1977); and J. Delobel, ed., *Logia: Les Paroles de Jésus — The Sayings of Jesus* (Festschrift for Joseph Coppens; BETL 59; Louvain: Uitgeverij Peeters/Louvain University Press, 1982). Among older studies, especially helpful are those by W. A. Beardslee, "Uses of Proverb in the Synoptic Gospels," *Int* 24 (1970) 61–73; and idem, "Wisdom Tradition in the Synoptic Gospels," *JAAR* 35 (1967) 231–40; see also his "Proverbs in the Gospel of Thomas," *Studies in New Testament and Early Christian Literature: Essays for A. P. Wikgren* (ed. D. E. Aune; NovTSup 33; Leiden: E. J. Brill, 1972) 92–103. J. D. Crossan offers a rare look at the history of the aphoristic tradition that includes data from the *Gospel of Thomas* (*In Fragments: The Aphorisms of Jesus* [San Francisco: Harper & Row, 1983]).

tian wisdom tradition that eventually produced these two documents. This common tradition is described and characterized in its particularity within the larger corpus of Jewish and Hellenistic wisdom tradition. Second, the documents themselves are considered. Of particular importance here is the way in which the common tradition is taken up and used toward a particular end in each document. In this way something is learned about the potential of wisdom theology to unfold in various ways under particular circumstances, and ultimately about the relationship between wisdom and two other theological paradigms current in earliest Christianity: apocalypticism and Gnosticism. Before all of this, however, the relative obscurity of these two texts necessitates a brief word of introduction to both.

THE SAYINGS SOURCE: Q

Q is an early Christian document widely held to have been used by Matthew and Luke in the composition of their respective Gospels. The Q hypothesis is one-half of the most commonly held explanation for the extensive parallels between the first three canonical Gospels: Matthew, Mark, and Luke. This hypothesis — commonly referred to as the two-source hypothesis — was made popular by Heinrich Julius Holtzmann in the late nineteenth century.[2] It holds that Matthew and Luke made independent use of two sources: the Gospel of Mark and a second source, Q.[3] This second source was composed mostly of sayings attributed to Jesus. Unfortunately it did not survive antiquity and must therefore be reconstructed on the basis of Matthew's and Luke's use of it.[4] However, that it was indeed a written document and not simply a

2. H. J. Holtzmann, *Die Synoptische Evangelien: Ihr Ursprung und geschichtliche Charakter* (Leipzig: Wilhelm Engelmann, 1863). Holtzmann did not really invent the hypothesis. C. H. Weisse, drawing upon the earlier work of Friedrich Schleiermacher and Karl Lachmann, had made a similar proposal already in 1838 in *Die evangelische Geschichte kritisch und philosophisch bearbeitet* (2 vols.; Leipzig: Breitkopf and Hartel, 1838). It was Holtzmann's work, however, that established the two-source hypothesis as a working scholarly consensus.

3. The siglum Q derives from *Quelle,* the word for "source" in German, the language in which the hypothesis was first proposed and discussed. On the use of "Q" to designate this document, see L. H. Silbermann, "Whence *Siglum* Q? A Conjecture," *JBL* 98 (1979) 287–88.

4. There have been many attempts to reconstruct the document Q. The first was by A. von Harnack in *Sprüche und Reden Jesu* (Leipzig: Hinrichs, 1907); Eng.: *The Sayings of Jesus* (trans. J. R. Wilkinson; New York: G. P. Putnam's Sons; London: Williams and Norgate, 1908). A recent critical tool for this work has been provided by J. Kloppenborg,

commonly shared body of oral tradition is suggested by the extensive verbal correspondence found in parallel texts ascribed to Q.[5] Further evidence for its existence as a written source can be adduced from the fact that while Matthew and Luke tend to insert sayings from Q into different contexts in the Markan narrative, they nonetheless frequently make use of Q sayings in the same relative order.[6] Though the actual document used by Matthew and Luke has been lost, scholarly convention assigns all of the parallel texts shared by Matthew and Luke, but not found in Mark, to this sayings source.[7] That Matthew and Luke made use of it necessitates a date for Q sometime before the mid-80s CE (the date normally assigned to Matthew), but Mark's probable knowledge of some Q texts makes a date of around 60 CE more likely, though an earlier date is not ruled out.[8]

THE *GOSPEL OF THOMAS*

The *Gospel of Thomas,* like Q, is a collection of sayings attributed to Jesus. And like Q, the *Gospel of Thomas* disappeared sometime after the close of the early Christian period. In fact, it was lost to the modern world until 1945, when a chance discovery in the sands of Egypt brought it once again into the light of day.[9] The fact that this noncanonical text shares so much in common with Matthew, Mark, and

Q Parallels: Synopsis, Critical Notes and Concordance (Foundations and Facets; Sonoma, Calif.: Polebridge, 1988). A major project toward this end is currently under way sponsored by the Society of Biblical Literature under the direction of James M. Robinson. The project's results are published yearly in the *Journal of Biblical Literature.*

5. For a discussion of the issue see J. Kloppenborg, *The Formation of Q* (Studies in Antiquity and Christianity; Philadelphia: Fortress Press, 1987) 42–47.

6. This discovery was made by V. Taylor; see his "The Order of Q," n.s., *JTS* 4 (1953) 27–31; and idem, "The Original Order of Q," *New Testament Essays: Studies in Honor of T. W. Manson* (Manchester: Manchester University Press, 1959) 246–49. Both articles are reprinted in V. Taylor, *New Testament Essays* (Grand Rapids, Mich.: Wm. B. Eerdmans Publishing Co.; London: Epworth, 1970) 90–94 and 95–118, respectively.

7. There are exceptions to this general rule, for occasionally the content of Mark and Q probably overlap. Such cases are identified by doublets (when Matthew or Luke contain the same story twice, in slightly different versions) or by agreements between Matthew and Luke against Mark. For a general treatment see R. Laufen, *Die Doppelüberlieferung der Logienquelle und des Markus-evangeliums* (BBB 54; Bonn: Peter Hanstein Verlag, 1980).

8. D. Lührmann makes a plausible case for a date in the 50s or 60s (*Die Redaktion der Logienquelle* [WMANT 33; Neukirchen-Vluyn: Neukirchener Verlag, 1969] 85–89).

9. For an account of this remarkable discovery see J. M. Robinson, "The Discovery of the Nag Hammadi Codices," and "Getting the Nag Hammadi Library into English," *BA* 42/4 (1979) 206–24 and 239–48, respectively.

Luke (about half of *Thomas*'s sayings are found also in the Synoptic Gospels) at once made it both the object of much attention and the center of much controversy. At issue were its relationship to the canonical tradition and its date. While a full-scale discussion of these important issues is not possible here, my own position may be summarized as follows:[10] the *Gospel of Thomas* derives for the most part from oral and written traditions that are parallel to, but not derived from the canonical Gospels and their sources. That this is true is indicated by the following facts: (1) *Thomas* shows no consistent patterns suggesting its use of Synoptic materials — no extensive verbal correspondence, no shared order,[11] and only rare instances where *Thomas* shares a detail thought to have been unique to one or another of the Synoptic authors.[12] (2) From a form-critical point of view, *Thomas*'s sayings are more primitive, or derive from forms that are more primitive, than their Synoptic counterparts.[13] (3) As a sayings collection, *Thomas* belongs in an early Christian genre that does not presuppose the development of the narrative gospel and that, if the fate of Q is instructive, seems to have died out after the end of the first century.[14] (4) Finally, there are Synoptic parallels for only about half of *Thomas*'s sayings; for the rest one must assume independent (oral or written) sources.[15] Cumulatively these factors indicate that *Thomas* represents an autonomous gospel tradition. While *Thomas* is notoriously difficult to date, all of these factors are relevant for this second question as well. The primitive nature of its sayings, its inde-

10. For a more thorough treatment of the problem see S. J. Patterson, *The Gospel of Thomas and Jesus* (Foundations and Facets; Sonoma, Calif.: Polebridge, 1993).

11. So R. McL. Wilson, *Studies in the Gospel of Thomas* (London: A. R. Mowbray, 1960) 50–51.

12. On the last point see the particularly helpful study by J. Sieber, *A Redactional Analysis of the Synoptic Gospels with Regard to the Question of the Sources of the Gospel According to Thomas* (Ann Arbor, Mich.: University Microfilms, 1966). Sieber's work is an important corrective to the earlier work of W. Schrage, *Das Verhältnis des Thomasevangeliums zur synoptischen Tradition und zu den koptischen Evangelienübersetzungen: Zugleich ein Beitrag zur gnostischen Synoptikerdeutung* (BZNW 29; Berlin: Töpelmann, 1964).

13. This is most evident in the parables tradition that is shared by *Thomas* and the Synoptic Gospels; see esp. H. Montefiore, "A Comparison of the Parables of the Gospel According to Thomas and the Synoptic Gospels," *NTS* 7 (1960–61) 220–48; also H. Koester, "Three Thomas Parables," *The New Testament and Gnosis: Essays in Honor of Robert McL. Wilson* (ed. A. H. B. Logan and J. M. Wedderburn; Edinburgh: T. & T. Clark, 1983) 195–203, and R. Cameron, "Parable and Interpretation in the Gospel of Thomas," *Forum* 2 (1986) 3–34.

14. On this see C.-H. Hunzinger, "Aussersynoptisches Traditionsgut im Thomas-Evangelium," *TLZ* 85 (1960) 843.

15. So, originally, O. Cullmann, "Das Thomasevangelium und die Frage nach dem Alter in ihm enthaltenen Tradition," *TLZ* 85 (1960) 334.

pendence from the canonical tradition, and its genre all suggest a date in the first century. Without a compelling reason to date it later, one should probably regard it as roughly contemporaneous with Q.[16]

Q AND *THOMAS* AS WISDOM GOSPELS

As a pair, then, Q and *Thomas* make up one of the earliest strata of Christian literary activity. Both documents are sayings collections. This fact has not gone unnoticed in the study of early Christianity, and its significance may be considerable. In 1964 James M. Robinson published an essay in which Q and *Thomas* are placed within the context of other sayings collections of Jewish and early Christian provenance.[17] This was Robinson's attempt to work out more systematically Rudolf Bultmann's treatment of sayings from the Synoptic tradition under the heading: "Logia (Jesus as a Teacher of Wisdom)."[18] Focusing on the sayings collection as a genre, and using its native vocabulary (*logoi* or *logia*) to follow its path, Robinson begins by tracing its development forward. The path leads to the *Gospel of Thomas,* whose *incipit* identifies it as one such sayings collection (*^{e}nshaje,* i.e., *logoi*). But Robinson, noting in *Thomas* the presence of a number of sayings of a more esoteric nature, argues that here the sayings genre had begun its modulation into a genre more typical of Gnosticism, namely, discourses of the risen Lord, a development continued in a work like *Thomas the Contender* and brought to completion in a text such as *Pistis Sophia,* in which traditional sayings are juxtaposed freely with esoteric interpretation and cast in the form of a discourse of the resurrected Lord with his disciples.[19] Robinson then reverses his direction, tracing the genre backwards from Q to other early Christian sayings collections, such as that found in *Didache* 1:3–6 or Mark 4:1–34, and pre-Christian collections imbedded in

16. For a thorough treatment of recent discussion of *Thomas*'s date, see J. M. Robinson, "On Bridging the Gulf from Q to the Gospel of Thomas (or Vice Versa)," *Nag Hammadi, Gnosticism, and Early Christianity* (ed. C. W. Hedrick and R. Hodgson, Jr.; Peabody, Mass.: Hendrickson, 1986) 142–64.

17. J. M. Robinson, "LOGOI SOPHON: Zur Gattung der Spruchquelle," *Zeit und Geschichte: Dankesgabe an Rudolf Bultmann* (ed. Erich Dinkler; Tübingen: J. C. B Mohr [Paul Siebeck], 1964) 77–96. A translated and revised edition of the essay was published as "LOGOI SOPHON: On the Gattung of Q," *Trajectories Through Early Christianity* (ed. J. M. Robinson and H. Koester; Philadelphia: Fortress Press, 1971). (All references are to the English translation.)

18. R. Bultmann, *History of the Synoptic Tradition* (trans. John Marsh; revised ed.; New York: Harper & Row, 1963) 69–108.

19. Robinson, "LOGOI SOPHON," 76–85.

the *Testaments of the Twelve Patriarchs*, the *Apocalypse of Adam*, and the *Similitudes of Enoch*.[20] Ultimately he locates its roots in Jewish wisdom literature, in particular the collections of *logoi* found in Prov 22:17–24:22, whose superscription lends a designation for the genre as a whole: *logoi sophon*, or "sayings of the sages."

Two things from Robinson's work stand out as important for the present study. First, in settling the literary context within which Q and *Thomas* are to be considered, Robinson also suggests a theological paradigm within which they are to be understood: wisdom. Second, Robinson notes that within early Christianity the use of the wisdom genre, *logoi sophon*, was not a static, but a dynamic phenomenon. *Thomas*, while continuing the tradition of collecting Jesus' sayings, moved this genre into the service of another theological paradigm, Gnosticism. *Thomas* is no longer simply a wisdom gospel, and Jesus in *Thomas* is no longer simply Wisdom's sage or prophet; he has become a Gnostic revealer. What Robinson did not notice was that Q in its present form likewise is not a wisdom gospel in any pure sense, but itself represents a development away from the idea of Jesus as Wisdom's sage or prophet. This was Helmut Koester's insight.

In two articles published shortly after Robinson's initial essay, Koester noticed that while *Thomas* indeed represents a secondary development away from the wisdom orientation suggested by its genre, when compared to Q, it shows some primitive traits as well.[21] More specifically, Koester points out that when one compares the content of Q and *Thomas*, one finds that conspicuously absent from *Thomas* is any of the apocalyptic expectation so typical of Q. There are, for example, no Son of man sayings in *Thomas*, so central to Q's own apocalyptic tradition.[22] This, in Koester's view, is not the result of a systematic purge of apocalyptic material from the sayings tradition in *Thomas*. Rather, building on the work of Philipp Vielhauer,[23] who had argued that the

20. Ibid., 106–9.

21. H. Koester, "GNOMAI DIAPHOROI: The Origin and Nature of Diversification in the History of Early Christianity," *HTR* 58 (1965) 279–318; and idem, "One Jesus and Four Primitive Gospels," *HTR* 61 (1968) 203–47. Both are reprinted in Robinson and Koester, *Trajectories*, 114–57 and 158–204, respectively. (All references are to *Trajectories*.)

22. Koester, "One Jesus," 168–70.

23. P. Vielhauer, "Gottesreich and Menschensohn in der Verkündigung Jesu," *Festschrift für Günther Dehn* (ed. W. Schneemelcher; Neukirchen: Kreis Moers, 1957) 51–79; and idem, "Jesus und der Menschensohn," *ZTK* 60 (1963) 133–77. Both are reprinted in P. Vielhauer, ed., *Aufsätze zum Neuen Testament* (Munich: Kaiser, 1965) 55–91 and 92–140, respectively.

earliest stages of the Synoptic tradition did not yet contain apocalyptic speculation about the Son of man, Koester suggests that *Thomas*'s lack of an apocalyptic element is a primitive feature deriving from the earliest stages in the sayings tradition. Q, with its Son of man apocalypticism, represents a secondary development.[24] Thus, while Q and *Thomas* are, in terms of genre, wisdom gospels, neither has retained wisdom as its operative hermeneutical paradigm: *Thomas* has moved the genre in the direction of Gnosticism while Q has moved it in the direction of apocalypticism.

KLOPPENBORG: Q^1 AND Q^2

Koester's hunches about Q were subsequently pursued by John Kloppenborg in his composition-critical study of Q.[25] Kloppenborg sought to clarify the redactional history of Q by posing the question in literary-critical terms: What principles of composition can be seen as formative for the Q document, and what elements appear to be redactionally secondary? Kloppenborg discovered that the compositional structure that underlies the Q document as a whole is a series of wisdom speeches: Q 6:20b–49;[26] Q 9:57–62; 10:2–16, 21–24; Q 11:2–4, 9–13; Q 12:1–12; Q 12:22–34; and Q 13:24–30, 34–35; 14:16–24, 26–27; 17:33; 14:34–35.[27] To this foundational layer in Q ($=Q^1$) are affixed, at irregular intervals, a number of sayings whose character may generally be described as "the announcement of judgment": Q 3:7–9, 16–17; Q 7:1–10, 18–23, 24–26, (16:16), 31–35; Q 11:14–26, 29–32, 33–36, 39–52; Q 12:39–40, 42–46, 49, 51–53, (54–56), 57–59; and Q 17:23, 24, 26–30, 34–35, 37.[28] It is Kloppenborg's hypothesis that this second redactional layer of Q ($=Q^2$) was added as the Q community came ever more to the realization that their initial preaching was not being received with enthusiasm. Their frustration with this course of events inspired the strains of judgment spoken against "this generation" so characteristic of

24. Koester, "One Jesus," 186–87.
25. Kloppenborg, *Formation of Q*.
26. By convention, texts from Q are cited using the versification of Luke, since Luke is generally considered to have preserved the original order of Q more faithfully. In the event that a Matthean text without a Lukan parallel is thought to have come from Q, it is cited as a Matthean text.
27. Kloppenborg, *Formation of Q*, 171–245.
28. Ibid., 102–70.

Kloppenborg's Q^2 materials.[29] As might be expected, all of the apocalyptic Son of man sayings Koester regarded as secondary to the Q tradition are found in this later redactional layer. Kloppenborg's composition-critical study of Q thus confirmed what Koester's comparison of Q and *Thomas* had suggested earlier: while Q in the form used by Matthew and Luke was an apocalyptic document, the Q tradition nonetheless had its origins in an early Christian sapiential tradition that focused not on judgment and an imminent, cataclysmic end to history, but on Jesus' words.

It seems clear from this work that in Q and *Thomas* we have the remnants of an early Christian tradition in which emphasis was placed on Jesus' words; this tradition is thus in the broadest sense sapiential. In its later manifestations — in *Thomas* and in Kloppenborg's Q^2 — this early sapiential orientation gave way to theological paradigms better known from later Christian generations: Gnosticism and apocalypticism, respectively. But questions linger. If Q and *Thomas* lie on diverging trajectories each grounded in, yet moving away from, an early sapiential tradition, what can be said about this early tradition itself? The quest for origins begins with the material common to both traditions; this common tradition will provide at least a minimal inventory of the tradition out of which the Q and *Thomas* trajectories emerged.

THE COMMON TRADITION

The tradition common to Q and *Thomas* may be inventoried as follows:

1. There are a number of sayings and parables that have not been recast by the respective hermeneutical tendencies at work in each trajectory (apocalypticism in Q, Gnosticism in *Thomas*). In both trajectories they appear to share the same basic meaning: *Thom* 6:3 || Q 12:2 (Hidden, Revealed); *Thom* 14:4 || Q 10:8–9 (Eat What Is Set Before You); *Thom* 20:2–4 || Q 13:18–21 (The Mustard); *Thom* 26:1–2 || Q 6:41–42 (Speck and Log); *Thomas* 32 || Matt 5:14 (City on a Hill); *Thom* 33:1 || Q 12:3 (Preach from Housetops); *Thom* 33:2–3 || Q 11:33 (Lamp on a Lamp Stand); *Thomas* 34 || Q 6:39 (Blind Leading the Blind); *Thomas* 36 (Coptic) || Q 12:22 (What You Shall Wear); *Thom* 45:1 || Q 6:44b (Grapes and Thorns); *Thom* 45:2–3 || Q 6:45 (Good Person, Good Heart); *Thom* 47:2 || Q 16:13 (Serving Two

29. Ibid., 167–68.

Masters); *Thomas* 54 || Q 6:20b (Blessed Are the Poor); *Thomas* 55 || Q 14:26–27 (Hating One's Family); *Thomas* 58 || Q 6:22 (Blessed the Sufferer); *Thomas* 63 || Q 12:16–21 (The Rich Fool); *Thom* 68:1–2 || Q 6:22–23 (Blessed Are the Persecuted); *Thom* 69:2 || Q 6:21a (Blessed Are the Hungry); *Thom* 72:1–2 || Q 12:13–14 (Jesus Not a Divider); *Thomas* 73 || Q 10:2 (The Harvest Is Great); *Thom* 76:3 || Q 12:33–34 (Abiding Treasure); *Thom* 86:1–2 || Q 9:58 (Foxes Have Holes); *Thomas* 94 || Q 11:9–10 (Seek and Find); *Thom* 95:1–2 || Q 6:34–35a (Lend Without Return); *Thom* 96:1–2 || Q 13:20–21 (The Leaven); *Thomas* 107 || Q 15:3–7 (The Lost Sheep); *Thomas* 113 || Luke 17:20–21 (The Present Reign of God).

2. A number of sayings and one parable are found in both *Thomas* and Kloppenborg's second redactional layer in Q (Q^2). However, even though they were added to Q at a time when the Q community was engaging in apocalyptic speculation, these sayings, when isolated from their secondary Q contexts, do not themselves connote an apocalyptic understanding of the world. What they do share in common, however, is a noteworthy polemical flavor: *Thomas* 24 || Q 11:33–36 (The Light Person); *Thom* 39:1–2 || Q 11:52 (Taking the Keys of Knowledge); *Thom* 44:1–3 || Q 12:10 (Blaspheming the Holy Spirit); *Thom* 46:1, 2b || Q 7:28 (None Greater Than John); *Thom* 64:1–12 || Q 14:15–24 (The Great Supper); *Thom* 78:1–3 || Q 7:24–26 (Why Have You Come Out?); *Thom* 89:1–2 || Q 11:39–41 (Washing the Outside).

3. Several sayings have been drawn into and recast in the service of the apocalypticism of Q^2; however, they survive in *Thomas* in a nonapocalyptic form: *Thomas* 10 || Q 12:49 (Fire on Earth); *Thom* 16:1–4 || Q 12:51–53 (A House Divided); *Thom* 35:1–2 || Q 11:21–22 (Binding the Strong Man); *Thom* 41:1–2 || Q 19:26 (Have and Receive); *Thomas* 91 || Q 12:56 (Reading the Moment); *Thomas* 103 || Q 12:39 (Expecting the Thief).

4. There are also several sayings that have been drawn into and recast in the service of Gnosticism in *Thomas*, but which survive in Q in a non-Gnostic form. Interestingly, all of these sayings are also attested elsewhere in *Thomas*, but in non-Gnostic forms: *Thomas* 2; 92 (cf. *Thomas* 94) || Q 11:9–10 (Seek and Find); *Thomas* 3 (cf. *Thomas* 113) || Luke 17:20–21 (The Present Reign of God); *Thom* 5:2 (cf. *Thom* 6:3) || Q 12:2 (Hidden, Revealed); *Thom* 69:1 (cf. *Thom* 68:1–2) || Q 6:22–23 (Blessed Are the Persecuted); *Thomas* 101 (cf. *Thomas* 55) || Q 14:26–27 (Hating Family).

5. Several sayings have undergone transformation in each trajec-

tory, Q recasting the saying in terms of apocalyptic judgment, *Thomas* in terms of Gnosticism: *Thom* 4:2 || Q 13:30 (First, Last); and *Thom* 21:3[30] || Q 12:39 (Expecting the Thief); *Thom* 61:1 || Q 17:34 (One Will Live, One Will Die); *Thom* 61:3 || Q 10:22a (Things Given of the Father).

From this material two things are evident. First, by far the largest category — i.e., category (1) — is that fund of common tradition upon which the apocalypticism of the Q trajectory and the esotericism of the *Thomas* trajectory have had little or no impact. This is remarkable considering that, as pointed out above, neither Q nor *Thomas* is in its present form a wisdom book in any pure sense. However, it confirms in a very concrete way the theoretical arguments of Robinson and Koester that Q and *Thomas* are rooted in an early Christian sayings tradition that is neither apocalyptic nor Gnostic. This is further suggested by categories 2, 3, and 4, in which each saying is preserved in an early form despite its having been appropriated either for Q's apocalypticism or *Thomas*'s Gnosticism. Laying the parallels out in this way makes it clear that Q and *Thomas* indeed lie on divergent trajectories — Q moving in the direction of apocalypticism, *Thomas* in the direction of Gnosticism — which are nonetheless rooted in a common tradition that is neither apocalyptic nor Gnostic.

The second thing that stands out from this data, however, is the lack of any clear pattern between the parallels that would suggest a specific and concrete relationship between Q and *Thomas* themselves. For example, there is no extensive verbal correspondence or residual cases of shared order that would suggest, as in the case of Matthew's and Luke's use of Q, an actual document shared by Q and *Thomas*. This raises two issues: (1) how to account for these extensive Q–*Thomas* overlaps, and (2) how to describe the corpus of overlapping sayings as any sort of meaningful whole.

The first of these questions is perhaps the easiest to answer. At this early stage in the development of the Jesus tradition it may not be supposed that the movement was yet very large. If Paul — the only early Christian preacher about whom we have any detailed knowledge — may be taken as illustrative of the situation early on, even he, who traveled to regions of the empire quite remote from the Eastern roots of the movement in Palestine and Syria, had intimate contact with its original leaders in the East (Gal 1:18–20; 2:1–14). Its seems probable that those

30. Note the more original form of the saying in *Thomas* 91.

who proffered the oral traditions that eventually found codification in Q and *Thomas*, respectively, simply knew one another and consequently shared traditions.

The second of these questions is more difficult. The lack of evidence for a document at such an early stage in the Jesus movement is not in itself surprising. It cannot be supposed that the Jesus movement, having begun in a culture whose rate of literacy was generally very low, was originally grounded primarily in texts and literary activity.[31] The Q–*Thomas* overlaps derive quite clearly from shared oral tradition. But how might one characterize this oral tradition? Does the fact that its earliest written codification took the form of *logoi sophon* suggest anything about its earlier oral character? Can one speak legitimately here of an early Christian wisdom tradition, or even a wisdom school? Is it meaningful to characterize an oral tradition in terms that normally imply a scribal or learned context? What is more, *sophia* ("wisdom") or its cognates are never mentioned in the common material. Nor, for that matter, is wisdom ever mentioned explicitly in the earliest written codifications of this tradition: *Thomas* and Q^1. The terminology specific to wisdom theology occurs first in Q^2 (Q 7:35; 10:21; 11:31; and 11:49). To answer these questions we must first learn more about this still obscure corner of Christian origins, beginning with a more precise description of the character of the tradition common to Q and *Thomas*. Once this has been done we can go on to look more carefully at how its subsequent tradition history is played out in the Q and *Thomas* trajectories.

31. See esp. W. V. Harris, *Ancient Literacy* (Cambridge, Mass.: Harvard University Press, 1989); also W. Kelber, *The Oral and the Written Gospel: The Hermeneutics of Speaking and Writing in the Synoptic Tradition* (Philadelphia: Fortress Press, 1983) 17–18; D. J. Wiseman, "Books in the Ancient Near East and in the Old Testament," *The Cambridge History of the Bible*, vol. 1: *From the Beginnings to Jerome* (Cambridge: Cambridge University Press, 1970) 37; and J. Goody (*The Domestication of the Savage Mind* [Cambridge: Cambridge University Press, 1977] 152–53), who argues that this state of affairs predominated even until the nineteenth century. Certainly prior to the rise of print technology one cannot assume that people shared the modern preoccupation with books and print, since such things were simply not available to the general public. Even among the literate elite of antiquity there was a distinct preference for the oral report over the written word (so W. Ong, *The Presence of the Word: Some Prolegomena for Cultural and Religious History* [New Haven and London: Yale University Press, 1967] 55–60; idem, *Orality and Literacy: The Technologizing of the Word* [New Accents; London and New York: Methuen, 1982] 79–80, 96–98). Thus, Papias's preference for the oral reports of elders over those of books (Eusebius *Hist. Eccl.* 3.39.3–4).

CHARACTERIZING THE COMMON TRADITION

Common Forms

In the absence of a specific document to which we could point as the source of this tradition, form criticism suggests itself as an appropriate point of departure for further investigation. While there may have been some written traditions prior to Q and *Thomas,* one must assume that this early phase of the Jesus movement for the most part cultivated its traditions orally. When one looks at the material common to Q and *Thomas* as a whole, the forms that predominate are from the wisdom tradition — the sort of forms Bultmann listed under the category "Logia (Jesus as the Teacher of Wisdom)." There are, for example, numerous *maxims,*[32] some formulated on the basis of the natural world (*Thom* 5:2 and 6:5–6 || Q 12:2; *Thom* 45:1 || Q 6:44b); some formulated on the basis of human experience (*Thom* 4:2 || Q 13:30; *Thomas* 24 || Q 11:34–36; *Thom* 33:2–3 || Q 11:33; *Thomas* 34 || Q 6:39; *Thom* 35:1–2 || Q 11:21–22; *Thom* 41:1–2 || Q 19:26; *Thom* 45:2–3 || Q 6:45; *Thom* 47:2 || Q 16:13; *Thom* 86:1–2 || Q 9:58); and others formulated as macarisms (*Thomas* 54 || Q 6:20b; *Thomas* 58 || Q 6:22; *Thom* 68:1–2 || Q 6:22–23; *Thom* 69:2 || Q 6:21a; *Thomas* 103 || Q 12:39).[33] There are also several *hortatory formulations*[34] (*Thom* 14:4 || Q 10:8–9; *Thom* 26:1–2 || Q 6:41–42; *Thomas* 36 || Q 6:39; *Thomas* 94 || Q 11:9–10; *Thom* 95:1–2 || Q 6:34–35a) and *sapiential questions* (*Thom* 89:1–2 || Q 11:39–41[35]). Finally, there are six *parables* (*Thomas* 20 || Q 13:18–19; *Thomas* 63 || Q 12:16–21; *Thomas* 64 || Q 14:15–24; *Thomas* 76 || Q 12:33–34; *Thomas* 96 || Q 13:20–21; and *Thomas* 107 || Q 15:3–7).

The large number of wisdom sayings in this common tradition has hermeneutical implications: it tells us that those who propagated the Jesus tradition in this way had before them a wisdom agenda. That is, they were about the quest for insight — insight into the nature of human existence and of the world and especially of humanity's proper stance in the world. The task is both bold and basic. For this reason the sages tended to formulate their insights in rather bold, universal-sounding terms using maxims, exhortations, and the like. However, as

32. Bultmann's term was *Grundsäzte* (*Die Geschichte der synoptischen Tradition* [9th ed.; Göttingen: Vandenhoeck & Ruprecht, 1979] 77).

33. The Q 12:39 version is probably secondary here; it has been reformulated to prepare for the hortatory conclusion appended in Q 12:40.

34. Bultmann's term was *Mahnworte* (*Geschichte,* 80).

35. Q's polemical formulation is probably secondary; so H. Koester, *Ancient Christian Gospels: Their History and Development* (Philadelphia: Trinity Press International; London: SCM Press, 1990) 91–92; see also Kloppenborg, *Formation of Q,* 149–50.

William Beardslee has argued, this should not lead one to conclude that the sage was typically focused on Truth writ large, universals that have no particular grounding in the historical reality of human existence.[36] For the sage, the key to true sagacity was the ability to be wise in a particular situation, to appropriate and properly apply insights derived from other situations of analogous quality. The sage was to be a master interpreter of human experience in the world. That is what the early Jesus movement that formulated its traditions in terms of the wisdom tradition was striving for: an interpretation of human experience.

Uncommon Content

By the first century, wisdom was a well-known theological and hermeneutical category within Judaism. But it was not limited to Jewish culture. Wisdom in antiquity was an international phenomenon; the work of the sage played a role in all of the ancient cultures of the Near East. The Greco-Roman world, too, had its instructional tradition, embodied especially in the philosophical schools of late antiquity, which codified their wisdom in collections of gnomologia.[37] Thus it is not unusual that the Jesus movement, with roots in the thoroughly Hellenized Jewish culture of lower Galilee, should choose to cultivate its own traditions in this form.[38] However, when one lays this early Christian wisdom tradition alongside its contemporary cousins, it is not without its own unique qualities.

Wisdom in the ancient Near East was for the most part a school tradition carried on under official sponsorship. Sages were retained in the employ of the royal court as a corps of educated elites, which used its learning to further the cause of the ruling family. As such, wisdom tended to be rather conservative. Its interests were those of the status

36. W. Beardslee, "Uses of Proverb," 65–66. Beardslee cites the earlier study by H. H. Schmid as decisive for his conclusion: *Wesen und Geschichte der Weisheit* (Berlin: Töpelmann, 1969). This squares well with the oral origins of the Synoptic tradition. Ong points out that "oral cultures must always conceptualize and verbalize all their knowledge with more or less close reference to the human life world, assimilating the alien, objective world to the more immediate, familiar interaction of human beings" (*Orality and Literacy*, 42).

37. For a convenient survey of Near Eastern and Greco-Roman instruction see Kloppenborg, *Formation of Q*, 263–316.

38. Lower Galilee was no cultural backwater; so J. A. Overman, "Who Were the First Urban Christians? Urbanization in Galilee in the First Century," and D. R. Edwards, "First Century Urban/Rural Relations in Lower Galilee: Exploring the Archaeological and Literary Evidence," *Society of Biblical Literature 1988 Seminar Papers* (ed. David Lull; SBLSP 27; Atlanta: Scholars Press, 1988) 160–68 and 169–82, respectively.

quo: moderation, order, hierarchy, wealth as a sign of divine favor, and so on. As James L. Crenshaw aptly summarizes: "The sages did not want anyone to rock the boat. Accordingly, they encouraged any means that would mollify anger, and they refused to become involved in efforts at social reform."[39] This generally conservative tendency of the wisdom tradition can be seen even in the small literary pretense used by the sages to present their material: as the collected insight of a parent passed along to the children.[40] The last generation's wisdom becomes that of the next, with all the legitimating power that can be conveyed only through the cultural codes of parental authority.

In comparing the wisdom of Q with the broader tradition of ancient Near Eastern instruction, Kloppenborg has called attention to two anomalous qualities in Q: (1) Q does not present its material in the guise of parental instruction. (2) Rather than sharing the generally conservative tone of most ancient Near Eastern instruction, "Q presents an ethic of radical discipleship which reverses many of the conventions which allow a society to operate, such as principles of retaliation, the orderly borrowing and lending of capital, appropriate treatment of the dead, responsible self-provision, self-defense and honor of parents."[41] This generally radical character of the early Christian sayings tradition may be illustrated in the common tradition no less than in Q. Here, too, family life is eschewed (*Thomas* 55 and 101:2–3 || Q 14:26–27) or depicted as disintegrating (*Thom* 16:1–4 || Q 12:51–53); poverty and begging are embraced (*Thomas* 54 || Q 6:20b; *Thom* 69:2 || Q 6:21a; *Thom* 14:4 || Q 10:8–9; *Thomas* 36 || Q 6:39; *Thom* 95:1–2 || Q 6:34–35a); homelessness is lamented, but accepted (*Thom* 86:1–2 || Q 9:58). More than that, the cultural codes that form the social boundaries between Jews and Gentiles here fall under attack (*Thom* 89:1–2 || Q 11:39–41; *Thom* 14:4 || Q 10:8–9).[42] No ordinary sages these. Despite the presence of a number of sayings of a more conventional quality,[43] here they are clearly not em-

39. J. L. Crenshaw, *Old Testament Wisdom: An Introduction* (Atlanta: John Knox Press, 1981) 20; see also n. 36 for further literature.

40. For this feature of wisdom see ibid., 33; Kloppenborg, *Formation of Q*, 274–75, 284, 301.

41. Kloppenborg, *Formation of Q*, 318.

42. In the latter saying, notice what is implied. The issue of whether or not to eat what is offered would have arisen primarily as itinerants wandered among Gentiles (see S. J. Patterson, "Paul and the Jesus Tradition: It Is Time for Another Look," *HTR* 84 [1991] 32–33).

43. The following sayings are more proverbial in character: *Thom* 6:5–6 || Q 12:2; *Thom* 26:1–2 || Q 6:41–42; *Thom* 33:2 || Q 11:33; *Thomas* 34 || Q 6:39; *Thom* 45:1–2 ||

ployed in the interest of the status quo. At least two of these proverbs seem to imply conflict (*Thom* 35:1–2 || Q 11:21–22; *Thomas* 103 || Q 12:39). There is criticism afoot (*Thom* 41:1–2 || Q 19:26; *Thom* 39:1–2 || Q 11:52; *Thom* 78:1–3 || Q 7:24–26; *Thomas* 91 || Q 12:56). "Boat rocking" is in the air (*Thom* 4:2 || Q 19:26; *Thomas* 10 || Q 12:49; *Thom* 16:1–2 || Q 12:51). Persecution is welcomed as the legitimation of faithfulness in the face of a hostile and unfaithful world (*Thom* 68:1–2 || Q 6:22–23).

THE KINGDOM OF GOD

As sayings of the sages these sayings are quite remarkable. Rather than enforcing the cultural codes and conservative comportment essential to the perpetuation of the status quo, they offer a radical critique of culture. This is obviously not the product of officially sanctioned activity. These early Christians were not operating in the normal setting for sages: the court of the king. However, even while noticing this our attention is drawn to a group of sayings in the common tradition having to do with the *basileia* ("kingdom").[44] To understand the full significance of these sayings it is important to recall that the term *basileia* is an overtly political term. This is the word used to refer to the ancient and legendary *kingdoms* of Egypt and the ancient Near East, and later those that succeeded Alexander the Great in the fourth century BCE. In choosing this term, these latter-day Q–*Thomas* sages understood what they were doing: though their attitude toward any official court can only be seen as indifferent at best and hostile at worst, they did see themselves as operating within a setting appropriate to the sage — the court service of a *basileia*.

Now, this in itself might have been seen as a radical position vis-à-vis the powers that be. In the first century the *basileia* was the empire, the Roman Empire. There could be no mistake about this. To speak of *another basileia*, an empire of God, or an empire of heaven, or an empire of the Father,[45] would have been rather daring in the deeply suspicious

---

Q 6:44b–45; *Thom* 47:2 || Q 16:13; *Thomas* 94 || Q 11:9–10; *Thomas* 24 || Q 11:34–36; *Thom* 35:1–2 || Q 11:21–22; and *Thomas* 103 || Q 12:39.

44. *Thomas* 3, 113 || Q 17:20–21; *Thom* 14:2 || Q 10:8–9; *Thom* 46:1, 2b || Q 7:28; *Thomas* 54 || Q 6:20b; *Thomas* 68 || Q 6:22–23; *Thomas* 76 || Q 12:33–34; *Thomas* 96 || Q 13:20–21; *Thomas* 20 || Q 13:18–21; *Thomas* 64 || Q 14:15–24 (a kingdom parable in Matthew's version of Q); and *Thomas* 107 || Q 15:3–7 (a kingdom parable in the *Thomas* version).

45. All these forms are attested in Q and *Thomas*, as well as the simple *basileia* without predication.

and oppressive atmosphere of Palestine under Roman rule.[46] For as Mack points out rhetorically, "Why, indeed, a kingdom symbol at all, unless kings, kingdoms, and social circumstances were up for discussion?"[47] And if up for discussion among the peasants of Galilee, surely it would have been a critical discussion. And this is precisely what the empire and its beneficiaries did not want.

This is without a doubt one of the reasons the term "kingdom of God" is so rare in the wider literature of late antiquity. When it does occur outside of the New Testament, the subject that is up for discussion is precisely the nature of just rule. In Jewish literature, for example, one finds it only in Philo[48] and the Wisdom of Solomon.[49] Both of these authors were writing in Alexandria during a period of particularly poor Roman administration, in which hundreds of Egyptian Jews lost their lives to angry Greek mobs.[50] Just rule was indeed up for discussion — as a matter of life and death. But their criticisms were not particularly risky in view of the fact that even the Romans recognized the irresponsibility, indeed treason, of Flaccus, the Roman governor in charge, and removed him from office.[51] When the Wisdom of Solomon says: "Because as servants of his kingdom you did not rule rightly,... he will come upon you terribly and swiftly, because severe judgment falls on those in high places" (6:4, 5), there was not a person in Rome who would have disagreed.

But there were others in the empire who also dared to speak of an ideal *basileia* and thereby engage in social criticism of the most ba-

46. The recent work of Richard Horsley provides an important corrective to earlier, more romantic accounts; see esp. *Jesus and the Spiral of Violence* (San Francisco: Harper & Row, 1987) 1–58 and (with John S. Hanson) *Bandits, Prophets and Messiahs: Popular Movements at the Time of Jesus* (1985; reprinted, San Francisco: Harper & Row, 1988).

47. B. L. Mack, *A Myth of Innocence* (Philadelphia: Fortress Press, 1988) 70.

48. In Philo the term "kingdom of God" actually occurs only once (*Spec.* 4.135–36); but he devotes considerable discussion to how just rule is rooted in the divine reality (*Mut.* 135–36; *Spec.* 1.207; *Abr.* 261). Elsewhere the sage is seen as a true king (*Opif.* 148; *Som.* 2.243–44; *Abr.* 261; *Agr.* 41; *Sob.* 57; *Post.* 138). See the discussion in J. D. Crossan, *The Historical Jesus: The Life of a Mediterranean Peasant* (San Francisco: HarperCollins, 1991) 288–89, and Mack, *Myth of Innocence,* 73 n. 16.

49. The kingdom of God occurs as a term in Wis 10:10; in 6:3–20 the author speaks of kingship as deriving from God. See the discussion in Crossan, *Historical Jesus,* 289–90.

50. For an account of the Jewish pogroms in Alexandria, see E. M. Smallwood's introduction to her edition of *Philonis Alexandrini: Legatio ad Gaium* (Leiden: E. J. Brill, 1961). Philo's role in the events is chronicled firsthand in this work (see also his *In Flaccum*). For the date of Wisdom of Solomon see J. J. Collins, *Between Athens and Jerusalem: Jewish Identity in the Hellenistic Diaspora* (New York: Crossroad, 1983) 182.

51. Philo *Flacc.* 104–15.

sic sort. In the various schools of popular philosophy contemporary to the emergence of the Jesus movement, much effort was spent on the topic of *basileia*. Philosophers operating from the periphery of public life explored the nature of just rule in treatises using kingship as the operative metaphor. Mack summarizes:

> Cynics also saw themselves as "kings" standing over against tyrants as well as against a society blindly following unreasonable rules. Using metaphors such as king, overseer, physician, gadfly, and teacher, Cynics understood themselves to be "sent" from God to preside over the human situation. Epictetus even refers to the Cynics' vocation as a reign (*basileia*, "kingdom") in order to catch up the challenging aspects of representing publicly a way of life grounded in the divine laws of nature.[52]

The parallels to the Q–*Thomas* tradition need not be elaborated.[53] The important point for now is that the Cynics were not greatly appreciated by the empire for these philosophical services. Nero, Vespasian, and Domitian all expelled the street philosophers from Rome as a threat to the social stability of the empire.[54]

There is not space here to discuss all of the kingdom sayings in the common tradition in detail. However, closer attention to two parables from this category will illustrate the slightly seditious character of the tradition's use of *basileia* language: the parable of the mustard (*Thomas* 20 || Q 13:18–21) and the parable of the leaven (*Thomas* 96 || Q 13:20–21). What is noteworthy about these two parables is their audacious comparison of the kingdom to proverbial symbols of nuisance and defilement. There is more to the parable of the mustard than the contrast between the smallness of the seed and the largeness of the plant. In fact, allusion to the noble cedar of Ezek 17:22–24 in the final line of the parable renders the mustard's size a mere parody by contrast.[55] At least as important for its parabolic content is what everyone knew about mustard: once you plant it in a place it soon takes over such that it is

52. Mack, *Myth of Innocence*, 72–73. The reference is to Epictetus *Disc.* 3.22.63, 76, 80. More extensive discussion is to be found in R. Hoistad, *Cynic Hero and Cynic King* (Uppsala: Bloms, 1948), and E. R. Goodenough, "The Political Philosophy of Hellenistic Kingship," *Yale Classical Studies I* (New Haven, Conn.: Yale University Press, 1928) 55–102 (as cited by Mack).

53. The Cynic sense of destiny might, by way of analogy, help to account for the several I-sayings found in the common tradition (e.g., *Thomas* 10 || Q 12:49; *Thomas* 16 || Q 12:51–53; and *Thom* 61:3b || Q 10:22a).

54. See D. R. Dudley, *A History of Cynicism from Diogenes to the 6th Century* A.D. (London: Methuen, 1937) 125–42.

55. So R. W. Funk, *Jesus as Precursor* (Semeia Studies; Philadelphia: Fortress Press, 1975) 23.

almost impossible to be rid of it.[56] So prolific was mustard that it was forbidden to plant it in a garden or in a field in more than a few small patches, lest it threaten to take over an entire area and crowd out the more desirable crops, such as grain.[57] It would be more to the point to call this the parable of the mustard *weed* rather than the mustard *seed*.[58] Add to this the parable's final stroke: and it attracts birds to nest in its branches (the last thing a farmer wants in a grain field!). This is what the kingdom of God is like: it grows from the smallest of seeds to become the most threatening of weeds — it can take over, overwhelm a neatly planted field, and, worst of all, attract unwanted guests. The image is hardly decorous.

The parable of the leaven has a similar, slightly threatening tone. Leaven in antiquity was a proverbial symbol of defilement and corruption.[59] One can see this in the New Testament itself, where its metaphoric use is confined to this negative range.[60] But throughout Jewish and Hellenistic culture it was also so regarded. A. R. S. Kennedy summarizes: "In the view of antiquity, Semitic and non-Semitic, panary fermentation represented a process of corruption and putrefaction in the mass of dough."[61] Leaven is a symbol of corruption. The parable of the leaven uses this negative symbol to conjure up a particularly seditious image: in each version the leaven is *hidden* in the flour — much flour![62] Presumably the prank would not have been discovered until one wished to use the flour, at which time the baker would have some-

56. Pliny *Nat. Hist.* 19.170.

57. J. Jeremias calls attention to the problem with sowing mustard in a garden in his *The Parables of Jesus* (2d ed., rev.; New York: Charles Scribner's Sons, 1972) 27, n. 11. For a more extensive discussion see B. B. Scott, *Hear Then the Parable* (Minneapolis: Fortress Press, 1989) 381–83.

58. So D. Oakman, *Jesus and the Economic Questions of His Day* (Studies in the Bible and Early Christianity 8; Lewiston, N.Y.: Edwin Mellen Press, 1986) 123–28, esp. 127: "It is hard to escape the conclusion that Jesus deliberately likens the rule of God to a weed."

59. See Scott's discussion, *Hear Then the Parable,* 374–75; also Windisch, "*Zumē, zumóō, ázumos,*" *TDNT* 2.903–6.

60. Cf. Matt 16:66 || Mark 8:15 || Luke 12:1; 1 Cor 5:6–8.

61. A. R. S. Kennedy, "Leaven," *Encyclopaedia Biblica* (ed. T. K. Cheyne and J. S. Black; New York and London: Macmillan, 1902) 3.2754 (as cited by Scott, *Hear Then the Parable,* 324).

62. Jeremias called attention to the great amount of flour indicated in "three measures" (*sáta tría*): "In the parable of the Leaven they drastically pictured the overflowing mass of dough by borrowing from Gen. 18.6 . . . the number of 3 *se a* (39.4 liters) — 3 *se a* are something like 50 pounds of flour, and the bread baked from this amount would provide a meal for more than 100 persons" (*Parables of Jesus,* 147). See also the discussion in Scott, *Hear Then the Parable,* 326–27.

thing of a surprise in store. A small thing can be a very large nuisance indeed.

In both of these parables, as with the *basileia* sayings in general, the new empire is not painted with broad, acceptably conventional strokes. Its form is irreverent and seditious, countercultural at a very basic level.

COUNTERCULTURAL WISDOM

The tradition common to Q and *Thomas* presents one with a dilemma. On the one hand, it makes overwhelming use of wisdom forms, which suggests a hermeneutic consistent with the (conservative) aims of the sages. On the other hand, it fills these forms with a content that is socially radical and confrontative, critical of the conventions that made ancient Jewish and Hellenistic social life possible.[63] This is precisely the opposite of what one would expect from a wisdom school. What are we to make of this curious combination of disparate traditions?

The radical content of the sayings tradition has not gone unnoticed. Eugene Boring and Helmut Koester have argued, for example, that this makes this tradition much more prophetic than sapiential in character.[64]

63. A qualification to this must be added: the tradition common to Q and *Thomas* is curiously silent about the temple. In the tradition common to *Thomas* and Mark there is the so-called Temple Word (*Thomas* 71 || Mark 14:57–58; cf. 13:2; 15:29), so that we need not suppose that the earliest Jesus movement was uninterested in such things, even from a critical standpoint. The omission, however, is curious.

64. M. E. Boring, *Sayings of the Risen Jesus: Christian Prophecy in the Synoptic Tradition* (SNTSMS 46; Cambridge: Cambridge University Press, 1982) 180–81. Boring suggests that Q is closer to Jeremiah than to Proverbs. Koester's position is more nuanced (*Ancient Christian Gospels,* 150–62). Noting the radicality of the tradition, Koester writes: "The behavior which Jesus requests is a demonstration of the kingdom's presence, i.e., of a society which is governed by new principles of ethics. This not only ascribes a kerygmatic quality to the ethical demands of Jesus, it presents Jesus as a prophet rather than a teacher of wisdom. Although formal claims of Jesus to prophetic authorization, such as a vision of a calling or the introductory formula 'thus says the Lord,' are missing, the prophetic role of Jesus is evident in the address of these ethical demands to a community, not just to individual followers" (p. 160). Richard Horsley, claiming that almost half of *Thomas*'s sayings are "prophetic and apocalyptic" material, proposes that Robinson's designation for the genre be adjusted to LOGOI PROPHETON ("Logoi Propheton? Reflections on the Genre of Q," *The Future of Early Christianity: Essays in Honor of Helmut Koester* [ed. B. A. Pearson et al.; Minneapolis: Fortress Press, 1991] 195–209, esp. 200–201). However, while there may be prophetic sayings (using Koester's ethical definition of "prophetic"), there are no apocalyptic sayings in *Thomas.* Of those Horsley names, six may be understood more readily in terms of speculative wisdom or Gnosticism (*Thomas* 11, 17, 18, 19, 85, and 111); the remaining saying is in fact antiapocalyptic (*Thomas* 51).

While there is some merit to this proposal,[65] there are problems with it as well. While the Jewish prophetic tradition is on the whole very specific, aiming its social criticism at particular persons or institutions or policies, the early Q–*Thomas* tradition is very general and hortatory.[66] In this sense the content, while socially radical, is still very wisdom-like. Gerd Theissen and Burton Mack have suggested Greco-Roman Cynicism as a particularly apt point of comparison for understanding this early tradition.[67] However, while there are indeed many instructive parallels between the Jesus movement and Cynicism, especially in terms of style of dress and public comportment, missing from the Jesus tradition is the one overarching theme that seems to characterize Cynicism as a whole: self-sufficiency.[68]

In my view, this tradition — even with all of its radicality — is still best described as wisdom. To be sure, in many ways it defies what we have come to expect of wisdom; however, in other respects it is very wisdom-like indeed. Most significantly, it shares wisdom's basic task: the interpretation of human existence as lived out in the intense historicity of everyday life.[69] A radical perspective like that of the Q–*Thomas* tradition could well have led to an utter disregard for the world and withdrawal into fantasies of a transcendent reality in which the ideals of the Jesus movement might be more fully realized. But in choosing familiar wisdom forms as the medium through which to present their social critique, those who propagated this tradition made the decision to remain rooted in their historical reality and engage their culture di-

65. There are many sayings from the common tradition that could be called sapiential or prophetic. One thinks, for example, of the saying in *Thomas* 17 || Q 10:23–24, in which Jesus speaks using the words of Isa 64:4. The parallel use in 1 Cor 2:9, however, suggests that early Christians understood this in terms of speculative wisdom. The classification of the Q–*Thomas* beatitudes is also problematic. Bultmann classified them as prophetic and apocalyptic sayings (*History,* 109–10), but the designation is much disputed (see the discussion in Kloppenborg, *Formation of Q,* 187–89). Kloppenborg uses the felicitous term "radical wisdom" to describe them (p. 189; cf. H. D. Betz, "The Beatitudes of the Sermon on the Mount [Matt. 5:3–12]," *Essays on the Sermon on the Mount* [Philadelphia: Fortress Press, 1985] 17–36, who calls them "anti-wisdom").

66. The exception is *Thom* 39:1–2 || Q 11:52, where the Pharisees are criticized. But this does not characterize the tradition as a whole. In this sense it is very much unlike Jeremiah.

67. G. Theissen, "Wanderradikalismus: Literatursoziologische Aspekte der Überlieferung von Worten Jesu im Urchristentum," *ZTK* 70 (1973) 255–56; also idem, *Sociology of Early Palestinian Christianity* (trans. John Bowden; Philadelphia: Fortress Press, 1978) 15; Mack, *Myth of Innocence,* 72–74, 84–87.

68. Cf. Crossan, *Historical Jesus,* 338–44.

69. So Beardslee, "Wisdom Tradition," 231–32.

rectly, even though what they had to say about that culture turned out to be quite unconventional by wisdom standards.[70] Rather than undergird the cultural systems that define human existence, this "wisdom" served to undermine culture. This was countercultural wisdom.

To define the tradition only negatively in this way leaves something to be desired. It tells us what the common tradition is against, but not what it is for; it tells us what it seeks to deconstruct, but not what it would erect in its place. But such a definition is in a sense true to the common tradition itself. Its proclivities are far more deconstructive than constructive. Yet something positive may be drawn even from this characterization: it tells us by whom and for whom this tradition was cultivated. The question, What next? — that is, the question of what shall replace the culture that is so critically undermined by the early Jesus movement — is a question that would arise only from those who were somewhat invested in the status quo. For such persons the demise of the status quo would present a crisis: How shall I survive?... How shall I exist?... What will my future be? But there are others in an agrarian culture, such as that from which this tradition originally emerged, for whom this would not be true. These are the persons whom Gerhard Lenski calls the "expendable class" — the beggars, the criminals, the itinerant and chronically underemployed.[71] For these "expendables," who had no stake whatsoever in culture, in the future, and in the empire, for whom survival already stood in question — for these persons it would have been enough to deconstruct the status quo and sweep it away.[72] It would matter little what shape this new empire of God would take — just so long as it belonged to the beggars (*Thomas* 54 || Q 6:20b), and no one asked them to wait for it (*Thomas* 113 || Q 17:20–21). Countercultural wisdom is wisdom pursued in the interest of the culturally marginalized.

70. This hypothesis is built upon that of Beardslee (see "Wisdom Tradition" and "Uses of the Proverb"). The point is also stressed by N. Perrin (*Jesus and the Language of the Kingdom: Symbol and Metaphor in New Testament Interpretation* [Philadelphia: Fortress Press, 1976] 48–54) and especially J. D. Crossan in his distinction between the conventional "proverbial" saying and the more radical, "dis-ordering" aphorism (*In Fragments,* 3–36).

71. G. E. Lenski, *Power and Privilege: A Theory of Social Stratification* (New York: McGraw-Hill Book Co., 1966) 281–82. We might also include here Lenski's "unclean and degraded classes" — prostitutes, tax collectors, etc. — familiar figures from the Synoptic tradition. Crossan suggests the appropriateness of Lenski's categories (*Historical Jesus,* 43–46, esp. 273).

72. Cf. Theissen's similar suggestion in "Wanderradikalismus," 252; also *Sociology,* 15–16.

FROM THE COMMON TRADITION TO Q AND *THOMAS*

Having described the foundational tradition out of which the Q and *Thomas* trajectories emerged, it is now possible to look at how the history of this tradition is played out as it reaches the literary phase of its two trajectories, Q and *Thomas.* In the case of Q, one may observe this process over a relatively extended period by noting how materials from the common tradition are incorporated into the two distinct phases of Q's history, Q^1 and Q^2. In the case of *Thomas* the possibilities are more limited since knowledge of the history of this document has not progressed beyond a monolithic conception of its composition, even though its form suggests an aggregative compositional history even more complicated than that of Q. Here a few general remarks must suffice.

Q^1: Training the Tradition

A majority of the sayings common to Q and *Thomas* were taken up into Q in its first redaction.[73] The continuity between oral and written tradition here is considerable. For example, in Q^1 the tradition has been arranged into a series of wisdom speeches. But one may suppose that the sages of earliest Christianity were constantly doing this *ad hoc* long before the writing of a particular set of speeches, as they sparred with, debated, and cajoled anyone who would care to join in on the streets and in the marketplaces of the ancient world. Nevertheless, the fact that the tradition has now been written down has implications. First, writing implies something about the social makeup of the group: someone in the group can now write. No longer is the community made up entirely of the socially marginalized. Literacy itself implies social standing and — presumably — social investment. These early Christians have made allies. Second, writing things down changes the nature of the tradition itself. In distinction from the fleeting, temporary character of the spoken word, the written word has a permanent, fixed form. It is subject to analysis, comparison, manipulation — it can be applied consistently toward a particular end. Its very existence can become a "statement" around which thoughts and actions can be organized.[74]

73. This comprises most of the sayings listed in category (1) in the inventory of Q–*Thomas* parallels above.

74. This seems to me to be one of the implications of Goody's observations about the nature of writing as over against spoken communication (*Domestication of the Savage Mind,* 37). Writing, that is, fixing a text in some permanent form, writes Goody,

The ramifications of these changes may be seen in the way Q[1] makes use of the common tradition in three of its speeches: the Q Sermon (Q 6:20–49), the discourse commonly titled "On Cares" (Q 12:22–32), and the Mission Discourse (Q 10:1–12).

Several sayings from the common tradition have been taken up into the Q[1] Sermon (Kloppenborg's "Inaugural Sermon" [Q 6:20–49]): *Thomas* 54 || Q 6:20b; *Thom* 69:2 || Q 6:21b; *Thomas* 68 || Q 6:22; *Thomas* 95 || Q 6:30; *Thomas* 34 || Q 6:39; *Thomas* 26 || Q 6:41–42; *Thomas* 45 || Q 6:43–45. The first three of these are beatitudes; they have been incorporated into the beatitude collection that begins the Q Sermon (Q 6:20–23). There is nothing here to distinguish them over against their significance as free sayings in the common tradition until v. 23, where Q attaches to the fourth beatitude (*Thomas* 68 || Q 6:22) the admonition: "Rejoice . . . for your reward is great in heaven." This changes things. A thought is given over to the future: a reward lies ahead. No longer simply a reflection on the existence of culturally marginalized persons, these sayings now express an ethic, a *program,* whose following merits a reward. Reflection on marginal living has become a radical ethic of the reign of God.[75] The saying in *Thomas* 95 || Q 6:30 is the closest thing to an admonition in the common tradition; it is used as such in the Q Sermon. With the remaining Q–*Thomas* sayings in the sermon, however, there is a considerable transformation to be observed. All three are at base simple wisdom sayings. Yet in Q they have been cast together with several other sayings (Q 6:39–45) as a kind of parenetic supplement to the instruction in the main body of the sermon (Q 6:20–38). Rather than offering general insight into the nature of human existence, each now addresses itself to the one who hears/reads this instruction: listen and learn lest *you* be as the blind who would attempt to lead in ignorance (*Thomas* 34 || Q 6:39), lest *you* stumble around with a log in your eye trying to remove specks from another's (*Thomas* 34 || Q 6:39; *Thomas* 26 || Q 6:41–42), lest *you* be found bearing bad fruit (*Thomas* 45 || Q 6:43–45).[76] No longer sim-

---

"encouraged, at the very same time, criticism and commentary on the one hand and the orthodoxy of the book on the other." I would add that it can encourage both the orthodox *character* of the book and the orthodox *status* of the book. Once something has been written down it can become a reference point around which organization can take place.

75. So Kloppenborg, *Formation of Q,* 189. Kloppenborg prefers the term "radical discipleship."

76. Kloppenborg (*Formation of Q,* 184–85) compares it to the parenesis in Rom 14:2–23 and Jas 4:11–12.

ple proverbs, these sayings have become the sanction for the radical ethic outlined in the sermon.

A similar transformation can be seen in the Q[1] speech commonly titled "On Cares" (Q 12:22–32). There are antecedents for this well-crafted discourse in the common tradition, but they are limited to an admonition not to worry about what clothing to wear (*Thomas* 36 [Coptic] || Q 12:22), or perhaps a Cynic-like general affirmation of nature's providential care (*Thom* 36:1–2 [Gk.] || Q 12:22, 27, 29).[77] As such the saying(s) provide sage advice to those struggling on the margins of social acceptability. In Q[1], however, the tone has shifted slightly; the addition of v. 31 makes all the difference. Here is a program: "Instead, seek his reign and these things will be added to you." The Q author does not entertain a kind of naive trust in the providential goodness of the universe, but rather a program: seeking the reign of God. It is through "seeking the reign" of God that care is provided.[78]

Finally, we might look at how Q[1] makes use of the common tradition in composing its version of the Mission Discourse (Q 10:1–12).[79] There are two identifiable sayings from the common tradition in this speech: *Thomas* 73 || Q 10:2 and *Thom* 14:4 || Q 10:8–9. The first of these is most instructive. In *Thomas* the saying stands alone, without any context to suggest its appropriateness to mission activity. Its frame of reference is broader: it has meaning to anyone fighting an uphill battle and in need of more help. Its appeal to anyone thinking and living counterculturally is readily explicable. In the case of Q, on the other hand, its

77. The tradition history here is complex and not yet fully understood. *Thomas* 36 exists in two versions, a shorter version (Coptic) and a longer version (Greek), which incorporates more of the material found in the Q version of the tradition (longer still than both *Thomas* versions). Under the theory that traditions expand over time, the Coptic version would be the oldest, followed by that of Greek *Thomas* and finally the Q version. But traditions do not always expand, and the propensity of oral tradition to preserve a tradition in multifarious forms is well known. Furthermore, the fact that two different *Thomas* manuscripts of relatively late date preserve the tradition differently shows that the oral tradition continued to affect the shaping of the tradition long after it was written down for the first time. Under such circumstances it may be impossible to determine which version stands closest to the "original."

78. So H. D. Betz, "Cosmogony and Ethics in the Sermon on the Mount," *Essays on the Sermon on the Mount*, 89–123, esp. 118.

79. It is possible that Q did not compose this discourse from scratch, but used a tradition it holds in common with Mark 6:8–13. However, the fact that only in Q 10:2–12 do we find parallels to the *Thomas* material suggests that at any rate, basic to Q's work was the incorporation of materials from the common oral tradition into this complex. Thus, Q[1]'s Mission Discourse provides an opportunity to examine how Q combines free sayings with a traditional complex.

use is somewhat awkward. It is placed on the lips of Jesus ostensibly in an address to missionaries being sent out to visit various cities and towns. In such a context, how is one to understand its final clause? ("Pray therefore the Lord of the harvest to send out laborers into his harvest.") As addressed to the laborers it makes little sense. One is left to agree with Mack's observation that although in the fictive pretext of the Q discourse this saying is addressed to those being sent out, in reality the Q author has in mind to address through this saying those who are to do the sending.[80] It has been employed to undergird a program of mission activity.

The other saying from the common tradition taken up by Q in this discourse has been similarly used. *Thom* 14:2 is sage advice for beggars: "When you go into any country and walk from place to place, when people receive you, eat what they serve you and heal the sick among them." Apart from its Q context the saying simply presumes an itinerant context in which begging is cast in the form of an exchange: food for care.[81] Q's use of the saying is more complex. Set now among a series of instructions for assessing the receptivity of households and towns (Q 10:5–11), it becomes part of the program of spreading the reign of God. The effect of this new context may be seen in the saying itself through the addition of the words, "And say to them, 'The kingdom of God has come near to you' " (10:9b). The entire Mission Discourse is an etiology for the organizational aspect of the program: even as travelers are commissioned, communities are asked to supply both more recruits for the task and support for those already engaged.[82]

In all three of these cases, the largely critical and dismantling agenda of the common tradition has been trained in the service of a program: the reign of God. To be sure, this program retains much of the countercultural impetus of the common tradition. The difference is that in Q^1 there are indications that considerable reflection has been given to the future, to establishing something. When one considers the shifting sociology of the group suggested first and foremost simply by the writing down of the tradition, the new developments become explicable. What was once the creation of a socially and culturally marginalized

80. See Mack, "The Kingdom That Didn't Come," *Society of Biblical Literature 1988 Seminar Papers* (ed. D. J. Lull; SBLSP 27; Atlanta: Scholars Press, 1988) 623.

81. Cf. Theissen's suggestion that the early Jesus movement engaged in "begging of a higher order" ("Wanderradikalismus," 260; *Sociology*, 14).

82. So Mack, "The Kingdom That Didn't Come," 623.

group has become meaningful to persons from a somewhat higher niche in society, persons whose cultural position has afforded them the rare possession of writing.[83] It is no longer enough to deconstruct the status quo. Some thought must now be given to training the tradition in the direction of a program, through which a new future is to be secured.

Q^2: Transcendentalizing the Tradition

When one turns to the texts assigned by Kloppenborg to Q's second edition (Q^2), two theological developments stand out. The first is that for the first time the language peculiar to the speculative side of Jewish wisdom literature is introduced (Q 7:35; 10:21–22; 11:31–32; and 11:49–51).[84] The second is the introduction of a number of passages whose general theme is judgment, whether this be in the form of a call to prepare for its imminent arrival (Q 3:7–9, 16–17; 12:39–40, 42–46, 49, 51–59), a description of its actual unfolding (Q 17:23, 24, 26–30, 34–35, 37), or criticism of those against whom it is ultimately aimed (Q 7:31–35; 11:29–32, 39–52).[85] The two developments are related.

Both of these developments, in contrast to the basically optimistic and confident strains of proverbial wisdom, reflect a profound sense of disappointment. Both traditions are used in Q^2 to sound a warning against those who have neglected to heed the Q group's preaching.[86] Both traditions are used to give expression to its despair at not having made more of an impression on its audience. On the nature of speculative wisdom, Beardslee writes:

83. Writing alone would indicate the presence of such persons in the group; in antiquity writing was the possession of a small elite (see n. 31, above). *Why* such persons would be attracted to the Jesus movement is another question. Theissen points to a number of factors — political, economic, and ecological — that might have threatened a broad segment of first-century Palestinian society (not just the poorest of the poor) with social up-rootedness and downward mobility. See esp. his "'Wir Haben Alles Verlassen' (Mc. X,28): Nachfolge und soziale Entwurzelung in der jüdisch-palästinischen Gesellschaft des 1. Jahrhunderts n. Chr.," *NovT* 19 (1977) 161–96; also *Sociology,* 39–46.

84. See the primary discussion by D. Lührmann (*Redaktion,* 97–100). All of these passages belong to Q^2. Note, however, that two seem to relate to wisdom tradition in a positive way (7:35 and 11:49), but the third seems very negative toward the sages (10:21), and a fourth seems to suggest that the teaching of the Jesus movement has now surpassed that of the sages (11:31). The implication is that while the Jesus movement on some level embraced wisdom tradition, it probably finds itself in competition with other Jewish groups that likewise have laid claim to its legitimate interpretation.

85. For discussion see esp. Kloppenborg, *Formation of Q,* 102–66; also Lührmann, *Redaktion,* passim.

86. On this relationship between apocalyptic and speculative wisdom in Q see Lührmann, *Redaktion,* 99–100.

> In this line of development, the despair of finding God's righteousness in the world, instead of leading back to the Law as a concrete revelation, stimulates a reaching beyond the world to a transcendent Wisdom not manifested in this world. This development leads to a reversal of the meaning of Wisdom. Instead of something to be identified through a sound understanding of the world, Wisdom becomes something unavailable to men, not existent in the world. It has come to men by some special knowledge.[87]

The despair of which Beardslee speaks is, of course, also at the root of the apocalypticist's strains of judgment spoken against "this generation." No longer confident of a reign of God to be realized in the present world of human endeavor, the apocalyptic redactor of Q^2 turns to the transcendent realm of the future, in which God's intervention sets things aright. The program so industriously pursued in the rhetoric of Q^1 is now given a contingent status as the Q community regroups and rethinks its agenda in the light of what must have been at best a lukewarm response to its preaching. Concerning this moment in the life of the Q community, Mack observes: "A program thought to be constructive was experienced as ineffective. In response to those whose rejection hindered the progress of the program, the mode of 'instruction' switched to the mode of defense, reproach, and threat of judgment."[88]

In this effort of regrouping and reinterpretation, the Q redactor goes once again to draw from the well of tradition, appropriating and transforming sayings from the common tradition in the service of this new apocalyptic paradigm. A number of instructive examples suggest themselves. For example, in Q 19:26 an originally free-standing saying about the rich getting richer while the poor grow poorer (cf. *Thom* 41:1–2) is given a more positive interpretation and attached to Q's parable of the talents, here read as an allegory for the coming judgment. In Q 11:39–41 an originally free-standing saying critical of popular piety is incorporated into a long polemical speech against the Pharisees (Q 11:14–26, 29–32, 33–36, 39–52). This critical attitude toward the Pharisees is not original to Q; at least one saying from the common tradition bears this mark early on. It too is incorporated into this Q speech (Q 11:52 || *Thom* 39:1–2). Four sayings from the common tradition are taken up into the

87. Beardslee, "Wisdom Tradition," 233 (also his n. 10).

88. Mack, "Kingdom That Didn't Come," 619. Mack here follows especially Kloppenborg, *Formation of Q*, 102–70 (esp. 167–68), 324–25.

Q speech calling for preparation before the coming judgment (Q 12:39–40, 42–46, 49, 51–53, [54–56], 57–59). In their Q contexts they all seem vaguely appropriate, yet when seen as independent sayings they do not necessarily connote that which is imposed upon them in Q. For example, Q 12:39 || *Thomas* 103 is an exhortation to watchfulness, but not necessarily a warning that apocalyptic judgment is near. Likewise, Q 12:56 || *Thomas* 91 speaks of recognizing the significance of the events in which this group is involved, but there is no indication here that the sage regards the moment as an apocalyptic one. Further, Q 12:49 || *Thomas* 10 has a more ominous tone, as does Q 12:51–53 || *Thom* 16:1–4, but it is Q that provides the apocalyptic framework in which these polemical sayings take on a more apocalyptic flavor.[89]

In Q^2 the sayings tradition takes a transcendental turn. The early tradition of countercultural wisdom, whose proverbial and aphoristic character suggests a hermeneutic grounded in the world of human experience, has been overlaid with traditions of a more speculative nature. Wisdom theology provides one of the new paradigms from which Q^2 draws. The other is provided by apocalypticism. It is into the latter that Q^2 is able to incorporate sayings from the common tradition, for there already one could find material of a polemical nature to augment — perhaps even suggest — the new theological strategy of divine judgment.

THOMAS: PERSONALIZING THE TRADITION

The *Gospel of Thomas* is a different sort of document than Q. To be sure, both are sayings collections, but in contrast to Q, with its elaborate speeches designed to weave its sayings into a rhetorically effective presentation, *Thomas* presents its sayings in a very simple serial format. It is much more like a list than the literary work that is Q. As such, functionally it lies much closer to the oral context of its genesis than does Q.[90] It still relies upon the skill of the sage to choose sayings wisely from its repertoire and combine them to form a persuasive argument. Thus, most of the sayings from the common tradition taken up by *Thomas* have

89. For a nonapocalyptic reading of this saying see S. J. Patterson, "Fire and Dissension: Ipsissima Vox Jesu in Q 12:49, 51–53?" *Forum* 5 (1989) 135.

90. For lists as a primary form of writing see Goody, *Domestication of the Savage Mind,* 74–111.

not been given a specifically "Thomean" interpretation;[91] it is the task of the sage schooled in the *Thomas* tradition to "discover" this (Thom 1).

Still, by fixing words in a permanent visual field, writing invites comparison, reflection, and ultimately manipulation of the word.[92] We must assume that many of *Thomas*'s sayings have been recast in forms congenial to the collector's own interpretation of the tradition. However, there are only a handful of sayings from the common tradition in which something of this process may be observed with any degree of control. These are sayings that have been drawn into and recast in the service of the esoteric theology peculiar to *Thomas,* but which survive in Q in a more original form. That Q indeed preserves a more original version in each case is confirmed by a second version of the saying in *Thomas* that reads roughly the same as that found in Q. This confirms that *Thomas* also knew these sayings originally in more or less their Q form. The sayings are: *Thomas* 2 and 92[93] || Q 11:9–10; *Thomas* 3[94] || Luke 17:20–21; *Thom* 5:2[95] || Q 12:2; *Thom* 69:1[96] || Q 6:22–23; and *Thomas* 101[97] || Q 14:26–27. They are instructive for clarifying *Thomas*'s own handling of the common tradition.

In *Thom* 6:3 and Q 12:2 there is a saying from the tradition common to these two texts. A third witness in Mark 4:22 (par. Luke 8:17) attests to its wide currency within the early Jesus movement. Its Q version reads:

> Nothing is covered that will not be revealed,
> or hidden that will not be known.

It is a flexible saying. It can be used as a caution against indiscreet talk (as in Q), or as an admonition to speak up so that the truth will out (as in Matthew's rendering of Q or Mark's use of the saying), or as a warning against private behavior one would not want exposed to divine scrutiny (as in *Thom* 6:3). In all instances it speaks of the inevitability of public disclosure. In *Thom* 5:3, however, it finds another use:

91. These sayings are listed under groups (1), (2), and (3) in the inventory of Q–*Thomas* parallels above.
92. So Goody, *Domestication of the Savage Mind,* 37; Ong, *Orality and Literacy,* 103–5.
93. Cf. the more original form of the saying in *Thomas* 94.
94. Cf. the more original form of the saying in *Thomas* 113.
95. Cf. the more original form of the saying in *Thom* 6:3.
96. Cf. the more original form of the saying in *Thom* 68:1–2.
97. Cf. the more original form of the saying in *Thomas* 55.

> Jesus said, "Know what is before your face, and what is hidden from you will be disclosed to you. For there is nothing hidden that will not be revealed."[98]

The saying is presented in truncated form so that its focus is tightly fixed on "revelation." More important, however, is the first part of the saying, to which our aphorism has been appended as interpretation. Of particular importance is the inclusion of three second-person, singular, male pronouns: *your* face (*pekho*); from *you* (*erok*); to *you* (*nak*). The saying cannot now refer to the inevitability of *public* disclosure. It has become a promise to an individual, a promise that understanding will come. The disclosure of which the aphorism now speaks is not public, but *private.*

The invitation to discovery is found also in the saying from the common tradition attested in Q 11:9–10 and, at its simplest, in Thom 94:

> Jesus [said]: "One who seeks will find, and to [one who knocks] it will be opened."

Its theme, the admonition to seek instruction, derives from the wisdom tradition.[99] Its place in the common tradition is therefore clearly explicable. However, in addition to *Thomas* 94, *Thomas* presents the saying in two other versions. The first is Thom 92:

> Jesus said, "Seek and you will find. In the past I did not tell you the things about which you asked me then. Now I am willing to tell them, but you are not seeking them."

Nothing is said here of the object of seeking, or the results of finding. The admonition to seek instruction is used simply to introduce the saying's more central focus: the one whose role it is to reveal wisdom, Jesus. In *Thomas* the quest for wisdom is not to be carried out in the world. Wisdom is inaccessible, hidden, not self-evident. It must be revealed, and the request for revelation must be timely.

A third version of the saying in *Thomas* reads as follows:

98. Cited according to the Coptic version. The version of the saying in POxy 654 contains what is probably a secondary expansion: "nor buried that will not be raised" (so H. W. Attridge, "Appendix: The Greek Fragments," *Nag Hammadi Codex II, 2–7 Together with XII, 2 Brit. Lib. Or. 4926 [1], and P. Oxv. 1. 654. 655;* Vol. 1: *Gospel According to Thomas, Gospel According to Philip, Hypostasis of the Archons, and Indexes* [ed. Bentley Layton; NHS 20; Leiden: E. J. Brill, 1989] 101).

99. Cf. Prov 8:17; Sir 6:27; Wis 6:12.

> Jesus said, "Let one who seeks not stop seeking until one finds. And when one finds, one will be disturbed. When one is disturbed, one will marvel, and will reign over the All."[100]

One is struck by how obtuse the saying appears. It speaks of the object of revelation, but only obliquely. Its language is not that of wisdom; it is esoteric language, coded for an audience who understands it. What is it that one discovers? Why does it disturb? What is its power? We do not know. The esotericism of the saying is impenetrable; its secrets are not for the outsider to know. Elsewhere (*Thomas* 77) *Thomas* equates Jesus with "the All," but in the next breath clarifies: "From [Jesus] did the All come forth." The deeper we dig, the more mystifying the tradition becomes.

The object of knowing is clearer in *Thomas* 3. This saying is based loosely upon the saying from the common tradition attested in *Thomas* 113 and Q 17:20–21. The earlier version speaks of the presence of the kingdom in a way that is quite at home in the earliest stratum of countercultural wisdom discussed above. Its *Thomas* version reads:

> His disciples said to him, "When will the kingdom come?" <Jesus said,> "It will not come by looking for it, nor will it do to say, 'Behold, over here!' or 'Behold, over there!' Rather, the kingdom of the Father is spread out upon the earth, but people do not see it."

The kingdom exists as potential, realizable whenever people chose to "see it." But *Thomas* 3 speaks differently of the kingdom:

> [1]Jesus said, "If your leaders say to you, 'Look, the kingdom is in the sky,' then the birds of the sky will precede you. [2]If they say to you, 'It is in the sea,' then the fish will precede you. [3]Rather, the kingdom is within you and it is outside you. [4]When you know yourselves, then you will be known, and you will understand that you are children of the living Father. [5]But if you do not know yourselves, then you live in poverty, and you are the poverty."

Whether this is in fact a version of the earlier saying or just a free composition based upon it is not of significance.[101] What is important is that here the kingdom is no longer something to be discovered "spread out

100. The POxy 654 version is slightly different. It omits any reference to the "All" and adds the sentence: "And [once one has ruled], one will [attain rest]."

101. The first part of the saying is a freehand burlesque of the popular Jewish motif of seeking after wisdom in the furthest reaches of the universe, taking Job 28:12–15 and Bar 3:29–4:1 as its point of departure (so T. F. Glasson, "The Gospel of Thomas 3, and Deuteronomy xxx, 11–14," *ExpTim* 78 [1976–77] 151–52; also S. Davies, *The Gospel of Thomas and Christian Wisdom* [New York: Seabury Press, 1983] 41–46).

upon the earth." It is "within" you as well as "outside" you. The transition from v. 3 to v. 4 is awkward and vague; however, it is apparent that the author wishes to identify the kingdom's disclosure somehow with self-disclosure and self-understanding. The content of this disclosure is one's true identity as a child "of the living Father."

This brings us close to the heart of the matter for *Thomas*. Now it is clear that we are not dealing with the wisdom tradition in a form similar to that attested in the tradition common to Q and *Thomas*, or even in the first redaction of Q. For *Thomas* the great truths about human existence are not to be discovered in the deconstruction of oppressive cultural systems, or in the pursuit of a culturally radical program (kingdom), but in awakening to words of revelation spoken by a redeemer who has come from God (*Thomas* 28; 38). Truth comes through private disclosure (*Thomas* 23; 62; 83–84; 108). It has to do with recognizing one's alien status in the world (*Thomas* 56; 80; 110) and recognizing the one whose words are revelation and life (*Thomas* 1; 13; 15; 43; 52:2; 59; 61:3; 77; 91; 111). The kingdom is no longer an earthly reality, even in potential terms, but a transcendent realm to which identity as its children constitutes entitlement. A brief catechism stands at the heart of the *Thomas* collection (*Thomas* 49–50):

> **49**[1]Jesus said, "Congratulations to those who are alone and chosen, for you will find the kingdom. [2]For you have come from it, and you will return there again." **50**[1]Jesus said, "If they say to you, 'Where have you come from?' say to them, 'We have come from the light, from the place where the light came into being by itself, established [itself], and appeared in their image.' [2]If they say to you, 'Is it you?' say, 'We are its children, and we are the chosen of the living Father.' [3]If they ask you, 'What is the evidence of your Father in you?' say to them, 'It is motion and rest.' "

The theological paradigm into which this sort of thinking fits most readily is Gnosticism. To be sure, *Thomas* does not contain much of the highly complex mythological structure considered to be typical of Christian Gnostic texts of the second century and later. Nonetheless, the rudiments of Gnostic thought are clearly in place: an expression of alienation to a world conceived of as evil; a revealer whose mission it is to disclose to human beings their true identity and origin in another realm; the call to awaken and return to the heavenly realm of their origin. This is rudimentary Gnosticism.

However, one should not therefore view developments on the *Thomas* side of the tradition in discontinuity with what we have already observed on the Q side of the tradition, that is, a gradual modulation into speculative wisdom and apocalypticism. The line between speculative wisdom, with its conviction that wisdom and righteousness have disappeared from the world and must now be revealed to faithful souls through Sophia's emissaries — the line between this and Gnosticism such as we have in *Thomas* is broad and fuzzy.[102] As Hans-Martin Schenke has shown, we have to do here not with two distinct religious phenomena, but with two very similar ways of thinking that lie close together on a continuum, a continuum whose extremes are the very optimistic parenetical forms of wisdom found in collections of proverbs, on the one hand, and, on the other, the elaborate Gnostic systems of late antiquity, whose pessimism about the world is enshrined in their extraordinarily complex accounts of how it got to be so bad.[103] Both *Thomas* and Q^2 — insofar as the latter entertains notions from the more speculative wisdom tradition — lie closer to the end of this continuum that is characterized by its pessimism about the world.[104] And even when considered in terms of its more dominant theological paradigm (apocalypticism), Q^2 shares with *Thomas* this basic pessimism about the world as the arena in which the reign of God is to be realized.[105] As Q's

102. S. Davies has argued that *Thomas* is more a work of speculative wisdom than of Gnosticism (*Gospel of Thomas,* 18–61). Davies is correct in pointing to certain affinities between *Thomas* and speculative Jewish wisdom and in pointing out that *Thomas* lacks some typically Gnostic characteristics, such as intricate descriptions of the world and of its creation, and most of all the figure of the Gnostic demiurge, responsible for the creation of an evil world. However, neither does *Thomas* share the characteristic vocabulary of speculative Jewish wisdom. For example, the Coptic words that might render the Greek *sóphos/sophía* (wise/wisdom) occur only four times in *Thomas* (*Thom* 8:1, 2; 13:3; and 76:2). Only in *Thom* 13:3 is Jesus called "wise," and this is in error. The word *gnōsis* (knowledge) is also rare in *Thomas* (only in 39:1), but the verbal forms for "knowing" (*souōn*) or "understanding" (*epistēmōn*) are relatively frequent (see esp. *Thom* 3:4, 5; 5:1; 18:3; 19:4; 21:8; 65:4; 67; 69:1; 80:1; 91:2; and 105). The point is that *Thomas* does not fit either characterization cleanly.

103. H.-M. Schenke, "Die Tendenz der Weisheit zur Gnosis," *Gnosis: Festschrift Hans Jonas* (ed. B. Aland; Göttingen: Vandenhoeck & Ruprecht, 1978) 351–72. See also G. W. MacRae, "The Jewish Background of the Gnostic Sophia Myth," *NovT* 12 (1970) 86–101. Schenke's work is offered as an adjustment to Robinson's thesis in "LOGOI SOPHON." Schenke argues that there is no automatic tendency toward Gnosticism within the wisdom sayings genre; rather, the flow of traditions between wisdom and Gnosticism runs both ways. The movement from wisdom to Gnosticism occurs particularly in an atmosphere of pessimism about the world (see esp. "Die Tendenz," 358–59).

104. Cf. Schenke, "Die Tendenz," 358–59.

105. One recalls the hypothesis of G. von Rad that apocalypticism emerged from out of the wisdom tradition in Israel (*Old Testament Theology* [New York: Harper & Row, 1965] 2.304–8). Von Rad, however, does not link these traditions through the development of pessimism or skepticism in wisdom, but through the quest for knowledge and the desire to deal with life's most pressing questions. The role that disappointment and

tradents came ever more to embrace apocalypticism as the appropriate theological expression of their experience, *Thomas*'s tradents chose Gnosticism. Thus, their respective theologies place them on divergent trajectories. However, they are united in their common experience of disillusionment and disappointment in the world. Each in its own way has turned to transcendence in an effort to keep hope alive.

CONCLUSIONS

At the base of the early Christian sayings tradition represented by Q and *Thomas* there lies a body of sayings (parables, proverbs, aphorisms, community rules, etc.). Among these sayings a predominance of wisdom forms suggests a hermeneutic consonant with wisdom tradition: they are about insight into human existence and what it means to live life faithfully toward God. The tradition is grounded in a quest for answers to the very real dilemmas of historical existence. Their insights, however, are quite radical and culturally critical. They are given to speaking of a reign of God, in which their cultural critique is most direct, as they lay out in parable and aphorism an alternative to common ways of ordering human existence. At first their critique is more negative than positive, without a clear program (the common tradition). With Q^1, however, a more positive program comes into view, as its now anonymous author, in composing a series of sapiential speeches, can be seen to lay out the radical ethic more clearly. In Q^2 the social radicalism that characterized the earlier sayings tradition is still intact; however, any hope for actualizing any of the movement's program, given the present state of affairs in the world, has evaporated. The redactor has turned to two other theological paradigms to give expression to this disappointment about the past and pessimism about the future: speculative wisdom and the closely related tradition of apocalypticism. On the *Thomas* side of the tradition our redaction-critical work has not progressed to the point of making us privy to any distinct phases in the history of this trajectory. However, when it is picked up in the latter part of the first century in the form of the *Gospel of Thomas*, it is clear that something not unlike what happened in the Q trajectory has happened here as well. Any of wisdom's optimism about finding meaning in the

---

pessimism play in the transition from wisdom to apocalypticism is the contribution of recent Q studies.

world of human existence has given way to a hope only for personal salvation. Through the theological paradigm of Gnosticism the reign of God has become a transcendent realm to which faithful, discerning souls will someday pass, leaving the world behind.

Wisdom is about the quest for insight into the nature of the world and human existence in it. If one experiences the world as a benevolent place, or if one at least sees this possibility, wisdom can be a theological exercise in optimism and confidence. But what if one's experience indicates that the best one can say about the world is that it is evil? Then there are other traditions close at hand that can be drawn upon to give this experience its own proper expression. When early Christians experienced the world in this way they turned to apocalypticism and Gnosticism. Apocalypticism and Gnosticism lie close to wisdom when the sage experiences the world as evil, and the quest for meaning in social structures, perceived as unalterable, collapses in despair. This is what happened ultimately to the early Christian wisdom movement that produced Q and *Thomas*.

12

WISDOM AND APOCALYPTICISM IN MARK

Richard Horsley

In the standard wisdom of New Testament scholarship, not only does the Gospel of Mark *have* an apocalypse — the "Synoptic Apocalypse" of Mark 13 — but it *is* itself apocalyptic. Since Johannes Weiss and Albert Schweitzer, not only Jesus but Mark as well have been understood as presupposing and articulating an apocalyptic view of the world. This has been argued or dealt with in somewhat different ways, nearly all of which now seem problematic.

The standard basis for categorizing Mark or any other piece of early Christian literature as apocalyptic has been the presence of features typical of apocalypticism. We are increasingly recognizing this as a questionable approach. But it is instructive to note what apocalyptic motifs and language are present or absent and, when present, whether they are functional and/or qualified in Mark.

Present are both the motif of resurrection and the figure of "the son of man." However, the occurrences of the term "the son of man" in Mark are diverse, with only a few referring to the future or "apocalyptic son of man" and even those differing significantly in function. Moreover, "resurrection" in Mark refers basically only to Jesus "rising again" in the three predictions in the middle section of the Gospel along with the empty tomb at the very end. Otherwise there is only the academic discussion of the implication of the laws of levirate marriage for belief in the resurrection initiated by the Sadducees, in 12:18–27. In striking contrast to Paul, Mark makes nothing of the general resurrection (of believers) or of Jesus' resurrection as its firstfruits.

Also present in Mark are a reference to "mysteries"[1] and plenty of "unclean spirits." However, the mysteries disclosed in the parables in Mark 4 do not appear comparable with the apocalyptic plan of God for the resolution of the major historical crisis, as in Daniel 2 (or the "wisdom in a mystery" of 1 Cor 2:6–7). And, besides not being distinctive to apocalyptic literature, the demons and Satan are not part of a more complete mythical or metaphysical scheme of spatial and temporal dualism. Mark has no transcendent world inhabited by angels, no angel-interpreter appears, no semidivine forces explain mysteries or assist a helpless humanity. Nor is there a temporal dualism. "This age" and "the age to come" appear in passing in 10:30, but the emphasis is explicitly on manifold social-economic restoration "now in this age." Mark simply does not trade in concepts or symbols such as the end time, the eschaton, or a new world of some sort. It is even difficult to claim a last judgment for Mark. The term "the son of man" appears in an apparent judgment scenario twice. But, as we shall see below, one of those sayings functions as a sanction on the disciples' readiness to suffer martyrdom for the cause (8:38), and the other functions as apparent vindication for Jesus as he is about to be sentenced to death by crucifixion (14:62). Mark is full of judgment, but in the form of Jesus' prophetic pronouncements and demonstration against the rulers and ruling institutions (11:12–23; 12:1–9, 38–40; 13:1–2). Furthermore, Mark gives no indications of pessimism, historical determinism, cosmic disorder, social anomie, or impending cosmic catastrophe. One might doubt that the mere presence of mysteries, demons, a rising Jesus, and a future "son of man" make Mark apocalyptic.[2]

1. In establishing the text of Mark, we must always keep in mind the possibility that the "common agreements" of Matthew and Luke against Mark may be rooted in an earlier version of Mark than the one behind our best manuscript evidence. See the compelling recent arguments for an *Urmarkus* in H. Koester, *Ancient Christian Gospels* (Philadelphia: Trinity Press International, 1990) 275–86.

2. The results are similarly negative when we measure Mark 13 and/or Mark as a whole against one of the standard synthetic lists of apocalyptic motifs, e.g., that in K. Koch, *The Rediscovery of Apocalyptic* (SBT 22; 2d series; London: SCM Press, 1972): (1) expectation of imminent end of earthly conditions: no; no; (2) the end as a cosmic catastrophe: no, not even 13:24–25; (3) periodization and determinism: "end" deemphasized in 13:7; (4) angels' and demons' activities: no, Mark 13; yes, Mark 1–9; (5) new salvation, paradisal: not even in Mark 10:2–9; (6) manifestation of kingdom of God: implied in 13:27? yes, 1:15, etc; (7) mediator with royal functions: son of man in 13:26? Christ! and (8) "glory": in passing, 13:26; but emphasis on suffering.

Redaction critics have found more sophisticated ways of arguing that Mark is apocalyptic. Werner Kelber makes the case not so much on the appearance of several apocalyptic motifs as on the basic scheme Mark presupposes and presents.[3] He finds Mark's overall agenda to be the progressive revelation of the kingdom. He then understands this as unfolding in terms of a modern scholarly construct of Christian apocalyptic eschatology: the kingdom, only partially realized and hidden during the ministry of Jesus, reaches its climactic events in the crucifixion and resurrection, but will finally be fully revealed only with the parousia of Jesus as the son of man. Reading the pericope 8:38–9:10 according to this scheme, Kelber finds the basic components in particular terms or symbols taken from the immediate framing or contents of the transfiguration story. Thus, for example, 8:38 turns out to be "the first explicit announcement of the parousia"; then the transfiguration itself is "a parousia epiphany."[4] The other two "future son of man sayings" (13:26; 14:62) also turn out to be references to the parousia. The result of such redaction criticism of Mark is an attractively compact eschatological-christological scheme. "This apocalyptic function of the parousia is of a piece with Mark's theology of the Kingdom. As the Kingdom arrived with Jesus, is hidden at present, but will be seen shortly *en dynamei* (9:1), so also did the Son of Man walk on earth with authority, is absent at present (2:20; 13:34; 14:25), but will be seen *meta dynameis polles* (13:26)."[5]

The scheme that Kelber reads into Mark might well be documented from Paul or Matthew, who do indeed write of the parousia. But Mark 8:38 is hardly an "explicit announcement of the parousia," nor are the other two references to the future "son of man." Read *in* literary context, 8:38, inseparable from 8:34–37, sanctions "taking up the cross and following" Jesus. Without the Matthean transformation of this and particularly other "future son of man sayings" it is difficult to find any parousia in Mark.

Those who have been embarrassed by the presence of apocalyptic elements or worldview in Mark have pursued one or another of two strategies. Some have attempted to deny or discount the apoc-

---

Are the presence of "the kingdom of God" and "the messiah" sufficient to render Mark apocalyptic?

3. W. Kelber, *The Kingdom in Mark* (Philadelphia: Fortress Press, 1974).
4. Ibid., 74, 76.
5. Ibid., 123.

alyptic motifs and perspective in Mark, assigning these to Synoptic traditions or more likely Jewish traditions that Mark used but reworked and mitigated. Others, most recently and critically Burton Mack,[6] acknowledging that Mark is apocalyptic in one way or another, have argued that the apocalyptic elements and/or ideology were developed by the Markan community or the author of the Gospel — thus freeing Jesus and/or the earliest followers of Jesus from features distasteful to modern sensibilities.

PROBLEMATIC CONCEPTS AND PROCEDURES

There are a number of problems with our standard assumptions, concepts, and procedures, however, when it comes to "apocalyptic." All of the above approaches are caught within and/or struggling against a synthetic modern scholarly construct of "apocalyptic." "Apocalyptic" and related concepts were constructed in highly synthetic fashion at the turn of the century by a theologically oriented scholarship that drew the components from ancient Jewish apocalyptic literature in various languages and ranging over a millennium in dates of origin. From this literature, read as descriptive and theological rather than as symbolic or visionary language, a particular "apocalyptic" worldview was constructed. Then that view of the world was found in a particular document or even fragment of literature when certain component motifs or terms were present.

Some of the problems with this would appear to be obvious. (1) Some of the language labeled "apocalyptic" may have been simply common cultural coin and not distinctive to apocalyptic literature and its worldview: hell/hades, angels, demons, divine judgment, and so on. Such terms appear in popular or prophetic discourse as well as in apocalypses. (2) With the synthetic modern construct in place, the tendency is to take particular passages or motifs out of their original literary context and to place them instead into the modern conceptual context. (3) The use of such an abstract synthetic construct means that a particular piece of literature such as Mark is being compared with a worldview that never existed in any particular document or community. It is unclear what might be learned from comparison with such a vague and wide-ranging cultural reification. (4) The misreading of

6. B. L. Mack, *A Myth of Innocence* (Philadelphia: Fortress Press, 1988).

visionary or other metaphorical or hyperbolic imagery as descriptive or metaphysical means that modern misconceptions (such as "cosmic catastrophe" or "antihistorical" or "end time") are imposed on ancient Jewish and Christian literature and its communities. For most of this century standard scholarly handbooks have insisted that Jewish apocalyptic literature was an unfortunate and unprecedented departure from biblical traditions and orientation.[7] The differences found, however, appear to have been merely differences constructed.

More critical analysis of the literary sources on which the synthetic modern construct was ostensibly based has only made the old conceptual apparatus seem all the more problematic. The more precise we become about what qualifies as an "apocalypse" — thanks to the incisive analysis of the SBL "Genre of Apocalypse" group[8] — the less satisfactory our points of comparison for dealing with the earliest "Christian" literature. Virtually no apocalypses other than the *Similitudes of Enoch* and perhaps an updated *Testament of Moses* are extant from the generations just prior to the time of Jesus and Mark. The *Psalms of Solomon* and *Testaments of the Twelve Patriarchs* do not qualify substantively or generically; most Qumran literature does not qualify generically; and 2 *Baruch* and 4 Ezra are later. We are left with Daniel and the early Enoch literature from two centuries earlier.

Adding considerations of the probable differences in social location between apocalyptic literature and Mark only complicates the problem further. Apocalyptic literature was almost certainly produced by and directed to intellectual strata, groups of scribes or sages. Although the author of Mark was obviously literate, the Jesus traditions Mark used were apparently of popular provenance and were orally performed and cultivated in popular communities. The Gospel itself, moreover, would have been read aloud in those popular communities. There is probably also an important regional difference between Mark and Jewish apocalyptic literature. That is, according to an emerging new consensus, Mark

7. See the brief critique in R. Horsley, *Jesus and the Spiral of Violence* (San Francisco: Harper & Row, 1987) 131–40; several critical and critically reconstructive articles by E. Schüssler Fiorenza, G. Nickelsburg, and others in *Apocalypticism in the Mediterranean World and the Near East* (ed. D. Hellholm; Tübingen: J. C. B. Mohr [Paul Siebeck], 1983); and the earlier critique of Koch, *Rediscovery of Apocalyptic*.

8. See *Semeia* 14 (1979); and J. J. Collins, *The Apocalyptic Imagination* (New York: Crossroad, 1984), chap. 1. In retrospect it seems ironic that scholarly definition of genre is based so exclusively on form and content when it comes to literature that was so deliberately functional for crises of history and/or faith.

comes from the Galilean or Syrian periphery — which of course it views as the center of significant action — while most apocalyptic literature is focused and oriented on the ruling center of Jerusalem, even when it is hostile to the rulers there.

ON USING JEWISH LITERATURE IN INTERPRETATION OF MARK

Recent analyses of apocalyptic literature in historical context have laid the basis for a far more adequate understanding of that literature and the situations and people addressed.[9] The question then is the way in which Jewish scribal apocalyptic literature may be used for comparisons with and elucidation of popular literature such as the Gospel of Mark. Certain comparisons and elucidations may be possible because, as I have noted in another context, the scribes who produced apocalyptic literature had come to experience a situation somewhat similar to that of the common people under alien imperial rule in late Hellenistic and early Roman Palestine.[10] Apocalypses such as Daniel and the various sections of *1 Enoch* were literature of resistance by persecuted communities of resistance. The relation of Mark to such apocalyptic literature is at best very indirect, however, and any comparisons must attend to the respective literary and historical social contexts.

Many of the same observations are appropriate to the assessment of "wisdom" in Mark. It is ironic, and a source of considerable divergence of scholarly energy, that wisdom and apocalyptic became separated so dramatically into different worlds and worldviews in New Testament scholarship. As John J. Collins points out in his essay above, Hebrew Bible/Old Testament scholarship does not so divide the two. Indeed, there is increasing consideration of von Rad's suggestion that "the real matrix from which apocalyptic literature originates" is wisdom. The progressively more precise understanding of wisdom traditions emerging in recent years makes credible the possibility that an apocalyptic wisdom may have developed out of mantic wisdom (in contrast with wisdom sayings, nature wisdom, and speculative or theological wisdom), as may be indicated in the book of Daniel (see the dream interpretation opening onto the "mystery" according to which

9. See especially Collins, *Apocalyptic Imagination*, and G. W. E. Nickelsburg, *Jewish Literature Between the Bible and the Mishnah* (Philadelphia: Fortress Press, 1981).

10. See further Horsley, *Jesus and the Spiral of Violence*, chap. 5.

God has planned the resolution of historical crisis in Daniel 2 and the parallel dream in Daniel 7) or in Enoch literature. Thus it makes no sense to maintain the wedge driven between the categories "sapiential" and "apocalyptic" according to which interpreters jump from the form of sayings both to separate literary genres and to whole different world-views or orientations to life supposedly expressed in those respective types of sayings. By pointing out the presence of wisdom sayings in apocalyptic literature and of apocalyptic elements in ostensibly sapiential literature, Collins has demonstrated how unwarranted is the basis of the recent separation of the sayings source Q into separate sapiential and apocalyptic layers.[11] Nevertheless, we must deal with the clear difference between a Sirach and a Daniel, between a collection of sayings from a scribe-sage who also interprets dreams and a collection of dream-visions with attendant interpretation for those undergoing the historical trauma to which they pertain.

Further consideration of the social role and location of both apocalyptic literature and sapiential literature may help elucidate both their differences and their possibly common background and provenance. We must begin with two apparent and determinative realities in ancient Near Eastern societies such as Judea: few people could write, and the social structure was relatively simple. Basically the only people who were literate and who produced literature were the scribes, and their role was, in subordination to and dependence on the rulers, to assist the rulers in governing the society. Ben Sira lays out a rather illuminating description of the fundamental social structure in 38:24–39:11. As long as the scribes and sages could serve under rulers who were either independent or were subject to Persian imperial sponsorship of local cultural and legal traditions, they could simply, as Ben Sira says (39:1–4), "study the law of the Most High,... preserve the discourse of notable men, and seek out the hidden meanings of proverbs," while serving "among great men and... rulers." But once the rulers compromised too much with an imperial situation politically and culturally or even assimilated to the dominant politics and culture, weakening or even abandoning the ancestral laws and customs, they also threatened or even eliminated the role and function of the

11. See also a parallel critique of the use of these categories as a basis for claiming different strata in Q in Horsley, "Questions about Redactional Strata and Social Relations Reflected in Q," SBLSP (Atlanta: Scholars Press, 1989) 186–203; and J. Kloppenborg's response, 204–15.

scribes/sages. It is precisely from the point at which the Judean rulers began to compromise and assimilate that apocalyptic literature such as the sections of *1 Enoch* and Daniel appears, and the thrust of that literature is against such compromise and total political and cultural domination by alien imperial forces. The authors of these apocalyptic visions and speculations were precisely the scribes and sages, the teachers and the wise (*maskilim,* etc.) who had to struggle for their lives as well as rights to continue to preserve proverbs and penetrate parables. It is only to be expected that sapiential proverbs or admonitions would appear in apocalyptic literature. The book of Daniel does indeed articulate a different worldview from the book of Sirach, because the world had changed. The scribes and sages wrote different literature in response to different situations. But rather than reify two different worlds of wisdom and apocalyptic on the basis of different types of sayings and genres, New Testament scholarship should attend to the historical circumstances that particular pieces of literature addressed, instead of pulling motifs and "aphorisms" out of their literary as well as historical context.

Discernment that both sapiential and apocalyptic literature come from people of the same social location and role — that is, scribes and sages who ordinarily served as "retainers" to the Judean rulers — means that for both we have the same problems of comparison with and relevance to popular literature such as Mark. One would only expect to find some overlap and contacts between scribal or learned wisdom and popular wisdom, between a more reflective and consciously systematized scribal explanation and a less reflective popular explanation of a common historical crisis. Sages would find popular maxims illuminating and utilize them or take up popular imagery and "order" it, while the people would likely be influenced at least in some way by their "teachers" despite a certain degree of suspicion and resentment. With both extant apocalyptic literature and extant sapiential literature there are problems of both temporal and regional distance with regard to Mark. Like Daniel and most of *1 Enoch,* Sirach is over two hundred years earlier. Nothing other than possibly the *Testaments of the Twelve Patriarchs* is chronologically close. And given that Galilee had been separated politically from Judea for centuries before the Hasmoneans conquered the area about a hundred years before Jesus, we might expect considerable regional variation. Nevertheless, Judean/Jewish apocalyptic and sapiential literature may provide some useful points of comparison and illumination of apocalyptic motifs and wisdom materials taken up by Mark.

MARK'S PLOTTING: WHAT IS THE GOSPEL ABOUT?

The kingdom and the Christ, indeed. But Mark is about the kingdom in a concrete political, or rather political-religious, sense.[12] Jesus preaches the kingdom and heals people in the *villages* of Galilee and the surrounding areas. He never goes into the ruling cities of Galilee or the surrounding areas. And his activity and preaching in Jerusalem constitute one aggressive prophetic condemnation after another against the ruling institutions of temple and high priesthood. Meanwhile, his preaching and manifestation of the kingdom in Galilean and other villages are unmistakably portrayed as a renewal of Israel. This is signaled clearly in the appointment of the Twelve as symbolic of the whole people of Israel. It is continued then more substantively in the two chains of miracle stories (chaps. 4–8) that clearly repeat the key facets of the founding and renewal of Israel under Moses and Elijah, in stories of sea crossings and wilderness feedings, healings and exorcisms.[13] The renewal of the people Israel is also consistently portrayed — in the alternative cures and forgiveness Jesus offers the people — as a challenge to the established political-religious system centered in Jerusalem, and Jesus is regularly challenged in turn by the representatives of the established system, who are already plotting "how to destroy him" by 3:6. The advent of the kingdom (or should we translate the "politics"?) of God as the renewal of the people of Israel is then further concretized in the renewal of local (covenantal) community. Chapters 8–10 may well be focused on "discipleship," but it is not the individualistic discipleship of much modern exegesis. If it is not already evident in the announcement of new "familial" community in 3:31–35, then the succession of passages (in Mark 10) dealing with the fundamental forms and dimensions of local community, marriage/family, membership, use

12. After the provocative recent studies in "narrative criticism," we simply can no longer read the Gospels piecemeal; nor can we read them primarily for their "theology," as in "redaction criticism." Among the many recent creative and critical analyses: C. Myers, *Binding the Strong Man* (Maryknoll, N.Y.: Orbis Books, 1989); and S. D. Moore, *The Gospels and Literary Criticism* (New Haven, Conn.: Yale University Press, 1990).

13. See Mack, *Myth of Innocence,* chap. 8, for critical elucidation of the miracle chains and their function in Mark.

of economic resources, the manifold restoration of "houses, families, and fields, *now in this age,*" and finally the egalitarian policy of leadership makes abundantly clear just how concrete the kingdom of God announced by Jesus is to be. These teachings about the concrete shape of the renewed community are juxtaposed with and sanctioned by precisely the predictions of the passion and resurrection. Meanwhile, in the pronouncement stories, or more particularly the controversies with the Pharisees and scribes, Mark has Jesus defend local prerogatives, customs, and claim to economic resources over against the representatives of the established system centered in Jerusalem and its efforts to supervise local life and extract economic resources for support of the temple and priesthood.

Closely linked with the main plotting of the preaching and manifestation of the kingdom of God is the role played by Jesus the proclaimer and healer-exorcist. Juxtaposed on the narrative at three crucial points, beginning, middle, and end, are identifications of Jesus as the messiah or Son of God. But Mark fleshes out his special understanding of the messiah's role and agenda not only with miracle chains and controversy stories but also with announcements of the necessity of "the son of man" suffering and dying for the cause and then being raised in vindication. The identification of the messiah with the prophet catalyzing the renewal of Israel (like Moses and Elijah) and with the son of man who must die and be raised is established precisely in the center of the Gospel in the juxtaposition of Peter's confession with Jesus' rebuke and the first announcement of death and resurrection with the transfiguration on the mountain.

MARK'S USE OF APOCALYPTIC MOTIFS

With some sense of the basic narrative or plotting of the Gospel, it may be possible to discern how features of Mark identified as apocalyptic are used or adapted. The place to start is surely at the end. It is not only a fearsome ending, but an open one, inviting the readers/hearers to make a new beginning. After thrice announcing his suffering, death, and rising again in the middle of the Gospel, Jesus then says pointedly, in Gethsemane after the Last Supper, "But after I am raised up, I will go before you to Galilee." Then, in the next to the last statement of the Gospel, the "young man" says not only "he has been raised" but (again) "he is going ahead of you to Galilee." Can there be any doubt that Mark, among all the Gospels, with no actual portrayal of the resurrection or appearances, means that the resurrection *is* Jesus going back to Galilee and leading his disciples (including the women!) to get back to the business of the kingdom that the whole Gospel has just been about? No standing around waiting for ascension, enthronement, Pentecost, or the general resurrection in Mark! Jesus' resurrection in Mark sends people right back to community renewal in Galilee.

What about Kelber's parousia? Far from being a Pauline crucifixion-resurrection kerygma with a long introduction, Mark may not even have known the Pauline gospel. Or if he did, he does not seem to have picked up the concept of parousia. The proof texts previously claimed for the parousia in Mark, as noted above, are "the apocalyptic son of man" sayings. The occurrence at three points in Q of "son of man" sayings classified as "apocalyptic" has recently been the principal basis for claiming a secondary redactional layer in Q. Even so, the occurrence at three points of similarly classified "son of man" sayings continues to be a principal basis for the apocalyptic reading of Mark.

Most of the "son of man" sayings in Mark, of course, have nothing to do with judgment or gathering the elect or influence of visionary imagery from Daniel 7. They are rather the three announcements of the suffering, death, and raising of Jesus (8:31; 9:31; 10:33–34) and four or five other references to Jesus' death or raising that appear to be Markan compositions related to those three formulaic sayings (9:9, 12; 14:21, 41, and possibly 10:45 as well). The sayings about the authority of "the son of man" in 2:10 and "the son of man" as lord of the Sabbath in 2:28 similarly pertain to the life or ministry — and perhaps also still have the general sense of humankind/people having authority to forgive/over the Sabbath. Thus it is only the other three "son of man" sayings that have provided a basis for the apocalyptic reading of Mark in general and the parousia motif in particular.

Although they are usually classified together somewhat vaguely as "future" or "apocalyptic," the formulations and the functions of the three sayings are rather different. In 8:38, a variation on the saying also found in Luke/Q 12:8–9, the "son of man" appears to be an advocate at the divine judgment in the attending company of the angels, and neither saves nor condemns people himself. Mark 13:26–27 alludes to the "coming with the clouds" of Dan 7:13, but in contrast with the "human-like one" of Daniel 7, which symbolized the people who are to be delivered, the "son of man" in Mark 13:26–27 presides over the deliverance, the gathering, of the elect. In Mark 14:62, with apparent quotation of "coming with the clouds of heaven" from Dan 7:13 and allusion to "seated at the right hand" from Ps 110:1 as well, "the son of man" appears to be the divine agent of judgment himself, ready to condemn the high-priestly court and vindicate Jesus.

In none of these sayings in Mark is Jesus identified with "the son of man." Indeed, in Mark 8:38 and 14:62 in particular, Jesus refers to a figure different from himself, in the latter text, a figure who will vindicate him. One could imagine that if Mark had wanted to identify clearly the "son of man" who is Jesus with the future "son of man" as advocate, agent of deliverance, or judge, he would have added a fourth step to the predictions: that is, "the son of man" would suffer, die, rise, and save/judge. We can surmise that the relationship between the two types of "son of man" is so unclear and indefinite in Mark because Mark is at pains to identify the messiah with the suffering "son of man" = Jesus, and/or because Mark is the first in the tradition in which he stands to imply that the two types of "son of man" were the same person. But even the three "future son of man" sayings in Mark are so different from one another that it is difficult to find a consistent image or to imagine that Mark intends them all as the same "title" of a clearly defined redeemer figure. And besides the absence of the term "parousia," there is no indication in these sayings that Mark had some sort of parousia in mind. Jesus had already "gone before them to Galilee." No parousia was to be expected in Mark.

Because there simply is no "end" or parousia in Mark, there is not even the possibility of the Gospel coordinating or juxtaposing such with the defeat of the demonic forces. Satan and numerous "unclean spirits" play a key role in Mark's drama. But they are already being "bound" or driven out by Jesus and disappear from the narrative before the climactic political confrontation of Jesus with the rulers in Jerusalem. Moreover, even though Satan appears as the tempter of Jesus himself and the adversary of the word early in the Gospel (1:13; 4:15), the dominant conflict even there is the religious-political one with the rulers and their retainers (see esp. 1:21–28; 2:1–12; 3:1–6; 4:30–32). This subordinate role and decisive defeat of Satan and the unclean spirits in Mark contrast sharply with the programmatic visualization in the Qumran *Community Rule* (1QS 4:18–25), where the destruction of Falsehood/Angel of Darkness is coordinated with the final intervention or "visitation" by God.

In fact, Mark's portrayal of the struggle between Jesus and the demonic forces contrasts with that in the Dead Sea Scrolls in a more general way, despite their similarities. Mark and the ethos from which Mark and the pre-Markan materials come share with the Qumran community the view that life as they know it is caught in a dualistic struggle between two superhuman forces; such is the assumption behind the "Beelzebul controversy" in Mark 3:22–27. And in both Mark and the Dead Sea Scrolls the "unclean spirits" or "Spirit of Falsehood/Angel of Darkness" (1QS 3–4; cf. "Prince of the Kingdom of Wickedness" [1QM 17]) symbolize the struggle of superhuman or divine forces that helps explain how social-political life could be so completely beyond comprehension in terms of ordinary human causation.[14] Moreover, in both the demonic forces are clearly reflections, as well as explanations, of the control of their lives by the Roman imperial forces; hence the defeat of the demonic forces has more or less direct political implications.[15] In the *War Scroll* from Qumran the defeat of the Prince of the Kingdom of Wickedness is simultaneously the defeat of the Roman imperial forces, and in Mark 5:1–20 the "unclean spirit(s)" are named "legion" and are driven into the sea to their destruction. In Mark, however, the "unclean spirits" appear to function in an ad hoc manner, possessing particular persons while being more or less "at large" as an ominous presence over the land. That Mark and pre-Markan materials simply reflect a common popular belief in demons and Satan is indicated by the scribes' accusation, in which they exploit the common belief to charge Jesus with witchcraft (3:22). The intellectuals at Qumran, on the other hand, had articulated a systematic demonology that helped explain all matters of life under the struggle between the two superhuman "spirits." Mark, originating in and addressed to a popular movement, does not appear to have assimilated much by way of the more systematic reflection cultivated among the scribal circles that produced the extant apocalyptic literature.

14. On the function of such apocalyptic symbolization in an imperial situation, see further my preliminary reflections in Horsley, *Jesus and the Spiral of Violence,* 129–45, and idem, *Sociology and the Jesus Movement* (New York: Crossroad, 1989) 96–99.

15. See further Horsley, *Jesus and the Spiral of Violence,* 184–90; and Myers, *Binding the Strong Man,* who suggests that Mark has even identified the demonic forces with the Jewish rulers and ruling system.

A "SYNOPTIC APOCALYPSE"?

But would not the presence of a "little apocalypse" or "the Synoptic Apocalypse" in Mark 13 make Mark apocalyptic? With all due respect to traditional scholarly labels, the use in this case may constitute, as it were, an academic self-fulfilling prophecy. Many of the standard topics of scholarly debate may simply be generated by the standard synthetic construct of "apocalyptic" presupposed when discussing the contents of Mark 13. Assuming that "Jews" and "early Christians" believed in something such as the end or the eschaton, modern scholars find it in the phrase "he who endures to the end" in 13:13. Assuming that ancient Jewish and Christian authors believed in a special period of time before the end, scholars find it in the editorial phrase that the gospel must be preached *before* or *first* in 13:10. Assuming that ancient Jewish and Jewish-Christian authors believed that Jerusalem was to be connected in some way with the end, and finding in "the desolating sacrilege" of 13:14 a reference to the Roman desecration of the temple and/or the destruction of Jerusalem in 70 CE, modern scholars conclude that Mark 13 is in some way struggling with the relation of the end of Jerusalem and the end in the larger sense. Or, assuming that ancient Christians believed in a sequence of "eschatological" events in which the parousia would happen in connection with the end, modern scholars find the whole scenario where they detect hints of parts of it. Kelber even finds Satan in Mark 13 simply on the basis that "the masculine participle *hestekota* endows the neuter *bdelygma* with a personal quality."[16]

In order to use the label "apocalyptic" for any motif or symbol in Mark 13, however, we would have to compare each particular motif with attention to its respective literary and historical contexts. Because we are still so heavily under the influence of the old synthetic construct, even the careful search for fundamental schemes on a less grandiose scale, as pursued by Lars Hartman, is problematic; as he himself warned, one rarely finds a whole scheme in a single text.[17]

That we may be reading schemes into ancient texts rather than out of them should make us skeptical about attempts to identify a pre-Markan "apocalypse" behind Mark 13. Debates continue on the extent and character of an apocalyptic "flier" or other *Vorlage* possibly used by Mark. A very careful recent analysis found that what appears in

16. Kelber, *Kingdom in Mark,* 119.
17. L. Hartman, *Prophecy Interpreted* (Lund: Gleerup, 1966).

13:7–8, 14–20, 24–27 was written by a Jewish-Christian prophet during the revolt of 66–70 CE to interpret Daniel's "desolating sacrilege" as the coming destruction of the temple.[18] It is clearly impossible to engage that debate here. But the whole procedure may be questionable for another reason. Isolating a pre-Markan *Vorlage* has meant taking Mark 13 out of the literary context of Mark as a whole, and then the *Vorlage* out of the context of Mark 13 — and ironically then interpreting Mark 13 and even Mark as a whole on the basis of the isolated *Vorlage.* But this procedure leaves no literary context on the basis of which to make judgments about historical context and the possible references in Mark 13 to particular situations and events! If anything we should proceed in the opposite manner, beginning with Mark and Mark 13 as a whole precisely in attempting to discern such references to historical situations.

In fact, in treating Mark 13 we should consider not only that it is an integral part of the Gospel, but also that images or motifs may well have been utilized previously or in other ways than in apocalyptic literature, and that there was escalating social conflict throughout the middle of the first century, from the time of Jesus' death through the outbreak of the great revolt against Roman and Jewish high-priestly rule.

It just so happens that the severe political-religious conflict portrayed by Mark as a whole closely matches the structural social conflict in Roman Palestine known through external sources such as Josephus. That conflict erupted into widespread revolt both a generation before and a generation after the ministry of Jesus, and it was manifested in numerous protests, social unrest, resistance movements, and official measures of repression during (the period of) the formation of pre-Markan traditions.[19] Much of the previous treatment of Mark 13 seems to assume that, somehow in contrast to the idyllic scene of Jesus' ministry, Mark 13 suddenly addresses a situation of conflict for Jesus' followers, and it assumes that the destruction of Jerusalem was utterly unanticipated. In Mark's portrayal, however, the ministry of Jesus was a sharp and escalating struggle against the repressive rulers and their retainers, with basically a similar struggle apparently continuing for Jesus' followers (e.g., 8:34–38). Thus the situation of class and regional

18. E. Brandenburger, *Markus 13 und die Apokalyptik* (FRLANT 134; Göttingen: Vandenhoeck & Ruprecht, 1984).

19. Sketched briefly in Horsley, *Sociology and the Jesus Movement,* chaps. 4–5. A fuller analysis is found in idem, *Jesus and the Spiral of Violence,* chaps. 2–4.

conflict in Palestine exacerbated by the overall imperial situation was continuous. And that is the general situation of structural social conflict that we must take into account when probing phrases in Mark 13 for possible references to particular events.

Insofar as there then appear to be several references to specific events in Mark 13, we are in the advantageous position of knowing of a number of major and minor conflicts or movements that occurred between 30 and 70 CE, but we may find it impossible to reach any degree of precision in relating particular possible references to particular possible events. For example, some find in 13:7 a reference to Gaius's order to erect his bust in the temple. Others suggest that the "desolating sacrilege" in 13:14 is a reference to that same event. Still others claim that the "desolating sacrilege" refers to the final destruction of Jerusalem, or to the impending attack on the temple by Titus. In relation to 13:21–22, there were a number of "prophets" active in Palestine roughly at midcentury, while certain "messianic pretenders" emerged at the beginning and during the midst of the great revolt of 66–70 CE.

If attempts to read Mark 13 as somewhat analogous to the rehearsal of past history in order to "set up" reassurance about a present crisis have any validity, then the discernment of 13:14 as the shift from past to present-and-future provides some criteria for the identification of references. On such a basis the "rumors of war" and "famine" of 13:7–8 could be references to the impact of Gaius's order to erect his bust in the temple and the disastrous effects of the severe drought in the late 40s. But that would not mean that the reference of 13:14–20 was necessarily to either the Jewish War of 66–70 CE or the Roman destruction of Jerusalem and the temple. Social conflict was escalating steadily during the 50s and 60s, and at several points the Roman governors sent out the military to suppress popular unrest. Moreover, people in Palestine had long experience — periodically from 63 to 37 BCE and again in 4 BCE — with how the Romans reacted to actual or perceived resistance with severe repressive measures, including "scorched earth" and "search and destroy" tactics in (re)conquering a people. Anytime after the dramatic events touched off by Gaius's order, a discerning prophet could have anticipated a scenario so suddenly devastating for the people that "one in the field must not turn back to get a coat." A prophet would not need to have experienced the Roman reconquest of Galilee or northern Judea in 67–68 CE to have composed the sayings in Mark 13:14b–18. Thus arguments that situate Mark prior to the actual revolt of 66 CE and the imminent destruction of the temple and Jerusalem are more persuasive than those that read Mark 13 as prophecy after the fact. Were Mark 13 *vaticinium ex eventu* ("prophecy after the fact"), then we would expect to find in the text a more precise reflection of the way in which the temple was actually destroyed. Moreover, if Jerusalem were already in ruins, then there would have been no longer a problem with potential false prophecy and false messiahs!

Thus, with regard to the particular, possible references of the statements usually listed as "apocalyptic" or ascribed to a pre-Markan "apocalypse," reasoning is necessarily somewhat circular. In order even to consider whether the phrases in 13:7–8 or the sayings in 13:14–20 refer to particular events or people, we must have some possibilities in mind. The phrases in 13:7–8 were apparently already stereotyped and could be simply apocalyptic rhetoric (4 Ezra 9:3; 13:31; *2 Baruch* 27; 70:8), and that in turn may even have been rooted in "prophetic" rhetoric (Isa 8:21; 13:13; 14:30; 19:2; Ezek 5:12; see any number of commentaries, articles, or monographs). On the other hand, in Palestine during the decades after Jesus' death, there was indeed a disastrous famine following a serious drought in the late 40s, and besides the rumors of war (e.g., in the wake of Gaius's mania), the Roman governors frequently sent out the army against any popular unrest, from banditry to would-be new Joshuas at Jericho or the Jordan. Whether particular references are intended, Mark's point is clear at the end of 13:7: such events must be expected and should not provoke any unusual excitement.

The sayings in 13:14b–18 appear to have far more specific reference, now clearly to future events. But they have no particular apocalyptic traits (unless it be "in those days" of 13:17). Even though not apparently written from the perspective of Jerusalem or even of Judea, they seem to have anticipated events in Judea in mind, events that threaten the lives of ordinary people with sudden disaster (i.e., apparently a Roman reconquest of the land). The anticipated scope of the firestorm, however, seems ominous from the sobering yet reassuring comments in 13:19–20. The style and substance of assurance here have more of an apocalyptic tone (Dan 12:1; *1 Enoch* 80:2). The puzzle of this section is what the *bdelygma* might refer to. In his historicizing transformation looking back on the Roman siege of Jerusalem, Luke has simply wiped out the term (21:20). Matthew makes explicit reference not only to Daniel but to the temple. Matthew's rewriting makes the vague simplicity of the Markan statement all the more striking. Nothing in the saying or immediate literary context suggests Jerusalem or the temple. And the masculine participle is as flimsy a basis for finding a reference to Titus as it is for reading Satan into the text. The "parenthetical" phrase "let the reader understand" should perhaps be a clue to us that the reader must possess much more understanding of the cultural lore of ancient Palestine than we do to "get" this one. We can certainly reason that referring the desolating sacrilege to (the threat of) the Roman destruction of the temple does not make sense for a community or Gospel so opposed to the temple.

The imagery in 13:24–25, often labeled "cosmic" and even read as reference to "cosmic catastrophe," is derived ultimately from prophetic tradition and is standard symbolization of "the Day of Yahweh," usually with connotations of God's judgment against foreign regimes (e.g., Isa 13:10; 34:4; Ezek 32:7–8; Joel 2:10). Apocalyptic literature simply continued the use of such imagery (*As. Mos.* 10:3–5). But it is not necessarily apocalyptic. And it is clearly symbolic language, such as hyperbole dramatizing just how ominous God's judgment would be. The two-step scene presented in Mark 13:24–25, 26–27 is reminiscent of Daniel 7 quite aside from the allusion to the "coming with the clouds" from Dan 7:13 in Mark 13:26. But we may doubt just how directly and explicitly Daniel 7 was in mind here, because in Daniel the "human-like one" symbolized the elect to be gathered, while in Mark "the son of man" presides over the gathering. The gathering of the elect from the four winds may come from Zech 2:6, not from Daniel, and the image of gathering the scattered people of Israel from the nations or ends of the world is fairly common in Hebrew biblical traditions.

All of these "apocalyptic" or simply prophetic predictions, however, are framed, balanced, and interpreted by the parenesis in 13:5–6, 9–13, and 28–37, particularly by the carefully positioned and repeated "watch" (*blepete*) in 13:5, 9, 23, 33 (cf. *gregoreite*, 13:35, 37). The main point of the parenesis, and thus of the material framed by the parenesis, seems to be, "Do not be diverted from the struggle by the difficulties attendant upon the struggle." The first main section of parenesis, 13:9–13, partly paralleled by similar exhortations elsewhere in the Synoptic tradition (Luke/Q 12:2–12; 12:51–53) as well as sayings earlier in Mark (8:34–38), focuses on the trials the movement is undergoing, internal dissension as well as external persecutions by rulers and local enemies. Far from being distracted by wars and famines (13:7–8), the members of the movement are to heed this advice: "Watch! Expect repressions, but do not worry! Expect to be hated by all, but endure!"

The second main section of parenesis follows up the prediction of sudden devastation (at least for those in Judea) and the promise of judgment and gathering of the elect in two steps. First are statements that the positive resolution of the crisis is near and that Jesus' words are sure, utterly credible (13:28–31). But neither here nor elsewhere does Mark appear to be emphasizing or giving special weight to "nearness." The only comparable saying, that the kingdom of God will come with power soon, also serves as a reassurance or sanction on remaining focused on the cause in a similar sequence (8:34–9:1). Then, after those words of reassurance, and as the final word in the section, comes the concluding point that no one, including the angels of "the Son" himself, knows when the crisis will be resolved, hence: "Watch! Keep alert! Keep awake!"

There appears to be no "little apocalypse" in Mark 13. Is the discourse in Mark 13, perhaps along with that in Mark 4, to be understood as esoteric apocalyptic teaching? Many of the motifs taken as evidence for an apocalypse here seem to disappear once we both abandon the old synthetic construct of "apocalyptic" and examine the motifs more critically. Mark 13 appears rather to be somewhat analogous to 1 Corinthians 13, where Paul is borrowing a certain style and a few associated motifs in order to turn the subject matter of esoteric spiritual wisdom on its head. Mark appears to be utilizing some apocalyptic motifs in order to caution readers against an apocalyptic reading of their own crisis situation. In Mark 13 the "apocalyptic" motifs serve two parenetic purposes: "rumors of war, famine," and so on characterize the current difficulties that are not to divert one from the struggle, and the impending coming of the son of man to gather the elect provides hope and reassurance that "summer is near," the crisis will not last forever. Mark 13, like the rest of the Gospel, is focused clearly on the historical struggle. Even in the context of a German theology focused on "the problem of history" thirty-five years ago, it was clear that Mark 13 "is not primarily concerned with speculating about the end (vv. 14–27), but rather with the struggles of the present time (vv. 5–13), the help of the Spirit (v. 11), and the exhortation to watch (vv. 28–37)."[20]

Because Mark's and the other Synoptic Gospels' statements ostensi-

20. J. M. Robinson, *The Problem of History in Mark* (London: SCM Press, 1957) 50.

bly about the destruction of Jerusalem and the temple have played such an important role in Christian ideology as well as biblical scholarship, we should at least clarify what Mark does not say in chap. 13, even if it may be impossible to discern exactly what Mark does say. There can be no question but that Mark sharply condemns the temple and high priesthood. Moreover, the prophecy of the destruction of Jerusalem in 13:2 follows immediately upon Jesus' prophetic demonstration and verbal attacks in chaps. 11–12, and then the double question of 13:3–4 ("When will these things be and what will be the sign . . . ?") appears to link what ensues in the rest of chap. 13 with the prophesied destruction of Jerusalem. Yet nothing in the rest of chap. 13 implies that the events prophesied have anything to do with Jerusalem. Judging from 13:14, these paragraphs must be written from a viewpoint outside of both Jerusalem and Judea (fleeing to the mountains in Judea would mean fleeing toward Jerusalem). Even if we were to read these sayings as pertaining to events that included Jerusalem, the author's main message is to refuse to be distracted by ostensibly earth-shaking events from the concerns of the movement. But the concerns of the movement were renewal of Israel centered in Galilee, with a rejection of temple and high priests as exploitative and unfaithful stewards. Hence, Mark is not rejecting Jerusalem rulers and ruling institutions because they had already been destroyed by Rome. Nor is Mark proclaiming God's judgment of Jerusalem and Jewish rulers in a vindictive way because they had killed Jesus. Rather, the conflict involving Jesus and the Jesus movement in Mark is rooted in and mirrors the structural social conflict of late Second Temple, Roman Palestine.

WISDOM IN MARK

With regard to wisdom in Mark, most striking is that the point of only the second story Mark tells at the opening of Jesus' ministry is to draw a sharp contrast between Jesus' teaching and that of the scribes. In distinction from the supposedly authoritative official teachers, Jesus teaches with *exousia,* that is, authority/power that is efficacious for and resonates with the people. In one of the major subplots of the Gospel, moreover, Mark further portrays Jesus as repeatedly challenging the authoritative wisdom of the scribes and Pharisees in several controversies in which Jesus appears to be building on traditional popular understandings or customs (e.g., 2:23–28; 7:1–23; 10:2–9). Mark thus provides us a clear sense of the structural social conflict in the context of which we must assess the presence or influence of wisdom in the Gospel.

Of the various types of wisdom mentioned above, there is simply no trace of theological or nature or mantic wisdom in Mark. The deciphering of parables in Mark 4:10–20 might well be compared with one of the traditional functions of scribes (see Sir 39:1–3), assuming that the earliest establishable text of Mark read "mysteries" in 4:11, with each of the parables representing or containing a mystery. Only if the original text read "mystery" in the singular, virtually a technical term for the apocalyptic plan of God, would we be inclined to view Mark 4 as a discourse in which Jesus was revealing esoteric apocalyptic wisdom. The relation of Jesus' parables to wisdom and their function in Mark has been dealt with extensively and critically in recent studies.[21]

Besides the parables, there is a handful of wisdom sayings or proverbs in Mark. Nearly every one of these appears to be from popular lore rather than from the learned sapiential circles — certainly those about the unshrunk cloth on an old garment and new wine in old wineskins and that about a lamp under a bushel, and probably also the proverb about prophets not without honor except in their hometown (2:21–22; 4:21; 6:4). Most of these wisdom sayings do not stand alone, but have been used in formation of "pronouncement stories" or "controversy stories": for example, "the well have no need of a physician" climaxing 2:15–17; the "unshrunk cloth" and "new wine" attached to 2:18–20; and the proverb/parable about first binding the strong man before plundering his house as the climax of the Beelzebul controversy (3:22–27). How these wisdom sayings have been developed into or linked with *chreiae* or pronouncement stories in the pre-Markan tradition and Mark is evident by contrast with their standing as isolated sayings or in a series of similar sayings in the *Gospel of Thomas* (e.g., 31b; 104; 47e; 47d; 35; 31a, respectively). Insofar as these very controversy stories, along with several others, are directed against the Pharisees and/or scribes, popular wisdom is utilized in Mark in a distinctive polemical argument against the officially sanctioned wisdom of the professional sages. Little influence of traditional professionally transmitted wisdom appears in Mark except in the negative sense: Mark's Jesus attacks it.

One suspects that the "apocalyptic" motifs in Mark, like the wisdom sayings, were simply common cultural coin. The presence of alien

21. See esp. B. B. Scott, *Hear Then the Parable* (Minneapolis: Fortress Press, 1989).

demonic forces that "possessed" particular people as well as provided an explanation for extreme social distress; the belief in resurrection; the symbol of "the son of man" as an advocate or judgmental figure in the divine judgment — these were more than likely all standard features of Galilean culture, the latter two only very indirectly connected with Daniel 7 and 12. Mark, like the tradition upon which he drew, used both common popular wisdom sayings and common beliefs in his portrayal of the political-religious struggle to bring renewal in concrete social terms to the people (Israel). Mark portrayed Jesus as having already "bound the strong man" and exorcized unclean spirits as part of the establishment of the kingdom of God among the people. He used the symbol of "the (future) son of man" in sayings of sanction on discipline and reassurance of vindication for those in the movement, and perhaps most originally Mark used the resurrection of Jesus to point the movement back to Jesus' agenda of concrete social renewal in Galilee.

13

THE GOSPEL OF MATTHEW: A SAPIENTIAL PERFORMANCE OF AN APOCALYPTIC DISCOURSE

Bernard Brandon Scott

Modern scholarship has barely faced up to the problem of the interface between apocalypticism and wisdom.[1] This question is reaching some urgency in New Testament studies, which have begun to flounder on the old paradigm with its watertight compartments and the presumed opposition of apocalyptic and wisdom. While studies of both apocalypticism and wisdom have developed their respective trajectories and bodies of scholarship, two methodological issues have stymied the debate. One arises with the effort to employ a temporal model that locates wisdom and apocalyptic at distinct points along a developmental path. Such a temporal model underlies the scholarship that develops out of Wilhelm Wrede and Albert Schweitzer, who claim that the earliest strands of Christianity were apocalyptic and that wisdom developed later.[2] Conversely, a number of recent studies of Jesus have stressed that he was a teacher of wisdom who was later interpreted apocalyptically.[3]

1. In one of the last conversations I had with John Gammie he told me how he was looking forward to working on the relation between apocalyptic and wisdom.

2. W. Wrede, *The Messianic Secret* (1901; reprint, Greenwood, S.C.: Attic, 1971); A. Schweitzer, *The Quest of the Historical Jesus: A Critical Study of Its Progress from Reimarus to Wrede* (trans. W. Montgomery; 1906; reprint, New York: Macmillan Co., 1968). E. P. Sanders (*Jesus and Judaism* [Philadelphia: Fortress Press, 1985]) follows in the tradition of Schweitzer.

3. B. L. Mack, *A Myth of Innocence: Mark and Christian Origins* (Philadelphia: Fortress Press, 1988); J. D. Crossan, *The Historical Jesus: The Life of a Mediterranean Jewish Peasant* (San Francisco: Harper & Row, 1991).

Likewise in the study of the Q material, many now propose that the earliest layers of Q were wisdom strata.[4] These studies retain Wrede and Schweitzer's divorce of apocalyptic and wisdom but reverse their temporal positions. But interpretation of the relevant textual data may not require a temporal scheme that designates for wisdom and apocalyptic discrete moments in a developmental process. As Roland Murphy has noted, "The relation between wisdom and apocalyptic and the extent to which the latter was influenced by the former also remains a moot point."[5] Rather, it may be possible to account for the interface between wisdom and apocalyptic without recourse to a temporal model.

A second problematic strategy for the study of the interface between apocalypticism and wisdom relies on predetermined definitions of sapiential and apocalyptic literary forms as necessarily representing the ideology of apocalyptic or wisdom. Literary form does not necessarily determine ideology,[6] especially when forms are mixed. Even more the characterization of apocalyptic literature as otherworldly and wisdom literature as this-worldly is too simplistic. In fact, wisdom and apocalyptic forms can coexist and even reinterpret each other in a particular performance.

Because of its prominent sapiential and apocalyptic features, Matthew's Gospel affords an instructive example of the interface of apocalypticism and wisdom. What follows is an investigation of the fifth and final discourse of that Gospel, where the interface between apocalyptic and wisdom is obvious. I will offer a close reading of the discourse based on the phenomenological observation of the narrator's self-description as a scribe, setting aside both temporal models and formal definitions of wisdom or apocalyptic.

ASSUMPTIONS

To proceed along this path, I will make a series of assumptions that I hope are not too controversial, although I recognize that today virtually no position has universal acceptance.

4. J. S. Kloppenborg, *The Formation of Q: Trajectories in Ancient Wisdom Collections* (Studies in Antiquity and Christianity; Philadelphia: Fortress Press, 1987).

5. R. Murphy, "Wisdom," *HBD* (ed. P. Achtemeier; San Francisco: Harper & Row, 1985) 1135–36.

6. "Ideology" is used in this essay in the sense of B. Uspensky, *A Poetics of Composition* (Berkeley: University of California Press, 1973) 8: "a general system of viewing the world conceptually. . . . [W]e are speaking about the deep compositional structure."

First, I assume that the author of Mark's Gospel "thinks in apocalyptic terms."[7] For our concerns one need not admit that Mark follows any particular apocalyptic schema, but only acknowledge that apocalypticism forms a primary element in the narrator's ideology, that the present difficulties that the implied readers are experiencing soon will be remedied by the climax of the imminent future with the coming of the end. Furthermore, Mark 13 portrays and warns about that impending apocalyptic climax. While cautioning about false signs of the end, the author nonetheless remains convinced of its imminent coming.

Second, I assume that the author of Matthew's Gospel is a scribe (or perhaps minimally the narrator presents himself as a scribe). Matthew 13:52 is an autobiographical reference: "Therefore every scribe who has been trained [*mathēteutheis*] for the kingdom of heaven is like the master of a household who brings out of his treasury what is new and what is old" (NRSV).[8] One might suppose that such a self-reference would help enormously, but we are not all that well informed about what it means to designate oneself and the members of one's community as scribes in the first century after the fall of the temple. David Orton, in a recent work, has made a number of interesting suggestions.[9] He distinguishes between what he calls a Pharisaic/rabbinic ideal and a nonrabbinic ideal. Rather than "ideal," "model" more accurately describes what Orton has constructed. He sees the nonrabbinic model emerging "from a joint Jewish and ancient Near Eastern — especially Babylonian — background, surfacing in Ezra, the Levites and the later prophets, and in a wide range of intertestamental scribal literature, especially Sirach, apocalyptic literature and Qumran."[10] Orton finds five characteristics of this scribe model as supported by Matthew:

(1) the exercise of wisdom and the gift of special "understanding" or insight; typically this is evidenced in the understanding of "parables" and "mysteries";

(2) the notion of authority, in the custody and maintenance of religious values, or true "righteousness" in the Jewish community;

7. N. Perrin and D. C. Duling, *The New Testament: An Introduction* (2d ed.; New York: Harcourt Brace Jovanovich, 1982) 238.

8. The commissioning likewise states that the community is to "make disciples" (*mathēteusate*) of all the heathen (*ethnē*). Thus the word "scribe" describes both the author/narrator and the reader/community.

9. D. Orton, *The Understanding Scribe: Matthew and the Apocalyptic Ideal* (JSNTSup 25; Sheffield: JSOT Press, 1989).

10. Ibid., 161.

(3) hence the notion of righteous teaching, including the right interpretation of the law and the prophets — the object being to inculcate "understanding" in others;

(4) a close association with true prophecy: the ideal scribe is a mantic, sharing the mission and commission of the prophets as well as their insights;

(5) related to (4), a sense of inspiration.[11]

One need not agree with all of Orton's conclusions to accept the basic argument as sound. The scribal tradition develops out of the ancient Near Eastern wisdom tradition. Minimally for Matthew, the scribe is one who has wisdom, understanding, and insight into the divine mysteries. Thus if Matthew's and the true disciple's primary self-definition is that of a scribe, then we would expect Matthew to bring scribal, wisdom insights to bear on the apocalyptic tradition.

My third assumption is perhaps the most controversial, depending upon presuppositions. While acknowledging the steady attack on the two-source theory for the past generation, along with a majority of scholars I judge it reasonable to assume that in the composition of the final discourse, the author of Matthew was using the Gospel of Mark. More specifically I assume that Mark 13 underlies the first element in the threefold structure of Matthew's final discourse.[12] Ockham's razor favors Mark as the source rather than Mark as an abbreviation of Matthew (or some combination of Luke).

My concern at this point is not to explore the intricacies of source criticism, but simply to establish a line of dependency so as to understand what Matthew is doing. Matthew performs the Markan text, initially in much the same way as any reader performs a text.[13] But I do not have in mind a modern reader with the conventions of silent reading. Rather, Matthew is an oral performer creating text to be heard or proclaimed, not seen and read silently (thus internalized) in print. Oral performance almost inevitably involves elements of homeostasis,

11. Ibid., 161–62.

12. While Koester's suggestion that Matthew (and Luke) employed a version of Mark different from canonical Mark is highly probable, the issue is irrelevant here because Matthew follows Mark 13 rather closely. See H. Koester, *Ancient Christian Gospels* (Philadelphia: Trinity Press International, 1990) 325–26.

13. The comparative move is also the first step of redaction criticism. But my aim diverges over the issue of performance. On performance, see W. Iser, *The Act of Reading: A Theory of Aesthetic Response* (Baltimore: Johns Hopkins University Press, 1978) 59. The theory of implied reader employed in this essay is strongly influenced by Iser.

by which an oral society keeps itself in equilibrium and thus constantly updates itself.[14] One should not view Matthew as a modern author creating *ex nihilo,* so to speak, nor as a copyist slaving over a manuscript of Mark's Gospel attempting to create a new theological synthesis, but as a traditional performer, a wise man, gathering the fragments of the tradition and re-forming them into a new story. He is, in the phrase of Lévi-Strauss, a *bricoleur,* or, in Matthew's own phrase, a scribe who "brings out of his treasury what is old and what is new."

STRUCTURE

Almost all commentators have perceived the sermon's tripartite shape. Jan Lambrecht, for example, divides the sermon into "The Phases of the Future" (24:4b–35); "Exhortations to Vigilance" (24:36–25:30); and "The Judgment of All the Nations" (25:31–46).[15] The formal elements of the three sections are distinct. Part 1 ("The Phases of the Future") follows closely the parallel discourse in Mark 13. Part 2 ("Exhortations to Vigilance") consists of a group of parables, mostly from Q, while Part 3 ("The Judgment of All the Nations") is unique to Matthew's Gospel. The sermon constitutes an elaborate speech of Jesus, the chief character, ostensibly foretelling the events of the end.

John Donahue has suggested that in form the discourse is an Apocalyptic Testament, comparable to those in the *Testaments of the Twelve Patriarchs.*[16] In this literary fiction a departing seer warns his followers about what is to happen. The use of the form in Matthew's narrative creates a special tension. Within story time, Jesus' speech responds to the disciples' question: "Tell us, when are these things going to happen and what will be the sign of your coming [*parousia*] and the end [*synteleia*][17] of the age?" (Matt 24:3). But the speech describes events that would make no sense to the fictional audience of disciples. Furthermore, some of these events already have happened outside story time and within the authorial[18] reader's lifetime, so that the implied reader impinges on

14. W. J. Ong, *Orality and Literacy: The Technologizing of the Word* (New Accents; London and New York: Methuen, 1982) 46.

15. J. Lambrecht, "The Parousia Discourse: Composition and Content in Mt XXIV-XXV," *L'Évangile selon Matthieu* (ed. M. Didier; BETL; Gembloux: J. Duculot, 1972) 312–13.

16. J. Donahue, *The Gospel in Parable* (Philadelphia: Fortress Press, 1988) 114.

17. *Synteleia* occurs only in the Gospels, in Matthew.

18. I am using the helpful distinction of M. A. Tolbert, *Sowing the Gospel: Mark's World in a Literary-Historical Perspective* (Minneapolis: Fortress Press, 1989) 53: "It too

the text in a very special way.[19] This is so true that the text even offers its "readers" specific directions for interpretation: "So when you see the 'devastating desecration' (as described by Daniel the prophet) standing 'in the holy place' (the reader had better figure out what this means)..." (Matt 24:15).[20] Unlike the Markan parallel, the Matthean seer makes clear to the reader exactly which text the reader must employ to make the correct interpretation. Thus the authorial reader is brought into the text much more directly and obviously than fiction normally allows. The fiction is actually broken by an incursion of the reader from a position other than story time.

Part 1: The Coming End

The first panel in the Apocalyptic Testament's triptych, as observed above, derives from Mark 13. This section's basic structure also comes from Mark, and the editing follows what one normally would expect from Matthew. However, since Matthew does not play down the nearness of the end's approach, this adaptation of the Markan apocalyptic perspective has occasioned very contrary evaluations of the speech's place in the overall structure of Matthew's thought. Lambrecht maintains that "The expectation of a near coming of the Lord, even the '*Naherwartung*,' is clearly expressed in XXIV, 4b–35, and this notwithstanding the fact that there are at the same time clear warnings against a wrong, hasty and heated apocalyptic unrest."[21] Lambrecht interprets Matthew as a literal reader of Mark's speech. F. W. Beare in his recent commentary argues that "the apocalyptic materials which are derived from Mark are subordinated to other modes of eschatological instruction."[22]

The positions of Lambrecht and Beare define the problem. As Lambrecht says, there are clear statements of the end's near coming.

---

is a heuristic literary construct, which we might conceive as the writer's vision of an ideal reader, the reader who would fulfill the reader's role in the way it was designed to be done." The advantage of the adjective "authorial" is that it indicates the implied reader is conditioned by the historical and cultural context of the author and text as distinguished from a dehistoricized implied reader or a modern implied reader.

19. J. D. Kingsbury, *Matthew as Story* (2d ed.; Philadelphia: Fortress Press, 1988) 107–10.

20. Translation from *The Complete Gospels* (ed. Robert J. Miller; Sonoma, Calif.: Polebridge Press, 1992). Remaining translations are from this edition unless otherwise noted.

21. Lambrecht, "Parousia Discourse," 325.

22. F. W. Beare, *The Gospel According to Matthew* (San Francisco: Harper & Row, 1981) 461.

Matthew is the only Synoptic Gospel to use the term *parousia.* Yet for Beare this apocalyptic material should not be taken literally because it is "subordinated" within the larger context of the five sermons in Matthew and the sermon's remaining two parts. The question, of course, is what does Beare mean by "subordinated" and what effect does subordination have on the apocalyptic language? This goes to the heart of this essay, of the interface between apocalypticism and wisdom. As a way of moving beyond the impasse as represented by Lambrecht and Beare, I will follow how this language functions: How does it want to be read? How does it structure its reading? The thesis that will emerge from this reading is that the apocalyptic form and language are reinterpreted by the ideology of wisdom.

The narrative beginning of the sermon has a number of terms that indicate a new beginning:[23] "And Jesus was leaving the temple area on his way out . . . " (24:1). Not only is there a change of place but also a change of audience when the disciples approach Jesus and point out the temple buildings. Even with these strong markers of a new beginning, the conclusion of the preceding scene deserves notice. Chapter 23 is the notorious speech in which the formulaic phrase "You scholars and Pharisees, you impostors! Damn you!" is the recurring structural pattern of the denunciation. But the denunciation's conclusion shifts attention from the scribes and Pharisees to a personified Jerusalem. This judgment oracle[24] from Q has four lines with an A–B pattern.

A Jerusalem, Jerusalem, the city that murders the prophets and stones those sent to her.

B How often I wanted to gather your children as a hen gathers her chicks under her wings and you wouldn't let me.

A Can't you see, your house is being abandoned as a ruin?

B So I tell you, you certainly won't see me from now on until you say, "Blessed is the one who comes in the name of the Lord."

In this A–B pattern the A terms are negative judgments while the B terms are *parakalesis,* encouragement by the voice of wisdom. The first term is negative while the second is positive, thus ending on a hopeful note. Further, by concluding the attack on the scribes and Pharisees with this oracle on Jerusalem, the narrator binds more closely the fate

23. D. Patte, *The Gospel According to Matthew: A Structural Commentary on Matthew's Faith* (Philadelphia: Fortress Press, 1987) 333.

24. Kloppenborg, *Formation of Q,* 237.

of Jerusalem with the Apocalyptic Testament that follows. The *polis,* the city Jerusalem, becomes the focus and not just or even the temple. The images are strongly personified.

The disciples initiate the sermon with a question that hints at stages: "Tell us, when are these things going to happen and what will be the sign of your coming and end of the age [*synteleias tou aiōnos*]?" (24:3). The question asks *when* (*pote*) these things will occur — that is, the destruction of the temple mentioned in the sermon and that of Jerusalem mentioned in the conclusion of the previous speech. These events have already occurred in the past history of the authorial reader, while still being future events for the fictional audience of disciples. The second part of the question asks *what* (*ti*) will be the sign of (1) "your coming" and (2) the "end of the age." Matthew's precise formulation of the question leads a reader to expect an apocalyptic drama foretold in exact stages.

The initial stage is described as the appearance of false messiahs, wars, famines, and earthquakes. "Now all these things mark the beginning of the final agonies [*ōdinōn*]" (v. 8). Literally *ōdin* means "birthpang," and its oddness deserves notice. Similar to the *Complete Gospels,* the RSV translates it as "suffering," assuming this meaning as a figurative extension of the literal meaning. While both Bauer and Louw and Nida support this understanding,[25] Bertram in his review of Greek and Septuagintal usage indicates that the sense of birth is central to the semantics of the word group.[26] If Matthew were uncomfortable with the initial sense of the term, he could have varied Mark's metaphor. The sense of the pain at the *beginning* should be maintained. There is an irony in the choice of metaphor because the speech deals with the end and yet it is only the "beginning of birthpangs."

Persecution of the community marks the second stage: "At that time they will turn you over for torture, and will kill you, and you will be universally [*hypo pantōn tōn ethnōn*] hated because of me" (v. 9). This section of part 1 of the final sermon does not follow Mark, contrary to the general tendency in this part of the sermon. Mark's sermon warns that "they will deliver you up to councils; and you will be

25. W. Bauer et al., *A Greek-English Lexicon of the New Testament and Other Early Christian Literature* (2d ed.; Chicago: University of Chicago Press, 1979) 895; J. P. Louw and E. A. Nida, *Greek-English Lexicon of the New Testament Based on Semantic Domains,* 2 vols. (2d ed.; New York: United Bible Societies, 1989) 1.24.7. The REB, the NAB, and the NRSV employ the birthpangs metaphor, *The Complete Gospels* agrees with the RSV.

26. G. Bertram, "Ōsin," *TDNT* 9.667–70.

beaten in synagogues; and you will stand before governors and kings" (Mark 13:9). This material occurs in Matthew in the second sermon, the Commissioning of the Disciples (Matt 10:17–22a).

This second stage in Matthew's version of the apocalyptic drama thrusts the community onto the stage of world history. The community is going to suffer internal turmoil, and many "will betray one another and hate each other" (24:10). The end result of this turmoil and betrayal within the community is that "mutual love will grow cool" (24:12). This phrase *hē agapē tōn pollōn* is somewhat odd in the Gospel. While this is the only use of the noun *agapē* in Matthew, the verb *agapaō* does occur in some interesting and enlightening passages. In the Sermon on the Mount, the final antithesis says, "As you know, we once were told, 'You are to love your neighbor' and 'You are to hate your enemy' " (5:43), the latter a nonextant quote in its present form.[27] The antithesis is "love your enemies and pray for your persecutors" (5:24). Jesus asks: What good is love directed only toward those who love us already? The narrator sets up a dilemma for the reader since the examples refer only to those who love those who love them. "If you love those who love you, why should you be commended for that? Even the toll-collectors do as much, don't they? And if you greet only your friends, what have you done that is exceptional? Even the pagans [*hoi ethnikoi*] do as much, don't they?" (5:46–47). The Matthean text is much more specific at this point than the Lukan (and apparently Q) parallel.[28] Where Q speaks of sinners and "those who do good to you," Matthew has toll collectors and pagans as a specification of the sinners and friends as a specification of those who love you. From the perspective of the implied Jewish reader the toll collector is a Jewish renegade and thus impure, and the *ethnē* is impure simply because he is *ethnē,* the other.

Thus the situation pictured in Matthew's final sermon is a complete breakdown of community. Not only are the *ethnē* handing the members over for death and hating them, but the community members' mutual love for each other has broken down. They are so offended by each other that they hate one another. They cannot even love each other,

27. R. H. Gundry, *Matthew: A Commentary on His Literary and Theological Art* (Grand Rapids, Mich.: Wm. B. Eerdmans Publishing Co., 1982) 96–97; Beare, *Gospel According to Matthew,* 160–61. G. Strecker (*The Sermon on the Mount: An Exegetical Commentary* [trans. O. C. Dean, Jr.; Nashville: Abingdon Press, 1988] 87) suggests that the negative antithesis is a composition of Matthew.

28. Kloppenborg, *Formation of Q,* 174–75.

like the pagans do. The situation is for Matthew *anomia,* the complete breakdown of law.[29]

To be saved, the reader must endure this breakdown of the community until the end (24:13). This marks an important shift in the conception of the stages of the apocalyptic drama. The drama has now moved into the internal conflicts and breakdown within the community. Now the end is foretold: "And this good news of Heaven's imperial rule [*Touto to evangelion tēs basileias*] will have been proclaimed in the whole inhabited world [*en holē tē oikoumenē*] so you can make your case to all peoples. And then the end will come" (24:14). *Touto to evangelion tēs basileias* is a peculiar Matthean phrase occurring here and in two Matthean summary phrases in 4:23 and 9:35. In the other two occurrences it is associated with traveling throughout Galilee, teaching in synagogues, proclaiming the gospel of the kingdom, and healing every disease. The threefold phrase — teaching, proclaiming, and healing — is a formulaic phrase in Matthew summing up Jesus' activity.[30] Yet the summary statements in 4:23 and 9:35 function differently than the summary statement here. The previous two are summary statements that form an *inclusio* for chaps. 5–9 defining what it is that the primary character does: teaching (Sermon on the Mount) and healing in chaps. 8–9, wherein Matthew has gathered together almost all of Jesus' wonder-working activity. But the current summary statement defines the future, outside story time, and so the context is no longer Galilee and the surrounding cities but the whole inhabited world. The stress falls not on teaching and healing but on proclaiming this gospel of the kingdom. Thus the Apocalyptic Testament prepares a reader for a shift in the ministry of the community from a ministry exclusively to the Jews, as was the case with Jesus, to a ministry among the *ethnē.* The quote from Isaiah (8:23–9:1) that introduces the ministry of Jesus refers to Galilee of the Gentiles (4:15), but that quote functions proleptically because Jesus goes only to the lost sheep of Israel (Matt 10:5–6; 15:24). Only after his resurrection, when Jesus returns to the mountain in Galilee, is the community commanded to go to all the nations. In the Apocalyptic Testament the proclaiming of the gospel of the kingdom to the whole world is demanded before the end will come.

29. In 7:23, 13:41, and 23:28 the sense of *anomia* would indicate a subversion of law, i.e., Torah. I would suggest that a similar sense applies here.

30. U. Luz, *Matthew 1–7: A Commentary* (EKKNT; Minneapolis: Augsburg Publishing House, 1989) 1.203.

Perhaps even more is at stake. Joseph Grassi has argued recently that the phrase "this gospel of the kingdom" is a reference to Matthew's book, and thus the narrator is warning that to read this book is to encounter the living voice of the seer.[31] If this is so, then it occurs in a section of the seer's testament in which references to its textual character are particularly strong.

The apocalyptic drama of predictable stages now switches back from the proclamation of the sufferings at the end to the desecration of the holy place with the sacrilege prophesied by Daniel. This text creates an enigma for the reader. First the reader is called upon to solve the reference, to understand, to pay attention. "The devastating desecration," as the narrator/author (not the seer) indicates, quotes or alludes to Daniel (9:27; 11:31; 12:11), where it refers to Antiochus IV Epiphanes building an altar to Zeus Ouranios in the Jerusalem temple. A description of the event is contained in 1 Macc 1:54. Because an exact event during the period under question has been difficult to ascertain,[32] some commentators have suggested that the holy place refers to the community that has been desecrated by the events of betrayal just described.[33] This is not necessarily an either/or situation, but should be left ambiguous.[34] The reader must understand how to interpret the prophet's words. Thus the text begins to question the literal character of the seer's Apocalyptic Testament. A reader's strategy to make sense, to form a consistency, out of the text is in danger. The textual world has begun to fall apart. The narrator/author has directly intervened, overwhelming the seer by making a direct appeal to the reader to understand, demanding wisdom and insight. This intervention causes ambiguity because the reference is unclear. The "devastating desecration" standing in the "holy place" (1) is literally a reference to a past event in another apocalyptic text, Daniel, where again it is a veiled reference; (2) now stands for a literal event in the history of the temple during the reader's lifetime; and/or (3) stands for the metaphorical event within the community's life. In the cacophony of textual voices it is difficult to ascertain who is talking to whom about what. This makes the reader's situation

31. J. A. Grassi, "Matthew as a Second Testament Deuteronomy," *BTB* 19 (1989) 23–29.

32. Beare, *Gospel According to Matthew,* 468.

33. F. W. Burnett, *The Testament of Jesus-Sophia: A Redaction-Critical Study of the Eschatological Discourse in Matthew* (Washington, D.C.: University Press of America, 1981) 300–338.

34. Patte, *Gospel According to Matthew,* 338.

precarious, so the reader is warned to take care. This intervention of the narrator into the seer's apocalypse demands of the implied reader wisdom to solve the dilemma.

With the deconstructive seeds planted, the seer continues to forecast the end's urgency and tribulation. Yet once again, as there was in the sermon's beginning, a warning occurs against false messiahs and prophets who will lead many astray. The seer states that these apocalyptic events in no sense will be hidden but will be perfectly obvious: "Look, I have warned you in advance. In fact, if they should say to you, 'Look, he's in the wilderness,' don't go out there; 'Look, he's in one of the secret rooms,' don't count on it. For just as lightning comes out from the east and is visible all the way to the west, that's what the coming of the son of Adam will be like. For wherever there is a corpse, that's where the vultures will gather" (24:25–28). The two analogies for obviousness come from opposite ends of the aesthetic scale, lightning and the vultures gathering over a corpse, but the point is well made — the coming of the Son of man will be unmistakable. Yet this obviousness does not alleviate the tension or trap for the reader who is supposed to interpret correctly the devastating desecration with its ambiguous meaning and not be one of those led astray by false messiahs and prophets.

The drama of the stages reasserts itself in v. 29, "immediately after the tribulation of those days." The seer now reaches the final stage, the sign of the Son of man (v. 30), which sign is the Son of man himself.[35] The authorial reader must avoid being led astray because the only true sign of the coming of the Son of man is the Son of man. The forecasting function of the Apocalyptic Testament begins to turn in on itself. While its stages should provide signs for the prediction of the end, yet just as the seer appears to predict the signs, he undercuts their sign character. The real sign is the Son of man, which should be as obvious as vultures gathering around a corpse.

If the reader's situation were not difficult enough, the conclusion of this first part of the seer's testament provides the ultimate deconstructive nod. The seer solemnly prophesies: "This generation certainly won't pass into oblivion before all these things take place" (24:34). First the reader must solve the reference to "this generation." Is it the disciples, the fictional audience of the testament, or the authorial audience?

35. Lambrecht, "Parousia Discourse," 324.

If the former, then the seer is mistaken; if the latter, then the seer is ambiguous.

Even though v. 36 opens the second panel of the sermon, ideologically it functions as a transition that undercuts the seer's own knowledge: "As for that exact day and minute: no one knows, not even heaven's messengers, nor even the son — no one, except the Father alone." The text accentuates the lack of knowledge by its grammatical construction.[36] *No one* (*oudeis*) knows, *neither* (*oude*) the messenger . . . *nor* (*oude*) the son *but only* (*ei mē ho pater monos*)[37] the Father. If no one knows the day or the hour, not even the seer himself, of what value is the prediction? This undercuts the testament's predictive aspect and deprives the implied reader of the son's knowledge to resolve the dilemma. The seer is not an unreliable narrator; quite the opposite, he is an honest narrator. But his honesty confounds the apocalyptic schema. Matthew not only accentuates the uniqueness of the Father's knowledge, but emphasizes it even more by making it the opening of the second panel of the sermon's triptych. While apocalyptic in form, this first part calls into question the very viability of apocalypticism's explanatory power, not by rejecting the form but by withdrawing the knowledge necessary to support it and demanding wisdom from the implied reader.

Part 2: The Parable Cluster/Interlude

This midpanel of the sermon is a carefully structured unit:[38]

A As for that exact day and minute: no one knows, not even heaven's messengers, nor even the son — no one, except the Father alone (24:36).
For as [*hōsper gar*] it was in the days of Noah (v. 37) . . .

Parable of two men and two women (vv. 40–41).

B Watch for you do not know on what day your Lord will come (v. 42).

Parable of the householder and the thief (v. 43).

A Therefore even you must be ready, for you do not expect the hour when the Son of man will come (v. 44).

Parable of the faithful and wise servant/the evil servant (vv. 45–50).

36. B. M. Metzger, *A Textual Commentary on the Greek New Testament* (New York: United Bible Societies, 1971) 62.

37. Matthew follows Mark except for *monos,* which indicates he understands and accentuates the point of the Father's unique knowledge.

38. B. B. Scott, *Hear Then the Parable: A Commentary on the Parables of Jesus* (Minneapolis: Fortress Press, 1989) 219–20.

C There people will weep and gnash their teeth (v. 51).

Parable of five wise and five foolish virgins (25:1–12).

B Watch, therefore, because you do not know the day or the hour (v. 13).

For as [*hōsper gar*] the parable of the two good and faithful servants and the third evil and slothful servant (vv. 14–19) . . .

C There people will weep and gnash their teeth (v. 30).

"For as" (*hōsper gar*) begins (24:37) and ends (25:14) this section. A series of parables all based on contrasting behavior provides the backbone. The stories' conclusions form the pattern A–B–A, C–B–C (i.e., two sets of chiasms built on the B member). There is even internal consistency within this arrangement. In the parable of the faithful and wise servant, one is faithful and wise, the other evil. In the parable of the ten virgins, one group is called wise, and in the parable of the talents, the servants whose talents increase are called good and faithful, but the one-talent man is evil. Set in series, the stories promote a stark either-or situation that prepares for the sermon's final scene of judgment.

The chiasmic structure makes clear the narrator's central point: watch because you do not know the day or the hour of the coming of the Son of man. This ignorance, of course, is due to the fact that not even the son knows the day or hour. Ignorance of the apocalyptic hour combines with a demand for wisdom to shift ideology from apocalypticism to wisdom. The vigilance required is not simple passive watching, but active service. Two of the parables contrast two sets of characters in which one set are wise and faithful because they have done the appropriate things, while the second set are foolish and slothful because they have only waited and done nothing. As Donahue says, "Vigilance is not simply waiting for the future but active engagement in the present which will determine the shape of the future."[39] This future that the present is determining is the future judgment whose scene remains yet to be described.

This active engagement of the present represents a shift in perspective within the sermon. The first part of the sermon kept its focus on the future, especially the future tribulations and its signs. Having questioned that effort, the sermon turns attention to the present and to activity in the present as the determinative factor of the future judgment. Three times the delay of the master is mentioned (24:48; 25:8,

39. Donahue, *Gospel in Parable*, 104–5.

19). Lambrecht sees these references as no "more than mere unstressed parable elements. But we are of the opinion that in Matthew's way of thinking 'near' and 'unexpected' go together."[40] This misses the point. As Günther Bornkamm has pointed out, in the parable of the wise and foolish virgins, the bridegroom's delay constitutes the test, and the preparation for the delay determines wisdom. The foolish virgins' illusion is precisely their expectation of his near return.[41] Again Donahue is closer to the point when he argues that "Matthew retains the critical urgency which was associated with the early Christian hope of the parousia without retaining its temporal immediacy."[42] Apocalypticism has been undercut in favor of wisdom by shifting the temporal focus from future to present. The midpanel continues Matthew's scribal reaction to an apocalyptic situation, while deemphasizing the apocalyptic drama and emphasizing being wise in the present time.

Part 3: The Judgment

The final panel in the triptych is the vivid judgment scene depicting the separation of the sheep and goats and the dramatic confrontation with the king who judges according to whether one has cared for him in the guise of the other. Yet it too has been the subject of recent debate. In the traditional interpretation, the standard of judgment is how one has treated those who are least, and as such the passage has been a powerful warrant for social concern. But recently this interpretation has come under critical attack. The context of this judgment scene is not the Christian community but all the nations (*panta ta ethnē*, v. 32), and those for whom one must care are "the least of my brothers" (v. 40). In the New Testament "brother," when not describing a physical relationship, denotes a fellow member of the community, a usage it shares with Judaism.[43] Matthew agrees with this usage, and the term "brother" is frequently used in the Gospel as a reference to describe how fellow Christians are to behave toward each other (5:22–24; 7:3–5; 18:15, 21, 35). Furthermore, in Matthew "the little ones" and "the least" are those who are the vulnerable members of the Christian community. On the basis of such observations, Lamar Cope has argued that the "least of

40. Lambrecht, "Parousia Discourse," 328.

41. G. Bornkamm, "End-Expectation and Church in Matthew," *Tradition and Interpretation in Matthew* (ed. G. Bornkamm et al.; London: SCM Press, 1963) 23.

42. Donahue, *Gospel in Parable*, 104.

43. H. von Soden, "Adelphos," *TDNT* 1.145–46.

the brothers" are Christian missionaries and that the pagan nations will be judged on how they have received these Christian missionaries. He sees the scene as sectarian, and it "*cannot* provide legitimate basis for Christian concern for the poor and the needy of the world."[44]

Cope's arguments do not directly concern us here except that they indicate how easily a text can be misread, if the total context of the narration is neglected. The judgment scene occurs only in Matthew, and while it may be dependent on a traditional parable,[45] it surely shows clear signs of Matthean redaction.

Previously (24:30–31) the sermon had clearly forecast the Son of man's coming as the sign of the end and likewise the gathering of all the nations (24:14). In fact, "this gospel of the kingdom" is to be proclaimed throughout the entire inhabited world (*oikoumenē*). To describe the nations as pagans, as Cope does, is to mistranslate. The world is the context for the activity of the community's preaching, just as Israel is the context for Jesus' ministry.[46] The nations are those to whom the witness (24:14) has been given.

The seer reports that the Son of man will separate the nations "as a shepherd segregates the sheep from the goats" (v. 32). The initial analogy, indicated by "as," now becomes a story in which a king puts the sheep on his right hand. The implied reader oscillates back and forth between an analogy about the judgment of the Son of man and a story about a king separating sheep. The line between the two is never very clear. The king addresses those sheep on his right hand as "blessed of my father," which indicates that the king, the Son of man, and the son are all the same and that the sheep are believers, members of the Christian community. The seer/narrator further describes the sheep as *hoi dikoioi* (v. 37), an important term in Matthew, first used of Joseph (1:19). The righteous address the king as "Lord," a prominent term in Matthew used of Jesus. When one considers the context

44. L. Cope, "Matthew XXV:31–46, The Sheep and the Goats Reinterpreted," *NovT* 11 (1969) 44.

45. Donahue (*The Gospel in Parable*, 161) attempts to isolate a pre-Matthean parable. While this is extremely problematic, the confusion of titles (Son of man, shepherd, king) at the narrative's beginning indicates independent tradition. So R. Bultmann, *The History of the Synoptic Tradition* (New York: Harper & Row, 1963).

46. A.-J. Levine (*The Social and Ethnic Dimensions of Matthean Social History: "Go Nowhere Among the Gentiles" [Matt. 10:5b]* [Studies in the Bible and Early Christianity 14; Lewiston, N.Y.: Edwin Mellen Press, 1988] 233–39) argues for the universalistic understanding of Matthew, chap. 8, and specifically in regard to the last judgment narrative.

of the sermon, it seems clear that Cope has overstated the evidence. The nations are indeed judged, but the nations are the context of Christian ministry and by their address to the Lord appear to be members of the Christian community. Cope has made the text too specific, too literal.

The criteria for judgment create a powerfully disturbing image in this scene and are thoroughly deconstructive. They are repeated in the scene four times, and such redundancy creates a vivid impression. "You may remember, I was hungry and you gave me something to eat; I was thirsty and you gave me something to drink; I was a foreigner and you showed me hospitality; I was naked and you clothed me; I was ill and you visited me; I was in prison and you came to see me" (vv. 35–36). The radical shock derives from the Son of man's hiddenness in these marginalized. This goes well beyond the point made in the contrasting parables of part 2 of the sermon. There the present serves as the criterion of the future. Yet as now becomes evident, the issue is not simply vigilance or caring for the entrusted talents. Rather the Son of man is hidden in and is the hungry, the thirsty, the foreigner, the naked, the sick, and the imprisoned. In part 1 the implied reader was forewarned that the sign of the Son of man would appear in heaven and that the nations would mourn (24:30). Now the seer reveals that the sign of the Son of man has already appeared and is hidden in those who are least.[47] The judgment is radically present now, and the seer pronounces judgment on all those who do not see. An apocalyptic drama serves the needs of wisdom's radical insight into the present.

At the Gospel's very beginning the narrator had quoted Isa 7:14: "Behold, a virgin will conceive a child and she will give birth to a son, and they will name him Emmanuel" (1:23). Then the narrator translated that Hebrew word for his Greek reader as "God with us" (*meth hēmōn ho theos*). While the first part of the quote was fulfilled in the birth narrative, Joseph did not name the child Emmanuel but Jesus. Thus the child has a hidden name, God with us, that functions as a presiding

47. Such an interpretation would allow a reader through retrospection (see S. Rimmon-Kenan, *Narrative Fiction: Contemporary Poetics* [New Accents; London and New York: Methuen, 1983] 122) to make sense of Matt 10:23b: "You will not finish all the cities of Israel until the Son of man comes." This saying creates an asymmetry for the reader because it is not literally true. The fictional characters of the disciples do not finish the cities of Israel before the coming of the Son of man. Yet by retrospection the reader can see that the saying is true because the Son of man has already come and judged in the hiddenness of the least.

symbol that the implied reader constructs throughout the story.[48] At the narrative's conclusion, Jesus promises, "And remember, *I am with you* [*egō meth hymōn eimi*] every day until the completion of the age [*eōs tēs syntheleias tou aiōnos*]" (28:20, my trans.). In the judgment scene the implied readers discover that Jesus is with them, God present to them, in the least.

The scribal reading of Mark's apocalyptic text leads Matthew to shift the future into the present. The apocalyptic crisis is now. Paradoxically the Son of man is hidden among the least, and that has been revealed by this gospel of the kingdom. But there is yet one more crisis for the implied reader. The reading of the text provides for the implied reader a solution for the puzzle of the sign of the Son of man, a sign as obvious as lightning or vultures gathering over a corpse. However, in the judgment scene, none of those judged knows whether he or she is righteous or cursed. "Not everyone who says to me, 'Master, Master,' will get into heaven's domain — only those who carry out the will of my Father who is in heaven. On that day many will address me, 'Master, Master, didn't we use your name when we prophesied? Didn't we use your name when we exorcised demons? Didn't we use your name when we performed all those miracles?' Then I will tell them honestly, 'I never knew you' " (7:21–23). This doubt is the final deconstruction of the apocalyptic form — the seer not only does not know the hour, but having given the sign of the Son of man, the seer plants doubts about one's certainty of its application.

As an example of the interface between apocalypticism and wisdom, Matthew's performance of Mark's apocalyptic sermon is instructive. It is evident that wisdom and apocalyptic forms can coexist. Even more, a wisdom interpretation need not abandon apocalyptic form. The shift can take place by means of a subtle reinterpretation in which the focus shifts from the future to the present. Matthew has the speaker shift from the future to the present as a rhetorical strategy to force the authorial reader to follow the authoritative speaker and thereby gain insight and unify the various ideological planes — author/narrator, speaker, authorial audience. Thus the presence of apocalyptic or wisdom forms is not telling; what is telling is the ideology that organizes these forms.

48. B. B. Scott, "The Birth of the Reader in Matthew," *Faith and History: Essays in Honor of Paul W. Meyer* (ed. J. Carroll et al.; Atlanta: Scholars Press, 1990) 162.

14

WISDOM AND APOCALYPTIC IN PAUL

E. Elizabeth Johnson

The search for wisdom in Paul's letters, like so many scholarly quests, has progressed by fits and starts, bumping up against methodological roadblocks and meandering through exegetical detours in pursuit of its goal. The largest roadblock has been erected by those who have posited an alternative theological ancestry for the apostle in apocalyptic Judaism, assuming that such a background necessarily precludes his substantive employment of wisdom thought. The most frequent detours have concerned the nature of Paul's Christology, which question is itself largely shaped by judgments about the extent of the authentic Pauline corpus. In the main, those who have looked for wisdom in Paul have wanted to find it globally in his Christology, and they have been less than universally persuasive since they tend to rely chiefly on Col 1:15–20, an admittedly sapiential passage but in a letter of disputed authorship. The scholars who have broadened the search for wisdom in Paul beyond his Christology have tended, with a few notable exceptions, to ignore the apocalyptic convictions he expresses in the same contexts. This essay seeks to examine the relationship between sapiential and apocalyptic language and traditions in a selection of Pauline texts without being either stopped short by a forced choice between wisdom and apocalyptic or detoured by presuppositions about Christology.

I

Hans Windisch argued vigorously at the beginning of this century for the primacy of Israel's wisdom tradition (defined in large measure by the classical wisdom corpus) in Paul's theological heritage,[1] and he has been joined since then by a small but notable company including Wilfred L. Knox, Ulrich Wilckens, Dieter Georgi, Robin Scroggs, Robert Hamerton-Kelly, and particularly Hans Conzelmann.[2] There is great diversity among these scholars regarding the focus of Paul's wisdom thought. For Windisch and Knox, Paul understands the Wisdom of God in personified terms (as in Job 28; Prov 8:22–31; Sirach 24; Bar 3:9–4:4; and Wisdom 9; cf. *1 Enoch* 42), and they claim this hypostatic portrait underlies Pauline Christology, most clearly in Col 1:15–20, but evident also in 1 Corinthians 1–3; 8:6; 10:4; Rom 10:6–9; and Eph 1:19–21.[3] Wilck-

1. H. Windisch, "Die göttliche Weisheit der Jüden und die paulinische Christologie," *Neutestamentliche Studien für Georg Heinrici* (ed. H. Windisch; Leipzig: J. C. Hinrichs, 1914) 220–34.

2. W. L. Knox, *St. Paul and the Church of the Gentiles* (Cambridge: Cambridge University Press, 1939). U. Wilckens, "Sophia," *TDNT* (1971) 7.465–528; and idem, *Weisheit und Torheit: Eine exegetisch-religions-geschichtliche Untersuchung zu I Kor. 1 and 2* (BHT 26; Tübingen: J. C. B. Mohr [Paul Siebeck], 1959). D. Georgi, *Die Geschichte der Kollekte des Paulus für Jerusalem* (Hamburg: Herbert Reich, 1965); idem, "Der vorpaulinische Hymnus Phil 2,6–11," *Zeit und Geschichte: Dankesgabe an Rudolf Bultmann zum 80. Geburtstag* (ed. E. Dinkler; Tübingen: J. C. B. Mohr [Paul Siebeck], 1964) 263–93. R. Scroggs, "Paul: SOPHOS and PNEUMATIKOS," *NTS* 14 (1967) 33–55. R. G. Hamerton-Kelly, *Pre-Existence, Wisdom, and the Son of Man: A Study of the Idea of Pre-Existence in the New Testament* (Cambridge: Cambridge University Press, 1973) 112–19. H. Conzelmann, "Paulus und die Weisheit," *NTS* 12 (1965) 231–43; idem, "Wisdom in the New Testament," *IDBSup* (1976) 956–60; idem, "The Mother of Wisdom," *The Future of Our Religious Past: Essays in Honor of Rudolf Bultmann* (ed. J. M. Robinson; New York: Harper & Row, 1964) 230–43. For a more thorough *Forschungsbericht* see E. Elizabeth Johnson, *The Function of Apocalyptic and Wisdom Traditions in Romans 9–11* (SBLDS 109; Atlanta: Scholars Press, 1989) 23–54.

3. The most recent revival of the argument by E. J. Schnabel essentially catalogues previous research without adding substantively to it (*Law and Wisdom from Ben Sira to Paul: A Tradition Historical Enquiry into the Relation of Law, Wisdom, and Ethics* [WUNT 2/16; Tübingen: J. C. B. Mohr (Paul Siebeck), 1985] 236–63). Schnabel's dissertation makes one curious innovation by *concluding* the case for hypostatized wisdom Christology with the hymn in Col 1:15–20 rather than *beginning* with it, as nearly everyone since Windisch has done. One wonders why, if Schnabel considers Colossians (although not Ephesians) authentically Pauline, he declines to offer his strongest evidence at the outset. The claims that Gal 4:4; 1 Cor 8:6; 10:4; Rom 10:6–7; 11:33–36; and Phil 2:6–11 all give voice to a fully developed wisdom Christology rest in large measure on the assumption that they are penned by the author (or quoter) of the Colossians hymn, a dubious assumption at best. The greatest assistance provided by Schnabel's study is that it gathers in one place the vast majority of literature on Paul and wisdom Christology.

J. D. G. Dunn surveys the landscape with a much more cautious and critical eye in *Christology in the Making: A New Testament Inquiry Into the Origins of the Doctrine of the Incarnation* (Philadelphia: Westminster Press, 1980) 163–97, although he too argues that

ens claims instead that Paul uses wisdom language in 1 Corinthians 1–3 as a polemic against the heretical Christology of the Corinthians, and that his own Christology is instead formed by an apocalyptic interpretation of the cross and resurrection.[4] Georgi and Conzelmann argue in much broader terms for a sapiential "school tradition" that Paul both inherits from his Jewish context and perpetuates in his Christian teaching, although neither Conzelmann nor Georgi limits the content of that wisdom teaching to Paul's Christology, and neither places much stock in the role apocalyptic traditions play in Pauline thought. Scroggs and Hamerton-Kelly both describe a more complex theological context from which Paul operates that does indeed attend to the apocalyptic as well as sapiential elements in the letters, but neither one examines the nature or result of the confluence of the two perspectives in Paul. This wider net cast by Conzelmann, Georgi, Scroggs, and Hamerton-Kelly carries the greatest promise of usefulness for understanding Paul's letters, it seems, and invites one to take up again the search for wisdom in Paul.

Since Albert Schweitzer's turn-of-the-century insistence on the radically apocalyptic nature of Paul's thought,[5] though, a striking majority of Pauline scholars has continued to argue that the apostle's closest theological kinfolk are not the heirs of the wisdom tradition but rather

"[t]he most plausible indications of a Wisdom christology in the Pauline letters remain those which ascribe a role to the cosmic Christ in creation" (187), by which he means the Colossians hymn, as well as 1 Cor 1:23, 30; 8:6. Although I find Dunn's exegesis of these passages most thoughtful and perceptive, his position is finally more christocentric than Paul's, and he limits Paul's understanding of the gospel too severely to the person and work of Christ.

4. Although U. Wilckens retracts significant points of his original argument in "Zu 1 Kor 2,1–16," *Theologia Crucis, Signum Crucis* (ed. C. Andresen and G. Klein; Tübingen: J. C. B. Mohr [Paul Siebeck], 1979) 501–37, the influence of *Weisheit und Torheit* has been significant. Wilckens has been joined by a host of scholars who have attempted to refute any and all claims of wisdom Christology in Paul, although few have been persuaded by Wilckens's particular reconstruction of the Corinthians' Christology. See B. A. Pearson, "Hellenistic-Jewish Wisdom Speculation and Paul," *Aspects of Wisdom in Judaism and Early Christianity* (ed. R. L. Wilken; Notre Dame, Ind.: University of Notre Dame Press, 1975) 43–66; idem, *The Pneumatikos-Psychikos Terminology in I Corinthians: A Study in the Theology of the Corinthian Opponents of Paul and Its Relation to Gnosticism* (SBLDS 12; Missoula, Mont.: Scholars Press, 1973). See also Johnson, *Apocalyptic and Wisdom Traditions*, 44–45, for a discussion of A. Van Roon, "The Relation Between Christ and the Wisdom of God According to Paul," *NovT* 16 (1974) 207–39.

5. Schweitzer himself credits R. Kabisch (*Die Eschatologie des Paulus in ihren Zusammenhängen mit dem Gesamtbegriff des Paulinismus* [Göttingen: Vandenhoeck & Ruprecht, 1883]) with having been the first to recognize the "real eschatological essence" of Pauline thought (*Paul and His Interpreters* [London: SCM Press, 1912 (1906)] 60); cf. also idem, *The Mysticism of the Apostle Paul* (New York: H. Holt, 1931 [1929]) 18. Schweitzer's concern to highlight the Jewish apocalyptic character of early Christianity was first voiced in his *The Quest of the Historical Jesus* (London: SCM Press, 1910 [1906]).

apocalyptic Jews who anticipate an imminent divine intervention that will bring human history to a close and usher in God's day of salvation.[6] Much in Paul's letters, of course, encourages this judgment. Beyond his frequent use of *apokalypto* (I reveal) and its cognates[7] is his claim to have received numerous revelations himself (2 Cor 12:1–7), some of which he apparently reveals to his churches (e.g., 1 Cor 15:51; Rom 11:25–27). Paul's urgent expectation of an imminent return of the Lord and the arrival of God's glory and judgment forms his apostolic consciousness and work in significant ways. "The appointed time has grown short," he warns the Corinthians, because "the present form of this world is passing away" (1 Cor 7:29, 31).[8] He claims his preaching is compelled by apocalyptic necessity (9:16), and he comforts the Thessalonians with the assurance that, although some among them have already died, "we who are alive, who are left until the coming of the Lord, will by no means precede those who have died" (1 Thess 4:15). Despite enormous scholarly debate about the precise character of Jewish apocalyptic thought and the nature of Paul's indebtedness to it,[9] there is substantial consensus that one can scarcely understand the apostle's letters without discerning the apocalyptic contours of his thought. Scholars continue to debate whether one rightly locates the focus of Paul's apocalyptic

6. Schweitzer's own *Forschungsbericht* is but the first of many in this century. See the discussion in W. G. Kümmel, *The New Testament: The History of the Investigation of Its Problems* (Nashville: Abingdon Press, 1972) 226–44. See also the select history of research into Paul's apocalyptic heritage in Johnson, *Apocalyptic and Wisdom Traditions*, 4–23.

7. Paul calls the Corinthians, for example, believers who "wait for the *apokalypsin* [revelation] of our Lord Jesus Christ" (1 Cor 1:7); he describes Christian worship as containing revelations (1 Cor 14:6, 26), and he says his gospel came to him by revelation rather than human communication (Gal 1:12; cf. 2:2). Paul sees the present moment transformed by the revelation of God's righteousness and wrath (Rom 1:17–18); God's wrath and glory, the children of God, and the work of church leaders will be revealed at the judgment day (Rom 5:2; 8:18, 19; 1 Cor 3:13); and people who hold theological stances different from the apostle's will have the error of their ways revealed to them by God (Phil 3:15). God's Spirit has already revealed to believers "what eye has not seen" (1 Cor 2:10); God revealed Christ to Paul (Gal 1:16), and *pistis* (faith) was revealed in the Christ event (Gal 3:23).

8. Unless noted otherwise, Bible translations in this essay are from the NRSV.

9. Most significant in this regard is E. P. Sanders's contribution in *Paul and Palestinian Judaism: A Comparison of Patterns of Religion* (Philadelphia: Fortress Press, 1977). R. E. Sturm surveys the critical investigation of apocalyptic literature and thought, particularly as that research concerns Paul's letters, and argues that the most helpful studies ask not only about the genre of literature defined by Daniel and Revelation, but about the conceptual world of those writers ("Defining the Word 'Apocalyptic': A Problem in Biblical Criticism," *Apocalyptic and the New Testament: Essays in Honor of J. Louis Martyn* [ed. J. Marcus and M. L. Soards; Sheffield: JSOT Press, 1989] 17–48).

eschatology in his hope of God's future glory[10] or his past experience of the cross and resurrection as the inauguration of the new age,[11] but the assumption that Paul owes some measure of debt to Jewish apocalyptic thought is widespread.

Several passages in Paul's letters, though, stubbornly refuse to be categorized as deriving from allegedly apocalyptic quarters. J. Christiaan Beker, for example, who has made the most spirited recent plea for understanding Paul as an apocalyptic interpreter of the gospel, nevertheless claims that the apostle's Jewish apocalyptic worldview undergoes "a profound modification" because of his experience of Christ.[12] This means to some of Beker's critics that he has too narrowly defined "apocalyptic thought" and therefore not clearly seen its presence in letters (like Galatians) where Paul neglects to discuss the imminent parousia and the approaching glory of God.[13] But to other readers of Paul's letters, such alleged "modification" is instead evidence of the influence of other, nonapocalyptic forces on Paul's thought — particularly from the wisdom literature.

II

By and large, then, these two groups of scholars make incompatible claims about the shape and focus of Paul's thought. The former describes the apostle's theology as singularly shaped by sapiential categories; the latter, by apocalyptic. The distance between these two groups of Pauline scholars is symptomatic of a long-standing assumption

10. J. C. Beker, *Paul the Apostle: The Triumph of God in Life and Thought* (Philadelphia: Fortress, 1980).

11. L. E. Keck, "Paul as Thinker," *Int* 47 (1993) 27–38. Cf. also Keck's "Paul and Apocalyptic Theology," *Int* 38 (1984) 229–41, in which he says, "Paul's theology (not the same as his gospel) is apocalyptic . . . because it shares with apocalyptic theology the perspective of discontinuity" (241).

12. Beker, *Paul the Apostle,* 145.

13. See particularly J. L. Martyn's review of Beker's book in *Word & World* 2 (1982) 194–98; idem, "Apocalyptic Antinomies in Paul's Letter to the Galatians," *NTS* 31 (1985) 410–24; and Sturm, "Defining the Word 'Apocalyptic,'" 35–36, 39. Keck chides Beker for attributing Paul's failure to use the language "this age and the age to come" to his "modification" of Jewish apocalyptic, and says, "whoever [like Paul] becomes convinced that the resurrection of Jesus has signaled the intrusion of the age to come into the present cannot be expected to speak of the age to come in the same way as he or she had done before. What the absence of 'the age to come' from Paul's vocabulary shows is not that two-age thinking has been marginalized but that thinking ex post facto about Jesus' resurrection made this phrase obsolete, while not annulling the two-age view of reality itself" ("Paul as Thinker," 30).

among students of the Old Testament and early Judaism that apocalyptic and sapiential ways of looking at the world and God and human life are mutually exclusive: one is either a sage or a seer, but not both. Here, too, there is reason to think such a thing. What could seem more different books than Proverbs and Daniel? If we approach the problem from a literary standpoint and begin with the traditional wisdom corpus and several first-century apocalypses,[14] a necessarily dichotomous picture emerges:

> 1. For the "ideal" sage, the meaning of life is immanent: accessible in the present, the mundane, the human experiences of God and nature. For the archetypal seer, meaning is virtually absent from those spheres, and is rather located in the future, the supramundane, the transcendent realms.
>
> 2. The wisdom writer finds meaning in the proper conduct of this life — social relations, personal integrity, the pursuit of happiness and prosperity. The apocalyptic writer, on the other hand, finds meaning in divine activity yet to occur and his own preparation for that activity.
>
> 3. Wisdom is available to all who seek it; revelations are granted only to specific persons. The sage finds wisdom by observation and active study; the seer receives revelations passively from otherworldly beings.
>
> 4. The wisdom writer experiences boundless confidence in the order, balance, and harmony of God's creation and his own rightful and appropriate place in that creation. His life can make sense if he aligns himself with the world's God-given order: virtue is rewarded, sin is punished. The writer of an apocalypse, on the other hand, despairs of all order this side of the eschaton: the godly seem to be punished and the wicked rewarded, and creation itself is decaying. His life makes no sense apart from his hope that God will soon break into human history and rescue him from his plight. For the sage, the present has great potential for experience of the good, and this life carries with it responsibility for faithful action that can bear fruit. For the seer, only the eschatological future is potentially good, and this life is a matter of (none-too-patient) waiting in which one's primary responsibility is to discern the signs of the times and prepare for divine visitation and redemption.[15]

Despite these stark differences, though, there are substantial points of continuity between these two types of literature, most of them first catalogued by Gerhard von Rad in his attempt, in *Old Testament Theology* and *Wisdom in Israel,* to demonstrate that the apocalyptic movement

14. Such as the documents isolated on the basis of genre by the Apocalypse Group of the SBL Genres Project and discussed in *Semeia* 14 (1979).

15. Johnson, *Apocalyptic and Wisdom Traditions,* 70–71.

derives from degenerate wisdom thinking.[16] Seers often call themselves wise men and their books "wisdom" books (e.g., *1 Enoch* 37:1); both sorts of book concern themselves with nature more than with history; and both give voice to the concept of determinism, relate dreams and oracles, employ questions and answers, and wrestle with the problem of evil.[17] On the strength of von Rad's observations, several studies have expanded the list of perspectives shared by wisdom and apocalyptic literature. John G. Gammie demonstrates that both traditions assume an absolute distinction between heaven and earth, between the righteous and the wicked;[18] Simon J. DeVries suggests that both share an idealized perspective of "timelessness";[19] John J. Collins finds in both a "cosmological conviction" that sees the "way to salvation . . . in understanding the structure of the universe and adapting to it."[20]

So despite the very evident differences between apocalyptic and sapiential literature, there remain numerous points at which authors refuse to acknowledge the boundaries. Although it was the two distinct halves of Daniel, chaps. 1–6 and 7–14, which seem to give expression to radically dissimilar kinds of religious experience,[21] that called von Rad's

16. G. von Rad, *Old Testament Theology* (New York: Harper & Row, 1965) 2.301–15; idem, *Wisdom in Israel* (Nashville: Abingdon Press, 1972) 263–83. Von Rad's argument has not been universally persuasive, and countless defenders of apocalyptic's prophetic heritage have risen up against it. P. D. Hanson expresses a majority view by saying, "That wisdom was drawn into apocalyptic and given a prominent position within that literature cannot be denied. That wisdom, however, accounts for the origin and circumscribes the essence of apocalyptic is an untenable hypothesis" ("Prolegomena to the Study of Jewish Apocalyptic," *Magnalia Dei: The Mighty Acts of God* [ed. F. M. Cross et al.; Garden City, N.Y.: Doubleday & Co., 1976] 401).

17. Von Rad, *Old Testament Theology,* 2.306–15.

18. J. G. Gammie, "Spatial and Ethical Dualism in Jewish Wisdom and Apocalyptic Literature," *JBL* 93 (1974) 356–85.

19. S. J. DeVries, "Observations on Quantitative and Qualitative Time in Wisdom and Apocalyptic," *Israelite Wisdom: Theological and Literary Essays in Honor of Samuel Terrien* (ed. J. G. Gammie et al.; New York: Union Theological Seminary, 1978) 263–76.

20. J. J. Collins, "Cosmos and Salvation: Jewish Wisdom and Apocalyptic in the Hellenistic Age," *HR* 17 (1977) 121–42. M. Küchler's dissertation goes so far as to claim that first-century apocalypticists espouse a particular wisdom teaching that is all their own, although the description of that wisdom teaching in Küchler's book ends up looking very much like an encyclopedic description of all the ways wisdom language appears in apocalyptic literature rather than a critical analysis of its function (*Frühjüdische Weisheitstraditionen: Zum Fortgang weistheitlichen Denkens im Bereich des Frühjüdischen Jahwehglaubens* [OBO 26; Göttingen: Vandenhoeck & Ruprecht, 1979]).

21. J. J. Collins ("The Court Tales in Daniel and the Development of Apocalyptic," *JBL* 94 [1975] 218–34) argues that the stories about Daniel the international courtier in chaps. 1–6 were transformed into the visions of chaps. 7–12 under the pressure of Antiochus Epiphanes's persecution of Palestinian Jews. Similarly, J. Z. Smith claims that the development of apocalyptic expectations is the product of wisdom speculation about

attention to the phenomenon in the first place, Daniel does not provide the most helpful point of departure for examining the confluence of wisdom and apocalyptic traditions. "Wisdom" is indeed granted the seer to "understand" his visions (e.g., Dan 9:22–23), and "the wise" are identified as those who will survive the holocaust (11:33; 12:3), but the content of their wisdom is nowhere defined as it is in the later works — like *1 Enoch* — that seem to have been inspired partly by Daniel. So also, the tales in Daniel 1–6 evidence in themselves no particularly "apocalyptic" concerns.[22] The Wisdom of Solomon, on the other hand, while its form is scarcely that of an apocalypse, contains an extended passage that is reminiscent of some apocalyptic writings describing the great assize and the elevation of the righteous in the presence of the wicked (4:10–5:23), and the apocalypses of *1 Enoch,* 4 Ezra, *2 Baruch,* and numerous Qumran texts make extensive use of language, imagery, and thought that are familiar from wisdom books. These texts repeatedly and consistently equate the wisdom of God with Torah as does Sirach, and they exhort "the wise" to heed divine revelations that are often labeled "wisdom." Furthermore, as John G. Gammie's essay on secondary genres demonstrates so clearly,[23] the habitually dichotomous pictures of apocalyptic and sapiential genres fails to take account of the substantial sharing of formal characteristics between the two types of literature: both employ admonitions, exhortations, parables, lists, riddles, and historical surveys as secondary genres.[24] A comparison of wisdom and apocalyptic literature that remains at the level of primary genre is limited from the start.

These persistent connections among books once thought to represent mutually exclusive worldviews therefore invite a different set of questions than the ones raised earlier by comparing disparate sorts of books. Rather than asking what an "ideal" sage or seer thinks in general and then comparing the two perspectives, we might ask in-

---

the ideal human ruler after the cessation of native kingship ("Wisdom and Apocalyptic," *Religious Syncretism in Antiquity: Essays in Conversation With Geo Widengren* [ed. B. A. Pearson; Missoula, Mont.: Scholars Press, 1975] 131–56).

22. In his very thoughtful review of my *Wisdom and Apocalyptic Traditions,* J. M. Scott objected to my decision not to examine Daniel along with *1 Enoch,* 4 Ezra, *2 Baruch,* and the Qumran library (*JBL* 110 [1991] 742–44). An extended footnote on pages 72–73 explains my decision, but I reiterate it here because I still see no way fruitfully to apply the same analysis to Daniel that I apply to the other texts.

23. J. G. Gammie, "Paraenetic Literature: Toward the Morphology of a Secondary Genre," *Semeia* 50 (1990) 41–77.

24. Ibid., 47.

stead how discreet documents address specific questions, most notably questions about the wisdom of God and its relation to human experience: (1) Where does the author locate God's wisdom? Does it reside in the creation and human relationships, or is it primarily a heavenly reality? (2) What does the author consider to be the content of God's wisdom? (3) Who, according to the author, has access to God's wisdom? (4) What potential does the author think exists for ordered and meaningful life before the eschaton? What is the value of the present for human life?

The picture rendered by answers to these questions is not a dichotomous one of mutually exclusive ways of talking about God and human experience but rather a continuum that might be described as traveling the spectrum between "immanence" and "transcendence."[25] Put most simply, there appears to be a correlation between an author's use of wisdom themes in "traditional" ways (that is, as measured by books like Proverbs and Sirach) and his conviction of the potential to find meaning accessible in this life, before the eschaton: the more an author considers God's wisdom to inhere in the creation and in Torah, and therefore to be universally accessible, the more the author anticipates fruitful human action in the present; the more an author considers God's wisdom to be hidden in esoteric interpretations of Torah or divine mysteries revealed by heavenly beings to select human beings, the more he despairs of meaningful human life this side of the eschaton.[26]

This spectrum of possibilities for talking about God and human experience calls into question the conclusions drawn by earlier studies that have investigated the wisdom traditions in Paul. Those conclusions have tended to claim that the apostle is *either* a sage *or* a seer, or else to posit a third option between the two extremes, in the language of Robin Scroggs, a hybrid "apocalyptic-wisdom theology"[27] that borrows characteristics from each but belongs properly to neither. It now appears more likely that the dichotomy between wisdom and apocalyptic modes of discourse is itself a scholarly construct that may not

25. Johnson, *Apocalyptic and Wisdom Traditions*, 71. The language of immanence and transcendence here refers only to an author's perception of where God's wisdom may be found, rather than a philosophical debate about divine immanence and transcendence.

26. See the extended discussions of Wisdom, *1 Enoch*, 4 Ezra, *2 Baruch*, and the Qumran library in ibid., 74–109.

27. Scroggs, "Paul," 35. Cases similar to Scroggs's are also made, with different nuances, by J. M. Reese, "Paul Proclaims the Wisdom of the Cross: Scandal and Foolishness," *BTB* 9 (1979) 147–53; and Hamerton-Kelly, *Pre-Existence*, 112–19.

have made sense to a first-century Jew like Paul, and that the alleged hybrid is itself the dominant species.

III

Paul uses the language of wisdom[28] most explicitly in three contexts: Rom 1:18–32, Rom 11:33–36, and 1 Corinthians 1–3. The first speaks of human possession and poverty of wisdom; the latter two discuss God's wisdom. The first two use sapiential language in ways most familiar from Jewish wisdom literature (indeed the second is a Jewish hymn); the third is the least familiar (or the most Christian) in its appropriation of sapiential language. But in all three instances, Paul's arguments are profoundly shaped by his apocalyptic convictions about the inbreaking of God's redemption as well as his reliance on wisdom traditions. It is impossible in each case to separate the sapiential traditions from the apocalyptic.

Romans 1:18–32

The force of Paul's argument is determined by the first word, *apokalyptetai* (is revealed). "The decisive perspective is the eschatological one," observes Ernst Käsemann, who draws attention to the similar language about God's wrath in *1 Enoch* 91:7; *2 Bar.* 54:17ff.; and *T. Naph.* 3:2–5.[29] The revelation of divine wrath is "the reverse side of the manifestation of [God's] righteousness" (*dikaiosyne . . . apokalyptetai* [righteousness . . . is revealed], 1:17), "God's divinity asserting itself where it is not recognized by human beings."[30] God's wrath falls on human beings who know but refuse to acknowledge God. They claim

28. *Sophia* (wisdom): Rom 11:33; 1 Cor 1:17, 19, 20, 21 (bis), 22, 24, 30; 2:1, 4, 5, 6 (bis), 7, 13; 3:19; 12:8. *Sophos* (wise): Rom 1:14, 22; 16:19, [27]; 1 Cor 1:19, 20, 25, 26, 27; 3:10, 18 (bis), 19, 20; 6:5. Cf. *moraino* (I am foolish): Rom 1:22; 1 Cor 1:20; *moria* (foolishness): 1 Cor 1:18, 21, 23; 2:14; 3:19; *moros* (foolish): 1 Cor 1:25, 27; 3:18; 4:10. The single occurrence outside 1 Corinthians, Romans 1, and Romans 11 is 2 Cor 1:12 (*ouk en sophia sarkike . . . anestraphemen* [we behaved . . . not by earthly wisdom]), which apparently reprises the discussion in 1 Corinthians 1–3 by contrasting authentic apostolic proclamation of God's grace with mere human perspicacity (cf. V. P. Furnish, *II Corinthians* [AB 32A; Garden City, N.Y.: Doubleday & Co., 1984] 128). A second reminiscence of 1 Corinthians in the same context is *epegnote hemas apo merous* (you . . . understood us in part) (2 Cor 1:14), which calls to mind *ek merous gar ginoskomen* (for we know . . . in part) (1 Cor 13:9).

29. E. Käsemann, *Commentary on Romans* (Grand Rapids, Mich.: Wm. B. Eerdmans Publishing Co., 1980) 37.

30. P. W. Meyer, "Romans," *HBC* (ed. J. L. Mays; San Francisco: Harper & Row, 1988) 1136.

to be wise, Paul says, but are really fools (1:22; cf. Wis 12:24) because their knowledge of God issues not in worship but contempt. Here Paul gives voice to the widespread Jewish assumption that God's wisdom inheres in the creation and reveals God's deity and glory, much as Pseudo-Solomon says:

> With you [O God] is Wisdom, she who knows your works
> and was present when you made the world;
> she understands what is pleasing in your sight
> and what is right according to your commandments.
> Send her forth from the holy heavens,
> and from the throne of your glory send her,
> that she may labor at my side,
> and that I may learn what is pleasing to you. (9:9–10)

But unlike Pseudo-Solomon, Paul also looks at the world the way Enoch does:

> The state of violence will intensify upon the earth; a great plague shall be executed upon the earth; all (forms of) oppression will be carried out; and everything shall be uprooted; and every arrow shall fly fast.... Then a great plague shall take place from heaven upon all these; the holy Lord shall emerge with wrath and plague in order that he may execute judgment upon the earth. (*1 Enoch* 91:5, 7)[31]

The optimism in Wis 9:9–10 about wisdom's ability to elicit proper worship of God is itself tempered by Pseudo-Solomon's awareness of idolatry. Indeed the entire picture in Romans 1 of human wickedness as the result of God's wrath, rather than its cause, reflects the picture in Wisdom 12–13 of idolaters who confuse the created order with its creator, who are not to be pardoned (*oud' suggnostoi* [not... to be excused], 13:8; cf. *anapologetos* [without excuse], Rom 1:20; 2:1), and who are therefore "punished by the very things by which one sins" (11:16) and "tormented through their own abominations" (12:23; cf. *paredoken* [gave them up], Rom 1:24, 26, 28).[32]

Here in Romans 1, then, Paul employs language that can be said to stand at the very hearts of both apocalyptic and wisdom contexts: God's eschatological wrath on idolatry, on the one hand, and the foolishness of idolatry, on the other. Their fusion in Paul's argument emphasizes

31. Meyer (ibid.) calls attention to "the background to Paul's use of this phrase [i.e., 'the wrath of God'] in apocalyptic and wisdom traditions as represented by 1 Enoch and the Wisdom of Solomon." See also Wis 16:5; 18:20; cf. Sir 5:6–7; 16:11–12; 36:8–9.

32. Cf. also *T. Gad* 5:10; *Jub.* 4:32; 1QS 4:11ff. (Käsemann, *Romans*, 43).

the present manifestation of God's wrath, which is revealed now in the gospel rather than anticipated only at the eschaton. Although he maintains with Enoch that there is yet "wrath to come" at the eschaton (1 Thess 1:10), for Paul the new age has already begun to intrude on the old in the proclamation of the righteousness of God (note the perfect tense of *apokalyptetai* [is revealed] in Rom 1:17, 18). This is why he can make such considerable use of Pseudo-Solomon's analysis of contemporary human experience without sharing either the sage's anthropology or his cosmology.[33]

Romans 11:33–36

The praise of God with which Paul concludes the first major section of his argument in Romans (1:18–11:32) is very likely a synagogue hymn in praise of God's wisdom.[34] Paul quotes the piece at this juncture because it gives thanks for the very wisdom revealed in the mystery of Rom 11:25–27 that provides for the redemption of both Jews and Gentiles.[35] The hymn combines with the introductory oath of Rom 9:1–5 to create a literary *inclusio* for chaps. 9–11, beginning and ending with ascriptions of praise to the omnipotent God (cf. *epi panton,* 9:5; *ta panta,* 11:36).

> Just as 11:28–32 conclude not only chapters 9–11 but the whole of Romans 1:16–11:27, so the hymn in 11:33–36 expresses Paul's awe and wonder at the miracle of God's redemption of the world.... God's dealings with the world by means of the gospel are utterly consistent with God's dealings with the world by means of Israel. It is that consistency, that trustworthiness, that simultaneous impartiality and faithfulness of God which drives the argument of Romans to its conclusion in 11:28–32. And because it is

33. Keck's discussion of Paul as a "two-age thinker" is here particularly germane. "The experienced tension between the Old and New Ages does not mean that the New is struggling to emerge out of the Old but that the intrusion of the New challenges the Old during the temporary overlap" ("Paul as Thinker," 31).

34. The intricacy of its structure, the apparently multiple sources of its traditions, the preponderance of *hapax legomenoi* or vocabulary used in uncommon ways, and its marked similarity to other poetic passages in praise of God's wisdom in *2 Bar.* 75:1–5 (cf. 14:8–10, where there are even verbal similarities, although the intention is quite different from Paul's) and 1QH 7:26–33; 10:3–7 combine to tip the scales in favor of pre-Pauline authorship.

35. On the use of *mysterion* (mystery) in early Judaism as a description of God's revealed counsel, see R. E. Brown, *The Semitic Background of the Term "Mystery" in the New Testament* (FBBS 21; Philadelphia: Fortress, 1968); D. Aune, *Prophecy in Early Christianity and the Ancient Mediterranean World* (Grand Rapids, Mich.: Wm. B. Eerdmans Publishing Co., 1983) 333; and for its function in Rom 11:25–27, Johnson, *Apocalyptic and Wisdom Traditions,* 129, 163.

God's wisdom — in the law and in the gospel which is the *telos* [end] of that law [Rom 10:4] — which remains consistent, Paul's doxological response in 11:33–36 cannot help but laud God's wisdom.[36]

Far from being a christological affirmation, as some have claimed,[37] the hymn describes divine wisdom as the ordering power of God's gracious sovereignty. Its language is "traditionally" sapiential, drawing on familiar Old Testament images and themes (the *bathos* [depth] of God, God's "judgments" and "ways," the citations of Isa 40:13 and Job 41:3) as well as the Stoic affirmation of divine sufficiency (*ta panta* [all things]) that is so often shared by Hellenistic Jews of the first century.[38] But Paul invokes this wisdom hymn precisely in response to a revelation concerning God's eschatological redemption, in much the way Baruch sings the praises of divine wisdom in response to his own receipt of a revelation concerning God's promised salvation (*2 Bar.* 75:1–5):

> Who can equal your goodness, O Lord?
> for it is incomprehensible.
> Or who can fathom your grace
> which is without end?
> Or who can understand your intelligence?
> Or who of those born can hope to arrive at these things,
> apart from those to whom you are merciful and gracious?

The hymns in praise of God's wisdom in the Qumran *Hôdāyôt* (hymns), particularly 7:26–33 and 10:3–7, similarly give thanks for the revelation of God's "mysteries" and the "counsel of God's truth" using the rhetorical questions so prominent in Baruch's hymn and the hymn Paul quotes in Romans 11.[39]

In the case of Rom 11:33–36, Paul's use of wisdom traditions is itself apparently quite traditional. Both Baruch and the Qumran psalmist(s) also offer praise of God's wisdom in response to apocalyptic mysteries, because those mysteries themselves make accessible to human beings

36. Johnson, *Apocalyptic and Wisdom Traditions*, 174.

37. See, for example, A. T. Hanson, *The New Testament Interpretation of Scripture* (London: SPCK, 1980) 21–96, and the response offered in Johnson, *Apocalyptic and Wisdom Traditions*, 48–49. Schnabel accepts Hanson's conclusions rather uncritically (*Law and Wisdom*, 250, 260–62).

38. E. Norden traces what he calls the "Bekenntnisformel der stoischen Theologie" (*Agnostos Theos: Untersuchungen zur Formengeschichte religiöser Rede* [Leipzig: Teubner, 1913] 240) throughout early Judaism and the New Testament (240–50). Further on the hymn see G. Bornkamm, "The Praise of God," *Early Christian Experience* (New York: Harper & Row, 1969) 105–11; R. Deichgräber, *Gotteshymnus und Christushymnus in der frühen Christenheit* (Göttingen: Vandenhoeck & Ruprecht, 1967) 60–64.

39. Johnson, *Apocalyptic and Wisdom Traditions*, 169–71.

the wisdom of God's counsel. For Baruch and the Qumran sectarians, God's counsel concerns the Torah and proper interpretation of it as well as God's wise plan for the future, while for Paul, God's counsel concerns the divine plan to save "all Israel" by means of the current "hardening" of some Jews to the gospel and the Christian faith of Gentiles. Both understandings of God's wisdom, though, see its function similarly: to order God's creation and set right its relation to God. Because Paul thus says of the gospel what his contemporaries say of God's law — that it embodies and makes accessible the wisdom of God — the hymn he quotes functions in the same way as Baruch's and the *Hôdāyôt do.*

1 Corinthians 1–3

Here, too, the wisdom of God is to be found in the gospel Paul preaches.[40] In response to the congregation's apparent assumption that wisdom is a human characteristic or possession, Paul asserts that the wisdom he preached to them is instead the "word of the cross" (1:18); "Christ crucified" (1:23; cf. 2:2); "Christ the power of God and the wisdom of God" (1:24); "Christ Jesus, whom God made our wisdom, our righteousness and sanctification and redemption" (1:30); "the wisdom of God in a mystery" (2:7; cf. 4:1); "words taught by the Spirit" (2:13). His proclamation is itself the *revealed* wisdom of God (2:10),[41] consisting of "what eye has not seen nor ear heard nor human heart conceived of, the things God prepared for those who love him" (2:9, my trans.).

Ever since publication of Wilckens's *Weisheit und Torheit,* most interpreters have decided that Paul and the Corinthians have competing Christologies, that what is at stake in the contest is the nature of Christ rather than the nature of Christian preaching and preachers. This is somewhat understandable, since Paul frequently uses the synecdoche "Christ" or "Christ crucified" to describe his gospel.[42] But to restrict the content of Paul's preaching solely to the person and work of Christ ignores the fundamentally *theo*centric quality of his thought in general[43] and the literary context of this specific passage, which confirms that

40. This section reiterates much of my argument in "The Wisdom of God as Apocalyptic Power," *Faith and History: Essays in Honor of Paul W. Meyer* (ed. J. T. Carroll, C. H. Cosgrove, and E. E. Johnson; Atlanta: Scholars Press, 1990) 137–48.

41. G. W. E. Nickelsburg, "Revealed Wisdom as a Criterion for Inclusion and Exclusion: From Jewish Sectarianism to Early Christianity," *"To See Ourselves as Others See Us": Christians, Jews, "Others" in Late Antiquity* (ed. J. Neusner and E. S. Frerichs; Chico, Calif.: Scholars Press, 1985) 73–91.

42. Hamerton-Kelly, *Pre-Existence,* 115.

43. Cf. Beker's insistence on Paul's theocentricity in *Paul the Apostle,* 351–67 (and

the dispute between the apostle and his church concerns the nature of Christian proclamation.[44]

Paul enumerates the elements of his gospel at 1 Cor 1:30 and 2:9. The *dikaiosyne te kai hagiosmos kai apolytrosis* (righteousness and sanctification and redemption) that define *sophia hemin apo theou* (for us wisdom from God) in 1:30 encompass the full spectrum of Paul's preaching, "the whole cosmic drama of God's creative sovereignty, justification of sinners, and redemption of the world,"[45] and therefore include not only the person of Jesus or the event of his death on the cross, but also *ha hetoimasen ho theos* (what God has prepared) (2:9), the riches of God's glory yet to be revealed (cf. Rom 8:18).[46]

At several other points in his letters in addition to these discussions of *sophia*, Paul speaks in ways that are reminiscent of the wisdom literature without using its vocabulary quite so explicitly. Several texts suggest the presence of wisdom traditions: the "wisdom chain" in Rom 5:3–5; the contrast between vessels of wrath and mercy in Rom 9:20–23; Rom 10:6–9, where Paul uses Baruch's exegesis of Deut 30:12–14 to call the gospel the near word of God's wisdom; and the assertion in Gal 4:4 and Rom 8:3 that God "sent" the Son, which is reminiscent of God's sending of wisdom into the world. In these passages too — just as in Romans 1, Romans 11, and 1 Corinthians 1–3 — the sapiential themes are bound inextricably to apocalyptic ideas.

Romans 5:3–5

After using the illustration of Abraham to dispense with the inappropriate boasting of human beings in (pseudo)righteousness of their own creation (Rom 4:1–25), Paul turns to a description of appropriate Christian boasting in 5:1–11, boasting in "our hope of God's glory"

---

passim), and a similar plea from N. A. Dahl, "The Neglected Factor in New Testament Theology," *Reflection* 73 (1975) 5–8.

44. Correctly N. A. Dahl, "Paul and the Church at Corinth," *Studies in Paul* (Minneapolis: Augsburg Publishing House, 1977) 40–61; R. W. Funk, "Word and Word in I Corinthians 2:6–16," *Language, Hermeneutic, and Word of God* (New York: Harper & Row, 1966) 275–305; G. Theissen, *Psychological Aspects of Pauline Theology* (Philadelphia: Fortress, 1987) 343–93. For all his otherwise very perceptive reading of the argument in 1 Corinthians 1–3, and his acknowledged distance from Wilckens, Dunn also collapses Paul's gospel into his Christology (*Christology in the Making*, 176–79).

45. Johnson, "Wisdom of God," 147.

46. Scroggs rightly insists that Paul's wisdom teaching is "not simply about Christ himself, but about the whole eschatological drama of the final time" ("Paul," 46).

(5:2, my trans.). The present manifestation of that hope in Christian experience is, paradoxically, boasting in tribulations (5:3).

Throughout early Judaism, and particularly in wisdom settings, exhortations abound to learn and otherwise profit from suffering.[47] Paul's connections of *thlipsis* (tribulation) with *hypomone, dokime, elpis* (endurance, character, hope), and *aischunomai* (I boast) are echoed in several wisdom texts like Sirach 2 or Wisdom 3,[48] which also like Paul attach *eirene* (peace) to *elpis* (hope) (3:3–4). Paul may even be deliberately alluding to such traditions by his use of *eidotes* (knowing), since such a very similar formulation occurs in part at Jas 1:3 (*dokimion . . . katergazetai hypomone* [testing . . . produces endurance]) and 1 Pet 1:7.[49]

In Sirach and Wisdom (as also frequently in 1 Maccabees) suffering is educative because the sufferer learns from experience that it can be endured and because God who has previously rescued Israel can be trusted again to save the righteous. For Paul, though, the hope that results from character, which is in turn produced by endurance, which is forged by suffering, is itself an eschatological reality[50] whose reliability rests not on proper faithful response to hardship but on God's love that has been "poured into our hearts through the Holy Spirit that has been given to us" (5:5). Hope is a mark of the end times because it is a product of the believer's living between Christ's resurrection and his parousia, experiencing the present reality of justification and life in the Spirit, but

47. C. H. Talbert nicely summarizes the evidence and provides an insightful analysis of the ways James, 1 Peter, Hebrews, and Luke-Acts make use of the traditions in *Learning Through Suffering: The Educational Value of Suffering in the New Testament and Its Milieu* (Collegeville, Minn.: The Liturgical Press [Michael Glazier], 1991).

48. E.g., in Sirach 2: "My child, when you come to serve the Lord, prepare yourself for testing. Set your heart right and be steadfast. . . . Accept whatever befalls you, and in times of humiliation be patient. For gold is tested in the fire, and those found acceptable, in the furnace of humiliation. Trust in him, and he will help you; make your ways straight, and hope in him. . . . Consider the generations of old and see: has anyone trusted in the Lord and been disappointed? Or has anyone persevered in the fear of the Lord and been forsaken? . . . Woe to you who have lost your nerve! What will you do when the Lord's reckoning comes?" (Sir 2:1–2a, 4–6, 10a-b, 14). In Wisdom 3: "For though in the sight of others they [the righteous] were punished, their hope is full of immortality. Having been disciplined a little, they will receive great good, because God tested them and found them worthy of himself; like gold in the furnace he tried them. . . . But the ungodly . . . who despise wisdom and instruction are miserable. Their hope is vain, their labors are unprofitable, and their works are useless" (Wis 3:4–6a, 10a, 11).

49. See L. Goppelt, *Der Erste Petrusbrief* (Göttingen: Vandenhoeck & Ruprecht, 1978) 101.

50. Cf. 8:20, 24; 12:12; 15:4, 13; 2 Cor 3:12; Gal 5:5; Phil 1:20; 1 Thess 2:19; 4:13; 5:8. Note particularly the connections of *elpis/elpizo* (hope/I hope) with *aischunomai* (I am put to shame) in both Rom 5:5 and Phil 1:20.

longing for the day of redemption (cf. Rom 8:18–30). Elsewhere when Paul speaks of *thlipsis,* it too carries an apocalyptic nuance,[51] just as in Jewish apocalyptic literature the end times are signaled by increased suffering. In the final analysis, Paul says the Christian's ability to boast in suffering[52] derives not from an attitude toward the world or a state of mind, but confidence in the God who raised Jesus from the dead and even now is bringing life from death. Christian hope is not optimism about a potentially positive future that makes present suffering a bearable, if necessary, evil. Hope is rather the stance of one who trusts God to complete what has begun at the cross.[53]

In Romans 5, particularly, the confluence of wisdom and apocalyptic traditions focuses on the fruitfulness of the time before the eschaton. Although clearly determined by the revelation of God's ultimate triumph in the cross and resurrection of Christ, the believer's ability to boast about tribulations depends also on the reality of human experience. The wisdom tradition that one can productively learn from suffering is sharpened by adding to it an apocalyptic starting point. "Suffering produces endurance" only when it is understood from the perspective of the cross. Without that perspective, suffering is just as likely to produce despair and resignation as hope in God's glory.

Romans 9:20–23

By recourse to two illustrations, one from history (the hardening of pharaoh in 9:14–18) and the second from the common experience of a potter, Paul in Romans 9 supports his claim that God's sovereignty is not capricious but serves the purposes of divine wrath and mercy.[54] Although God's sovereignty is commonly portrayed by the prophets with the metaphor of the potter,[55] Paul is clearly more influenced by a wisdom use of the image in this context. In neither Isaiah 29 nor Jeremiah 18 are there two sorts of vessels created for different uses such as we

51. E.g., Rom 2:9; 12:12; 2 Cor 1:3–11; 4:8, 17.

52. See Käsemann's very clear description of why *kauchasthai en thlipsesin* (to boast in tribulations) cannot be taken locatively but must describe tribulation as the "object of boasting" (*Romans,* 134).

53. See the discussion in J. C. Beker, *Suffering and Hope: The Biblical Vision and the Human Predicament* (Philadelphia: Fortress, 1987) 57–79.

54. Johnson, *Apocalyptic and Wisdom Traditions,* 132–33, 147–50.

55. Cf. Isa 29:16, from which the question of Rom 9:20a is taken, and Isa 45:9–13; Jer 18:1–11; 19:1–15.

find in Sir 33:12–13 and Wis 15:7.[56] In the prophetic contexts, a pot's defiance of a potter highlights the absurdity of Israel's defiance of divine judgment. In the sapiential contexts, however, what is at stake is not the rightness of God's judgment but God's freedom to elect some and not others, precisely the point under discussion in Romans 9.

This traditional illustration, which Paul seems to use in its sapiential rather than prophetic incarnation, nevertheless stands in the service of an argument that finds its closest affinities with apocalyptic writers. God's *endeixasthai ten orgen kai gnorisai ton dynaton autou* (to show his wrath and to make known his power) (9:22) is nothing else than the revelation of *dikaiosyne* (righteousness) and *orge* (wrath) with which Paul begins his argument at Rom 1:17, 18, the mark of the new age inaugurated by the death and resurrection of Christ and its announcement in Paul's gospel. It is precisely here, for the first time in Romans 9, that Paul makes a distinctly Christian claim.[57] All of 9:6–23 is entirely consistent with Jewish election theology, but at 9:24 Paul includes among the vessels of mercy not only Jews but also Gentiles who are called by God. This new thing God has done in calling Gentiles on the same basis as Jews is of course *consistent* with God's past dealings with Israel, which is why Paul invokes the biblical proofs he does at 9:25–29. It is nevertheless *new* insofar as it is embodied in Paul's apostolic commission (cf. 1:13–17).

So this sapiential metaphor of the potter who freely makes two sorts of pots serves the apocalyptic affirmation that God freely elects some (both Jews and Gentiles) and not others, which affirmation prepares for the questions Paul raises at 9:30 about Gentile faith and the unbelief of some Jews.

Romans 10:6–9

Paul's *pesher* exegesis (cf. *tout' estin* [that is], 10:6, 7, 8) of Deut 30:12–14 in Rom 10:6–8 is frequently chastised by interpreters who accuse Paul of turning the plain sense of the text against itself, but his reading of Deuteronomy has most likely been filtered through that of Bar 3:29–30.[58]

56. Käsemann, *Romans*, 272; C. E. B. Cranfield, *The Epistle to the Romans* (ICC; Edinburgh: T. & T. Clark, 1979) 491–92.

57. Johnson, *Apocalyptic and Wisdom Traditions*, 148–49.

58. See ibid., 133–37. Windisch was the first to notice the similarities ("Die göttliche Weisheit," 224), and the case has since been made most compellingly by M. J. Suggs, "'The Word Is Near to You': Romans 10:6–10 Within the Purpose of the Letter," *Chris-*

> Whereas the point in Deuteronomy is admonitory, that Israel hear and do the law, the point in Baruch is polemical, that Israel enjoys a privileged status vis-à-vis the nations in having access to the law. Paul's interpretation of the same passage [in Deuteronomy] serves to demonstrate that the gospel is equally near to the whole world . . . and further functions to interpret Lev 18:5.[59]

Paul's exegetical point is that God has already accomplished what human beings are incapable of doing for themselves, that is, making close at hand the righteousness of God that alone can save. No one can bring Christ down from heaven or raise Christ from the dead, nor does anyone need to, because "the word of faith which we preach" (10:8, my trans.) brings that saving righteousness near. In a very similar way, Sirach claims that God's wisdom is *eggus* (near) (51:26) as an incentive to seek it for oneself.

Yet once again, Paul claims for his apostolic proclamation what his contemporaries claim for God's wisdom made accessible in Torah, something he has already stated at 10:4, although he is so maddeningly brief there as to be enigmatic. To assert that *telos gar nomou Christos* (Christ is the end of the law) is not to make a christological affirmation,[60] since here again, as in 1 Cor 1:23, 30, *Christos* (Christ) stands as a shorthand reference to *logos staurou* (word of the cross), but to claim that the gospel of God's impartial righteousness is equally accessible to Jews and Gentiles, which is the divinely ordained goal of the law.[61] God's wisdom in the law reaches its eschatological destination in the proclamation that "Jesus is Lord" and "God raised him from the dead" (10:9).

Galatians 4:4; Romans 8:3

Eduard Schweizer has pursued a thirty-year quest for the sapiential background to the phrase "God sent his Son,"[62] finding the closest

---

tian History and Interpretation: Studies Presented to John Knox (ed. W. R. Farmer et al.; Cambridge: Cambridge University Press, 1967) 289–312.

59. Johnson, *Apocalyptic and Wisdom Traditions*, 134–35.

60. P. W. Meyer sees this clearly in "Romans 10:4 and the 'End' of the Law," *The Divine Helmsman* (ed. J. L. Crenshaw and S. Sandmel; New York: KTAV Publishing House, 1980) 59–78. Meyer retracts his initial equation of the stone of stumbling in 9:33 with the law in his later "Romans" essay (1157) to say Paul means it to refer to God. It still seems to me more likely that the stone that trips Israel up is the gospel.

61. Cf. "to the Jew first, but also to the Greek" (1:16; 2:9–11; cf. 3:9, 22, 29–30; 4:11–12; 10:12; 15:7–12). Johnson, *Apocalyptic and Wisdom Traditions*, 151–59.

62. E. Schweizer, "Zur Herkunft der Präexistenzvorstellung bei Paulus," *EvT* 19 (1959) 65–70; idem, "Aufnahme und Korrektur jüdischer Sophiatheologie im Neuen

parallels in Wis 9:10, 17, where God is requested to send Wisdom and the Spirit. Although Schweizer concludes that the background of this phrase, which occurs in both Pauline and Johannine contexts,[63] "is certainly a kind of Wisdom or Logos christology,"[64] he frames Paul's use of the tradition in much more nuanced terms than are demanded by Paul's emphatic monotheism, which is never permitted to be absorbed by Christology. Whenever it is used, the phrase precedes a purpose clause naming Jesus' death as the explicit reason he is sent. This means that for Paul, God's sending of the son encompasses all of God's prior relationship with the creation and with Israel, God's justification of sinners by the word of faith, and God's ultimate victory that yet awaits consummation. Schweizer's most recent proposal of his argument is careful to avoid claiming that Paul attributes hypostatic or even personified Wisdom to Christ:

> In using the expression "his son," we describe the relation of God to Jesus as a unique nearness. This excludes both a mere commission of a human being (a prophet) and a sending of a being that is no "partner" of God (either a subordinate being, such as an angel, or the spirit, word, and wisdom of God, which are not really distinguishable from him). What encounters us in Jesus is God's very life, indeed God's wisdom, word, love, and motion towards his creation.[65]

As we have seen previously, so also in Paul's reference to divine wisdom in the phrase "God sent his son" he understands wisdom to be Christian proclamation, present in the world as God's eschatological means of reclaiming the world.[66] Its function is therefore remarkably

---

Testament," *Hören und Handeln: Festschrift für E. Wolf* (Munich: C. Kaiser, 1962) 330–40; idem, "Zum religionsgeschichtlichen Hintergrund der 'Sendungsformel' Gal 4,4f; Rom 8,3f; Joh 3,16f; 1 Joh 4,9," *ZNW* 57 (1966) 199–210; idem, "Huios, ktl," *TDNT* (1972) 8.374–76; and idem, "What Do We Really Mean When We Say 'God Sent His Son . . .'?" *Faith and History: Essays in Honor of Paul W. Meyer* (ed. J. T. Carroll, C. H. Cosgrove, and E. E. Johnson; Atlanta: Scholars Press, 1990) 298–312.

63. John 3:16, 1 John 4:9; cf. also the motif of "sending" in the Synoptic tradition.

64. Schweizer, "What Do We Really Mean?" 310.

65. Ibid., 311.

66. Further "christological" texts remain to be examined from this perspective, not least the hymn Paul quotes in Phil 2:6–11, which, as D. Georgi would have it, may derive from the motif of the wise person's humiliation and exaltation in Wisdom 2–3 ("Der vorpaulinische Hymnus Phil 2,6–11," *Zeit und Geschichte: Dankesgabe an Rudolf Bultmann zum 80. Geburtstag* [ed. E. Dinkler; Tübingen: J. C. B. Mohr (Paul Siebeck), 1964] 263–93). A lively debate about the hymn's religio-historical ancestry (e.g., E. Käsemann, "Kritische Analyse von Phil. 2:5–11," *Exegetische Versuche und Besinnungen* [Tübingen: J. C. B. Mohr (Paul Siebeck), 1964] 1.51–95) continues without eliciting much consensus as yet. See the diverse positions represented by the literature cited in Schnabel, *Law*

similar to the function of wisdom in non-Christian texts contemporary with Paul, particularly the most apocalyptic of them like *1 Enoch* and 4 Ezra, for whom revelations of esoteric interpretations of Torah and heavenly mysteries constitute God's wisdom.

IV

In all these texts, Paul talks about the wisdom of God and employs exegetical and theological traditions familiar from wisdom books *at the very same time* that he expresses convictions he shares with Jewish apocalypticists. We can conclude from this that Paul, much as some of his Jewish contemporaries, refuses to respect the boundaries between what scholars have labeled wisdom and apocalyptic. Rather than locating him in one camp or another, this survey of Paul's letters forbids a stark dichotomy between the two. Their formal and ideological characteristics overlap in significant ways that, while not eliminating the distinctiveness of each, limit and add precision to the discussions of both.

Paul is therefore both sage and seer, as customarily defined, but he is finally neither. He calls himself *apostolos* (apostle), and his commission to preach the gospel impels him to make use of the whole of his religious heritage to understand and appropriate God's action in Christ. In ways that can scarcely be overestimated, Paul's interpretation of the cross and resurrection is shaped by the apocalyptic categories of God's revelation, the turning of the eras, and the inauguration of God's cosmic redemption. But Paul identifies his gospel with God's wisdom in much the ways his contemporaries identify God's Torah with wisdom. The ordering function of wisdom assigned to Torah throughout first-century Judaism Paul claims for his apostolic proclamation that makes present God's faithfulness and impartiality even before the eschaton will bring it to completion.

---

and Wisdom, 251–55. So also, Paul apparently appropriates in 1 Cor 10:1–4 an exegetical tradition found in Philo *Leg. All.* 2.86 and Sir 15:3 that interprets the rock of Exod 17:6; Num 20:8–11 as the wisdom of God.

15

WISDOM AND APOCALYPTIC IN THE APOCALYPSE OF JOHN: DESIRING SOPHIA

Tina Pippin

> The Apocalypse is the way the world looks after the ego has disappeared.
> — Northrop Frye, *The Great Code*

Sit back, but not comfortably, and watch the enactment of the end of the world. Your guide is the seer who calls himself John. He is going to take you through his visions of the future: the storming of the earth and its powers by the powers of heaven. The fates of the sinful and the righteous and the destruction of the old earth and the creation of the new are all presented as flesh and blood reality. This journey is not for the squeamish. There is war, rape, cannibalism, burning flesh, martyrdom, the burning of the earth, the terrorizing by seven-headed beasts, and the dead coming back to life. Your seat is conveniently placed at the edge of the bottomless pit, the abyss of chaos. But look around — there is a heavenly liturgy and a wedding feast and a beautiful city of hope. John is telling you what your choices are. He is telling you what you have to do to reach utopia. John has the wisdom of the end time: "I warn everyone who hears the words of the prophesy of this book: if anyone adds to them, God will add to that person the plagues described in this book; if anyone takes away from the words of the book of this prophecy, God will take away that person's share in the tree of life and in the holy city, which are described in this book" (Apoc 22:18–19).[1] Any questions?

1. Bible quotations throughout this essay are from the NRSV.

The tension between chaos and creation is central in the Apocalypse of John. This tension and the resulting ethical dualism call the hearers and readers of the book to patient endurance and testimony. The connection of wisdom traditions in the Mediterranean (especially North Africa) and Mesopotamia (manticism) with apocalyptic is found by scholars in the context of the ethical. The value system and the ethical demands of choosing good over evil are at stake. The point is not to find an evolutionary link of prophecy to wisdom to apocalyptic; but there are connections between apocalyptic and wisdom in the Apocalypse of John.

Jonathan Z. Smith makes the connection between wisdom and apocalyptic by examining the *Babyloniaka* of Berrossus, a priest of Marduk (ca. 290–280 BCE).[2] Smith is interested in the author of this text, a priestly scribe of an elite, well-educated class. Of these mantic scribes Smith notes, "They hypostatized the scribe and scribal activities in the figure of Divine Wisdom. They speculated about hidden heavenly tablets, about creation by divine word, about the beginning and the end and thereby claimed to possess the secrets of creation."[3] Thus, two main "influences" of the wisdom tradition (which can also be said about the prophetic) are the role of the seer/sage and the passage of time (beginnings and endings).

The seer of the Apocalypse of John claims wisdom, the knowledge of the mysteries of the heavens as revealed to him. John is told to "write in a book what you see and send it to the seven churches" (Apoc 1:11). John fearfully faces the mysteries and reports (accurately, of course) what he sees. According to Kurt Rudolph, "Wisdom was originally a practical matter, namely 'insight' into certain connections existing in human life and in the world and modes of behavior derived from this insight and put into the service of instruction and education.... A person's wisdom depends on what he or she has seen and thereby come

2. J. Z. Smith, "Wisdom and Apocalyptic," *Religious Syncretism in Antiquity: Essays in Conversation with George Widengren* (ed. B. A. Pearson; Missoula, Mont.: Scholars Press, 1975) 132.

3. Ibid., 135. On the wisdom sage as mantic scribe (and the work of the scribe as a cultic activity), see P. R. Davies, "The Social World of Apocalyptic Writings," *The World of Ancient Israel: Sociological, Anthropological and Political Perspectives* (ed. R. E. Clements; New York: Cambridge University Press, 1989) 260ff. Davies uses *1 Enoch*, Daniel, and Ben Sira as Jewish examples. Davies states, "The plausible *Sitz im Leben* for this erudite yet speculative discourse is an intellectual one" (265). See also J. Collins, "The Sage in the Apocalyptic and Pseudepigraphic Literature," *The Sage in Israel and the Ancient Near East* (ed. J. G. Gammie and L. G. Perdue; Winona Lake, Ind.: Eisenbrauns, 1990) 343–54.

to know."[4] In the Apocalypse of John seeing (and hearing) is believing, and believing is seeing (and hearing). Experiencing the secrets of the end is more than cathartic; ethical action is required once one "sees" and "knows" and "hears." The wise have sight (and at least one ear to hear) and will triumph; the fool is blind and deaf and will fall.

John Gammie focused on this relationship of "prudentialism to apocalypticism,"[5] which developed from a concern for family and king (Proverbs) to include divine election and warnings against idolatry (Sirach and Wisdom of Solomon). Gammie also incorporates Leo Perdue's work with Victor Turner's theory of liminality, noting that wisdom literature focuses on crisis periods or turning points.[6] According to Turner's studies, through the liminal experience the community participates in a ritual of role reversals, but liminality also refers to crossing individual thresholds in life, such as the entry into adulthood. Apocalyptic literature operates in a liminal zone, representing the ultimate and final crisis of the person and the universe. The Apocalypse of John crosses *the* major threshold — of the end of the world and the creation of God's new order. Anyone who disrupts God's order (and the final *communitas*) is destroyed. Social deviants (Jezebel, the Whore, the Beast, any unbelievers, to name a few) are considered dangerous. In the apocalyptic liminal zone the abyss is the "final" place of those who are impure. The "ritual process" (to borrow from Turner) is set by God in the Apocalypse. Anyone who refuses to play by God's rules is out. And the seer wants the Christian community to know and understand these rules.

"These are the words" begins each of the letters to the seven churches. Wisdom is given through the words and by the Word, the Son of man, "who holds the seven stars in his right hand" (Apoc 2:1); "the first and last, who was dead and came to life" (2:8); "who has the sharp two-edged sword" (2:12); "who has eyes like a flame of fire, and whose feet are like burnished bronze" (2:18); "who has the seven spirits of God and the seven stars" (3:1); "the holy one, the true one" (3:7); and "the Amen, the faithful and true witness, the origin of God's creation" (3:14). The description of the Son of man in 1:13–16 is amplified and expanded throughout these messages to the seven churches. The angels announce,

4. K. Rudolph, "Wisdom," *The Encyclopedia of Religion* (1987) 15.393.

5. J. Gammie, "From Prudentialism to Apocalypticism: The Houses of the Sages amid the Varying Forms of Wisdom," in Gammie and Perdue, *Sage in Israel*, 497.

6. Ibid., 483. See L. G. Perdue, "Liminality as a Social Setting for Wisdom Instructions," *ZAW* 93 (1981) 114–26.

John reports, and Jesus Christ (bloody lamb, sword-wielding savior) gives testimony with his awesome and terrifying presence (1:1–2). The words are from Jesus through intermediaries (twenty-four elders, angels, an eagle, and John). These words have power over both believer and unbeliever and over all the earth. The authority behind the words is God.

In the Apocalypse of John there are four major passages associated with wisdom influences: 5:12 and 7:12 (both are hymns), and 13:18 and 17:9. In these passages wisdom is specifically discussed. From discussions of these sections I want to move into a broader discussion of the interfacing of wisdom and apocalyptic in the text through the concepts of ethics, the threat (or threat as perceived by different parties), the goddess Sophia, and finally chaos (the abyss) and creation (the new Jerusalem).

APOCALYPSE 5:12 AND 7:12: HYMNS TO THE THRONE OF WISDOM

> Then I looked, and I heard the voice of many angels surrounding the throne and the living creatures and the elders; they numbered myriads of myriads and thousands of thousands, singing with a full voice, "Worthy is the Lamb that was slaughtered to receive power and wealth and wisdom and might and honor and glory and blessing!" (Apoc 5:11–12)

> And all the angels stood around the throne and around the elders and the four living creatures, and they fell on their faces before the throne and worshiped God, singing,
>
> "Amen! Blessing and glory and wisdom
> and thanksgiving and honor
> and power and might
> be to our God forever and ever! Amen."
>
> Then one of the elders addressed me, saying, "Who are these, robed in white, and where have they come from?" I said to him, "Sir, you are the one that knows." (Apoc 7:11–14)

In these hymns from the heavenly liturgy, God and the Lamb are the ones worthy to receive wisdom. Wisdom dwells with God. The throne and the heavenly choir of elders, angels, and four living creatures sing praises on the bestowing of wisdom and other attributes on the Lamb and the one who sits on the throne. Thus, the Lamb and God possess wisdom, and wisdom in turn comes from the throne. The throne is the place of highest wisdom.[7] Power, might, wealth, blessing, and honor are heaped onto God by the heavenly choir. The choir chants the truth. Participating in wisdom becomes a cultic activity. Heaven is a poetic (and musical) place.

From the throne God is a divine judge. God's actions throughout the narrative are defended. God's involvement in the suffering of the world is justified in the Apocalypse. James Crenshaw relates that "in wisdom thought, creation functions primarily as defense of divine justice."[8] Since God is destroying the evil powers in the process of destroying the earth, God's actions are justified. The tension between destruction (chaos) and creation is heightened by this judgment.

The agents of revelation are the ones who speak (or sing) in the Apocalypse. In 7:13 one of the twenty-four elders poses a question to the seer. John defers to the heavenly authority with his reply, "Sir, you are the one who knows" (7:14). The authority of the ones in the inner circle of heaven nearest the throne of God is emphasized. If one is to possess wisdom, one must imitate the wise ones nearest the throne (the elders singing praise to God, the martyrs under the altar, the two witnesses, Jesus the slain Lamb).

Furthermore, one is to also imitate the seer, John, by respecting the visions and seeking to understand God's revelation. John obediently follows the instructions from the heavenly guides. In 10:8–11 when the angel asks John to eat the scroll, he eats. John reports: "So I took the little scroll from the hand of the angel and ate it; it was sweet as honey in my mouth, but when I had eaten it, my stomach was made bitter" (10:10).[9] The act begins a new wave of prophesy, as it does for the prophet Ezekiel (Ezek 2:8–3:3). So John chews, grinds with his teeth, swallows, and digests the scroll. Lips, mouth, teeth, tongue, stomach, and bowels are all involved in the eating and digestive process. John's

7. E. Johnson notes that "the more transcendent is God's wisdom, and the more it is hidden in heavenly mysteries, the more the author locates hope for meaningful life in the disjunctive future" (*The Function of Apocalyptic and Wisdom Traditions in Romans 9–11* [Atlanta: Scholars Press, 1989] 207). On the throne as central, see E. Schüssler Fiorenza, *Revelation: Vision of a Just World* (Proclamation Commentaries; Minneapolis: Fortress Press, 1991) 120: "Revelation's central theological query is: To whom does the earth belong? Who is the ruler of this world? The book's central theological symbol is therefore the *throne,* signifying either divine and liberating or demonic and death-dealing power."

8. J. L. Crenshaw, "Prolegomenon," *Studies in Ancient Israelite Wisdom* (ed. J. L. Crenshaw; New York: KTAV Publishing House, 1976) 27.

9. Schüssler Fiorenza (*Revelation,* 76) states that the bitter scroll symbolizes death.

desire to know all the heavenly secrets leads to a bit of indigestion. Tibor Fabriny notes that the act of swallowing notes absorption or incorporation: "The reader is absorbed by the vision and recreated by it,"[10] just as John is. This is inspired eating.

APOCALYPSE 13:18: THE THREAT OF MONSTERS

> This calls for wisdom: let anyone with understanding calculate the number of the beast, for it is the number of a person. Its number is six hundred sixty-six. (Apoc 13:18)

The monster in the Apocalypse is the political state. Rather than worshiping the Son of man, the whole earth worships the monsters (13:4). The dragon and the beast of the earth and the beast of the sea are like the four beasts of Daniel 7; here the different national powers are combined into one imperial power with different forms. To discern who the beast is requires wisdom, since most of the inhabitants of the earth follow the beast blindly, marking their foreheads or right hands as slaves (13:16).

The number of the beast who rises out of the earth is 666. The believers are to calculate this number so that they know which person is represented. This use of *sophia* (wisdom) is linked to "the specific Christian-apocalyptic sense of esoteric knowledge."[11] The number of the beast remains a mystery, although valiant efforts have been made to decipher the code.[12] John is telling secrets and revealing mysteries, and "anyone with understanding" will know how to live in the world before the eschaton. The sets of opposites — the Son of man/Lamb with the Beast; the Bride and the Woman Clothed with the Sun with the Whore and the Jezebel — lead the believers to see the different ethical choices. There is also a "confusion of values."[13] The beasts are hypnotic, and

10. T. Fabriny, *The Lion and the Lamb: Figuralism and Fulfillment in the Bible, Art and Literature* (New York: St. Martin's, 1992) 76–77.

11. U. Wilckens, "Sophia," *TDNT* (1971) 7.524. He states that in 13:18 and 17:8–18 *sophia* "is the knowledge which is reserved for Christian confessors and which enables them to perceive the true meaning and ramifications of the events which were taking place on earth in their day."

12. P. Boyer (*When Time Shall Be No More: Prophecy Belief in Modern American Culture* [Cambridge, Mass.: Harvard University Press, 1992] chap. 8) traces the manifestations of 666 in popular culture and the interpretations by conservative Christian groups. The main focus is on the political situation in the Middle East and the European Common Market.

13. C. Camp, *Wisdom and the Feminine in the Book of Proverbs* (Sheffield: Almond

the Whore of Babylon is amazingly seductive. She also has a name of mystery on her forehead, "Babylon the great, mother of whores and of earth's abominations" (Apoc 17:5). The Bride is also seductive, in a different way, of course.

The results of following the beasts or the Lamb are made clear. The threat of the earthly political (and economic) power is great until its overthrow. But the threat of death at the hands of the earthly power is not as great as the threat of chaos. God's threat is bigger. Those who do or follow evil will eventually (very soon) meet the judgment of God. Only those who are not confused but understand the mysteries as explained by John can be counted as insiders in the "utopia of wisdom," a place where everyone shares the special wisdom. All war, death, and famine have ended, and all the enemies have perished. The wisdom of the empire is in tension with God's wisdom throughout the Apocalypse. The two thrones compete for the allegiance of humanity. As Claudia Camp notes concerning Ben Sira: "This sage addresses an educated, well-to-do, but — as far as political, economic, and social matters are concerned — persistently threatened audience."[14] By enacting all these different threats in the narrative, the Apocalypse becomes motivational rhetoric.

The threat is part of the ethical variable of the perception of the situation, according to ethicist Glen Stassen. The threat is measured in terms of its "nature, degree, and linkage with other elements."[15] The perception of the threat from different ethical players is important. John sees the imperial threat differently than some of the seven churches (e.g., the Nicolaitans). The imperial power perceives yet a different threat — from colonials who are rebellious — from the attack by God's army. The heavenly powers see the threat from the political power and all who make themselves impure by following it. Readers of the Apocalypse have experienced the threat in their own contexts. How the threat is perceived determines both interpretation and action. For example, Daniel Berrigan and Ernesto Cardenal stress the present threat of the imperialistic policies of the United States and urge the radical ethi-

---

Press, 1985) 17–18. She is referring to the language in Proverbs 1–9 and the use of seductive feminine imagery for the strange woman.

14. C. Camp, "The Female Sage in Ancient Israel and in the Biblical Wisdom Literature," in Gammie and Perdue, *Sage in Israel*, 198.

15. G. Stassen, "Critical Variables in Christian Social Ethics," *Issues in Christian Ethics* (ed. P. D. Simmons; Nashville: Broadman, 1980) 68.

cal action of choosing Christ over "Caesar." In the Apocalypse there are threats from many sides (e.g., the imperial power; seductive, evil women; God's judgment), but only one true promise.

APOCALYPSE 17:9: SOPHIA DISPLACED

> This calls for a mind that has wisdom: the seven heads are seven mountains on which the woman is seated; also, they are seven kings . . . ; they will make war on the Lamb, and the Lamb will conquer them, for he is Lord of lords and King of kings, and those with him are called and chosen and faithful. (Apoc 17:9 and 14)

The great Whore who thinks to herself, "I rule as a queen" (18:7), is discerned and destroyed. The angel gives a detailed explanation of the mystery of the Whore. The believers are called to come out of the Whore and to enter the Bride, the new Jerusalem.[16] Again, the choices are participation in the new creation or in chaos, the destruction of the earth. The Whore is dethroned, as the beast was. The Lamb alone rules in the new heaven and earth.

In Proverbs 1–9, Wisdom, personified as a woman, is a counselor, lover, and administrator of divine justice, and she is given the power of indirection, where women's intellect is praised.[17] Wisdom is a goddess — a wise goddess who passes her wisdom on to wise men. Wisdom (*sophia*) is Maat,[18] Aphrodite, Astarte, the queen of heaven, and the daughter of the father god (Gnosticism). By the Apocalypse there is a return to the King God, the King of kings and Lord of lords. Wisdom is displaced from the throne, or at least co-opted into the Son of man figure and the Woman Clothed with the Sun and the Bride. The Woman Clothed with the Sun is the mother of the messiah (Mary), and her astrological surroundings of a "moon under her feet, and on her head a crown of twelve stars" (12:1) resemble those of Wisdom. The Bride of the Lamb becomes the city of the new Jerusalem; otherwise she might be a queen and co-monarch. However, in medieval artistic representations

16. See the discussion of gender and misogyny in my *Death and Desire: The Rhetoric of Gender in the Apocalypse of John* (Louisville: Westminster/John Knox Press, 1992).

17. Camp, *Wisdom and the Feminine,* 274–81.

18. The Egyptian goddess Maat "symbolized truth, justice, and order in cosmos and society." This order "existed and is known . . . with an unbroken confidence in the act-consequence connection. Modesty, uprightness, self-control, subordination, silence, are virtues of the wise." Maat is eventually replaced by the sun god Re (Rudolph, "Wisdom," 396).

the Bride is often crowned as a queen but is known only in relation to her husband.

So what happens to Sophia in the Apocalypse? Is she part of Jesus and God, since wisdom is bestowed upon them? In the first and second century CE, Jesus was portrayed as Sophia, from the wisdom sayings of Jesus (in Q and Gnostic Gospels) to extracanonical apocalyptic literature. The main story line is that Sophia is rejected on earth and returns to heaven. In the *Similitudes of Enoch,* "Wisdom went out in order to dwell among the sons of men, but did not find a dwelling; wisdom returned to her place and took her seat in the midst of the angels" (42:2).[19] Is Sophia the Bride or the Bride and the Spirit (Apoc 22:17)? Is the Bride the consort made legitimate? James M. Robinson relates that the Holy Spirit "is feminine in Semitic languages and at times is interchangeable with Sophia."[20] In any event, the powerful Sophia of Proverbs is personified in many figures and thus is disempowered. Susan Cady, Marian Ronan, and Hal Taussig point to "Sophia's muted status in the New Testament,"[21] which certainly is the case in the Apocalypse.

Another aspect of Sophia is her antithesis, the Jezebel and the Whore. As in Proverbs 1–9, the counsel of a "strange" woman is dangerous. There is a female threat in the Apocalypse. The sexually aggressive female is the most threatening. Giving in to her seduction leads to death: "And I will strike her children dead" (2:23). Following the dangerous female also leads to the abyss. The term for the abyss or the bottomless pit is female in Greek.[22] The abyss represents the ultimate chaos. The abyss is the female hell mouth (the vagina with teeth), portrayed by the large mouth of the beast in certain medieval representations. In the

19. See the discussions of Jesus as Sophia in J. M. Robinson, "Jesus as Sophos and Sophia: Wisdom Tradition and the Gospels," *Aspects of Wisdom in Judaism and Early Christianity* (ed. R. L. Wilken; Notre Dame, Ind.: University of Notre Dame Press, 1975) 1–16. Also see especially E. Schüssler Fiorenza, *In Memory of Her: A Feminist Theological Reconstruction of Christian Origins* (New York: Crossroad, 1983) 130–40, and S. Cady, M. Ronan, and H. Taussig, *Sophia: The Future of Feminist Spirituality* (San Francisco: Harper & Row, 1986).

20. Robinson, "Jesus as Sophos and Sophia," 6.

21. Cady, Ronan, and Taussig, *Sophia,* 50.

22. Camp shows that the Strange Woman in Proverbs 1–9 is related to Death and Sheol: "The language of death, shades, and Sheol, which may have had its origin in the cult of a goddess (so Blenkinsopp) or some other chthonic deity (so McKane), is transformed in Proverbs to articulate a force — defined here as female — that will ultimately split the religious cosmos of Judaism and Christianity into a dualistic moral system in which woman can come out on only one side" ("What's So Strange about the Strange Woman?" *The Bible and the Politics of Exegesis* [ed. D. Jobling, P. Day, and G. Sheppard; Cleveland: Pilgrim Press, 1991] 29–31).

Apocalypse of Paul 4, the hell mouth is the place of eternal punishment. The angels with Paul say to each other, "Open the mouth of the well that Paul, God's dearly beloved, may look in, because power has been given him to see all the punishments of the underworld. And the angel said to me: Stand at a distance, for you will not be able to bear the stench of this place." There is fire in this well, like the lake of fire and sulfur ("the second death" [20:14]) in the Apocalypse of John. Were the seers expressing castration anxiety? What is the effect of pulling the readers/ hearers to the edge of the abyss? Do we nervously peer inside the pit?

CONCLUSION: THE PIT AND THE THRONE

> Then I saw a new heaven and a new earth; for the first heaven and the first earth had passed away, and the sea was no more. And I saw the holy city, the new Jerusalem, coming down out of heaven from God, prepared as a bride adorned for her husband. (Apoc 21:1–2)

All chaos is removed to the "outside" in the Apocalypse — the sea, the dangerous women, the evil monsters, all the unfaithful, and death. A new Eden is created as a new paradise with the tree of life restored.[23] Where is the tree of the knowledge of good and evil, the wisdom tree? Where is the wise serpent?

The need for wisdom is in the time before the end of time. "Anyone who has an ear to hear" is given the chance to gain wisdom and discernment enough to make the choice for good and against the powers of evil. Both powers are seductive and mysterious. Paradise is the reward for making the wise choice. But where is Wisdom, the female personification and deity, in the Apocalypse? The goddess both is and is not in the text; that is, she is not present in the form we know from Proverbs 1–9, as the powerful creatrix, teacher, and judge. She is subdued and passive, deferring to the male authorities (Jesus and God). The queen of heaven gives birth to the messiah (the Woman Clothed with the Sun) and later marries the messiah (the Bride). Her body is laid out

23. Cf. 4 Ezra 8:52: "Because it is for you that paradise is opened, the tree of life is planted, the age to come is prepared, plenty is provided, a city is built, rest is appointed, goodness is established and wisdom perfected beforehand." Anthropologist Bruce Lincoln says that in many cultures the concept of paradise is an inversion of the world: "Of the otherworld, all that can be said is that things there are totally *other,* completely opposed to all of this earth" (*Death, War, and Sacrifice: Studies in Ideology and Practice* [Chicago: University of Chicago Press, 1991] 29).

(and marked and measured by the seer) as the heavenly city and the new creation. Wisdom loses her place in the pantheon. She exists in the future world in a different form; or rather, she has been re-formed.

Do you doubt the wisdom of the Apocalypse? Then fall, fall, fall into the abyss,[24] the bottomless pit, the great endless gulf, the void. The fall is unavoidable. You were on the threshold, at the edge of the opening of the mouth. Were you thrown? Or did you get too close to the edge, straining to peer in? You will fall forever, free-fall in eternal flight. You will be at the opposite end of heaven, falling further from its salvation with every second. You are in hell, Sheol, the underworld, the place of darkness, of the dark, dangerous female. You are eternally outside of heaven, the new Jerusalem, that place of light and material delights, paradise regained. You have found the void, the *tabula rasa,* nothingness, the dark, deep innards of earth. You are in no place (*ou topos*), utopia.

24. An alternative meaning of abyss is "intellectual or spiritual profundity."

INDEX OF SCRIPTURAL AND DEUTEROCANONICAL REFERENCES

OLD TESTAMENT

Genesis

9:25 *161*
18:6 *204 n. 62*
18:22–33 *2*
41:8 *21 n. 4, 116 n. 4*

Exodus

1:14 *40*
2:11 *40*
2:12 *40*
2:15–16 *40*
2:18 *40*
3:12 *35 n. 21*
3:14–15 *35 n. 21*
5:2 *92*
7:1 *21 n. 4*
8:22 *83*
10:1 *161*
10:2 *102*
12:26 *102*
17:6 *151, 283 n. 66*
23:8 *24*
32 *83*
32–34 *32, 36*
32:1–34:10 *35*
32:7 *35*
32:11 *35*
32:11–12 *40*
32:12 *35, 40 n. 34, 40 n. 35, 42 n. 41*
32:14 *40 n. 34, 42 n. 41*
33:13 *35, 36*
33:16 *35, 38*
33:17–19 *36*
33:18 *38, 44 n. 48*
33:19 *35, 49*
34:5–9 *36*
34:6 *35, 35 n. 22, 36, 37, 38, 39, 40, 44, 44 n. 48, 45 n. 49, 45 n. 51, 46, 46 n. 56, 47, 48 n. 59*
34:6–7 *2, 4, 32, 33, 34, 34 n. 17, 36, 42, 46, 47, 48, 49*
34:7 *41 n. 38, 42*
34:14 *40, 47*
36:1 *138 n. 15*

Levitcus

18:5 *281*

Numbers

4:3 *29 n. 30*
8:24 *29 n. 30*
11:16 *103*
14:13–19 *40 n. 35*
14:20 *40 n. 35*
16:1–17:15 *29 n. 29*
20:8–11 *283 n. 66*
22:4–7 *103*
22:30 *69*

Deuteronomy

1:16–17 *25*
1:16–18 *24*
4 *136 n. 11*
4:1 *23 n. 12*
4:1–40 *27*
4:5 *23 n. 12*
4:5–8 *136*
4:6 *25*
4:6–8 *23*
4:9 *102*
4:10 *23 n. 13*
4:14 *23 n. 12*
5:1 *23 n. 13*
5:31 *23 n. 12*
6:1 *23 n. 12*

Deuteronomy (*continued*)
6:7 *102*
7:16–26 *28*
7:25 *25*
9:1–6 *28*
9:20 *28 n. 28*
10:6 *28 n. 28*
11:14 *58*
11:19 *23 n. 13*
12:12 *28 n. 26*
12:18–19 *28 n. 26*
14:27 *28 n. 26*
14:29 *28 n. 26*
16:11 *28 n. 26*
16:14 *28 n. 26*
16:18 *25*
16:18–19 *24*
17:8–13 *24, 25*
17:9 *28 n. 27*
17:12 *28 n. 27*
17:14–20 *25*
17:18–19 *23 n. 13*
18:6–7 *28 n. 26*
19:12 *103*
19:17 *28 n. 27*
20:21 *102*
21:5 *28 n. 27*
21:19 *103*
22:13–21 *103*
24:8 *28*
25:7–8 *103*
26:3–4 *58*
26:11–13 *28 n. 26*
27:14 *28*
28:1–14 *143 n. 35, 145 n. 44*
29:28 *23*
30 *136 n. 11*
30:11–14 *23*
30:12–14 *277, 280*
31:3–8 *28*
31:9–13 *28 n. 27*
31:13 *23 n. 13*
31:19 *23 n. 12*
31:22 *23 n. 12*
31:25–26 *28 n. 27*
32 *136 n. 11*
32:50 *28 n. 28*
33:4 *135*
33:8–11 *28 n. 27*
33:29 *55 n. 17*

Joshua
1:8 *59*
3:3 *28*
20:4 *103*
24:19 *47*

Judges
1–9 *291, 292, 293, 294*
8 *103*
8:5–6 *103*
8:14 *103*
8:16 *103*
8:21 *104*
9:28, 38 *92*
11:5–11 *103*
14:18b *123 n. 18*

Ruth
4 *103*

1 Samuel
6:15 *28*
8:4 *103*

2 Samuel
3:17 *103*
8:17 *52 n. 5*
11 *105*
13:3 *117, 146 n. 47*
14 *105 n. 14*
15:24 *28*
16:15–17:14 *105*
20:25 *52 n. 5*
24:14 *5*

1 Kings
2 *105*
4:32 *53 n. 9*
8:4 *28*
10:8 *55 n. 17*
12:6–11 *103*
20:7–12 *103*

2 Kings
12:10 *105*
14:25 *44, 45*
17 *42*
18:18–19 *52 n. 5*
22:8–10 *52 n. 5*
23:2 *30*

1 Chronicles
1–9 *19*
3 *19*
9:33–34 *29 n. 30*
10:13 *23 n. 15*
12:33 *26*
15:16–22 *29 n. 30*
15:22 *24 n. 18*
16:40 *23 n. 15*
22–27 *22*
22–29 *22*
22:12 *24 n. 17*
22:12–13 *23 n. 15, 24*
22:14 *22*
23:2–32 *29 n. 30*
23:3 *29 n. 30*
23:24 *29 n. 30*
23:27 *29 n. 30*
25:1–31 *29 n. 30, 30*
25:6–7 *24 n. 18*
25:8 *24 n. 18*
26:1–19 *29 n. 30*

Index of Scriptural and Deuterocanonical References

27:17 *29*
27:32 *105*
28:7 *23 n. 15*
28:19 *23 n. 15, 24 n. 17*
29:29 *21 n. 5*

2 Chronicles
1:7–12 *25*
1:10–12 *24 n. 16*
2:11 *24 n. 16, 24 n. 17*
5–10 *23 n. 15*
5:4–12 *29*
7:6 *29*
9:7 *55 n. 17*
9:29 *21 n. 5*
12:15 *21 n. 5*
13:22 *21 n. 5*
14:3 *25 n. 19*
14:7 *25 n. 19*
15:1–7 *30*
17:4 *25 n. 19*
17:7–9 *24, 27, 29*
19:3 *25 n. 19*
19:4–11 *24, 29*
19:8 *29*
19:11 *25*
20:4 *25 n. 19*
20:13–19 *30*
20:34 *21 n. 5*
21:12–15 *27*
22:9 *25 n. 19*
26:5 *24 n. 18*
26:22 *21 n. 5*
29:34 *29*
30:1 *27*
30:6–10 *27*
30:19 *27*
30:21 *29*
30:22 *24 n. 17*
31:4 *29*
31:21 *25 n. 19*
32:32 *21 n. 5*
33:10–13 *26*
33:19 *21 n. 5*
34:3 *25 n. 19*
34:12 *24 n. 18*
34:30 *30*
35:3 *24 n. 18, 28, 29*

Ezra
1:11 *27 n. 23*
2:1 *27 n. 23*
2:40–41 *29 n. 30*
2:70 *29 n. 30*
3:8 *27 n. 23*
4:1 *27 n. 23*
6:16 *27 n. 23*
6:19–21 *27 n. 23*
7:6–12 *52*
7:7 *29 n. 30*
7:10 *52*
7:11–26 *25*
7:14 *25*
7:25 *25*
7:26 *25*
8:15 *29*
8:18 *24 n. 17*
8:35 *27 n. 23*
10:7 *27 n. 23*
10:8 *27 n. 23*
10:16 *27 n. 23*

Nehemiah
5:15 *20 n. 2*
7:6 *27*
7:43–44 *29 n. 30*
7:73 *29 n. 30*
8 *29*
8:1–13 *52*
8:2–3 *24 n. 18*
8:7–9 *24 n. 18*
8:8 *24 n. 17*
8:12 *24 n. 18*
8:13 *24 n. 17*
9:16–37 *40*
10:1 *29*
12:26–36 *52*
13:10 *29 n. 30*

Job
1–2 *2, 81*
1:1 *82*
1:1–3 *142 n. 32*
1:8 *82*
2:3 *82*
3 *80, 92*
3–31 *81*
3:9 *69*
4:7–8 *122 n. 15*
4:7–11 *88*
4:8 *122 n. 16, 177*
4:12–21 *76*
4:13 *70 n. 56*
4:17–21 *85*
4:19 *159*
5:7 *85*
5:8–16 *85, 88*
5:8–27 *86*
8:8–10 *170*
8:11–12 *21*
9:1 *5*
9:6–10 *21*
9:30 *67*
10:11 *69*
11:5–6 *87*
11:5–8 *22 n. 7*
11:6 *4, 69*
11:7 *123 n. 18*
12–14 *89*
12:6 *90*
12:7–9 *21*
12:7–12 *90*

Job (*continued*)
12:12 *103*
12:13 *137 n. 12*
12:13–25 *90*
12:20 *103*
12:36–37 *21*
13:18 *67*
15:2–4 *87*
15:5 *87*
15:14–16 *87*
16:17 *67*
17:8 *69*
19:25 *66*
19:25–26 *68*
19:26–27 *66*
20:2 *70 n. 56*
21:26 *66*
21:27 *86*
21:34 *67*
22:21 *69*
26:7 *71*
26:7–14 *21*
27:13–23 *22 n. 7*
28 *13, 21, 95, 98, 120, 149, 168, 264*
28:7–8 *22*
28:12–15 *217 n. 101*
28:13 *22*
28:22 *96*
28:26 *151 n. 8*
28:28 *63, 96*
29 *88*
29:7–25 *145 n. 42*
31 *94*
31:1–40 *67*
32:1–33:33 *65*
33:24 *66*
33:33 *69*
34:2 *65*
37:4–18 *71*
37:13 *5*
37:19–24 *71*
37:23 *123 n. 18*
38 *21*
38–41 *168*
38–42 *76*
38:1–40:2 *92*
38:1–42:6 *13, 81*
38:8–11 *94*
38:12–15 *69*
38:39–39:30 *93*
40:3–5 *95*
40:6–41:26 *93*
40:8 *94*
40:15 *94*
40:15–41:5 *64 n. 36*
41:3 *275*
41:11 *16*
42:1–6 *95*
42:7–17 *81*
42:10–15 *142 n. 32*
45:7 *94*

Psalms
1 *57*
1:1 *55, 55 n. 16*
1:2 *55, 59, 59 n. 24*
1:3 *58, 60*
1:4–6 *55, 60*
1:5 *38 n. 27, 58*
2:12 *55*
3–41 *72*
5:10 *83*
8 *60 n. 26*
8:19 *71*
9:17 *59*
15 *72*
16 *72*
17 *72*
18 *72*
19 *57, 60 n. 26, 61, 62, 63, 71*
19:2–7 *61*
19:8–10 *61*
19:13–14 *61*
19:14 *61*
19:15 *59, 59 n. 24, 61*
20–21 *72*
22 *72*
22:6 *145 n. 43*
23 *72*
24 *72*
25 *37, 37 n. 26*
25:2–3 *145 n. 43*
25:4–13 *38*
25:20 *145 n. 43*
25:22 *38*
27:31 *59*
29 *60 n. 26*
31:4 *59*
32:10–11 *55*
33:1 *55*
33:1–5 *145 n. 46*
33:2 *55*
33:6–7 *56*
33:9 *56*
34:2–7 *56*
34:4 *55*
34:8–11 *56*
34:9 *55*
34:12–15 *56*
37 *15*
37:25 *122 n. 16*
37:30 *59 n. 24*
37:30–31 *25*
37:35–36 *122 n. 16*
40:5 *55*
40:9 *55*
41:4 *55*
42–43 *53 n. 8*
42–72 *72*
44 *53 n. 8*

Index of Scriptural and Deuterocanonical References

45:2 *54 n. 11*
47:7 *57 n. 21*
49 *15, 53 n. 8, 65 n. 38, 67*
49:1 *66*
49:2–3 *65*
49:4–5 *57 n. 21, 65*
49:8–9 *66*
49:13 *66*
49:15 *66*
49:16 *67*
49:21 *66*
50:9 *59*
50:10–12 *16*
51 *85*
51–72 *53 n. 8*
63:7 *59*
65:6–9 *56*
65:6–14 *56*
73 *15, 72*
73–89 *72*
73:1 *67*
73:1–9 *67*
73:11 *67*
73:13 *67*
73:15 *67*
73:16 *67*
73:17 *67*
73:18–20 *67*
73:21–26 *68*
73:23–24 *66*
73:26 *68*
73:28 *68*
77:13 *59*
78 *57 n. 20*
78:1–2 *56*
78:2 *57 n. 21*
78:3–4 *57*
78:5–59 *57*
78:70–72 *57*
84–85 *53 n. 8*
84:7 *58*
87–88 *53 n. 8*
88 *53 n. 8*
89 *32 n. 3*
89:10–16 *56*
89:12–13 *71*
89:16 *55*
89:31–33 *55*
89:47–49 *56*
90 *36 n. 24, 72*
90–106 *72*
91 *36 n. 24*
92:4 *59*
92:13–15 *60*
94:12 *55*
94:19 *70 n. 56*
94:20–23 *55*
102:26 *71*
103:3–13 *38*
104:2–30 *71*
104:31–35 *71*
105:21–22 *103*
106 *36 n. 24*
106:3 *55*
106:40–43 *55*
107–50 *72*
107:40–43 *36 n. 24*
109:6 *82*
110:1 *234*
111 *32 n. 8, 63*
111:4b *32 n. 8*
111:10 *64, 142 n. 33*
112 *32 n. 8, 63*
112:1 *55*
112:1–2 *64*
112:4b *32 n. 8*
113:1–3 *71*
118:135 *62*
119 *57, 57 n. 22, 62, 62 n. 30, 67*
119:1 *55*
119:2 *55*
119:6 *145 n. 43*
119:8 *62*
119:12 *62*
119:17 *62*
119:18 *62*
119:19 *63*
119:23 *62, 62 n. 29*
119:24 *60*
119:26 *62*
119:27 *62*
119:37 *62*
119:46 *145 n. 43*
119:54 *61, 65*
119:55 *55*
119:61 *55*
119:64 *62*
119:68 *62*
119:73 *62*
119:77 *60*
119:81–86 *63*
119:84 *62 n. 29*
119:85 *62 n. 29*
119:92 *60*
119:94 *63*
119:97 *60*
119:98 *25*
119:99–100 *63*
119:120 *63*
119:124 *62*
119:132 *62*
119:143 *60*
119:154 *62 n. 29*
119:165 *60*
119:175 *62*
119:176 *60, 63*
128:1–2 *56*
136:6 *71*
139 *68*
139:1 *70*

Psalms (*continued*)
139:3 *69*
139:5 *69*
139:6 *69, 120*
139:7 *70*
139:8 *69*
139:9 *69*
139:13 *69*
139:13–18 *70*
139:19 *69*
139:19–22 *68, 70*
139:20 *70*
139:21–22 *70*
139:23 *70 n. 56*
139:23–24 *70*
139:24 *71*
143:5 *59*
144:12–15 *56*
145 *36 n. 24*
146:5–6 *56*
146:16–18 *56*
148:7 *71*
148:11–14 *145 n. 46*

Proverbs
1–9 *17, 79, 100, 106 n. 18, 107, 110, 113, 291 n. 14, 292, 293*
1:1 *20*
1:1–19 *101 n. 6*
1:2–6 *107*
1:2–7 *77*
1:6 *21 n. 6*
1:7 *63, 77, 112, 142 n. 33*
1:8 *58, 102, 102 n. 7*
1:10 *102 n. 7*
1:15 *102 n. 7*
1:20–33 *79, 110*
2:1 *57, 102 n. 7*
2:1–16 *144 n. 39*
2:1–22 *101 n. 6, 110*
2:4 *113*
2:4–5 *120*
2:5 *119 n. 1*
2:5–7 *112*
2:6 *137 n. 12*
2:6–15 *113*
2:16–19 *110*
3:1 *57, 58, 102 n. 7, 109*
3:1–12 *101 n. 6*
3:9–10 *82*
3:11 *102 n. 7*
3:13–20 *110*
3:15 *113*
3:16 *113*
3:18 *113*
3:19 *113*
3:19–20 *112*
3:21 *102 n. 7*
3:21–35 *101 n. 6*
3:22 *113*
3:29 *103*
3:35 *147 n. 50*
4:1–4 *102*
4:1–9 *101 n. 6*
4:2 *58*
4:6 *113*
4:6–8 *113*
4:7 *113*
4:9 *113*
4:10 *102 n. 7*
4:10–19 *101 n. 6*
4:20 *102 n. 7*
4:20–27 *101 n. 6*
4:26 *83*
5:1–6 *109, 110*
5:1–23 *101 n. 6*
5:10 *103*
5:13 *58*
5:15–23 *109*
6:1 *102 n. 7*
6:3 *102 n. 7, 103*
6:16–19 *109*
6:20 *58, 102, 102 n. 7*
6:20–35 *101 n. 6, 110*
6:23 *58*
6:23–24 *109*
6:29 *103*
6:31 *103*
7:1 *102 n. 7*
7:1–27 *101 n. 6*
7:2 *58*
7:4 *113*
7:6–27 *110*
8 *168*
8:1–11 *79*
8:1–32 *112*
8:1–36 *110*
8:11 *113*
8:12–21 *79*
8:14 *92*
8:17 *114, 120, 216 n. 99*
8:19 *113*
8:22 *150*
8:22–23 *137 n. 12*
8:22–31 *23 n. 10, 71, 74, 79, 114, 264*
8:24 *151 n. 8*
8:30 *137 n. 12*
8:30–31 *60*
8:32–36 *60*
8:34 *113*
8:35a *114*
9:1–6 *79, 110*
9:10 *63, 112, 119 n. 1, 142 n. 33*
9:13–18 *110*
10–21 *174*
10–30 *168*
10:1 *102*
10:1–22:16 *100, 106 n. 18*
10:7 *145 n. 45*
10:29 *37*
11:14 *106*

Index of Scriptural and Deuterocanonical References

12:4 *102*
12:5 *86*
12:11 *103*
12:20 *106*
13:2 *112*
13:15 *112*
14:1 *102*
14:4 *103*
14:8 *112*
14:17 *46*
14:20–21 *103*
14:24 *113*
14:29 *46*
14:31 *177*
15:6 *103*
15:8 *82*
15:20 *102*
15:21–24 *112*
15:22 *106*
15:29 *82*
15:33a *112*
16:1–22:16 *105*
16:15 *109*
16:22 *113*
18:4 *113*
18:20–21 *111*
18:22 *102*
19:1–29:27 *99*
19:8 *112, 113*
19:13 *102*
19:14 *102*
19:18 *102*
19:21 *86*
19:27 *102 n. 7*
20:13 *109*
20:20 *102*
20:22 *109*
20:27 *109*
20:29–35 *109*
21:9 *102*
21:19 *102*
21:20 *103*
21:27 *82*
21:30 *112*
21:31 *112*
22:6 *102*
22:8 *112, 177*
22:11 *145 n. 42*
22:15 *102*
22:17 *21 n. 6*
22:17–24:22 *101 n. 6, 105, 106 n. 18, 110, 192*
23:10–11 *8*
23:15 *102 n. 7*
23:19 *102 n. 7*
23:22 *102*
23:25 *102*
23:26 *102 n. 7*
24:3–4 *103*
24:5–6 *112*
24:6 *106*
24:7 *113*
24:13 *102 n. 7*
24:19–20 *67*
24:21 *102 n. 7*
24:27 *103*
24:28 *103*
25–29 *106 n. 18*
25:1 *20, 104*
25:1–29:27 *105*
25:2–3 *109*
25:8 *103*
25:9 *103*
25:17 *103*
25:18 *103*
26:19 *103*
26:27 *112*
27:10 *103*
27:11 *102 n. 7*
27:12 *112*
27:14 *103*
27:20 *109*
28:9 *82*
28:10 *112*
28:13 *4*
28:19 *103*
28:24 *102*
29:5 *103*
30:1–4 *7*
30:3 *119*
30:4 *119 n. 1, 172*
30:5–6 *119 n. 1*
30:11 *102*
30:15–33 *109*
30:17 *102*
31:1 *20*
31:1–9 *10, 21, 101 n. 6, 102, 110*
31:10–31 *100, 102, 110*
31:25 *58*
31:26 *102*

Qoheleth (Ecclesiastes)

1:1 *20*
1:4 *181*
1:12 *121*
1:12–17 *128*
1:12–18 *121*
1:13 *121, 126, 127 n. 27*
1:13–2:26 *125 n. 22*
1:14 *127 n. 27*
1:16 *117, 120, 121, 124, 127 n. 27*
1:17 *121*
1:17a *126*
1:17b-18 *126*
1:18 *117, 126 n. 25*
2:1–2 *127 n. 26, 128*
2:1–10 *121*
2:3 *118*
2:3–9 *122*
2:9 *118*
2:12 *127 n. 27*

Qoheleth (*continued*)
2:13 *127, 127 n. 27*
2:13–14 *127 n. 28*
2:15–16 *125*
2:16 *125*
2:17 *125*
2:18–19 *124*
2:19 *118*
2:21 *118, 125*
2:21–23 *122*
2:22 *123 n. 19*
2:26 *124*
3 *115*
3:3 *49*
3:5–6 *181*
3:11 *14, 123, 149*
3:12 *127*
3:21 *172*
3:22 *127*
4:1–2 *122 n. 14*
4:3 *128*
4:11–13 *181*
4:13–14 *118*
4:14 *122 n. 14*
4:14–16 *125*
5:7–8 *122*
5:12–13 *122 n. 14*
5:13 *124*
5:18 *127*
5:19 *128*
6:1–2 *122 n. 14*
6:1–6 *126*
7:2 *127*
7:4 *127*
7:8 *46*
7:10 *119, 119 n. 9*
7:12 *118, 119*
7:14 *119 n. 9, 126*
7:14b *123*
7:15 *126, 128*
7:15–16 *122 n. 14*
7:16 *126, 128*
7:19 *119 n. 10*
7:23 *121, 124 n. 20*
7:23–24 *124*
7:23b *121*
7:24 *121*
7:24–26 *123*
7:25 *121*
7:25–26 *150*
7:27 *121*
7:27–29 *118*
8:1b *119*
8:5 *119*
8:9 *122 n. 14*
8:10 *122 n. 14*
8:15 *127*
8:16 *121, 124, 124 n. 20*
8:16–17 *123 n. 19*
8:17 *121, 123, 124, 124 n. 20, 124 n. 21*
8:17b *123 n. 18*
9:1 *128*
9:5 *127*
9:7–10 *127*
9:10 *127*
9:11 *125*
9:12 *125*
9:13–15 *117, 125*
9:16 *118*
9:16b *125*
9:17 *119*
9:18 *118, 124*
9:23 *126*
10:1 *119, 124*
10:6 *126*
10:12 *119, 145 n. 42*
11 *128*
11:6 *127*
11:9–10 *127*
12:9 *104*
12:9–14 *130*
12:11 *9, 21 n. 6*
12:12–14 *21*
12:13 *131*

Isaiah
2:1–5 *37*
5:19 *92*
7:14 *261*
8:21 *239*
10:5–27 *48 n. 61*
13:10 *240*
13:13 *239*
14:30 *239*
19:2 *239*
19:11–12 *21 n. 4*
22:15 *52 n. 5*
28:9 *92*
29 *279*
29:14 *117, 117 n. 6*
29:16 *279 n. 55*
30:15 *55 n. 17*
32:20 *55 n. 17*
33:18 *59*
34:4 *240*
36:3 *52 n. 5*
38:14 *59*
40:13 *275*
42:21 *58*
44:25 *21, 116 n. 4, 117 n. 6*
44:28 *59*
45:9–13 *279 n. 55*
46:10 *92*
47:8–13 *21*
47:10 *117*
51:3 *145 n. 44*
51:7 *59*
53:11 *123 n. 19*
55:7 *86*
56:1–7 *145 n. 44*
56:2 *55 n. 17*

Index of Scriptural and Deuterocanonical References

58:3–4 *20 n. 2*
59:6 *20 n. 2*
59:7 *86*
59:9–15 *20 n. 2*
64:4 *206 n. 65*

Jeremiah
4:23–26 *10*
8:8–9 *52*
9:11 *36 n. 24*
9:12 *58*
10:7 *21 n. 4*
11:19 *60*
15:15 *62 n. 29*
16:11 *58*
17:5–8 *60*
17:7–8 *58*
18 *279*
18:1–11 *279 n. 55*
18:20 *62 n. 29*
19:1–15 *279 n. 55*
20:14–18 *80*
23:18 *87*
25:29 *41 n. 38*
26:17–19 *103*
36:1–2 *62 n. 29*
36:4–18 *105*
50:34 *62 n. 29*
50:35 *21 n. 4*
51:57 *21 n. 4*

Ezekiel
2:8–3:3 *289*
5:12 *239*
7:26 *103, 105*
9 *105*
14:12–20 *80, 83*
17:5–8 *60*
28 *87*
28:5 *117*
32:7–8 *240*
40–48 *29*
44:10–14 *29 n. 29*
48:11 *29 n. 29*

Daniel
1–6 *269*
1:4 *116 n. 4*
2 *224, 229*
7 *184, 229, 240, 244, 290*
7–14 *269*
7:13 *233, 234, 240*
9:22–23 *270*
9:27 *255*
11 *174*
11:31 *255*
11:33 *270*
12 *244*
12:1 *239*
12:3 *270*
12:11 *255*
12:12 *55 n. 17*

Hosea
1:4–5 *36*
1:5 *35, 36 n. 23*
1:6 *35*
1:9 *34 n. 17, 35, 35 n. 21*
2:1 *35*
2:1–3 *35 n. 22*
2:2 *36*
2:3 *35*
2:6 *35*
2:8 *40*
2:16–17 *35 n. 20*
2:21–22; 4:1 *35 n. 22*
2:25 *35*
4:1 *119 n. 11*
5:4 *35 n. 20*
6:3 *35 n. 20*
6:6 *119 n. 11*
8:4–5 *34 n. 17*
12:5 *35 n. 20*
13:2 *34 n. 17*
13:4 *35 n. 20*
14:4 *34 n. 17*
14:10 *33, 36, 36 n. 24, 37, 38, 39, 46, 46 n. 54*

Joel
1–2 *43*
1:1–2:22 *40*
1:1–2:27 *39*
2:10 *240*
2:11 *36*
2:12 *42 n. 42*
2:12–14a *40*
2:14 *38, 39, 42 n. 41*
2:17 *40*
2:19 *40*
2:23 *58*
3:1–4:21 *39*
3:5 *43*
4:4 *43*
4:7 *43*
4:14 *43*
4:16 *41, 42*
4:16–20 *42*
4:18 *41*
4:20 *41*
4:21 *41, 42, 47 n. 58*

Amos
1:2 *41, 42*
2:7 *43*
3:1–2 *45*
3:1–8 *42*
3:1–9 *42*
4 *42 n. 42*
4:6–11 *40 n. 32*
4:12 *42 n. 42*
4:13 *42 n. 42, 43*

Amos (*continued*)
5 *42 n. 42*
5:1 *42*
5:1–17 *43 n. 42*
5:1–20 *36, 42 n. 42*
5:4–5 *42 n. 42*
5:8 *43*
5:12 *57 n. 21*
5:14–15 *42 n. 41, 42 n. 42*
5:16–20 *42*
5:18 *42 n. 40*
5:18–20 *42, 43 n. 42, 45*
6:1 *45*
6:3 *42 n. 40*
6:3–6 *45*
7:1–6 *42 n. 42*
7:3 *42 n. 41*
7:15 *42*
8:2–3 *42*
8:3 *36*
8:8 *43*
8:9–10 *36, 42, 45*
8:13 *36*
9:5–6 *43*
9:7 *45*
9:12 *43*
9:13 *41*

Obadiah
7–8 *43*
8 *21 n. 4*
10–14 *43*
15 *43*
15–18 *43*
17 *43*

Jonah
1–2 *20 n. 2*
1:1–3 *45*
1:2 *48 n. 59*
1:6 *38*
3:2 *48 n. 59*
3:3 *48 n. 59*
3:4 *45*
3:5 *40*
3:5–10 *45*
3:7–8 *40*
3:9 *38, 39, 40, 42 n. 41*
3:10–4:2 *38*
4 *2*
4:1 *48 n. 59*
4:1–2 *45*
4:2 *48, 48 n. 59*
4:3–11 *45*
4:11 *48 n. 59*

Micah
2:7 *46*
2:8–8a *46*
4:1–5 *37*
4:2 *37*
4:5 *37, 37 n. 25, 38, 46*
4:12 *46*
6–7 *47*
6:7–17 *37*
6:8 *37 n. 25*
7:7–10 *38*
7:7–20 *47 n. 57*
7:10 *40*
7:18 *39*
7:18–20 *36, 37, 38, 46, 47*

Nahum
1:2b-3a *47*
1:3 *42 n. 39*
1:3a *32 n. 7, 47, 48, 48 n. 59*

Haggai
1:6 *20 n. 2*
1:8–11 *20 n. 2*

Zechariah
1:2–6 *48*
2:6 *240*
7:9–10 *10*
8:10 *20*

Malachi
2:13–16 *20*
3:10–11 *20*

DEUTEROCANONICAL BOOKS

Baruch
3:9–4:4 *136, 264*
3:29–30 *280*
3:29–4:1 *217 n. 101*

4 Ezra
7:132–40 *44 n. 48*

1 Maccabees
1:54 *255*

Sirach
1:1 *137*
1:2–6 *137*
1:4 *151*
1:8 *181*
1:8–10 *137*
1:9–10 *141 n. 27*
1:11–30 *143 n. 37*
1:14 *142*
1:16 *143*
1:18 *143*
1:20 *143*
1:24 *151 n. 8*
1:26 *148*
1:27 *148*
2 *278*
2:1–2a *278 n. 48*
2:4–6 *278 n. 48*
2:7–18 *45 n. 49*

Index of Scriptural and Deuterocanonical References

2:10a-b *278 n. 48*
2:12–14 *136 n. 10, 140, 176*
2:14 *278 n. 48*
2:15 *148*
3:25 *138, 141 n. 25*
3:29 *141 n. 25*
4:11–13 *145 n. 45*
4:12–16 *148*
5:6 *4*
5:6–7 *273 n. 31*
5:11 *46*
6:18 *142 n. 30, 143 n. 38*
6:18–22 *140*
6:18–37 *140*
6:24–27 *141*
6:27 *216 n. 99*
6:32–36 *141*
6:32–37 *143 n. 37*
6:34 *142 n. 30, 143 n. 38*
6:37 *141*
8:8–9 *141 n. 25, 142, 143 n. 38*
9:14 *141 n. 25*
9:15–16 *141 n. 27*
10:23 *142*
10:31 *142*
11:1 *142 n. 32*
14:20–27 *144*
14:20–15:10 *144*
14:23 *144*
15:1–10 *145*
15:3 *283 n. 66*
15:4 *145*
15:5 *145*
15:6 *145*
15:9–10 *145*
15:11–20 *141 n. 28*
16:5–14 *122 n. 16*
16:11–12 *273 n. 31*
16:11–14 *4*
16:24–25 *141 n. 25, 142 n. 29*
17:9–10 *145 n. 46*
18:8–14 *4*
18:13 *4, 9*
18:27–29 *142 n. 29*
18:28–29 *141 n. 25*
19:20 *136 n. 10, 146*
19:20a *147*
19:20b *147*
19:22 *147*
19:22–25 *136 n. 10, 146*
19:24 *147*
19:24a *147*
21:11 *143 n. 34, 148*
21:14–16 *144 n. 40*
21:17 *145 n. 42*
21:18–19 *144 n. 40*
21:20 *144 n. 40*
21:21 *141 n. 25, 142 n. 29*
21:23–24 *144*
21:25–26 *144 n. 40*
22:1–2 *144 n. 40*
22:1–3a *138*
22:6 *144 n. 40*
22:9–18 *144 n. 40*
24 *79 n. 12, 264*
24:1–29 *23 n. 10*
24:6–8 *135*
24:9 *151*
24:11–12 *135*
24:18–23 *60*
24:19 *135*
24:22–23 *135*
24:23 *31*
24:23–29 *143 n. 37*
24:23bc *135 n. 7*
24:33 *31*
25:3 *143*
25:3–6 *142 n. 30*
25:6 *143*
25:10–11 *143*
28:2–4 *4*
29:9 *4*
29:12 *4*
31:8–11 *142 n. 32*
31:22 *123 n. 18*
32:3 *143 n. 38*
33:12–13 *280*
33:18 *137*
34:1–8 *172*
34:9 *141 n. 25*
34:9–12 *122, 137*
34:18–35:26 *82*
35:12 *4*
36 *16*
36:1–17 *5*
36:8–9 *273 n. 31*
37:22–26 *147*
37:26 *145 n. 45*
38:6 *141 n. 27*
38:24 *31, 45*
38:24–39:11 *20, 138, 229*
38:32 *138*
38:34cd *138*
39:1 *45*
39:1–2 *172*
39:1–3 *31, 243*
39:1–4 *137, 229*
39:1–8 *139*
39:8–11 *147 n. 50*
39:9–11 *145 n. 45*
39:44–50 *31*
40:19ab *142 n. 32*
41:4 *172*
41:8–9 *176*
41:8–10 *136 n. 10, 140 n. 21*
43:33 *141 n. 27*
44–51 *16*
44:14 *145 n. 45*
46:11d *145 n. 45*
47:12–21 *146 n. 47*

Sirach (*continued*)
49:1 *145 n. 45*
49:10 *35 n. 22*
50:27–29 *134*
51:17 *141 n. 27*
51:23 *104, 138*
51:26 *281*
51:30 *5*

Wisdom of Solomon
1:4 *162*
1:6 *158*
1:12–15 *160*
1:16 *160*
2–3 *282 n. 66*
2:24 *160*
3 *278, 278 n. 48*
3:4–6a *278 n. 48*
3:9 *5, 160*
3:10a *278 n. 48*
3:11 *278 n. 48*
4:10–5:23 *270*
6:4 *202*
6:5 *202*
6:12 *216 n. 99*
6:16 *160*
6:18 *157*
6:22 *151, 151 n. 8*
7:16 *157*
7:17 *157*
7:17–21 *156*
7:22–24 *152*
7:23 *158*
7:25 *151*
7:26–27 *137 n. 12*
7:27 *154, 155, 157, 162*
8:3 *153*
8:4 *153*
8:5–6 *153 n. 12*
8:7 *157*
8:8 *157*
8:9–13 *157*
8:17–18 *155*
9 *264*
9:1–2 *153*
9:4 *137 n. 12*
9:6 *137 n. 12*
9:8 *153*
9:9 *153*
9:9–10 *273*
9:10 *154, 282*
9:17 *157, 282*
10 *157*
10:1–21 *155*
11:4 *163 n. 24*
11:16 *273*
11:23 *5*
11:24 *158, 161*
11:26 *158*
12–13 *273*
12:1 *158*
12:10–11 *161*
12:12–18 *5*
12:19 *158*
12:19–22 *163*
12:20–21 *5*
12:23 *273*
12:24 *273*
13:8 *273*
14:2 *157*
14:3 *157*
15:7 *280*
16:3 *163 n. 24*
16:5 *273 n. 31*
18:4 *157*
18:9 *157*
18:20 *273 n. 31*
19:4–5 *161*

NEW TESTAMENT

Matthew
1:19 *260*
1:23 *261*
4:15 *254*
4:23 *254*
5–9 *254*
5:3–12 *206 n. 65*
5:12 *194*
5:22–24 *259*
5:24 *253*
5:43 *253*
5:46–7 *253*
7:3–5 *259*
7:21–23 *262*
7:23 *254 n. 29*
8:23–9:1 *254*
9:35 *254*
10:5–6 *254*
10:17–22a *253*
10:23b *261 n. 47*
10:39 *183*
13:41 *254 n. 29*
13:52 *247*
15:34 *254*
16:66 *204 n. 60*
18:15 *259*
18:21 *259*
18:35 *259*
23 *251*
23:28 *254 n. 29*
24:1 *251*
24:3 *249, 252*
24:4b-35 *249*
24:8 *252*
24:9 *252*
24:10 *253*
24:12 *253*
24:13 *254*
24:14 *254, 260*

Index of Scriptural and Deuterocanonical References

24:15 *250*
24:25–28 *256*
24:29 *256*
24:30 *256, 261*
24:30–31 *260*
24:34 *256*
24:36 *257*
24:36–25:30 *249*
24:37 *257, 258*
24:40–41 *257*
24:42 *257*
24:43 *257*
24:44 *257*
24:45–50 *257*
24:48 *258*
24:51 *258*
25:1–12 *258*
25:8 *258*
25:13 *258*
25:14 *258*
25:14–19 *258*
25:19 *258*
25:30 *258*
25:31–46 *249*
25:32 *259, 260*
25:35–36 *261*
25:37 *260*
28:20 *262*

Mark

1:13 *234*
1:15 *224 n. 2*
1:21–28 *234*
2:1–12 *234*
2:10 *233*
2:15–17 *243*
2:18–20 *243*
2:20 *225*
2:21–22 *243*
2:23–28 *242*
2:28 *233*
3:1–6 *234*
3:6 *231*
3:22 *235*
3:22–27 *235, 243*
3:31–35 *231*
4 *224*
4–8 *231*
4:1–34 *191*
4:10–20 *243*
4:11 *243*
4:15 *234*
4:21 *243*
4:22 *215*
4:30–32 *234*
5:1–20 *235*
6:4 *243*
6:8–13 *210 n. 79*
7:1–23 *242*
8–10 *231*
8:15 *204 n. 60*
8:31 *233*
8:34–37 *225*
8:34–38 *237, 240*
8:34–9:1 *241*
8:38 *224, 225, 233, 234*
8:38–9:10 *225*
9:1 *225*
9:9 *233*
9:12 *233*
9:31 *233*
10:2–9 *224 n. 2, 242*
10:30 *224*
10:33–34 *233*
10:45 *233*
11:12–23 *224*
12:1–9 *224*
12:18–27 *223*
12:38–40 *224*
13 *223, 224 n. 2, 237, 238, 239, 241, 247*
13:1–2 *224*
13:2 *205 n. 63, 242*
13:3–4 *242*
13:5 *240*
13:5–6 *240*
13:5–13 *241*
13:7 *224 n. 2, 238*
13:7–8 *238, 239, 240*
13:9 *240, 253*
13:9–13 *240*
13:10 *236*
13:11 *241*
13:11–12 *242*
13:13 *236*
13:14 *238, 242*
13:14–20 *237, 238, 239*
13:14–27 *241*
13:14b-18 *238, 239*
13:17 *239*
13:19–20 *239*
13:21–22 *238*
13:23 *240*
13:24–25 *224 n. 2, 240*
13:24–27 *237*
13:26 *224 n. 2, 225, 240*
13:26–27 *233, 240*
13:27 *224 n. 2*
13:28–31 *241*
13:28–37 *240, 241*
13:33 *240*
13:34 *225*
13:35 *240*
13:37 *240*
14:21 *233*
14:25 *225*
14:41 *233*
14:57–58 *205 n. 63*
14:62 *224, 225, 234*
15:29 *205 n. 63*

INDEX OF SCRIPTURAL AND DEUTEROCANONICAL REFERENCES

Luke

6 *182*
8:17 *215*
12:1 *204 n. 60*
17:20–21 *195, 215*
17:33 *183*
21:20 *239*

Q

3:7–9 *193, 212*
3:16–17 *193, 212*
6:20–23 *209*
6:20–38 *209*
6:20–49 *209*
6:20b *195, 198, 200, 201 n. 44, 207, 209*
6:20b-49 *193*
6:21a *195, 198, 200*
6:21b *209*
6:22 *195, 198, 209*
6:22–23 *195, 198, 201, 201 n. 44, 215*
6:30 *209*
6:34–35a *195, 198, 200*
6:39 *194, 198, 200, 200 n. 43, 209*
6:39–45 *209*
6:41–42 *194, 198, 200 n. 43, 209*
6:43–45 *209*
6:44b *194, 198*
6:44b-45 *200 n. 43*
6:45 *194, 198*
7:1–10 *193*
7:18–23 *193*
7:24–26 *193, 195, 201*
7:28 *195, 201 n. 44*
7:31–35 *193, 212*
7:35 *197, 212*
9:57–62 *193*
9:58 *195, 198, 200*
10:1–2 *210*
10:1–12 *209*
10:2 *195, 210*
10:2–12 *210 n. 79*
10:2–16 *193*
10:5–11 *211*
10:8–9 *194, 198, 200, 201 n. 44, 210*
10:9b *211*
10:21 *197*
10:21–22 *212*
10:21–24 *193*
10:22a *196, 203 n. 53*
10:23–24 *206 n. 65*
11:2–4 *193*
11:9–10 *195, 198, 201 n. 43, 215, 216*
11:9–13 *193*
11:14–26 *193, 213*
11:21–22 *195, 198, 201, 201 n. 43*
11:29–32 *193, 212, 213*
11:31 *197*
11:31–32 *212*
11:33 *194, 198, 200 n. 43*
11:33–36 *193, 195, 213*
11:34–36 *198, 201 n. 43*
11:39–41 *195, 198, 200, 213*
11:39–52 *193, 212, 213*
11:49 *197*
11:49–51 *212*
11:52 *195, 201, 206 n. 66, 213*
12:1–12 *193*
12:2 *194, 195, 198, 200 n. 43, 215*
12:2–12 *240*
12:3 *194*
12:8–9 *233*
12:10 *195*
12:13–14 *195*
12:16–21 *195, 198*
12:22 *194, 210*
12:22–32 *209, 210*
12:22–34 *193*
12:27 *210*
12:29 *210*
12:33–34 *195, 198, 201 n. 44*
12:39 *195, 196, 198, 201, 201 n. 43, 214*
12:39–40 *193, 212, 214*
12:42–46 *193, 212, 214*
12:49 *193, 195, 201, 203 n. 53, 212, 214*
12:51 *201*
12:51–53 *193, 195, 200, 203 n. 53, 214, 240*
12:51–59 *212*
12:54–56 *193, 214*
12:56 *195, 201, 214*
12:57–59 *193, 214*
13:18–19 *198*
13:18–21 *194, 201 n. 44*
13:20–21 *195, 198, 201 n. 44*
13:24–30 *193*
13:30 *196, 198*
13:34–35 *193*
14:15–24 *195, 198, 201 n. 44*
14:16–24 *193*
14:26–27 *193, 195, 200, 215*
14:34–35 *193*
15:3–7 *195, 198, 201 n. 44*
16:13 *194, 198, 201 n. 43*
16:16 *193*
17:20–21 *201 n. 44, 207, 217*
17:23 *193, 212*
17:24 *193, 212*
17:26–30 *193, 212*
17:33 *193*
17:34 *196*
17:34–35 *193, 212*
17:37 *193, 212*
19:26 *195, 198, 201, 213*

John

1:14–18 *44 n. 48*
3:16 *282 n. 63*

Index of Scriptural and Deuterocanonical References

Acts
7:35–38 *155 n. 14*

Romans
1 *272 n. 28, 273, 277*
1:13–17 *280*
1:14 *272 n. 28*
1:16 *281 n. 61*
1:16–11:27 *274*
1:17 *272, 274, 280*
1:17–18 *266 n. 7*
1:18 *274, 280*
1:18–11:32 *274*
1:18–32 *272*
1:20 *273*
1:22 *272 n. 28, 273*
1:24 *273*
1:26 *273*
1:28 *273*
2:1 *273*
2:9 *279 n. 51*
2:9–11 *281 n. 61*
3:3–4 *278*
3:9 *281 n. 61*
3:22 *281 n. 61*
3:29–30 *281 n. 61*
4:1–25 *277*
4:11–12 *281 n. 61*
5 *279*
5:1–11 *277*
5:2 *266, 278*
5:3 *278*
5:3–5 *277, 278*
5:5 *278 n. 50, 278*
8:3 *277, 281*
8:18 *266, 277*
8:18–30 *279*
8:19 *266*
8:20 *278 n. 50*
8:24 *278 n. 50*
9 *279, 280*
9:1–5 *274*
9:5 *274*
9:6–23 *280*
9:14–18 *279*
9:20–23 *277, 279*
9:20a *279 n. 55*
9:22 *280*
9:24 *280*
9:25–29 *280*
9:30 *280*
10:4 *275, 281*
10:6 *280*
10:6–7 *264 n. 3*
10:6–8 *280*
10:6–9 *264, 277, 280*
10:7 *280*
10:8 *280, 281*
10:9 *281*
10:12 *281 n. 61*
11 *272 n. 28, 277*
11:25–27 *266, 274, 274 n. 35*
11:28–32 *274*
11:33 *272 n. 28*
11:33–36 *264 n. 3, 272, 274, 275*
11:36 *274*
12:12 *278 n. 50, 279 n. 51*
14:2–23 *209 n. 76*
15:4 *278 n. 50*
15:7–12 *281 n. 61*
15:13 *278 n. 50*
16:19 *272 n. 28*
16:27 *272 n. 28*

1 Corinthians
1–3 *264, 265, 272, 272 n. 28, 276, 277*
1–30 *277*
1:7 *266 n. 7*
1:17 *272 n. 28*
1:18 *272 n. 28, 276*
1:19 *272 n. 28*
1:20 *272, 272 n. 28*
1:21 *272 n. 28*
1:22 *272 n. 28*
1:23 *265 n. 3, 272 n. 28, 276, 281*
1:24 *272 n. 28, 276*
1:25 *272 n. 28*
1:26 *272 n. 28*
1:27 *272 n. 28*
1:30 *265 n. 3, 272 n. 28, 276, 277, 281*
2:1 *272 n. 28*
2:2 *276*
2:4 *272 n. 28*
2:5 *272 n. 28*
2:6 *272 n. 28*
2:6–7 *224*
2:6–16 *277 n. 44*
2:7 *272 n. 28, 276*
2:9 *206 n. 65, 276, 277*
2:10 *266 n. 7, 276*
2:13 *272 n. 28, 276*
2:14 *272 n. 28*
3:10 *272 n. 28*
3:13 *266 n. 7*
3:18 *272 n. 28*
3:19 *272 n. 28*
3:20 *272 n. 28*
4:1 *276*
4:10 *272 n. 28*
5:6–8 *204 n. 60*
6:5 *272 n. 28*
7:29 *266*
7:31 *266*
8:6 *264, 264 n. 3, 265 n. 3*
9:16 *266*
10:1–4 *283 n. 66*
10:4 *264, 264 n. 3*
12:8 *272 n. 28*
13 *241*
13:9 *272 n. 28*

1 Corinthians (*continued*)
14:6 *266 n. 7*
14:26 *266 n. 7*
15:51 *266*

2 Corinthians
1:3–11 *279 n. 51*
1:12 *272 n. 28*
1:14 *272 n. 28*
3:12 *278 n. 50*
4:8 *279 n. 51*
4:17 *279 n. 51*
11:19 *137 n. 13*
12:1–7 *266*

Galatians
1:12 *266 n. 7*
1:16 *266 n. 7*
1:18–20 *196*
2:1–14 *196*
2:2 *266 n. 7*
3:23 *266 n. 7*
4:4 *264 n. 3, 277, 281*
5:5 *278 n. 50*

Ephesians
1:19–21 *264*

Philippians
1:20 *278 n. 50*
2:6–11 *264 n. 3, 282 n. 66*
3:15 *266 n. 7*

Colossians
1:15–20 *263, 264, 264 n. 3*

1 Thessalonians
1:10 *274*
2:19 *278*
4:13 *278*
4:15 *266*
5:8 *278*

Hebrews
11 *155 n. 14*

James
1:3 *278*
3:13–18 *147 n. 49*
4:11–12 *209 n. 76*

1 Peter
1:7 *278*

1 John
4:9 *282 n. 63*

Revelation (Apocalypse)
1:1–2 *288*
1:11 *286*
1:13–16 *287*
2:1 *287*
2:8 *287*
2:12 *287*
2:18 *287*
2:23 *293*
3:1 *287*
3:7 *287*
3:14 *287*
5:11–12 *288*
5:12 *288*
7:11–14 *288*
7:12 *288*
7:13 *289*
7:14 *289*
10:8–11 *289*
10:10 *289*
12:1 *292*
13:4 *290*
13:16 *290*
13:18 *288, 290*
17:5 *291*
17:9 *288, 292*
17:14 *292*
18:7 *292*
20:14 *294*
21:1–2 *294*
22:17 *293*
22:18–19 *285*

INDEX OF MODERN AUTHORS

Achtemeier, P., 246 n. 5
Ackroyd, P. R., 23 n. 11, 30 n. 31
Aland, B., 219 n. 103
Albertz, R., 8 n. 15, 71 n. 59, 89 n. 19
Albright, W. F., 52 n. 4
Aletti, J.-N., 56 n. 19, 68 n. 52
Al-Fayyumi, S.B.J., 16 n. 23
Allen, L. C., 36 n. 24, 41 n. 38, 43 n. 45, 46 n. 56
Alt, A., 52 n. 3
Amir, Y., 162 n. 20
Anderson, B. W., 53 n. 6
Anderson, F. I., 177 n. 41
Anderson, G. W., 51 n. 1
Andresen, C., 265 n. 4
Attridge, H. W., 216 n. 98
Auffret, P., 68 n. 52, 71 n. 58
Aune, D., 274 n. 35

Baldry, H. C., 158 n. 17
Balentine, S. E., 35 n. 19
Barth, Ch., 65 n. 38, 72 n. 61
Barton, G. A., 127 n. 28
Bauer, W., 252 n. 25
Bauer-Kayataz, C., 150 n. 4
Baumgartner, W., 68 n. 48
Beardslee, W. A., 187 n. 1, 199 n. 36, 206 n. 69, 207 n. 70, 213 n. 87
Beare, F. W., 250, 250 n. 22, 253 n. 27, 255 n. 32
Begrich, J., 54 n. 12
Beker, J. C., 267, 267 n. 10, 267 n. 12, 267 n. 13, 276 n. 43, 279 n. 53
Benages, N. C., 148 n. 52
Berger, K., 180, 180 n. 50
Berger, P., 78 n. 9
Bergler, S., 40 n. 33, 43 n. 44, 62 n. 28
Berlin, A., 41 n. 37
Bernhardt, K.-H., 69 n. 54, 71 n. 58, 101 n. 3
Bertram, G., 252 n. 26
Betz, H. D., 182 n. 55, 206 n. 65, 210 n. 78
Birkeland, H., 67 n. 42
Black, J. S., 204 n. 61
Blank, S., 67 n. 43
Blenkinsopp, J., 17, 17 n. 25, 19 n. 1, 23 n. 14, 25 n. 20, 27 n. 24, 136 n. 8, 293 n. 22
Bois, H., 151 n. 8
Bonkamp, B., 62 n. 28
Bonnard, P. E., 58 n. 23
Boring, M. E., 205, 205 n. 64
Bornkamm, G., 259, 259 n. 41, 275 n. 38
Box, G. H., 150, 150 n. 2
Boyer, P., 290 n. 12
Brandenburger, E., 237 n. 18
Braun, R., 122, 122 n. 17
Bream, H. N., 53 n. 7
Brekelmans, C., 53 n. 7
Briggs, Ch., 62 n. 28
Briggs, E. G., 62 n. 28
Brown, R. E., 274 n. 35
Brueggemann, W. A., 100 n. 2
Bryce, G. E., 60 n. 25
Buber, M., 67 n. 43
Bühlmann, W., 111 n. 27
Bultmann, R., 191 n. 18, 198 n. 32, 198 n. 34, 206 n. 65, 260 n. 45
Burkett, D., 7 n. 13

INDEX OF MODERN AUTHORS

Burnett, F. W., 255 n. 33
Buttenwieser, M., 68 n. 50

Cady, S., 113 n. 30, 293, 293 n. 19, 293 n. 21
Cameron, R., 190 n. 13
Camp, C., 100 n. 1, 105 n. 14, 107 n. 19, 112, 112 n. 29, 290 n. 13, 291 n. 14, 292 n. 17, 293 n. 22
Campbell, A. F., 57 n. 20
Camus, A., 129
Caquot, A., 52 n. 4, 67 n. 43, 68 n. 48
Carlston, C. E., 187 n. 1
Carroll, J. T., 262 n. 48, 276 n. 40, 282 n. 62
Carroll, R. P., 57 n. 20
Ceresko, A. R., 54 n. 12, 56 n. 19
Charlesworth, J. H., 171 n. 26
Cheyne, T. K., 204 n. 61
Claasen, W., 39 n. 31
Clements, R. E., 32 n. 4, 33, 33 n. 11, 33 n. 14, 35 n. 22, 39 n. 30, 48 n. 60, 286 n. 3
Clifford, R. J., 32 n. 4, 71 n. 59
Clines, D.J.A., 60 n. 26
Coats, G. W., 32 n. 4
Collins, A. Y., 182 n. 53
Collins, J. J., 162 n. 22, 167 n. 15, 167 n. 16, 170 n. 25, 171 n. 26, 173 n. 31, 175 n. 35, 175 n. 37, 177 n. 41, 178 n. 42, 180 n. 47, 184 n. 62, 202 n. 50, 227 n. 8, 228, 228 n. 9, 229, 269, 269 n. 20, 269 n. 21, 286 n. 3
Conzelmann, H., 264, 264 n. 2, 265
Cope, L., 259, 260, 260 n. 44
Cosgrove, C. H., 276 n. 40, 282 n. 62
Craigie, P. C., 37 n. 26, 38 n. 27
Cranfield, C.E.B., 280 n. 56
Crenshaw, J. L., 6 n. 10, 10 n. 17, 15 n. 21, 33 n. 10, 38 n. 28, 43 n. 43, 53 n. 7, 55 n. 17, 67 n. 43, 74 n. 3, 101 n. 4, 106 n. 18, 111 n. 28, 121 n. 12, 168 n. 19, 169, 169 n. 22, 174 n. 33, 200, 200 n. 39, 200 n. 40, 289 n. 8
Cross, F. M., 167 n. 12, 269 n. 16
Crossan, J. D., 187 n. 1, 202 n. 48, 202 n. 49, 206 n. 68, 207 n. 70, 207 n. 71, 245 n. 3
Crüsemann, F., 8 n. 15, 36 n. 24
Cullmann, O., 190 n. 15

Dahl, N. A., 277 n. 43, 277 n. 44
Danell, G. A., 69 n. 54
Davidson, R., 54 n. 12, 58 n. 23
Davies, P. R., 27 n. 24, 172 n. 27, 180 n. 47, 286 n. 3
Davies, S., 217 n. 101, 219 n. 102
Day, P. L., 110 n. 26, 293 n. 22
Deichgräber, R., 275 n. 38
Deissler, A., 60 n. 26, 62 n. 28
Deist, F. E., 39, 39 n. 31, 40 n. 32
Delcor, M., 180 n. 46
Delitsch, F., 72 n. 61
Delobel, J., 187 n. 1
Dentan, R. C., 32, 32 n. 8, 46 n. 53
De Vries, S. J., 31, 269, 269 n. 19
Didier, M., 249 n. 15
Di Lella, A. A., 133 n. 1, 133 n. 2, 134 n. 4, 139 n. 19, 140 n. 22, 140 n. 23, 143 n. 35, 173 n. 29
Dimant, D., 164, 164 n. 28
Dinkler, E., 264 n. 2, 283 n. 66
Donahue, J., 249, 249 n. 16, 258, 258 n. 39, 259, 259 n. 42, 260 n. 45
Donner, H., 47 n. 57
Dozeman, T. B., 32 n. 9, 33 n. 13, 34 n. 17, 44, 44 n. 47, 45, 45 n. 51
Drubbel, A., 51 n. 2
Dudley, D. R., 203 n. 54
Duling, D. C., 183 n. 58, 247 n. 7
Dunn, J.D.G., 264 n. 3, 277 n. 44
Dupont, J., 55 n. 18

Eaton, J., 71 n. 57
Edwards, D. R., 199 n. 38
Eissfeldt, O., 57 n. 20, 108 n. 22
Elgoin, T., 180 n. 46
Engnell, I., 58 n. 23, 60 n. 25
Eslinger, L., 39 n. 29
Ewald, H., 151 n. 8, 166 n. 9

Fabriny, T., 290 n. 10
Farmer, W. R., 281 n. 58
Fensham, F. C., 39 n. 31, 55 n. 18
Fichtner, J., 3, 3 n. 5, 4, 7, 18, 53 n. 6, 126 n. 24
Fiorenza, E. S., 227 n. 7, 289 n. 7, 289 n. 9, 293 n. 19
Fischer, I., 60 n. 26
Fishbane, M., 32 n. 4, 32 n. 9, 34 n. 17, 39 n. 29, 46 n. 56
Fohrer, G., 21 n. 4
Fontaine, C. R., 74 n. 4, 101 n. 3, 103 n. 8, 103 n. 9, 103 n. 10, 104 n. 11, 106 n. 17, 109 n. 23, 109 n. 25, 168 n. 20
Fox, M. V., 15 n. 21, 115 n. 1, 121 n. 13, 122 n. 15, 126 n. 24, 127 n. 26, 130 n. 31
Frerichs, E. S., 276 n. 41
Frost, S. B., 69 n. 54
Funk, R. W., 203 n. 55, 277 n. 44
Furnish, V. P., 272 n. 28

Index of Modern Authors

Gammie, J. G., 2 n. 3, 11 n. 18, 15 n. 21, 32 n. 4, 54 n. 12, 64 n. 36, 67 n. 43, 74 n. 2, 74 n. 4, 74 n. 5, 75 n. 6, 89 n. 19, 100 n. 2, 101 n. 3, 105 n. 14, 167 n. 13, 168, 168 n. 18, 245 n. 1, 269, 269 n. 18, 269 n. 19, 270, 270 n. 23, 270 n. 24, 286 n. 3, 287, 287 n. 5, 287 n. 6, 291 n. 14
Gardner, H., 129 n. 30
George, A., 55 n. 18
Georgi, D., 264, 264 n. 2, 265, 282 n. 66
Gerstenberger, E. S., 55 n. 18, 56 n. 19, 101 n. 3, 176 n. 39
Gilbert, M., 53 n. 6, 53 n. 7, 62 n. 28, 67 n. 41, 101 n. 4, 135 n. 7, 139 n. 17
Gilpin, W. C., 81 n. 14
Ginsberg, H. L., 119 n. 10, 121 n. 13, 123 n. 19, 124 n. 21
Girard, M., 56 n. 19
Girard, R., 18, 18 n. 27
Glass, G. T., 60 n. 26
Glasson, T. F., 217 n. 101
Godlovich, S., 116 n. 3
Goethe, J. W. von, 18
Goodenough, E. R., 203 n. 52
Goodrick, A.T.S., 151 n. 8
Goody, J., 197 n. 31, 208 n. 74, 214 n. 90
Goppelt, L., 278 n. 49
Gordis, R., 127 n. 27
Gottwald, N. K., 101 n. 5, 106 n. 18
Goulder, M. D., 53 n. 7
Gowan, D. E., 33 n. 12
Grassi, J. A., 255 n. 31
Grimm, C.L.W., 151 n. 8
Gross, H., 60 n. 26
Gundry, R. H., 253 n. 27
Gunkel, H., 47 n. 57, 54 n. 12
Gunneweg, A.H.J., 29 n. 29

Habel, N., 87 n. 18
Hadidian, D. Y., 125 n. 23
Hamerton-Kelly, R. G., 264, 264 n. 2, 265, 271 n. 27, 276 n. 42
Hanhart, R., 47 n. 57
Hanson, A. T., 275 n. 37
Hanson, J. S., 202 n. 46
Hanson, P. D., 170 n. 25, 269 n. 16
Harnack, A. von, 188 n. 4
Harrelson, W., 7 n. 13, 53 n. 6
Harris, W. V., 197 n. 31
Hartman, L., 236 n. 17
Haspecker, J., 133 n. 1, 143 n. 36
Hayes, J. H., 74 n. 3, 174 n. 33
Hayward, R., 135 n. 6
Hellholm, D., 227 n. 7
Hengel, M., 168 n. 21
Hermisson, H. J., 101 n. 4
Heschel, A., 49 n. 62
Hillers, D. R., 46 n. 52, 46 n. 55, 46 n. 56
Hoglund, K. G., 60 n. 26, 113 n. 29
Hoistad, R., 203 n. 52
Holladay, W. C., 58 n. 23
Hollander, H. W., 178 n. 44
Holman, I., 68 n. 52
Hölscher, G., 166 n. 9
Holtzmann, H. J., 188 n. 2
Horsley, R., 202 n. 46, 205 n. 64, 227 n. 7, 228 n. 10, 229 n. 11, 235 n. 14, 235 n. 15, 237 n. 19
Horst, P. W. van der, 175 n. 36, 180 n. 49
House, P. R., 32 n. 5, 34 n. 15
Humbert, P., 71 n. 58
Hunzinger, C.-H., 190 n. 14
Hurvitz, A., 54 n. 15, 55 n. 17
Hussey, E., 22 n. 8

Irwin, W. R., 66 n. 39
Iser, W., 248 n. 13
Iwry, S., 123 n. 18

Jackson, J. J., 54 n. 12, 67 n. 41
Jacobsen, T., 9 n. 16
Janzen, W., 55 n. 18
Jeremias, J., 204 n. 57, 204 n. 62
Jobling, D., 293 n. 22
Johnson, E. E., 264 n. 2, 265 n. 4, 266 n. 6, 268 n. 15, 271 n. 25, 274 n. 35, 275 n. 36, 275 n. 37, 275 n. 39, 276 n. 40, 277 n. 45, 279 n. 54, 280 n. 57, 281 n. 59, 281 n. 61, 282 n. 62, 289 n. 7
Jonge, M. de, 178 n. 44
Junker, F. H., 57 n. 20

Kabisch, R., 265 n. 5
Käsemann, E., 272 n. 29, 273 n. 32, 279 n. 52, 280 n. 56, 282 n. 66
Käser, W., 55 n. 18
Keck, L. E., 267 n. 11, 267 n. 13, 274 n. 33
Keel, O., 11 n. 18
Kelber, W., 197 n. 31, 225, 225 n. 3, 225 n. 4, 225 n. 5, 236 n. 16
Keller, C., 55 n. 18
Kennedy, A.R.S., 204, 204 n. 61
Kessler, M., 54 n. 12, 67 n. 41
Kilian, R., 69 n. 54
Kingsbury, J. D., 250 n. 19
Klein, G., 265 n. 4
Kloppenborg, J. S., 166, 166 n. 5, 166 n. 6, 174 n. 34, 181, 181 n. 52, 182, 182 n. 54, 183, 183 n. 56, 183 n. 57, 183 n. 59, 183 n. 60, 184, 184 n. 61, 184 n. 62, 185,

Kloppenborg, J. S. (*continued*) 188 n. 4, 189 n. 5, 193, 193 n. 25, 193 n. 27, 193 n. 28, 194 n. 29, 198 n. 35, 199 n. 37, 200 n. 40, 200 n. 41, 206 n. 65, 209 n. 75, 209 n. 76, 212 n. 85, 213 n. 88, 229 n. 11, 246 n. 4, 251 n. 24, 253 n. 28
Knibb, M. A., 167 n. 14
Knox, W. L., 264, 264 n. 2
Koch, K., 6 n. 9, 224 n. 2
Koester, H., 21 n. 6, 165, 165 n. 3, 166 n. 4, 190 n. 13, 191 n. 17, 192 n. 21, 192 n. 22, 193, 193 n. 24, 198 n. 35, 205, 205 n. 64, 224 n. 1, 248 n. 12
Koole, J. L., 68 n. 51
Kovacs, B. W., 106 n. 18
Krasovec, J., 58 n. 23
Kraus, H.-J., 37 n. 26, 57 n. 22, 60 n. 26, 67 n. 40
Küchler, M., 165 n. 2, 174 n. 34, 180 n. 46, 180 n. 48, 269 n. 20
Kümmel, W. G., 266 n. 6
Kuntz, J. K, 54 n. 12, 67 n. 41

Lambert, W. G., 149 n. 1, 249 n. 15
Lambrecht, J., 249 n. 15, 250, 250 n. 21, 256 n. 35, 259, 259 n. 40
Landes, G. M., 45 n. 50
Landsberger, B., 53 n. 9
Lang, B., 100 n. 1, 101 n. 4
Larcher, C., 152 n. 8
Laufen, R., 189 n. 7
Le Deaut, R., 26 n. 21
Lee, T. R., 16 n. 22
Lemaire, A., 74 n. 4, 100 n. 2, 101 n. 4, 105 n. 16
Lemke, W., 167 n. 12
Lenski, G. E., 207, 207 n. 71
Levenson, J. D., 2 n. 2, 57 n. 22, 96 n. 22
Levine, A.-J., 260 n. 46
Lewy, H., 152 n. 9
Lichtenberger, H., 180 n. 46
Lieberman, S., 26 n. 22
Lincoln, B., 294 n. 23
Lindars, B., 23 n. 11
Lindblom, J., 53 n. 6, 67 n. 40
Lipinski, E., 55 n. 18
Lods, A., 52 n. 4
Logan, A.H.B., 190 n. 13
Long, B. O., 32 n. 4, 51 n. 1, 54 n. 14
Louw, J. P., 252 n. 25
Luckmann, T., 78 n. 9
Lührmann, D., 189 n. 8, 212 n. 84, 212 n. 85, 212 n. 86
Lull, D., 199 n. 38
Luyten, J., 54 n. 13, 67 n. 41, 67 n. 44
Luz, U., 254 n. 30

Maag, V., 57 n. 21
McBride, S. D., 170 n. 25
McCann, J. C., Jr., 58 n. 22, 72 n. 60
McCurley, F. R., Jr., 53 n. 7
MacDonald, D. B., 123 n. 19
Mack, B. L., 16 n. 22, 79 n. 12, 166, 166 n. 7, 166 n. 8, 172 n. 28, 173 n. 29, 182, 202 n. 47, 202 n. 48, 203 n. 52, 206, 206 n. 67, 211, 211 n. 80, 211 n. 82, 213, 213 n. 88, 226 n. 6, 231 n. 13, 245 n. 3
McKane, W., 53 n. 6, 293 n. 22
MacRae, G. W., 219 n. 103
Malfroy, J., 53 n. 7
Mannati, M., 68 n. 46, 68 n. 48
Marböck, J., 133 n. 1, 139 n. 17
Marcus, J., 266 n. 9
Martin, J. D., 172 n. 27
Martyn, J. L., 267 n. 13
Mays, J. L., 47 n. 57, 58 n. 22, 106 n. 18
Meinhold, A., 60 n. 26
Mettinger, T., 8 n. 14, 13 n. 19
Metzger, B. M., 257 n. 36
Meyer, P. W., 272 n. 30, 273 n. 31, 281 n. 60
Michel, D., 122 n. 15, 127 n. 27
Middendorp, T., 173 n. 29
Milgrom, J., 60 n. 26
Miller, D. G., 32 n. 4
Miller, D. M., 62 n. 28
Miller, P. D., Jr., 6, 6 n. 11, 58 n. 22, 167 n. 12, 170 n. 25
Miller, R. J., 250 n. 20
Mohr, J. C. B., 264 n. 2, 264 n. 3, 265 n. 4
Montefiore, H., 190 n. 13
Moore, S. D., 231 n. 12
Morgan, D. F., 53 n. 7
Mowinckel, S., 54 n. 10, 54 n. 11, 54 n. 12, 58 n. 23
Müller, H.-P., 68 n. 52, 81 n. 15, 167 n. 11
Murphy, R. E., 6, 37 n. 26, 54 n. 12, 77 n. 7, 108 n. 20, 109 n. 24, 111 n. 27, 125 n. 23, 128 n. 29, 136 n. 9, 167 n. 14, 169, 169 n. 23, 174 n. 33, 246, 246 n. 5
Mussner, F., 60 n. 26
Myers, C., 231 n. 12, 235 n. 15

Neusner, J., 276 n. 41
Newsom, C. A., 17 n. 26, 103 n. 8, 110 n. 26, 180 n. 46
Nickelsburg, G.W.E., 171 n. 26, 176 n. 38, 176 n. 40, 227 n. 7, 228 n. 9, 276 n. 41
Nida, E. A., 252 n. 25
Noack, L., 166 n. 9

Index of Modern Authors

Norden, E., 155 n. 14, 275 n. 38
Nordheim, E. von, 178 n. 43, 178 n. 45

Oakman, D., 204 n. 58
O'Callahan, R. T., 68 n. 48
O'Connor, M., 41 n. 38
Oesch, M., 60 n. 26
Oesterly, W.O.E., 150, 150 n. 2
Offerhaus, U., 151 n. 8, 152 n. 8
Ogden, G. S., 15 n. 21
Ong, W., 197 n. 31, 249 n. 14
Orton, D. E., 172 n. 27, 247, 247 n. 9, 247 n. 10, 248, 248 n. 11
Overman, J. A., 199 n. 38

Pardee, D., 41 n. 37
Parker, K. I., 146 n. 47
Patte, D., 251, 255 n. 34
Patterson, S. J., 190 n. 10, 200 n. 42, 214 n. 89
Pautrel, R., 65 n. 38
Pearson, B. A., 205 n. 64, 265 n. 4, 270 n. 21, 286 n. 2
Perdue, L. G., 31, 32 n. 4, 53 n. 9, 54 n. 12, 57 n. 21, 64 n. 35, 64 n. 36, 65 n. 38, 66 n. 39, 67 n. 40, 67 n. 43, 74 n. 2, 74 n. 4, 74 n. 5, 75 n. 6, 78 n. 8, 78 n. 10, 79 n. 13, 81 n. 14, 82 n. 16, 89 n. 19, 100 n. 2, 101 n. 3, 105 n. 14, 107 n. 19, 168, 168 n. 18, 286 n. 3, 287 n. 6, 291 n. 14
Perlitt, L., 28 n. 28
Perrin, N., 183 n. 58, 184 n. 62, 207 n. 70, 247 n. 7
Petersen, D. L., 35 n. 17
Peuch, E., 182 n. 55
Pinto, B. de, 57 n. 22
Piper, R. A., 174 n. 34, 187 n. 1
Pippin, T., 292 n. 16
Pliny, 204 n. 56
Plumptre, E. H., 127 n. 28
Pope, M., 87 n. 18
Preuss, H. D., 3, 3 n. 7

Rad, G. von, 6 n. 8, 27, 27 n. 25, 29, 108, 108 n. 21, 111 n. 28, 126 n. 24, 133 n. 1, 145 n. 46, 165 n. 1, 167 n. 10, 168 n. 17, 219 n. 105, 228, 268, 269 n. 16, 269 n. 17, 269
Rankin, O. S., 143 n. 35
Reese, J. M., 271 n. 27
Reindl, J., 72 n. 61
Renaud, B., 67 n. 43
Rendsburg, G. A., 53 n. 8
Rimmon-Kenan, S., 261 n. 47
Ringe, S. H., 103 n. 8
Ringgren, H., 67 n. 43, 68 n. 48, 79 n. 12, 150, 150 n. 3, 150 n. 5, 162 n. 21
Robert, A., 57 n. 22
Robert, J., 26 n. 21
Roberts, J.J.M., 34 n. 16, 48 n. 59
Robertson, D., 95 n. 21
Robinson, J. M., 21 n. 6, 165 n. 3, 166 n. 4, 174 n. 34, 189 n. 4, 189 n. 9, 191 n. 16, 191 n. 17, 191 n. 19, 192 n. 20, 219 n. 103, 241 n. 20, 264 n. 2, 293, 293 n. 19, 293 n. 20
Ronan, M., 113 n. 30, 293, 293 n. 19, 293 n. 21
Ross, F. G., 67 n. 43
Rudolph K., 286, 287 n. 4
Rudolph, W., 35 n. 21, 35 n. 22, 36 n. 23, 46 n. 55, 46 n. 56, 47 n. 59, 292 n. 18
Rüger, H.-P., 180 n. 51
Rylaarsdam, J. C., 3, 3 n. 6

Sanders, E. P., 245 n. 2, 266 n. 9
Sanders, J. A., 57 n. 22
Sanders, J. T., 139 n. 18
Scharbert, J., 32 n. 8
Schechter, S., 180 n. 50
Schenke, H.-M., 219, 219 n. 103, 219 n. 104
Schiffmann, L. H., 180 n. 47
Schildenberger, J., 57 n. 20
Schmid, H. H., 6, 6 n. 12, 18, 18 n. 27, 52 n. 4, 55 n. 18, 78 n. 11, 199 n. 36
Schmidt, J. M., 166 n. 9
Schmidt, L., 2 n. 4
Schnabel, E. J., 264 n. 3, 275 n. 37, 282 n. 66
Schneemelcher, W., 192 n. 23
Schneider, D. A., 32 n. 5, 40, 40 n. 33
Schrage, W., 190 n. 12
Schulthess, J., 151 n. 8
Schüngel-Straumann, H., 69 n. 53
Schweitzer, A., 223, 245, 245 n. 2, 246, 265, 265 n. 5, 266 n. 6
Schweizer, E., 281–82, 281 n. 62, 282 n. 64, 282 n. 65
Scott, B. B., 204 n. 57, 204 n. 59, 204 n. 61, 204 n. 62, 243 n. 21, 257 n. 38, 262 n. 48
Scott, J. M., 270 n. 22
Scott, R.B.Y., 52 n. 4, 150, 150 n. 6
Scroggs, R., 264, 264 n. 27, 265, 271, 271 n. 27, 277 n. 46
Seitz, C. R., 32 n. 4
Sheppard, G. T., 31 n. 1, 36, 36 n. 24, 72 n. 61, 74 n. 2, 135 n. 7, 136 n. 11, 293 n. 22
Shupak, N., 101 n. 4
Sieber, J., 190 n. 12

INDEX OF MODERN AUTHORS

Silbermann, L. H., 188 n. 3
Simonsen, D., 44 n. 48
Skehan, P. W., 133 n. 1, 133 n. 2, 134 n. 4, 139 n. 18, 140 n. 22, 140 n. 23
Slotki, J. J., 65 n. 38
Smallwood, E. M., 202 n. 50
Smend, R., 47 n. 57
Smith, J. Z., 269 n. 21, 286, 286 n. 2
Smith, R. L., 46 n. 56
Soards, M. L., 266 n. 9
Soden, H., von, 259 n. 43
Soll, W., 62 n. 28
Spieckermann, H., 34 n. 17, 57 n. 20
Stassen, G., 291, 291 n. 15
Stone, M. E., 167 n. 12
Strecker, G., 253 n. 27
Strum, R. E., 266 n. 9, 267 n. 13
Suggs, M. J., 280 n. 58

Talbert, C. H., 278 n. 47
Tardieu, M., 152 n. 9
Taussig, H., 113 n. 30, 293, 293 n. 19
Taylor, V., 189 n. 6
Terrien, S., 64 n. 31, 64 n. 32, 64 n. 33, 64 n. 34, 66 n. 39, 68 n. 46, 68 n. 47, 68 n. 49, 68 n. 52, 71 n. 59
Theissen, G., 206, 206 n. 67, 207 n. 72, 211 n. 81, 212 n. 83, 277 n. 44
Tobin, T. H., 180 n. 46
Todd, R. B., 153 n. 11
Tolbert, M. A., 249 n. 18
Tournay, R. J., 67 n. 43
Tromp, N. J., 43 n. 42, 65 n. 38
Trublet, J., 54 n. 15, 56 n. 19, 68 n. 52
Tsevat, M., 93 n. 20
Tucker, G. M., 35 n. 17
Turner, V., 287
Tuttle, G., 33 n. 12

Uspensky, B., 246 n. 6

Van der Ploeg, J.P.M., 62 n. 28, 65 n. 38
Van Leeuwen, R. C., 32 n. 4, 32 n. 6, 106 n. 18
Van Roon, A., 265 n. 4
Vermeylen, J., 53 n. 6
Vielhauer, P., 192, 192 n. 23
Volz, P., 65 n. 38
Voort, A. van der, 71 n. 58

Waard, J. de, 43 n. 42
Wagner, S., 69 n. 54
Wallis, G., 57 n. 22
Waltke, B. K., 41 n. 38
Weber, M., 20, 20 n. 3
Wedderburn, J. M., 190 n. 13
Weinfeld, M., 14, 14 n. 20
Weiss, J., 223
Weisse, C. H., 188 n. 2
Wellhausen, J., 22, 22 n. 9
Westermann, C., 1, 1 n. 1, 14, 14 n. 20, 16, 52 n. 3, 55 n. 18, 65 n. 37, 101 n. 3, 168 n. 20
Whedbee, J. W., 53 n. 6, 176 n. 39
Whybray, R. N., 8 n. 15, 15 n. 21, 20 n. 4, 21 n. 6, 54 n. 13, 55 n. 17, 73 n. 1, 100 n. 2, 101 n. 4, 105 n. 13, 105 n. 14, 105 n. 15, 106 n. 18
Wilckens, U., 174 n. 34, 264, 264 n. 2, 265 n. 4, 276, 277 n. 44, 290 n. 11
Wilcox, J. T., 16 n. 24
Wilken, R. L., 265 n. 4, 293 n. 19
Williams, J. G., 95 n. 21, 187 n. 1
Williamson, H. G. M., 26 n. 21
Willis, J. T., 47 n. 57, 106 n. 18
Wilson, G. H., 31, 31 n. 3, 31 n. 3, 36 n. 4, 72 n. 61
Wilson, R. McL., 190 n. 1
Wilson, R. R., 35 n. 17
Windisch, H., 204 n. 59, 264, 264 n. 1, 280 n. 58
Winston, D., 159 n. 18, 160 n. 19, 163 n. 24, 163 n. 25, 163 n. 26, 164 n. 27
Winton, A. P., 187 n. 1
Wiseman, D. J., 197 n. 31
Wolff, H. W., 44 n. 46, 46 n. 56, 53 n. 6, 55 n. 18
Wrede, W., 245 n. 2, 246
Würthwein, E., 68 n. 48, 69 n. 53, 69 n. 55

Young, E. J., 69 n. 54

Zaehner, R. G., 152 n. 10
Zeller, D., 187 n. 1
Zigler, J., 133 n. 1
Zimmerli, W., 32 n. 8, 111 n. 28, 126 n.24
Zyl, H. A. van, 60 n. 26